D0048387

O'AHU

WITH HONOLULU, WAIKĪKĪ & THE NORTH SHORE

1st Edition

**Where to Stay and Eat
for All Budgets**

**Must-See Sights
and Local Secrets**

Ratings You Can Trust

Portions of this book appear in Fodor's Hawai'i
Fodor's Travel Publications   New York, Toronto, London, Sydney, Auckland
www.fodors.com

FODOR'S O'AHU

Editor: Mary Beth Bohman

Editorial Production: Linda Schmidt
Editorial Contributors: Wanda Adams, Don Chapman, Andy Collins, Jack Jeffrey, Katherine Nichols, Chad Pata, Cathy Sharpe, Cheryl Tsutsumi, Amy Westervelt, Shannon Wianecki, Maggie Wunsch, Katie Young
Maps & Illustrations: David Lindroth, William Wu, Ed Jacobus, with additional cartography provided by Henry Columb, Mark Stroud, and Ali Baird, Moon Street Cartography; Rebecca Baer and Bob Blake, *map editors*
Design: Fabrizio La Rocca, *creative director*; Siobhan O'Hare, *art director*; Chie Ushio, *designer*; Moon Sun Kim, *cover designer*; Melanie Marin, *senior picture editor*; William Wu, *illustrations*
Production/Manufacturing: Angela L. McLean
Cover Photo: Ken Ross/viestiphoto.com

First Edition

ISBN-10: 1–4000–1641–X

ISBN-13: 978–1–4000–1641–9

ISSN: 1559–0771

SPECIAL SALES

This book is available for special discounts for bulk purchases for sales promotions or premiums. Special editions, including personalized covers, excerpts of existing books, and corporate imprints, can be created in large quantities for special needs. For more information, write to Special Markets/Premium Sales, 1745 Broadway, MD 6-2, New York, New York 10019, or e-mail specialmarkets@randomhouse.com.

AN IMPORTANT TIP & AN INVITATION

Although all prices, opening times, and other details in this book are based on information supplied to us at press time, changes occur all the time in the travel world, and Fodor's cannot accept responsibility for facts that become outdated or for inadvertent errors or omissions. So **always confirm information when it matters,** especially if you're making a detour to visit a specific place. Your experiences—positive and negative—matter to us. If we have missed or misstated something, **please write to us.** We follow up on all suggestions. Contact the Hawai'i editor at editors@fodors.com or c/o Fodor's at 1745 Broadway, New York, NY 10019.

PRINTED IN THE UNITED STATES OF AMERICA

10 9 8 7 6 5 4 3 2 1

Be a Fodor's Correspondent

Your opinion matters. It matters to us. It matters to your fellow Fodor's travelers, too. And we'd like to hear it. In fact, we *need* to hear it.

When you share your experiences and opinions, you become an active member of the Fodor's community. That means we'll not only use your feedback to make our books better, but we'll publish your names and comments whenever possible. Throughout our guides, look for "Word of Mouth," excerpts of your unvarnished feedback.

Here's how you can help improve Fodor's for all of us.

Tell us when we're right. We rely on local writers to give you an insider's perspective. But our writers and staff editors—who are the best in the business—depend on you. Your positive feedback is a vote to renew our recommendations for the next edition.

Tell us when we're wrong. We're proud that we update most of our guides every year. But we're not perfect. Things change. Hotels cut services. Museums change hours. Charming cafés lose charm. If our writer didn't quite capture the essence of a place, tell us how you'd do it differently. If any of our descriptions are inaccurate or inadequate, we'll incorporate your changes in the next edition and will correct factual errors at fodors.com *immediately.*

Tell us what to include. You probably have had fantastic travel experiences that aren't yet in Fodor's. Why not share them with a community of like-minded travelers? Maybe you chanced upon a beach or bistro or B&B that you don't want to keep to yourself. Tell us why we should include it. And share your discoveries and experiences with everyone directly at fodors.com. Your input may lead us to add a new listing or highlight a place we cover with a "Highly Recommended" star or with our highest rating, "Fodor's Choice."

Give us your opinion instantly at our feedback center at www.fodors.com/feedback. You may also e-mail editors@fodors.com with the subject line "Hawai'i Editor." Or send your nominations, comments, and complaints by mail to Hawai'i Editor, Fodor's, 1745 Broadway, New York, NY 10019.

You and travelers like you are the heart of the Fodor's community. Make our community richer by sharing your experiences. Be a Fodor's correspondent.

Aloha!

Tim Jarrell, Publisher

CONTENTS

O'AHU IN FOCUS

ABOUT THIS BOOK

Our Ratings

Sometimes you find terrific travel experiences and sometimes they just find you. But usually the burden is on you to select the right combination of experiences. That's where our ratings come in.

As travelers we've all discovered a place so wonderful that its worthiness is obvious. And sometimes that place is so experiential that superlatives don't do it justice: you just have to be there to know. These sights, properties, and experiences get our highest rating, **Fodor's Choice,** indicated by orange stars throughout this book.

Black stars highlight sights and properties we deem **Highly Recommended,** places that our writers, editors, and readers praise again and again for consistency and excellence.

By default, there's another category: any place we include in this book is by definition worth your time, unless we say otherwise. And we will.

Disagree with any of our choices? Care to nominate a place or suggest that we rate one more highly? Visit our feedback center at www.fodors.com/feedback.

Budget Well

For attractions, we always give standard adult admission fees; reductions are usually available for children, students, and senior citizens. Want to pay with plastic? **AE, D, DC, MC, V** following restaurant and hotel listings indicate if American Express, Discover, Diner's Club, MasterCard, and Visa are accepted.

Restaurants

Unless we state otherwise, restaurants are open for lunch and dinner daily. We mention dress only when there's a specific requirement and reservations only when they're essential or not accepted—it's always best to book ahead.

Hotels

Hotels have private bath, phone, TV, and air-conditioning and operate on the European Plan (a.k.a. EP, meaning without meals), unless we specify otherwise. We always list facilities but not whether you'll be charged an extra fee to use them, so when pricing accommodations, find out what's included.

Many Listings

★ Fodor's Choice
★ Highly recommended
⊠ Physical address
✛ Directions
⌂ Mailing address
☎ Telephone
🖷 Fax
⊕ On the Web
✆ E-mail
🎫 Admission fee
☉ Open/closed times
► Start of walk/itinerary
☰ Credit cards

Hotels & Restaurants

🏨 Hotel
🛏 Number of rooms
♨ Facilities
✕ Restaurant
🪑 Reservations
👔 Dress code
🚭 Smoking
🍸 BYOB
✕🏨 Hotel with restaurant that warrants a visit

Outdoors

🏌 Golf
⚠ Camping

Other

☺ Family-friendly
🛂 Contact information
⇨ See also
⊠ Branch address
☞ Take note

Experience O'ahu

WORD OF MOUTH

"Why I love O'ahu? .˙. . the magic I feel when my toes first sink into the warm sand as I head off on my maiden walk on Waikīkī beach, looking toward Diamond Head and heading straight for the Banyan Bar at the Moana!"

—bashfulLV

"Our place was just a couple miles east of Hale'iwa and on a wonderful stretch of beach that displayed very few footprints on any given day."

—bogart04

WELCOME TO O'AHU

Getting Oriented

Traveling to Hawai'i is as close as an American can get to visiting another country while staying within the United States. O'ahu—where Honolulu and Waikīkī are—is the third largest Hawaiian island and has 75% of the state's population. Honolulu is the perfect place to experience the state's indigenous culture, the hundred years of immigration that resulted in today's blended society, and the tradition of aloha. The museums and historic and cultural sites will ground you, at least a bit, in Hawai'i history. The widest range of restaurants as well as the best nightlife scene in the Islands are here, too.

But O'ahu is not just Honolulu and Waikīkī. It is looping mountain trails on the western Wai'anae and eastern Ko'olau ranges. It is monster waves breaking on the golden beaches of the North Shore. It is country stores and beaches where turtles are your swimming companions. O'ahu, with its knife-edged mountain ranges, verdant green valleys, territorial-era architecture, and ring of white-sand beaches, is just the Hawai'i you came to see.

West O'ahu—which includes Central O'ahu highlands, the Leeward coast and the Hawaiian communities of Nānākuli and Wai'anae—is finding a new identity as a "second city" of suburban homes and tech firms, coexisting with agriculture and traditional lifestyles.

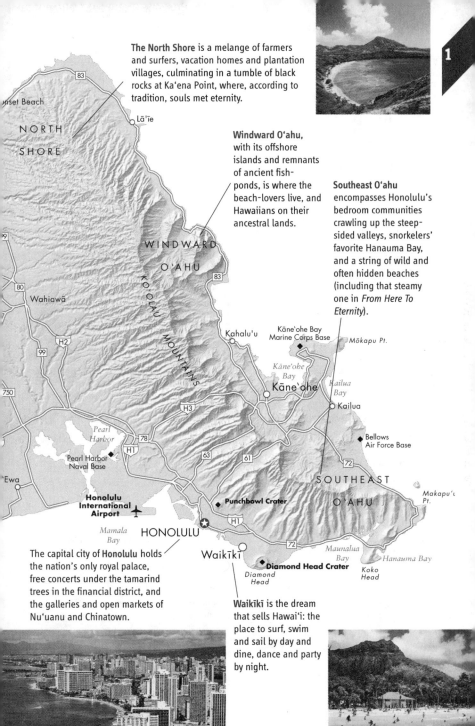

The North Shore is a melange of farmers and surfers, vacation homes and plantation villages, culminating in a tumble of black rocks at Ka'ena Point, where, according to tradition, souls met eternity.

Windward O'ahu, with its offshore islands and remnants of ancient fish-ponds, is where the beach-lovers live, and Hawaiians on their ancestral lands.

Southeast O'ahu encompasses Honolulu's bedroom communities crawling up the steep-sided valleys, snorkelers' favorite Hanauma Bay, and a string of wild and often hidden beaches (including that steamy one in *From Here To Eternity*).

The capital city of **Honolulu** holds the nation's only royal palace, free concerts under the tamarind trees in the financial district, and the galleries and open markets of Nu'uanu and Chinatown.

Waikīkī is the dream that sells Hawai'i: the place to surf, swim and sail by day and dine, dance and party by night.

O'AHU PLANNER

When You Arrive

Honolulu International Airport is 20 minutes from Waikīkī (40 during rush hour). Car rental is across the street from baggage claim. A cumbersome and inefficient airport taxi system requires you to line up to a taxi wrangler who radios for cars (about $25 to Waikīkī). Other options: TheBus ($2, one lap-size bag allowed) or public airport shuttle ($8). ■ TIP→→ Ask the driver to take H1, not Nimitz Highway, at least as far as downtown, or your introduction to paradise will be Honolulu's industrial backside.

Set the Stage

Head to Longs or Wal-Mart on your first day and buy a cheap Styrofoam cooler, grass beach mats, beach towels, floats for the kids, sun protection, and bottled water. What to do with all this stuff when you head for home? Leave it in the hotel room (you'll have gotten your money's worth). Better yet—look for a group that's just checking in and make a welcome gift of your survival kit.

What's New

O'ahu is under much-needed renovation with Waikīkī hotels and streets, the H-1 freeway, the Bishop Museum, and Pearl Harbor all affected. Enquire closely about renovation near the hotel you choose. And anytime you visit an attraction, call ahead to be sure hours haven't changed, and the particular things you want to see aren't closed.

Get out of Town

They'll tell you, wrongly, that O'ahu means "the gathering place." But scholars agree that no one knows what this ancient word really means. In any case, the island is a literal gathering place—for 800,000-plus residents and several thousand more visitors every day. If noise, traffic and crowding in Waikīkī and Honolulu get to you, head in any direction—you'll soon see that O'ahu has a rural side of exceptional beauty and even tranquility.

Car Rentals

Waikīkī and Honolulu can realistically be done without a car. Public buses and free shuttles reach most important sites. If you want to see the North Shore or the Windward beaches, you'll need to rent a car.

TIPS→→

■ If you are staying in Waikīkī, rent a car only on the days when you wish to go farther afield. You don't need a car in Waikīkī itself, and inconveniently-located hotel parking garages charge everyone (even hotel guests) close to $20 a day, plus tips.

■ Renting a Mustang convertible is a sure sign that you're a tourist and practically begs "come burglarize me." A good rule of thumb: When the car is out of your sight even for a moment, it should be empty of anything you care about.

To Island-Hop or Stop?

Should you try to fit another island into your trip or stay put in O'ahu? Tough call. Although none of the islands is more than 30 minutes away from another by air, security hassles, transport and check-in all swallow up precious vacation hours. If you've got less than a week, do O'ahu well and leave the rest for the next trip. With a week, you can give three good tour days to O'ahu (Pearl Harbor, Honolulu, and one rural venture), then head to a Neighbor Island for some serious beach time and maybe an adventure or two. If you do decide to island-hop, book in advance; you'll get a better fare by packaging your travel.

■ **TIP→→** If you want to get along on the Neighbor Islands, don't compare them to Honolulu and never call them "the outer islands"—that's insultingly O'ahu-centric.

Will It Rain?

There's a reason why Hawai'i's most-watched TV news show doesn't have a weather forecaster. Weather here is blissfully predictable: Mid to low 80s, morning showers at high elevations and in misty valleys, trade winds 5 to 15 miles per hour. The only reason anyone listens to the weather is to find out if the surf is up (especially in winter) and when low tide will be (for fishing).

Timing Is Everything

When to visit? Winter is whales (November through March) and waves (surf competitions December through February). In fall, the Aloha Festivals celebrate island culture in September. In summer, the Islands honor the king who made them a nation, Kamehameha I, on June 11, with parades and events on all islands. O'ahu's one-of-a-kind Pan Pacific Festival backs up to the Kamehameha Day, bringing together hundreds of performers from Japan's seasonal celebrations.

Guided Activities

When it comes to surfing, you come to O'ahu. For a much less exhausting trip beyond the breaks, try a short sail on a beach catamaran from Waikīkī. This chart lists average prices per person for O'ahu's most popular guided activities.

ACTIVITY	COST
Aerial Tours (1/2 hr.)	$100–$140
Beach Catamaran Sails	$12–$20
Deep Sea Fishing (1/2 day)	$120–$150
Golf (Green Fee)	$40–$165
Kayak Tours	$75–$100
Lū'au	$56–$195
Shark Encounters	$120
Snorkel Cruises (2–3 hrs.)	$50–$100
Surfing Lessons (1–2 hrs.)	$50–$100
Whale Watching (2–3 hrs.)	$100–$120

TOP OʻAHU
EXPERIENCES

That Beach

(A) Kailua is the beach you came to Hawaiʻi for: wide and gently sloped, glowing golden in the sun, outfitted with a couple of well-placed islets to gaze at, and fronted by waters in ever-changing shades of turquoise. The waves are gentle enough for children. Kayakers are drawn to the Mokulua Islands offshore. Grocery stores and restaurants are within walking distance. And there's just enough wind to keep you from baking. Paradise, but civilized. ⇨ *page 78.*

Finding Shangri La

(B) Wealth allowed heiress Doris Duke to acquire the lavish seaside estate she called Shangri La. For most, that would have been enough. But Duke had a passion—Islamic art and architecture—and determination as well as money. She had a vision of courtyards and pleasure gardens and rooms that are themselves works of art. And she

presided over every detail of the never-quite-finished project. The property, now a center for Islamic studies, is utterly unique and quite simply not to be missed. ⇨ *page 54.*

Oʻahu After Hours

(C) Yes, you can have an umbrella drink at sunset. But in the multicultural metropolis of Honolulu, there's so much more to it than that. Sip a glass of wine and listen to jazz at Formaggio, join the beach-and-beer gang at Duke's Canoe Club, or head to Zanzabar, where DJs spin hip-hop and techno. Sample the sake at an izakaya or listen to a performance by a Hawaiian musician. Snack on pūpū, and begin your journey toward that unforgettable tropical sunrise. ⇨ *page 156.*

Hiking to Kaʻena Point

(D) If we had but one day to spend in rural Oʻahu, we'd spend it walking the back road along the rocky shore at the

island's northern tip. Ka'ena, a state park as well as a protected Natural Area, comprises 850 acres of undeveloped coastline that centers on the point where it is said the souls of the ancient dead leapt into the eternal darkness. The views are incomparable; shells can be scavenged in keyhole coves in calm weather; whales spout offshore during winter; and threatened native plants flourish. It's a trek that will change your mind about O'ahu being "too crowded." ⇨ page 119.

Catching a Wave

(E) Taking a surfing lesson from a well-muscled beach boy has been a Honolulu must-do since the first gay divorcée stepped off the first cruise ship. Waikīkī, with its well-shaped but diminutive waves, remains the perfect spot for grommets (surfing newbies), though surf schools operate at beaches around the island. Most companies guarantee

at least one standing ride in the course of a lesson. And catching that first wave? We guarantee you'll never forget it. ⇨ page 99.

Exploring Chinatown

(F) Chinatown is like one of those centerpiece lazy susans: turn it this way, and you find one thing; turn it another, and there's something else. The various guided tours of this compact and busy neighborhood each offer up a different dish: one focuses on food and restaurants, another shines a light on cultural attractions, and the occasional architect-led AIA tour delves into the area's design character. Take your pick or wander on your own. Just don't miss this unique mixed plate. ⇨ page 33.

Hula with Heart

(G) Professional hula dancers–the ones in poolside hotel shows and dinner extravaganzas—are perfection: hands like undulating waves, smiles that never

waiver. But if you want to experience hula with heart, scan the newspapers for a hula school fundraiser, or ask the activities desk about local festivals. You may see some missteps and bumbles, but you'll also experience different hula styles and hear songs and chants deeply rooted in the culture, all the while surrounded by the scents of a hundred homemade lei. ⇨ *page 148.*

Listening to a Living Legend

(H) Auntie Genoa Keawe can hold a note longer than anyone. Drop by the Moana Terrace of the Waikīkī Marriott hotel any Thursday between 6 and 9 to hear for yourself. Keawe is an octogenarian dynamo and the living embodiment of the falsetto singing style that Hawaiians so relish. You'll feel like you dropped in on a backyard party. ⇨ *page 157.*

A Sail on the Wild Side

(I) Who wouldn't want these memory snapshots to take home: the unblinking and seemingly amused eye of a spinner dolphin as it arcs through the wake of the catamaran in which you're riding; the undulating form of an endangered green sea turtle swimming below you; the slap and splash and whoosh of a humpback whale breaching in full view on indigo seas. Wild Side Specialty Tours can't promise these specific encounters, but their ecologically conscious daily excursions in a quiet, uncrowded catamaran do guarantee good memories. ⇨ *page 90.*

A Day on the North Shore

(J) "Hano Hano, Haleiʻwa," the song says—Beautiful Haleʻiwa. Also fun, funky, fast-moving, family-friendly Haleʻiwa—an easy place in which to while away half a day. Visit the quirky surf museum, wander through the surf shops, choose from half a dozen good but cheap restaurants, suck up some refreshing shave ice, find one-of-a-kind

clothes and gifts, charter a catamaran or fishing boat. Then head back to town along a route that takes you past world-renowned surf spots. ⇨ *page 60.*

A Trip to Japan

(K) Little known outside O'ahu's growing community of Japanese nationals is a class of small restaurant/bars called *izakaya* or Japanese taverns. Even newer on the scene are *okonomi*, hip spots that specialize in Osaka-style grilled omelets and potent Japanese spirits. Both are like a visit to Japan, minus the long plane ride, and, though pricey, the à la carte menus are unfailingly excellent—if distinctly odd. A must-notch in any foodie's belt. ⇨ *page 155.*

A Plate Lunch Picnic

(L) Take a break the way the locals do: get a plate lunch, then find a park or beach. Don't pack a ton of stuff, don't stick to a schedule. Eat, talk-story, take a nap, or people-watch—then explore,

walk, swim, or snorkel. Some options: Mitsu-Ken Catering, then a picnic on the grounds of the nearby Bishop Museum; Fukuya Delicatessen, then Kahala Beach Park; Diamond Head Market and Grill, then Waikīkī Beach or Kapi'olani Park; L&L Drive-Inn, then Kailua Beach. ⇨ *page 168.*

Walking in the Rain Forest

(M) Wend your way through the hillside neighborhood of 'Āiea, northwest of Honolulu, and suddenly you're in a cool, green park, scented with astringent eucalyptus. This is the 3.5-mile 'Āiea Loop Trail and if you're committed to squeezing a hike into a short O'hu stay, you couldn't do better for glimpses of hidden valleys and the experience of an island forest. ⇨ *page 108.*

WHEN TO GO

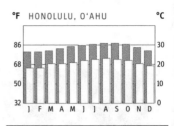

Long days of sunshine and fairly mild year-round temperatures make Hawaiʻi an all-season destination. Most resort areas are at sea level, with average afternoon temperatures of 75°F–80°F during the coldest months of December and January; during the hottest months of August and September the temperature often reaches 90°F. Higher "Upcountry" elevations typically have cooler and often misty conditions. Only at mountain summits does it reach freezing.

Moist trade winds drop their precipitation on the north and east sides of the islands, creating tropical climates, while the south and west sides remain hot and dry with desertlike conditions. Rainfall can be high in winter, particularly on those north and east shores.

Most travelers head to the Islands in winter, specifically from mid-December through mid-April. This high season means that fewer travel bargains are available; room rates average 10%–15% higher during this season than the rest of the year.

Climate

The following are average maximum and minimum temperatures for Honolulu; the temperatures throughout the Hawaiian Islands are similar.

🅵 Forecasts **Weather Channel Connection** ⊕ www.weather.com.

Only in Hawaiʻi Holidays

If you happen to be in the Islands on March 26 or June 11, you'll notice light traffic and busy beaches—these are state holidays not celebrated anywhere else. March 26 recognizes the birthday of Prince Jonah Kūhio Kalanianaʻole, a member of the royal line who served as a delegate to Congress and spearheaded the effort to set aside homelands for Hawaiian people. June 11 honors the first island-wide monarch, Kamehameha I; locals drape his statues with lei and stage elaborate parades. May 1 isn't an official holiday, but it's the day when schools and civic groups celebrate the quintessential Island gift, the flower lei, with leimaking contests and pageants. Statehood Day is celebrated on the third Friday in August (Admission Day was August 21, 1959). Another holiday much celebrated is Chinese New Year, in part because many Hawaiians married Chinese immigrants. Homes and businesses sprout bright red good luck mottoes, lions dance in the streets, and everybody eats gau (steamed pudding) and jai (vegetarian stew). The state also celebrates Good Friday as a spring holiday, a favorite for family picnics.

GREAT ONE-DAY ITINERARIES

To experience even a fraction of O'ahu's charms, you need a minimum of four days and a bus pass. Five days and a car is better: Waikīkī is at least a day, Honolulu and Chinatown another, Pearl Harbor the better part of another. Each of the rural sections can swallow a day each, just for driving, sight-seeing, and stopping to eat. And that's before you've taken a surf lesson, hung from a parasail, hiked a loop trail, or visited a botanical garden. The following itineraries will take you to our favorite spots on the island.

First Day in Waikīkī

You'll be up at dawn due to the time change and dead on your feet by afternoon due to jet lag. Have a dawn swim, change into walking gear, and head east along Kalākaua Avenue to Monsarrat Avenue, and climb Diamond Head. After lunch, nap in the shade, do some shopping, or visit the nearby East Honolulu neighborhoods of Mō'ili'ili and Kaimukī, rife with small shops and good, little restaurants. End the day with an early, interesting, and inexpensive dinner at one of these neighborhood spots.

Southeast & Windward Exploring

For sand, sun, and surf, follow H1 east to keyhole-shaped Hanauma Bay for picture-perfect snorkeling, then round the southeast tip of the island with its wind-swept cliffs and the famous Hālona Blowhole. Fly a kite or watch body surfers at Sandy Beach. Take in Sea Life Park. In Waimānalo, stop for local-style plate lunch, or punch on through to Kailua, where there's intriguing shopping and good eating.

The North Shore

Hit H1 westbound and then H2 to get to the North Shore. You'll pass through pineapple country, then drop down a scenic winding road to Waialua and Hale'iwa. Stop in Hale'iwa town to shop, to experience shave ice, and to pick up a guided dive or snorkel trip. On winding Kamehameha Highway, stop at famous big-wave beaches, take a dip in a cove with a turtle, and buy fresh Island fruit at roadside stands.

Pearl Harbor

Pearl Harbor is an almost all-day investment. Be on the grounds by 7:30 AM to line up for Arizona Memorial tickets. Clamber all over the USS *Bowfin* submarine. Finally, take the free trolley to see the Mighty Mo battleship. If it's Wednesday or Saturday, make the 5-minute drive mauka (toward the mountains) for bargain-basement shopping at the sprawling Aloha Stadium Swap Meet.

Town Time

If you are interested in history, devote a day to Honolulu's historic sites. Downtown, see 'Iolani Palace, the Kamehameha Statue, and Kawaiaha'o Church. A few blocks east, explore Chinatown, gilded Kuan Yin Temple, and artsy Nu'uanu with its galleries. On the water is the informative Hawai'i Maritime Center. Hop west on H1 to the Bishop Museum, the state's anthropological and archeological center. And a mile up Pali Highway is Queen Emma Summer Palace, whose shady grounds were a royal retreat. Worth a visit for plant lovers: Foster Botanical Garden.

WEDDINGS & HONEYMOONS

With everything from turquoise bays surrounded by perfect white crescents to hidden waterfalls tucked into tropical rainforests, it's easy to see why Hawai'i is such a popular destination for all things romantic—weddings, honeymoons, anniversaries, you name it. The weather is perfect; the people are warm; the scenery is beautiful; there's an easy, laid-back feel to everything; and, let's face it, everyone looks fantastic after a few days lounging on a beach. Planning a destination wedding, the perfect honeymoon, or an anniversary that brings back all the old magic can seem daunting at first, but Hawai'i has been in the love business for years, and there are many people and places just waiting to help celebrate yours.

Wedding Planning

The logistics. You must apply in person for a wedding license in Hawai'i, but you can download, fill in, and print the application from the State government's website: http://www.hawaii.gov/health/vital-records/vital-records/marriage/index.html. There is no waiting period and no blood test required. The cost is $60, which must be paid in cash. The license is valid for 30 days. Your certificate of marriage will be mailed to you after the wedding; for $10 you can put a rush on the certificate, which can be very useful for brides intending to change their last names.

The ceremony. The idea of planning a wedding in a strange place, thousands of miles away, may be enough to cause night sweats for some, but fear not. Hawai'i is home to some of the world's best wedding planners, many of whom are employed by—go figure—the more popular destination wedding resorts. Narrow your locations down and contact a few planners for quotes. Many planners work in conjunction with caterers and florists and offer packages; the resort-based planners have a variety of packages on offer. They're all used to people shopping around, so don't be afraid to haggle.

Those wishing to steer clear of the resort wedding and tap into old Hawai'i may also want to seek the help of a local planner, unless they have personal knowledge of their chosen destination or trustworthy friends or family in the area who can help taste food, scout locations, and meet potential officiants. There are certain things that are just too difficult to research from a distance, and having a wedding planner doesn't mean that your wedding will be expensive, nor does it mean that you'll end up with a Mainland wedding in Hawai'i or some sort of Hawaiian kitsch wedding (unless of course that's what you want!). These are people who know Hawai'i well and can help you find the perfect secluded beach, the local florist with the most beautiful orchids, or a house on the water for you and your inner circle, and the best caterer to roast a pig for you in the backyard.

The traditions. Most people who wed on Hawai'i incorporate local traditions to some extent. These can include Hawaiian music, ancient Hawaiian chants and blessings, and traditional Hawaiian food at the reception.

A simple lei exchange is customary for most couples—some include only the bride and groom, others splurge and get leis for everyone. Typically green maile garlands are for grooms, and strands of pink and white pīkake flowers are for brides. In a traditional Hawaiian wedding ceremony, the officiant, called the *kahuna pule* in

Hawaiian, binds the couple's hand together with a maile lei.

■ **TIP→** Almost everything is less expensive in Hawai'i during the off-season (September to mid-December), and weddings are no exception. Since the weather is perfect all year round, there's no reason to hold out for the more expensive summer months.

Honeymoon Planning

Hawai'i is a popular destination not only for everything it's got going for it, but for everything it's not as well—it's not all that far away; it's not outside the U.S. yet seems like another country; and it's not outrageously expensive if you plan well.

As for romance, yes, Hawai'i's romantic clichés—sunsets, beach strolls, moonlit walks—still work their magic, but there are also plenty of more unique ways to experience the romance of Hawai'i, whether you're looking to explore or just veg out together for awhile (swim with sea turtles, lounge on the beach, skinny dip in waterfall pools).

Almost as important as your choice of island is your accommodation choice. Although Hawai'i is home to dozens of world-class resorts all waiting to anticipate your every need, there are also several secluded B&Bs that are the perfect blend of luxury and total privacy. Most B&Bs have a honeymoon room or suite, and many of them offer stand-alone cottages. For even more privacy, there are several homes for rent throughout the islands, many of which are in stunning locations and often rent for less per night than rooms at the big resorts. Each island has its own B&B association, which inspects properties and lists the best of them.

■ **TIP→** Hawai'i's tourism bureaus spend a lot of money every year to keep people coming back for all things related to romance. Part of that entails running regular promotions in bridal magazines and on websites, so be sure to take a look at the usual suspects for the latest offers before booking your trip (go to www.gohawaii. com, then click on the individual sites from there).

Romantic Notions

• **Sunset on the North Shore in the winter.** Way more than just the average sunset—it's the usual scorching red sun and beautiful beach, but add to that the biggest waves you've ever seen, and killer local surfers catching the last few rides before dark.

• **Catering from Alan Wong's Pineapple Room, Ala Moana.** Delicious bits of 'ahi and onaga and Waimea tomatoes from one of the stars of Pacific Rim fusion make any reception extra special, and uniquely Hawaiian.

• **The Vera Wang Suite at the Halekūlani, Waikīkī.** Who else to design the perfect honeymoon suite but the designer made famous by her wedding dresses?

• **The Royal Hawaiian Hotel, Waikīkī.** The pink palace just screams Blue Hawai'i.

• **Surprise your spouse by saying "I do" all over again.** Many hotels offer vow-renewal ceremonies, making it a snap to be spontaneous.

• **Turtle Bay Resort, North Shore.** Ocean views from every room, 880 ocean-front acres on the North Shore, 5 mi of beaches, and 12 mi of ocean-front trails are all here, at a price well below that of most of the resorts in the islands.

A SNAPSHOT OF HAWAI'I

Any description of Hawai'i's beauty is a cliché by now—we've all seen the postcards and the movies, heard stories from friends, and read the guidebooks. Still, when you experience Hawai'i first hand, it's hard not to gush about the long perfect beaches, dramatic cliffs, greener than green rain forests, and that unbelievable plumeria perfume that hangs over it all. Add to that the fresh pineapple, the amazing marine life, the fascinating culture and history of the Hawaiian people, the location (at nearly 1,900 miles from the next continent, the Hawaiian islands are the most isolated in the world—talk about getting away from it all), and the fact that Hawai'i is one of the only places on Earth where you can watch an active volcano create new land, and it's easy to see why these islands have been such a popular destination for so long.

The Neighbor Islands

Maui. The second largest island in the chain, Maui's 727 square miles are home to only 118,000 people but host approximately 2 million tourists every year. Both Lāna'i and Moloka'i are just off the coast of Maui (west and north coasts, respectively), making day trips to either island easy and popular. With its restaurants and lively nightlife, Maui is the only island that competes with O'ahu in terms of entertainment; its charm lies in the fact that while entertainment is available, Maui's towns still feel like island villages.

Hawai'i (The Big Island). Once home to the state's capital, the Big Island has the second largest population of the islands (159,000) but feels sparsely settled due to its size. It's 4,038 square miles and growing—all of the other islands could fit onto the Big Island and there would still be room left over. The southernmost island in the chain, the Big Island is home to Kīleau, the most active volcano on the planet.

Kaua'i. The northernmost island in the chain, Kaua'i is, at approximately 540 square miles, the fourth largest of all the islands and the least populated of the larger islands, with just under 55,000 residents. Known as the Garden Isle, Kaua'i claims the title "wettest spot on Earth" with an annual average rainfall of 460 inches. Lush and peaceful, it's the perfect escape from the modern world.

Moloka'i. Moloka'i is Hawai'i's fifth largest island, encompassing 380 square miles. Moloka'i is very sparsely populated, with just under 7,000 residents, the majority of whom are native Hawaiians. Most of Moloka'i's 450,000 annual visitors travel from Maui or O'ahu to spend the day exploring its beaches, cliffs, and former leper colony.

Lāna'i. Lying just off Maui's western coast, Lāna'i looks nothing like its sister islands, with pine trees and deserts in place of palm trees and beaches. Still, the tiny 140-square-mile island is home to nearly 2,500 residents and draws an average of 70,000 visitors each year to two resorts (one in the mountains and one at the shore), both now operated by the Four Seasons.

Geology

The Hawaiian Islands comprise more than just the islands inhabited and visited by humans. A total of 19 islands and atolls constitute the State of Hawai'i, with a total landmass of 6,423.4 square miles. The islands are actually exposed peaks of a submersed mountain range called the Hawaiian-Emperor seamount chain. The range was formed as the Pacific plate moved very slowly (around 32 miles every million years) over a "hotspot" in the Earth's man-

tle. Because the plate moved northwestwardly, the islands in the northwest portion of the archipelago (chain) are older, which is also why they're smaller—they have been eroding longer.

The Big Island is the youngest, and thus the largest, island in the chain. It is built from seven different volcanoes, including Mauna Loa which is the largest shield volcano on the planet. Mauna Loa and Kīlauea are the only Hawaiian volcanoes still in the phase of development where explosions occur with any sort of frequency. Mauna Loa last erupted in 1984, and Kīlauea is currently erupting and has been since 1983. Mauna Kea (Big Island), Hualālai (Big Island), and Haleakalā (Maui) are all in what's called the Post Shield stage of volcanic development—eruptions decrease steadily for up to 250,000 years before ceasing entirely. Kohala (Big Island), Lāna'i (Lāna'i), and Wai'anae (O'ahu) are considered extinct volcanoes, in the erosional stage of development; Ko'olau (O'ahu) and West Maui (Maui) volcanoes are extinct volcanoes in the rejuvenation stage—after lying dormant for hundreds of thousands of years, they began erupting again, but only once every several thousand years. There is currently an active undersea volcano called Lo'ihi that has been erupting regularly. If it continues its current pattern, it should breach the ocean's surface in tens of thousands of years.

Flora & Fauna

Though much of the plantlife associated with Hawai'i today (pineapple, hibiscus, orchid, plumeria) was brought there by Tahitian, Samoan, or European visitors, Hawai'i is also home to several endemic species, like the koa tree and the yellow hibiscus. Long dormant volcanic craters are the perfect hiding place for rare plants (like the silversword, a rare cousin of the sunflower, which grows in Maui's Haleakalā crater and in few other places on Earth). Many of these endemic species are now threatened by the encroachment of introduced plants and animals. Hawai'i is also home to a handful of plants that have evolved into uniquely Hawaiian versions of their original selves. Mint, for example, develops its unique taste to keep would-be predators from eating its leaves. As there were no such predators in Hawai'i for hundreds of years, a mintless mint evolved; similar stories exist for the islands' nettle-less nettles, thorn-less briars.

Hawai'i's climate is well suited to growing several types of flowers, most of which are introduced species. Plumeria creeps over all of the islands; orchids run rampant on the Big Island; bright orange 'ilima light up the mountains of O'ahu. These flowers give the Hawaiian leis their color and fragrance.

As with the plantlife, the majority of the animals in Hawai'i today were brought here by visitors. Axis deer from India roam the mountains of Lāna'i. The Islands are home to dozens of rat species, all stowaways on long boat rides over from Tahiti, England, and Samoa; the mongoose was brought to keep the rats out of the sugar plantations. Most of Hawai'i's birds, like the nēnē (Hawai'i's state bird) and the Po'ouli owl are endemic; unfortunately about 80% are also endangered.

The ocean surrounding the Islands teems with animal life. Once scarce manta rays have made their way back to the Big Island; spinner dolphins and sea turtles can be found off the coast of all the Islands; and every year from December to May, the

humpback whales migrate past Hawai'i in droves.

History

Anthropologists believe that the Hawaiian Islands were initially settled by Polynesians from the Marquesas and Society Islands in approximately 300 AD. They were followed not long after by Tahitian settlers who quickly booted the Polynesians from the Islands. For whatever reason, exploration in this part of the world ceased for hundreds of years, and there are very few documented stories of any visitors to Hawai'i from the arrival of the Tahitians in the 300s to the arrival of British explorer Captain James Cook in 1778.

Frequent battles between warring chiefs dominated Hawaiian life throughout its first few centuries. In 1810, the chief Kamehameha from the Big Island united all of the Islands and tribes into one kingdom, just in time to protect the land and the culture from European explorers and Catholic missionaries. Though Cook and his compatriots are vilified now in Hawaiian history, they were welcomed as gods upon their initial arrival, and the natives bought guns and ammunition from the newcomers.

Under Kamehameha (from 1810 to 1872), the kingdom was relatively peaceful, despite the arrival of settlers from both Europe and America. Foreigners were accepted into the society, and they even participated in high levels of government. After the last of King Kamehameha's family had died without an heir, Kalakaua was appointed ruler (a great lover of hula, King Kalakaua was also known as the Merrie Monarch, which is where Hawai'i's yearly hula festival gets its name). Unfortunately, Kalakaua was coerced into signing the Bayonet Constitution, which

rendered the monarchy powerless. In 1893 Queen Lili'uokalani (Kalakaua's sister and heir to the throne) threatened to repeal the Bayonet Constitution and was subsequently overthrown by a group of American and European businessmen and government officials, aided by an armed militia. This led to the creation of the Republic of Hawai'i, which quickly became a Territory of the United States through resolutions passed by Congress (rather than through treaties). Hawai'i remained a territory for 60 years; Pearl Harbor was attacked as part of the United States in 1941 during World War II. It wasn't until 1959, however, that Hawai'i was officially admitted as the 50th State.

Legends & Mythology

Ancient deities play a huge role in Hawaiian life today—not just in daily rituals, but in the Hawaiians' reverence for their land. All of the gods and goddesses are associated with particular parts of the land, and most of them are connected with many parts thanks to the body of stories built up around each.

The goddess Pele lives in Kīlauea Volcano and rules over the Big Island. She is a feisty goddess known for turning enemies into trees or destroying the homes of adversaries with fire. She also has a penchant for gin, which is why you'll see gin bottles circling some of the craters at Volcanoes National Park. It's not the litter it appears to be, but rather an offering to placate the Volcano goddess. The Valley Isle's namesake, the demigod Maui, is a well-known Polynesian trickster. When his mother Hina complained that there were too few hours in the day, Maui promised to slow the sun. Upon hearing this, the god Moemoe teased Maui for boasting, but undeterred, the demigod wove a strong cord and lassoed

the sun. Angry, the sun scorched the fields until an agreement was reached: during summer, the sun would travel more slowly. In winter, it would return to its quick pace. For ridiculing Maui, Moemoe was turned into a large rock that still juts from the water near Kahakualoa.

One of the most important ways the ancient Hawaiians showed respect for their gods and goddesses was through the hula. Various forms of the hula were performed as prayers to the gods and as praise to the chiefs. Performances were taken very seriously, as a mistake was thought to invalidate the prayer, or even to offend the god or chief in question. Hula is still performed both as entertainment and as prayer; it is not uncommon for a hula performance to be included in an official government ceremony.

Hawai'i Today

After a long period of suppression, Hawaiian culture and traditions have experienced a renaissance over the last few decades. An unexpected result of rapid development fueled by mainland and Asian investments has been a resurgence of Hawaiian pride. There is a real effort to maintain traditions and to respect history as the Islands go through major changes and welcome more and more newcomers every day. New developments are required to have a Hawaiian cultural expert on staff to ensure cultural sensitivity and to educate newcomers.

Nonetheless, development remains a huge issue for all Islanders—land prices are skyrocketing, putting many areas out of reach for the native population. Traffic is becoming a problem on roads that were not designed to accommodate all the new drivers, and the Islands' limited natural resources are being seriously tapped. The government, though sluggish to respond at first, is trying to make development in Hawai'i as sustainable as possible. Rules for new developments protect natural as well as cultural resources, and local governments have set ambitious conservation goals (Honolulu's mayor wants to reduce energy usage by at least 20% by 2007). Despite all efforts to ease its effect on the land and its people, large-scale, rapid development is not anyone's ideal, and Islanders are understandably less than thrilled with the prospect of a million more tourists visiting every year or buying up property that residents themselves can't afford.

That said, the aloha spirit is alive and well. Though you may encounter the occasional "howlie" hater (howlie is pidgin for Mainlander or non-Hawaiian), the majority of Islanders are warm, a welcoming people who are proud that their home draws so many visitors and who are eager to share their culture with those who respect it.

Exploring O'ahu

Green sea turtles, Lanikai Beach

WORD OF MOUTH

"When and if you're tired of the city, just drive around the island a bit, and you will find wonderful little towns and beautiful scenery."
—crefloors

"Pu'uomahuka Heiau . . . is very sacred to the Hawaiians, and when you visit you will have beautiful views of Waimea Bay and the coastline. You will see many tiny bundles wrapped in ti leaves at the site where locals still come and leave them."
—sunbum1944

By Wanda
Adams

SHOULD YOU EVEN BOTHER WITH O'AHU? Aren't the Neighbor Islands where the real beauty of Hawai'i lives? Isn't Honolulu just another traffic-clogged city and Waikīkī just another tourist trap? To answer, we present these O'ahu scenes:

• The broad golden sands and turquoise waters of Kailua Beach.

• The shops of Chinatown noisy with a half-dozen languages, stacked with mysterious goods, redolent of steaming pastries and jasmine lei.

• The creaking wooden floors of the Queen Emma Summer Palace and the hushed voice of a guide who seems to be speaking of beloved friends, transporting you back 100 years.

• Sunset Beach on a winter morning, the power of the waves communicating itself in the throbbing sand under your feet, the surfers slicing furrows through the walls of water.

• A looping, easy trail through a cool forest above 'Āiea, a sharma thrush imitating your whistle, the perfume of ferns, a sudden view into an untouched emerald valley.

• Darkness and the hair-raising call of the ancient nose flute introducing a hula—not a tourist show but a recital by an amateur troupe that dances for love.

• A catamaran off the Wai'ane Coast, slapping through mischievous winter waves while spinner dolphins wheel and turn in the froth, seeming to eye you with intelligent interest.

• An outdoor stage just yards from the beach where a twentysomething island hipster is demonstrating why 'ukulele means "jumping flea," reinterpreting rock.

In short, O'ahu is one-stop Hawai'i—all the allure of the Islands in a chop-suey mix that has you kayaking around offshore islets by day and sitting in a jazz club 'round midnight, all without ever having to take another flight or repack your suitcase.

It has more museums, staffed historic sites, and walking tours than any other island. And only here do a wealth of renovated buildings and well-preserved neighborhoods so clearly spin the story of Hawai'i history. It's the only place to experience island-style urbanity, since there are no other true cities in the state. And yet you can get as lost in the rural landscape and be as laid-back as you wish.

Planning Your Time
But how to go about savoring O'ahu's many delights? Try alternating relaxing days with strenuous, city days with country, museum tours with adventure excursions.

If we were ranking O'ahu regions in order, it would look like this:

• **Downtown and Chinatown.** Tour 'Iolani Palace and the Mission Houses Museum, go on to Chinatown, shop and eat.

- North Shore and Windward Side. Head north and catch Windward (Kāneʻohe, Kailua) on the way back, or go north from Windward—your choice. Shop, eat, surf-watch, snorkel, see surfers and turtles.

- East Oʻahu, Makapuʻu, and Waimānalo. Visit Hanauma Bay, the Hālona Blow Hole, Bellows Beach—a beach clothes, plate lunch day.

- Central and Leeward Oʻahu. Visit a living history museum chronicling the plantation era, then beaches, sacred sites, whale-watching in winter. Be alert for car and beach thefts, racial tensions.

Each of these quadrants is a good day's exploring, as is the Pearl Harbor Memorial—especially if you add in the "Mighty Mo" and the *Bowfin* submarine (both much more fun for kids than the Memorial). Go on Wednesday to combine Pearl Harbor with a Swap Meet crawl at the Aloha Stadium, the place for tacky souvenirs, cheap T-shirts, and casual wear.

And if you're not staying in Waikīkī, do reserve a half-day to walk the storied beach, take a surf lesson, check out a show, and shop.

Some caveats for 2007: Oʻahu is under much-needed renovation with Waikīkī hotels and streets, the H-1 freeway, the Bishop Museum, and the Pearl Harbor Memorial all affected. Enquire closely about renovation near the hotel you choose; if there's anything going on within a few doors, pick another hotel. And anytime you plan to visit an attraction, call ahead to be sure hours haven't changed, and the particular things you want to see aren't closed.

DIAMOND HEAD & KAPIʻOLANI PARK
A NATURAL WONDER & A KING'S GIFT

Diamond Head Crater is perhaps Hawaiʻi's most recognizable natural landmark. It got its name from sailors who thought they had found precious gems on its slopes; these later proved to be calcite crystals, fool's gold. Hawaiians saw a resemblance in the sharp angle of the crater's seaward slope to the oddly shaped head of the ʻahi fish and so called it Lēʻahi, though later they Hawaiianized the English name to Kaimana Hila. It is commemorated in a widely-known hula—"A ʻike i ka nani o Kaimana Hila, Kaimana Hila, kai mai iluna/We saw the beauty of Diamond Head, Diamond Head set high above."

Kapiʻolani Park lies in the shadow of the crater. King David Kalākaua established the park in 1887, named it after his queen, and dedicated it "to the use and enjoyment of the people." Kapiʻolani Park is a 500-acre expanse where you can play all sorts of field sports, enjoy a picnic, see wild animals at the Honolulu Zoo, or hear live music at the Waikīkī Shell or the Kapiʻolani Bandstand. It's also the start and finish point for many weekend walks; check local newspapers or gohawaii.com.

Top Attractions
❶ Diamond Head State Monument and Park. Panoramas from this 760-foot extinct volcanic peak, once used as a military fortification, extend from

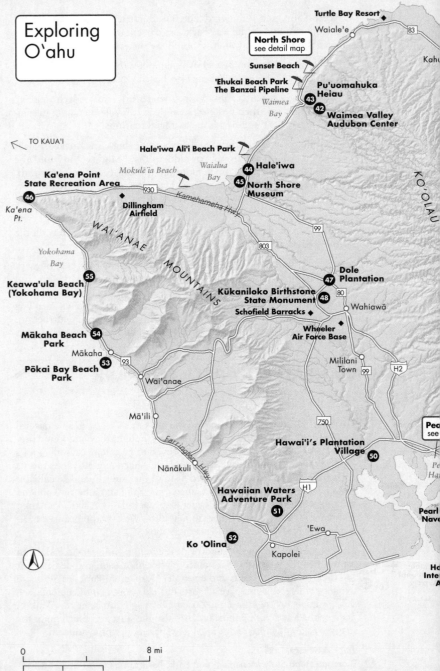

Exploring O'ahu

TO KAUA'I

Turtle Bay Resort

Waiale'e

83

Kahu

North Shore
see detail map

Sunset Beach

'Ehukai Beach Park
The Banzai Pipeline

43

Pu'uomahuka Heiau

Waimea Bay

42

Waimea Valley Audubon Center

Hale'iwa Ali'i Beach Park

Mokulē'ia Beach

Waialua Bay

44 **Hale'iwa**

45 **North Shore Museum**

Ka'ena Point State Recreation Area

46

Ka'ena Pt.

930

Kamehameha Hwy.

Dillingham Airfield

KO'OLAU

99

803

Yokohama Bay

WAI'ANAE MOUNTAINS

Dole Plantation

47

Keawa'ula Beach (Yokohama Bay)

55

Kūkaniloko Birthstone State Monument

48

80

Wahiawā

Schofield Barracks

Mākaha Beach Park

54

Mākaha

53

93

Wheeler Air Force Base

Pōkai Bay Beach Park

Wai'anae

Mililani Town

99

H2

Mā'ili

Farrington Hwy.

750

Nānākuli

Hawai'i's Plantation Village

50

Pea
see

Hawaiian Waters Adventure Park

H1

Pe
Ha

51

Pearl
Nav

Ko 'Olina

52

'Ewa

Kapolei

Ho
Inte
A

0   8 mi

0   8 km

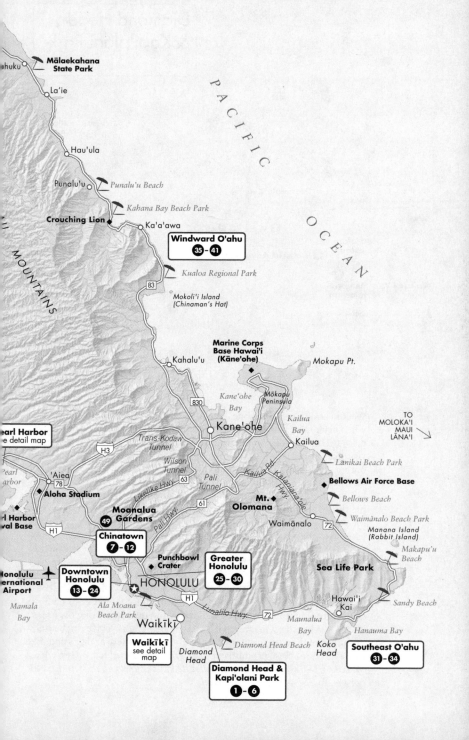

**Mālaekahana
State Park**

ʻahuku

Laʻie

PACIFIC

Hauʻula

Punaluʻu

Punaluʻu Beach

Kahana Bay Beach Park

Crouching Lion

Kaʻaʻawa

OCEAN

**Windward Oʻahu
35-41**

Kualoa Regional Park

83

*Mokoliʻi Island
(Chinaman's Hat)*

**Marine Corps
Base Hawaiʻi
(Kāneʻohe)**

Kahaluʻu

Mokapu Pt.

HAU MOUNTAINS

830

*Kaneʻohe
Bay*

*Mōkapu
Peninsula*

*Kailua
Bay*

Kaneʻohe

TO
MOLOKAʻI
MAUI
LĀNAʻI

Pearl Harbor
ee detail map

H3

*Trans-Kodaw
Tunnel*

*Wilson
Tunnel*

63

*Pali
Tunnel*

Kailua Rd

Kailua

Lanikai Beach Park

*Pearl
arbor*

ʻAiea

Bellows Air Force Base

78

Likelike Hwy

61

**Mt.
Olomana**

Bellows Beach

Aloha Stadium

l Harbor
val Base

H1

**Moanalua
Gardens**
49

Pali Hwy

Waimānalo

Waimānalo Beach Park

72

*Manana Island
(Rabbit Island)*

**Chinatown
7-12**

*Makapuʻu
Beach*

onolulu
ernational
Airport

**Downtown
Honolulu
13-24**

*Punchbowl
Crater*

**Greater
Honolulu
25-30**

Sea Life Park

*Mamala
Bay*

HONOLULU

H1

**Hawaiʻi
Kai**

Sandy Beach

*Ala Moana
Beach Park*

Lunalilo Hwy

72

*Maunalua
Bay*

*Koko
Head*

Hanauma Bay

Waikīkī

Waikīkī
see detail
map

*Diamond
Head*

Diamond Head Beach

**Southeast Oʻahu
31-34**

**Diamond Head &
Kapiʻolani Park
1-6**

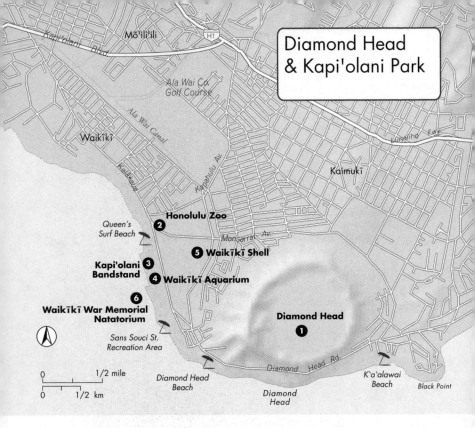

Honolulu Zoo

Queen's
Surf Beach

Monsarrat Av.

Waikīkī Shell

Kapi'olani
Bandstand

Waikīkī Aquarium

Diamond Head

Waikīkī War Memorial
Natatorium

Sans Souci St.
Recreation Area

0   1/2 mile

0   1/2 km

Diamond Head
Beach

Diamond
Head Rd.

Kʻaʻalawai
Beach

Black Point

Diamond
Head

Waikīkī and Honolulu in one direction and out to Koko Head in the other, with surfers and windsurfers scattered like confetti on the cresting waves below. This 360-degree perspective is a great orientation for first-time visitors. On a clear day, look to your left past Koko Head to glimpse the outlines of the islands of Maui and Moloka'i. To enter the park from Waikīkī, take Kalākaua Avenue east, turn left at Monsarrat Avenue, head a mile up the hill, and look for a sign on the right. Drive through the tunnel to the inside of the crater. The ¾-mi trail to the top begins at the parking lot. New lighting inside the summit tunnel and a spiral staircase eases the way, but be aware that the hike to the crater is a strenuous upward climb; if you aren't in the habit of getting much exercise, this might not be for you. Take bottled water with you to ensure that you stay hydrated under the tropical sun. ■ TIP→ To beat the heat and the crowds, rise early and make the hike before 8 AM. As you walk, note the color of the vegetation; if the mountain is brown, Honolulu has been without significant rain for a while; but if the trees and undergrowth glow green, it's the wet season when rare Hawaiian marsh plants revive on the floor of the crater. Keep an eye on your watch if you're there at day's end, because the gates close promptly at 6. ⊠ *Diamond Head Rd. at 18th Ave., Waikīkī* ☎ *808/587–0285* ⊕ *www.state.hi.us/dlnr/dsp/oahu.html* ☞ *$1 per person, $5 per vehicle.* ⊙ *Daily 6–6.*

Also Worth Seeing

2 Honolulu Zoo. To get a glimpse of the endangered nēnē, the Hawaiʻi state bird, check out the Kipuka Nēnē Sanctuary. Though many animals seem to prefer to remain invisible, the monkeys appear to enjoy being seen and are a hoot to watch. It's best to get to the zoo right when it opens, since the animals are livelier in the cool of the morning. There are bigger and better zoos, but this one, though showing signs of neglect due to budget restraints, is a lush garden and has some great programs. On Wednesday evenings in summer, there's The Wildest Show in Town, a series of $1 admission concerts. On weekends look for the Zoo Fence Art Mart, on Monsarrat Avenue on the Diamond Head side outside the zoo, for affordable artwork by contemporary artists. The offerings for families are also appealing. Consider a family sleepover inside the zoo during Snooze in the Zoo events, which take place on a Friday or Saturday night every month. Or just head for the petting zoo, where kids can make friends with a llama and meet Abbey, the zoo's resident monitor lizard. There's also an exceptionally good gift shop. Metered parking is available all along the makai side of the park and in the lot next to the zoo. TheBus (routes 22 and 58) makes stops here along the way to and from Ala Moana Center and Sea Life Park. ⊠ *151 Kapahulu Ave., Waikīkī* ☎ *808/971–7171* ⊕ *www.honoluluzoo.org* ⌨ *$6* ⊙ *Daily 9–4:30.*

3 Kapiʻolani Bandstand. An interpretation of the Victorian Kapiʻolani Bandstand, which was originally built in the late 1890s, is Kapiʻolani Park's centerpiece for community entertainment and concerts. The nation's only city-sponsored band, the Royal Hawaiian Band, performs free concerts on Sunday afternoons. Local newspapers list entertainment information. ⊠ *Near the intersection of Kalākaua and Monsarrat Aves., Waikīkī.*

4 Waikīkī Aquarium. This amazing little attraction harbors more than 2,500 organisms and 420 species of Hawaiian and South Pacific marine life, endangered Hawaiian monk seals, sharks, and the only chambered nautilus living in captivity. The Edge of the Reef exhibit showcases five different types of reef environments found along Hawaiʻi's shorelines. Check out the Sea Visions Theater, the biodiversity exhibit, and the self-guided audio tour, which is included with admission. Programs include Exploring the Reef at Night, Shark Nites, Stingray Tracking, and Aquarium After Dark activities. Give the aquarium an hour, including 10 minutes for a film in its Sea Visions Theater. ⊠ *2777 Kalākaua Ave., Waikīkī* ☎ *808/923–9741* ⊕ *www.waquarium.org* ⌨ *$9* ⊙ *Daily 9–4:30.*

> **UNDER THE STARS**
>
> Waikīkī's entertainment scene isn't just dinner shows and lounge acts. There are plenty of free or nearly free offerings right on the beach and at Kapiʻolani Park. Queen's Surf Beach hosts the popular Sunset on the Beach, which brings big-screen showings of recent Hollywood blockbusters to the great outdoors. Also, during the summer months, the Honolulu Zoo has weekly concerts, and admission is just $1. (⇨ See Entertainment & Nightlife *in Chapter 7.*)

5 **Waikīkī Shell.** Local people bring picnics and grab one of the 6,000 "grass seats" (lawn seating) for music under the stars (there are actual seats, as well). Concerts are held May 1 to Labor Day, with a few winter dates, weather permitting. Check newspaper Friday entertainment sections to see who is performing. ⌧ *2805 Monsarrat Ave., Waikīkī* ☎ *808/924–8934* ⊕ *www.blaisdellcenter.com.*

6 **Waikīkī War Memorial Natatorium.** This 1927 World War I monument, dedicated to the 102 Hawaiian servicemen who lost their lives in battle, stands proudly—its 20-foot archway, which was completely restored in 2002, is floodlighted at night. The 100-meter saltwater swimming pool, the training spot for Olympians Johnny Weissmuller and Buster Crabbe and the U.S. Army during World War II, is closed as the facility has fallen into disrepair while a debate rages within city government about whether to refurbish the pool or leave only the archway monument. ⌧ *2777 Kalākaua Ave., Waikīkī.*

■ **NEED A BREAK?**

According to legend, Robert Louis Stevenson once sat beneath the eponymous *hau* tree in the courtyard of the **Hau Tree Lānai** (⌧ 2863 Kalākaua Ave. ☎ 808/921-7066). You can enjoy the same shade, plus breakfast, lunch, or dinner, at this find in the New Otani Kaimana Beach Hotel, next to the Natatorium.

WAIKĪKĪ See Page 27

HONOLULU

Here is Hawai'i's only true metropolis, its seat of government, center of commerce and shipping, entertainment and recreation mecca, a historic site and an evolving urban area–conflicting roles that engender endless debate and controversy. For the visitor, Honolulu is an everyman's delight: hipsters and scholars, sightseers and foodies, nature lovers and culture vultures all can find their bliss.

Once there was the broad bay of Mamala and the narrow inlet of Kou, fronting a dusty plain occupied by a few thatched houses and the great Pakaka *heiau* (shrine). Nosing into the narrow passage in the early 1790s, British sea captain William Brown named the port Fair Haven. Later, Hawaiians would call it Honolulu–"sheltered bay." As shipping traffic increased, the settlement grew into a Western-style town of streets and buildings, tightly clustered around the single fresh water source, Nu'uanu Stream. Not until piped water became available in the early 1900s did Honolulu spread across the greening plain. Long before that, however, Honolulu gained importance when King Kamehameha I, reluctantly abandoning his home on the Big Island, built a chiefly compound near the harbor in 1804 to better protect Hawaiian interests from the Western incursion.

Continued on page 33

INS & OUTS OF WAIKĪKĪ

Waikīkī is all that is wonderful about a resort area, and all that is regrettable. On the wonderful side: swimming, surfing, parasailing, and catamaran-riding steps from the street; the best nightlife in Hawai'i;

shopping from designer to dime stores; and experiences to remember: the heart-lifting rush the first time you stand up on a surfboard, watching the old men play cutthroat checkers in the beach pavilions, eating fresh grilled snapper as the sun slips into the sea. As to the regrettable: clogged streets, body-lined beaches, $5 cups of coffee, tacky T-shirts, $20 parking stalls, schlocky art-work, the same street performers you saw in Atlantic City, drunks, ceaseless construction—all rather brush the bloom from the plumeria.

Modern Waikīkī is nothing like its original self, a network of streams, marshes, and islands that drained the inland valleys. The Ala Wai Canal took care of

that in the 1920s. More recently, new landscaping, walkways, and a general attention to infrastructure have brightened a façade that had begun distinctly to fade.

But throughout its history, Waikīkī has retained its essential character: an enchantment that cannot be fully explained and one that, though diminished by high-rises, traffic, and noise, has not yet disappeared. Hawaiian royalty came here, and visitors continue to follow, falling in love with sharp-prowed Diamond Head, the sensuous curve of shoreline with its baby-safe waves, and the strong-footed surfers like moving statues in the golden light.

WAIKĪKĪ WEST

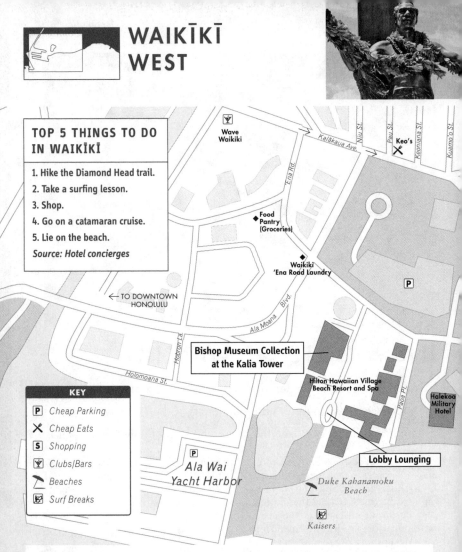

TOP 5 THINGS TO DO IN WAIKĪKĪ

1. Hike the Diamond Head trail.
2. Take a surfing lesson.
3. Shop.
4. Go on a catamaran cruise.
5. Lie on the beach.

Source: Hotel concierges

Wave Waikiki

Kalakaua Ave.

Niu St.

Pau St.

Keoniana St.

Kuamo'o St.

Keo's

Food Pantry (Groceries)

Ena Rd.

Waikīkī 'Ena Road Laundry

P

← TO DOWNTOWN HONOLULU

Ala Moana Blvd.

Hotront La.

Bishop Museum Collection at the Kalia Tower

Holomoana St.

Hilton Hawaiian Village Beach Resort and Spa

Paoa Pl.

Halekoa Military Hotel

KEY

P *Cheap Parking*
✕ *Cheap Eats*
S *Shopping*
Ⓨ *Clubs/Bars*
⚐ *Beaches*
⚑ *Surf Breaks*

P

Ala Wai Yacht Harbor

Lobby Lounging

Duke Kahanamoku Beach

Kaisers

CHEAP EATS

Keo's, 2028 Kūhiō: Breakfast.

Malia Cafe, 2211 Kūhiō: American/local diner.

Pho Old Saigon, 2270 Kūhiō: Vietnamese.

Japanese noodle shops: Try Menchanko-Tei, Waikīkī Trade Center; Ezogiku, 2164 Kalākaua.

■ TIP → Thanks to the many Japanese nationals who stay here, Waikīkī is blessed with lots of cheap, authentic Japanese food, particularly noodles. Plastic representations of food in the window are an indicator of authenticity and a help in ordering.

SHOP, SHOP, SHOP/PARTY, PARTY, PARTY

2100 Kalākaua: Select high-end European boutiques (Chanel, Gucci, Yves Saint Laurent).

Island Treasures Antique Mall: Hawaiian collectibles from precious to priceless. 2145 Kūhiō Ave. 808/922-8223.

Wave Waikīkī: This multi-story madhouse of sound and writhing bodies is a bit rough around the edges but hugely popular with locals. 1877 Kalākaua Ave. 808/941-0424.

Zanzabar: Upscale Zanzabar is a different club every night–Latin, global, over 30, under 18.

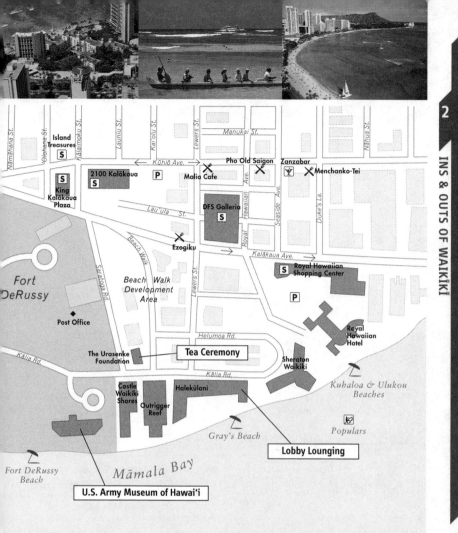

Fort DeRussy

Post Office

Fort DeRussy Beach

Māmala Bay

Island Treasures S

King Kalākaua Plaza S

2100 Kalākaua S P

Pho Old Saigon

Malia Cafe

Zanzabar Menchanko-Tei

Kūhiō Ave.

Manukai St.

Lau'ula St.

DFS Galleria S

Ezogiku

Kalākaua Ave.

Royal Hawaiian Shopping Center S

P

Beach Walk Development Area

Helumoa Rd.

The Urasenke Foundation

Tea Ceremony

Kālia Rd.

Kālia Rd.

Castle Waikīkī Shores

Outrigger Reef

Halekūlani

Sheraton Waikiki

Royal Hawaiian Hotel

Kuhaloa & Ulukou Beaches

Populars

Lobby Lounging

Gray's Beach

U.S. Army Museum of Hawai'i

Waikīkī Trade Center, 2255 Kūhiō Ave. 808/924-3939.

RAINY DAY IDEAS

Lobby Lounging: Among Waikīkī's great gathering spots are Halekūlani's tranquil courtyards with gorgeous flower arrangements and glimpses of the famous and the Hilton Hawaiian Village's flagged pathways with koi ponds, squawking parrots, and great shops.

Bishop Museum Collection at the Kalia Tower, Hilton Hawaiian Village: 8,000-square-foot branch of Hawai'i's premier cultural archive

illuminates life in Waikīkī through the years and the history of the Hawaiian people. 2005 Kalia Rd. 808/947-2458. $7. Daily 10-5.

Tea Ceremony, Urasenke Foundation: Japan's mysterious tea ceremony is demonstrated. 245 Saratoga Rd. 808/923-3059. $3 donation. Wed., Fri. 10-noon.

U.S. Army Museum of Hawai'i: Exhibits, including photographs and military equipment, trace the history of Army in the Islands. Battery Randolph, Kalia Rd., Fort DeRussy. 808/438-2821. Free. Tues.-Sun. 10-4:15.

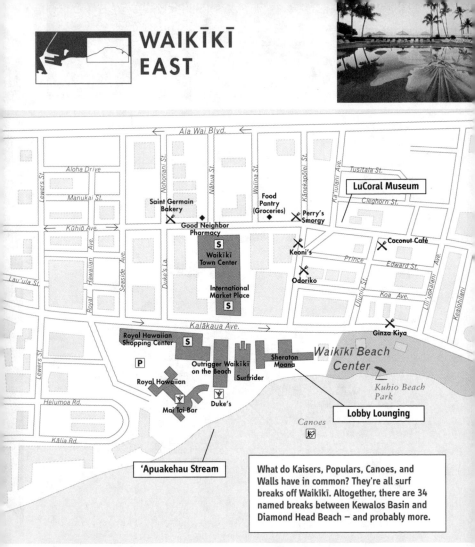

WAIKĪKĪ EAST

LuCoral Museum

Lobby Lounging

'Apuakehau Stream

What do Kaisers, Populars, Canoes, and Walls have in common? They're all surf breaks off Waikīkī. Altogether, there are 34 named breaks between Kewalos Basin and Diamond Head Beach — and probably more.

CHEAP EATS

Coconut Café, 2441 Kūhiō: Burgers, sandwiches under $5; fresh fruit smoothies.

Ginza Kiya, 2464 Kalākaua: Japanese noodle shop.

Keoni's, Outrigger East Hotel, 150 Kaiulani Ave.: Breakfasts at rock-bottom prices.

Odoriko, King's Village, 131 Kāiulani Ave.: Japanese noodle shop.

Perry's Smorgy Restaurant, 2380 Kūhiō: family-friendly American food; brunch under $10.

■ TIP → To save money, go inland. Kūhiō, one block toward the mountains from the main drag

of Kalākaua, is lined with less expensive restaurants, hotels, and shops.

SHOP, SHOP, SHOP/PARTY, PARTY, PARTY

Sheraton Moana Surfrider: Pick up a present at Noeha Gallery or Sand People. Then relax with a drink at the venerable Banyan Veranda. The radio program *Hawai'i Calls* first broadcast to a mainland audience from here in 1935.

Duke's Canoe Club, Outrigger Waikīkī: Beach party central.

Mai Tai Bar at the Royal Hawaiian: Birthplace of the Mai Tai.

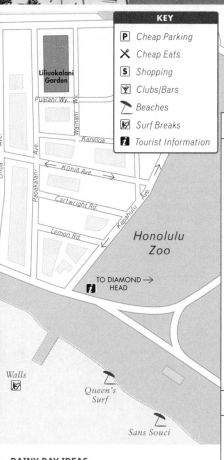

KEY

P	*Cheap Parking*
✕	*Cheap Eats*
S	*Shopping*
☂	*Clubs/Bars*
☂	*Beaches*
🏄	*Surf Breaks*
ℹ	*Tourist Information*

Liliuokalani Garden

Pualani Wy.

Waimani Wy.

Kaneloa

Ohua Ave.

Paoakalani Ave.

Kūhiō Ave.

Cartwright Rd.

Kapahulu Ave.

Lemon Rd.

Honolulu Zoo

TO DIAMOND → HEAD
ℹ

Walls
🏄

Queen's Surf

Sans Souci

RAINY DAY IDEAS

Lobby lounging: Check out the century-old, period-furnished lobby and veranda of the Sheraton Moana Surfrider Hotel on Kalākaua.

LuCoral Museum: Exhibit and shop explores the world of coral and other semi-precious stones; wander about or take $2 guided tour and participate in jewelry-making activity. 2414 Kūhiō.

WHAT THE LOCALS LOVE

Paid-parking–phobic Islanders usually avoid Waikīkī, but these attractions are juicy enough to lure locals:

■ **Auntie Genoa Keawe**, old-style lū'au music Thursdays at the Waikīkī Beach Marriott Resort and Spa.

■ **Pan-Pacific Festival-Matsuri in Hawaii**, a summer cultural festival that's as good as a trip to Japan.

■ **Aloha Festivals in September**, the legendary floral parade and evening show of contemporary Hawaiian music.

■ **The Wildest Show in Town**, $1 summer concerts at the Honolulu Zoo.

■ **Sunset on the Beach**, free films projected on an outdoor screen at Queen's Beach, with food and entertainment.

'APUAKEHAU STREAM

Wade out just in front of the Outrigger Waikīkī on the Beach and feel a current of chilly water curling around your ankles. This is the last remnant of three streams that once drained the inland valleys behind you, making of Waikīkī a place of swamps, marshes, taro and rice paddies, and giving it the name "spouting water." High-ranking chiefs surfed in a legendary break gouged out by the draining freshwater and rinsed off afterward in the stream whose name means "basket of dew." The Ala Wai Canal, completed in the late 1920s, drained the land, reducing proud 'Apuakehau Stream to a determined phantom passing beneath Waikīkī's streets.

WHAT'S NEW & CHANGING

Waikīkī, which was looking a bit shop-worn, is in the midst of many makeovers. Ask about noise, disruption, and construction when booking. In addition to fresh landscaping and period light fixtures along Kalākaua and a pathway that encircles Ala Wai Canal, expect:

1. BEACH WALK: Virtually every structure in the area bounded by Beach Walk, Lewers Street, and Kalia and Saratoga Roads is coming down or dressing up in a $460 million, 7.9-acre project masterminded by an arm of the local Outrigger Hotel chain. Two older hotels will emerge as newly branded Embassy Suites and Fairfield properties, along with a "dynamic and diverse" retail complex of local and name-brand shops and restaurants (completion late 2006).

2. ROYAL HAWAIIAN SHOPPING CENTER AND INTERNATIONAL MARKETPLACE: The fortress-like Royal Hawaiian Shopping Center in the center of Kalākaua Avenue will become an open, inviting space with a palm grove and a new mix of shops and restaurants (completion 2006). And tacky International Marketplace shops will give way to a low-rise compound of entertainment spaces, kiosks, and water features, with many historic trees preserved (completion 2007).

3. CIRQUE HAWAI'I: This acrobatic show with an international cast is so new at this writing that there's no way to predict its staying power, though local reviews have been good. 325 Seaside Ave., 808/922-0017, $55-$95.

GETTING THERE

It can seem impossible to figure out how to get to Waikīkī from H-1. The exit is far inland, and even when you follow the signs, the route jigs and jogs; it sometimes seems a wonder that more tourists aren't found starving in Kaimuki.

FROM EASTBOUND H-1 (COMING FROM THE AIRPORT):
1. To western Waikīkī (Ft. DeRussy and most hotels): Take the Punahou exit from H-1, turn right on Punahou and get in the center lane. Go right on Beretania and almost immediately left onto Kalākaua, which takes you into Waikīkī.

2. To eastern Waikīkī (Kapi'olani Park): Take the King Street exit, and stay on King for two blocks. Go right on Kapahulu, which takes you to Kalākaua.

FROM WESTBOUND H-1:
Take the Kapi'olani Boulevard exit. Follow Kapi'olani to McCully, and go left on McCully. Follow McCully to Kalākaua, and you're in Waikīkī.

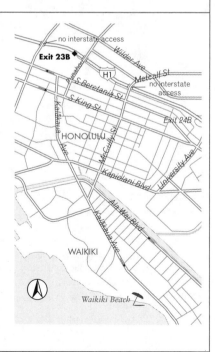

Two hundred years later, the entire island is, in a sense, Honolulu–the City and County of Honolulu. The city has no official boundaries, extending across the flatlands from Pearl Harbor to Waikīkī and high into the hills behind.

Chinatown

2

Honolulu's 15-Block Melting Pot

The name Chinatown has always been a misnomer. Though three-quarters of Oʻahu's Chinese lived closely packed in these 25 acres in the late 1800s, even then the neighborhood was half Japanese. Today, you hear Vietnamese and Tagalog as often as Mandarin and Cantonese, and there are touches of Japan, Singapore, Malaysia, Korea, Thailand, Samoa, and the Marshall Islands, as well.

Perhaps a more accurate name is the one used by early Chinese: Wah Fau, "Chinese port," signifying a landing and jumping-off place. Chinese laborers, as soon as they completed their plantation contracts, hurried into the city to start businesses here. It's a launching point for today's immigrants, too: Southeast Asian shops almost outnumber Chinese; stalls carry Filipino specialities like winged beans and goat meat; and in one tiny space, knife-wielding Samoans skin coconuts to order.

In the half-century after the first Chinese laborers arrived in Hawaiʻi in 1851, Chinatown was a link to home for the all-male cadre of workers who planned to return to China rich and respected. Merchants not only sold supplies, they held mail, loaned money, wrote letters, translated documents, sent remittances to families, served meals, offered rough bunkhouse accommodations, and were the center for news, gossip, and socializing.

Though much happened to Chinatown in the 20th century—beginning in January, 1900, with almost the entire neighborhood burned to the ground to halt the spread of bubonic plague—it remains a bustling, crowded, noisy, and odiferous place bent primarily on buying and selling and sublimely oblivious to its status as a National Historic District or the encroaching gentrification on nearby Nuʻuanu Avenue.

Its architectural signature was two-story wooden buildings with overhanging porches shading the sidewalks below. Businesses occupied the first floor, with living quarters above and hidden courtyards in the center. Although none today are original, buildings retain this profile, though in brick and stucco.

Chinatown's business district was made up of dry goods and produce merchants, tailors and dressmakers, barbers, herbalists, and dozens of restaurants. The meat, fish, and produce stalls remain but the mix is heavier now on gift and curio stores, lei stands, jewelry shops and bakeries with a smattering of noodle makers, travel agents, Asian-language video stores—and, of course, dozens of restaurants.

TIMING   Chinatown occupies 15 blocks immediately north of downtown Honolulu—it's flat, compact, and easily explored in half a day.

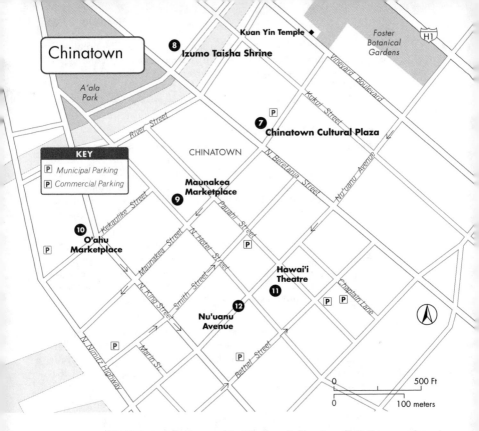

■ **TIP→** The best time to visit Chinatown is morning, when the *popos* (grand-mas) shop—it's cool, and you can enjoy a cheap dim sum breakfast. Chinatown is a seven-day-a-week operation. Sundays are especially busy with families sharing dim sum in raucous dining hall–size restaurants.

A caution: Hotel Street was Honolulu's red light district and A'ala Park, just across the Nu'uanu stream, shelters many homeless people and more than a few drug users. A police station in the heart of the district has tamped down crime, and the area is perfectly safe by day—even panhandling is rare. But at night, park in a well-lighted place, travel with the crowds, and be alert.

■ **TIP→** Look for well-marked municipal parking lots on Smith, Bethel, Nu'uanu, and Beretania; these charge a third of what the private lots demand.

If you're here between January 20 and February 20, check local newspapers or gohawaii.com for Chinese New Year activities. Bakeries stock special sweets, stores and homes sprout bright red scrolls, and lion dancers cavort through the streets feeding on *li-see* (money envelopes). The Narcissus Queen is chosen, and an evening street fair draws crowds.

Weekly tours of Chinatown are offered on Tuesdays by the Chinese Chamber of Commerce (⇨ O'ahu Sightseeing Tours *later in this chapter*).

Top Attractions

7 **Chinatown Cultural Plaza.** This sprawling multi-story shopping square surrounds a courtyard with an incense-wreathed shrine and Moongate stage for holiday performances. The Chee Kung Tong Society has a beautifully decorated meeting hall here; a number of such *tongs* (meeting places) are hidden on upper floors in Chinatown. ✉ *100 N. Beretania, Chinatown.*

8 **Izumo Taisha Shrine.** From Chinatown Cultural Plaza, cross a stone bridge to visit Okuninushi No Mikoto, a *kami* (god) who is believed in Shinto tradition to bring good fortune if properly courted (and thanked afterward). ✉ *N. Kukui and Canal, Chinatown* ☎ *No phone.*

Kuan Yin Temple. A couple of blocks *mauka* (toward the mountains) from Chinatown is the oldest Buddhist temple in the Islands. Mistakenly called a goddess by man, Kuan Yin, also known as Kannon, is a bodhisatva—one who chose to remain on earth doing good even after achieving enlightenment. Transformed from a male into a female figure centuries ago, she is credited with a particular sympathy for women. You will see representations of her all over the Islands: with a lotus flower (beauty from the mud of human frailty), as at the temple; pouring out a pitcher of oil (like mercy flowing), or as a sort of Madonna with a child. Visitors are permitted but be aware this is a practicing place of worship. ✉ *170 N. Vineyard, Downtown* ☎ *808/533–6371.*

9 **Maunakea Marketplace.** On the corner of Maunakea and Hotel streets is this plaza surrounded by shops, an indoor market, and a food court. Within the Marketplace, the **Hawaiian Chinese Cultural Museum and Archives** (✉ $2 ⊙ Mon.–Sat. 10–2) displays historic photographs and artifacts. ■ **TIP→ If you appreciate fine tea, visit the Tea Hut, an unpretentious counter inside a curio shop.** ✉ *1120 Maunakea St., Chinatown* ☎ *808/524–3409.*

★ 10 **O'ahu Marketplace.** Here is a taste of old-style Chinatown, where you're likely to be hustled aside as a whole pig (dead, of course) is wrestled through the crowd and where glassy-eyed fish of every size and hue lie stacked forlornly on ice. Try the bubble tea (juices and flavored teas with tapioca bubbles inside) or pick up a bizarre magenta dragonfruit for breakfast. ✉ *N. King St., at Kekaulike, Chinatown.*

SHOPS

You'll find ridiculously inexpensive gifts throughout Chinatown: folding fans for $1 and coconut purses for $5 at **Maunakea Marketplace,** for example. Curio shops sell everything from porcelain statues to woks, ginseng to Mao shoes. If you like to sew, or have a yen for a brocade cheong sam, visit **Imperial Tailors and Gifts and 1010 Fabrics** (North King Street and Maunakea). Narrow, dim, and dusty **Bo Wah Trading Co.** (1037 Maunakea) is full of inexpensive cooking utensils. **Chinatown Cultural Plaza** offers fine-quality jade. Chinatown is Honolulu's lei center, with shops strung along Beretania and Maunakea; every local has a favorite where they're greeted by name. In spring, look for gardenia nosegays wrapped in ti leaves.

Also Worth Seeing

⓫ **Hawai'i Theatre.** Opened in 1922, this theater earned rave reviews for its neoclassical theme with Corinthian columns, marble statues, and plush carpeting and drapery. Nicknamed the "Pride of the Pacific," the facility was rescued from demolition in the early 1980s and underwent a $30-million renovation. Listed on both the State and National Register of Historic Places, it has become the centerpiece of revitalization efforts of Honolulu's downtown area. The 1,200-seat venue hosts concerts, theatrical productions, dance performances, and film screenings. ✉ *1130 Bethel St., Chinatown* ☎ *808/528–0506* ✍ *$5* ⏲ *1-hr guided tours held every Tues. at 11.*

> **NEED A BREAK?**
>
> A world of small, inexpensive restaurants exists within Chinatown, among them:
> - **Golden Palace:** $1.50 dim sum
> - **Yusura:** Homey Japanese
> - **Ba-Le:** Vietnamese sandwiches
> - **Urumi:** Japanese noodles
> - **Grand Café & Bakery:** Retro diner
> - **Mabuhay:** Filipino standards
> - **Sweet Basil:** Thai buffet

⓬ **Nu'uanu Avenue.** Nu'uanu Avenue forms Chinatown's southern border. There and on Bethel Street are clustered art galleries, restaurants, a wine shop, an antiques auctioneer, a dress shop or two, one tiny theater space (The Arts at Mark's Garage), and one historic stage (the Hawai'i Theatre). **First Friday** art nights, when galleries stay open in the evening, draw crowds. ✉ *Nu'uanu Ave., Chinatown.*

Downtown Honolulu

The Capitol District

Honolulu's past and present play a delightful counterpoint throughout the downtown sector. Post-modern glass-and-steel office buildings look down on the Aloha Tower, built in 1926 and, until the early 1960s, the tallest structure in Honolulu. Hawai'i's history is told in the architecture of these few blocks: the cut-stone turn-of-the-century storefronts of Merchant Street, the gracious white-columned "American-Georgian" manor that was the home of the Islands' last queen, the jewel box palace occupied by the monarchy before it was overthrown, the Spanish-inspired stucco and tile-roofed Territorial-era government buildings, and the 21st-century glass pyramid of the First Hawaiian Bank Building.

TIMING Plan a couple of hours for exploring downtown's historic buildings, more if you're taking a guided tour or walk. The best time to visit is in the cool and relative quiet of the morning or on weekends when downtown is all but deserted except for the historic sites. To reach Downtown Honolulu from Waikīkī by car, take Ala Moana Boulevard to Alakea Street and turn right; three blocks up on the right, between South King and Hotel, there's a municipal parking lot in Ali'i Place on the right. You can also take Route 19 or 20 of TheBus to the Aloha Tower Marketplace or take a trolley from Waikīkī.

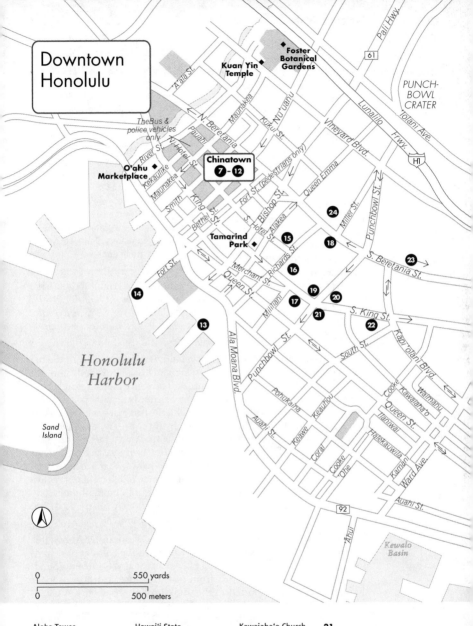

Downtown Honolulu

PUNCH-BOWL CRATER

Foster Botanical Gardens

Kuan Yin Temple

TheBus & police vehicles only

O'ahu Marketplace

Chinatown 7 - 12

Tamarind Park

Honolulu Harbor

Sand Island

Kewalo Basin

550 yards

500 meters

Top Attractions

16 **'Iolani Palace.** America's only royal

residence was built in 1882 on the site of an earlier palace, and it contains the thrones of King Kalākaua and his successor (and sister) Queen Lili'uokalani. Bucking the stereotype of the primitive islander, the palace had electricity and telephone lines installed even before the White House did. Downstairs galleries showcase the royal jewelry, and kitchen and offices of the monarchy. The palace is open for guided tours only, and reservations are essential.

■ TIP➔ If you're set on taking a tour, it might be worthwhile to call for reservations a few weeks in advance. Take

A HAWAIIAN SERVICE

Native Hawaiians who adopted Christianity brought with them a keen appreciation of protocol and a love of the poetic turn of phrase. Sunday worship at Kawaiaha'o Church affirms this with its greeters in white holokū, lei for visitors, and blessings and songs in Hawaiian. In this cradle of Protestant Christianity in the Islands, a prerequisite for the pastor is fluency in both languages. Don't worry; sermons are in English.

a look at the gift shop, formerly the 'Iolani Barracks, built to house the Royal Guard. ⊠ *King and Richards Sts., Downtown Honolulu* ☎ *808/ 522–0832* ⊕ *www.iolanipalace.org* ☶ *Grand Tour $20, downstairs galleries only $6* ⊙ *Grand Tour Tues.–Sat. 9–2, with tours beginning on half-hr; Galleries tour, Tues.–Sat. 9–4.*

17 **Kamehameha I Statue.** This downtown landmark pays tribute to the Big Island chieftain who united all the warring Hawaiian Islands into one kingdom at the turn of the 18th century. The statue, which stands with one arm outstretched in welcome, is one of three originally cast in Paris, France, by American sculptor T. R. Gould; the original—which was lost at sea for a time and had to be replaced by this one—was salvaged and now is in Kapa'au, on the Big Island, near the king's birthplace. Each year on the king's birthday, June 11, the statue is draped in fresh lei that reach lengths of 18 feet and longer. There's a parade that processes past the statue, and Hawaiian civic clubs, the women in hats and impressive long holokū dresses and the men in sashes and cummerbunds, pay honor to the leader whose name means "The Lonely One." ⊠ *417 S. King St., outside Ali'iōlani Hale, Downtown Honolulu.*

21 **Kawaiaha'o Church.** Fancifully called Hawai'i's Westminster Abbey, this 14,000-coral-block house of worship witnessed the coronations, weddings, and funerals of generations of Hawaiian royalty. Each of the building's coral blocks was quarried from reefs offshore at depths of more than 20 feet and transported to this site. Interior woodwork was created from the forests of the Ko'olau Mountains. The upper gallery has an exhibit of paintings of the royal families. The graves of missionaries and of King Lunalilo are adjacent. Services in English and Hawaiian are held each Sunday, and the church members are exceptionally welcoming, greeting newcomers with lei; their affiliation is United Church of Christ. Although there are no guided tours, you can look around the church at no cost. ⊠ *957 Punchbowl St., at King St., Downtown Hon-*

olulu ☎ *808/522–1333* ✉ *Free* ⊙ *English service Sun. at 8 AM and Wed. at 6 PM, Hawaiian service Sun. at 10:30 AM.*

Also Worth Seeing

ⓒ ⓮ **Aloha Tower Marketplace.** Two stories of shops and kiosks sell island-inspired clothing, jewelry, art, and home furnishings, as well as indoor and outdoor restaurants and live entertainment. For a bird's-eye view of this working harbor, take a free ride up to the observation deck of Aloha Tower. Cruise ships dock at Piers 9 and 10 and are often greeted and sent out to sea with music and hula dancing at the piers' end. ⊠ *1 Aloha Tower Dr., at Piers 8, 9, and 10, Downtown Honolulu* ☎ *808/ 528–5700, 808/566–2337 for entertainment info* ⊕ *www.alohatower. com* ⊙ *Mon.–Sat. 9–9, Sun. 9–6.*

★ ⓒ ⓭ **Hawai'i Maritime Center.** The story of the Islands begins on the seas. The **Kalākaua Boat House** has interactive exhibits where you can learn about Hawai'i's whaling days, the history of Honolulu Harbor, the Clipper seaplane, and surfing and windsurfing in Hawai'i. Moored next to the Boat House is the ***Falls of Clyde.*** Built in 1778, this four-masted, square-rigged ship once brought tea from China to the U.S. west coast and is now used as a museum. When it's not sailing, the voyaging canoe ***Hokule'a*** is docked at the end of the pier. The building of this vessel, which helped spark the Hawaiian cultural renaissance, proved that Hawaiians were masters of craftmanship and navigation. It has made numerous traditional-style voyages between islands and even to the Marquesas and Rapa Nui (Easter Island). ⊠ *Ala Moana Blvd. at Pier 7, Downtown Honolulu* ☎ *808/536–6373* ⊕ *www.bishopmuseum. org/exhibits/hmc/hmc.html* ✉ *$7.50* ⊙ *Daily 8:30–5.*

NEED A BREAK? In a vintage brick building at the corner of Nu'uanu Street and Merchant, **Murphy's Bar & Grill** (⊠ 2 Merchant St., Downtown Honolulu ☎ 808/531–0422) is an old-fashioned Irish pub, sports bar, and kamā'aina-style family restaurant. Comfort food is the order of the day.

⓯ **Hawai'i State Art Museum.** Hawai'i was one of the first states in the nation to legislate that a portion of the taxes paid on commercial building projects be set aside for the purchase of artwork. For this reason, the state's art holdings are extensive, but for many years, there was no place to routinely display the works. A few years ago, the state purchased an ornate period-style building (built to house the headquarters of a prominent developer) and dedicated 12,000 feet on the second floor to the art of Hawai'i in all its ethnic diversity. The **Diamond Head Gallery** features new acquisitions and thematic shows from the State Art Collection and the State Foundation on Culture and the Arts. The **'Ewa Gallery** houses more than 150 works documenting Hawai'i's visual-arts history since becoming a state in 1959. Also included are a sculpture gallery as well as a café, a gift shop, and educational meeting rooms. ⊠ *250 S. Hotel St., 2nd fl., Downtown Honolulu* ☎ *808/586–0300* ⊕ *www.hawaii.gov/sfca* ✉ *Free* ⊙ *Tues.–Sat. 10–4.*

⓲ **Hawai'i State Capitol.** The capitol's architecture is richly symbolic: the columns are meant to resemble palm trees, the legislative chambers are shaped like volcanic cinder cones, and the central court is open to the sky, representing Hawaiʻi's open society. Replicas of the Hawaiʻi state seal, each weighing 7,500 pounds, hang above both its entrances. The building, which in 1969 replaced ʻIolani Palace as the seat of government, is surrounded by reflecting pools, just as the Islands are embraced by water. A pair of statues, often draped in lei, flank the building: one of queen Liliʻuokalani and the other of the sainted Fr. Damien de Veuster. ⊠ *215 S. Beretania St., Downtown Honolulu* ☎ *808/586–0146* ✉ *Free* ☉ *Guided tours on request weekday afternoons.*

❶ Hawaiʻi State Library. This beautifully renovated main library was originally built in 1913. Its Samuel M. Kamakau Reading Room, on the first floor in the mauka courtyard, houses an extensive Hawaiʻi and Pacific book collection and pays tribute to Kamakau, a missionary student whose 19th-century writings in English offer rare and vital insight into traditional Hawaiian culture. ⊠ *478 King St., Downtown Honolulu* ☎ *808/ 586–3500* ✉ *Free* ☉ *Tues., Fri., and Sat. 9–5, Wed. 10–5, Thurs. 9–8.*

❷ Honolulu Academy of Arts. Originally built around the collection of a Honolulu matron who donated much of her estate to the museum, the academy is housed in a maze of courtyards, cloistered walkways, and quiet low-ceilinged spaces. The Academy has an impressive permanent collection that includes Hiroshige's *ukiyo-e* Japanese prints, donated by James Michener; Italian Renaissance paintings; and American and European art. The newer Luce Pavilion complex has a traveling-exhibit gallery, a Hawaiian gallery, and a gift shop. ■ **TIP➜ The Pavilion Cafe is an excellent choice for lunch.** The Academy Theatre screens art films. This is also the jumping-off place for tours of Doris Duke's estate, Shangri La (⇨ Shangri La CloseUp). ⊠ *900 S. Beretania St., Downtown Honolulu* ☎ *808/532–8700* ⊕ *www.honoluluacademy.org* ✉ *$7 Academy, free 1st Wed. of month* ☉ *Tues.–Sat. 10–4:30, Sun. 1–5.*

❸ Honolulu Hale. This Mediterranean Renaissance–style building was constructed in 1929 and serves as the center of city government. Stroll through the shady, open-ceiling lobby with exhibits of local artists, and time your visit to coincide with one of the free concerts sometimes offered in the evening, when the building stays open late. During the winter holiday season, the Hale becomes the focal point for the annual Honolulu City Lights, a display of lighting and playful holiday scenes spread around the Honolulu Hale campus. ⊠ *530 S. King St., Downtown Honolulu* ☎ *808/523–4654* ✉ *Free* ☉ *Weekdays 8–4:30.*

❹ Mission Houses Museum. The determined Hawaiʻi missionaries arrived in 1820, gaining royal favor and influencing every aspect of island life. Their descendants became leaders in government and business. You can walk through their original dwellings, including a white-frame house that was prefabricated in New England and shipped around the Horn— it's Hawaiʻi's oldest wooden structure. Certain areas of the museum may be seen only on a one-hour guided tour. Costumed docents give an excellent picture of what mission life was like. Rotating displays showcase such arts as Hawaiian quilting. ⊠ *553 S. King St., Downtown*

Honolulu ☎ *808/531–0481*
⊕ *www.lava.net/~mbm* ✉ *$10*
☺ *Tues.–Sat. 10–6; guided tours at*
11, 1, 2:45 and 4:30.

②④ Washington Place. For many years
the home of Hawai'i's governors,
this white-columned mansion was
built by sea captain John Dominis,
whose son married the woman who
became the Islands' last queen,
Lili'uokalani. Deposed by Ameri-
can-backed forces, the queen returned to the home—which is in

WHERE DO I PARK?

The best parking downtown is
street parking along Punchbowl
Street—when you can find it. There
are also public parking lots (75¢
per half hour for the first two
hours) in buildings along Alakea
Street, Smith, Beretania, and
Bethel Streets (Gateway Plaza on
Bethel Street is a good choice).

sight of the royal palace—and lived there until her death. The non-profit
Washington Place Foundation operates the gracious estate now, opening it for tours weekday mornings and on special occasions. Reservations required, 48 hours in advance. ⊠ *320 S. Beretania St., Downtown*
Honolulu ☎ *808/586–0248* ✉ *None, donations accepted.*

Around Honolulu

Exploring the Neighborhoods

Downtown Honolulu and Chinatown can easily swallow up a day's walking, sight-seeing, and shopping. Surrounding the city's core are another
day's worth of attractions. To the north, just off H–1 in the tightly-packed
neighborhood of Kalihi, explore a museum gifted to the Islands in memory of a princess. Immediately mauka, off Pali Highway, are a renowned
resting place and a carefully-preserved home where royal families retreated
during the doldrums of summer. To the south, along King Street and
Wai'alae Avenue, find a pair of neighborhoods chock-a-block with interesting restaurants and shops. Down the shore a bit from Diamond Head,
visit O'ahu's ritziest address and an equally upscale shopping center.

One reason to venture farther afield is the chance to glimpse Honolulu
neighborhoods. Note the several species of classic Hawai'i homes: the
tiny green-and-white plantation-era house with its corrugated tin roof,
two windows flanking a central door and small porch; the breezy bun-
galow with its swooping Thai-style roofline and two wings flanking
screened French doors through which breezes blow into the living room.
Note the tangled "Grandma-style" gardens and many *'ohana* houses–small
homes in the back yard or perched over the garage, allowing extended
families to live together. Carports, which rarely house cars, are the Island version of rec rooms, where parties are held and neighbors sit to
"talk story." Sometimes you'll see gallon jars on the flat roofs of garages
or carports: these are pickled lemons fermenting in the sun. Also in the
neighborhoods, you'll find the folksy restaurants and takeout spots favored by Islanders (⊳ *See* Takeout *in* Chapter 8, Where to Eat).

■ **TIP➔** If you have a Costco card, you'll find the cheapest gas on the island
at the Costco station on Arakawa Street between Dillingham Boulevard and Nimitz
Highway. Gas gets more expensive the farther you are from town.

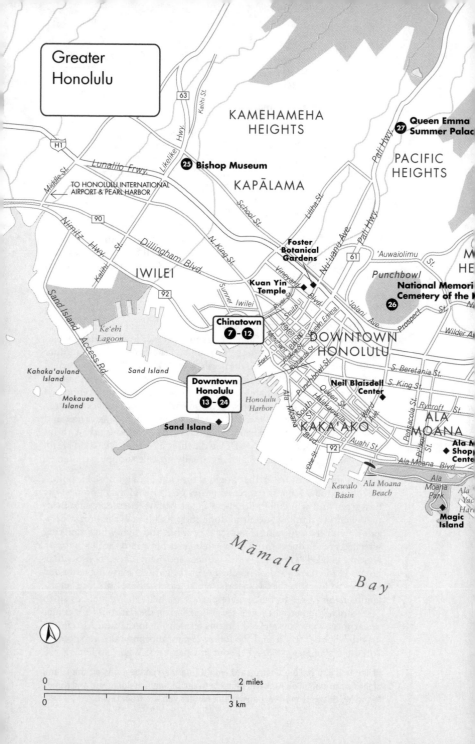

Greater Honolulu

KAMEHAMEHA HEIGHTS

27 **Queen Emma Summer Palac**

PACIFIC HEIGHTS

25 **Bishop Museum**

KAPĀLAMA

TO HONOLULU INTERNATIONAL AIRPORT & PEARL HARBOR

Foster Botanical Gardens

'Auwaiolimu

Punchbowl

National Memori Cemetery of the I

IWILEI

Kuan Yin Temple

Chinatown
7–**12**

26

Wilder A

DOWNTOWN HONOLULU

Ke'ehi Lagoon

Sand Island

Kahaka'aulana Island

Mokauea Island

Downtown Honolulu
13–**24**

Honolulu Harbor

Neil Blaisdell Center

S. King St.

S. Beretania St.

Rycroft St.

ALA MOANA

Sand Island

KAKA'AKO

Ala M Shop Cente

Auahi St.

Ala Moana Blvd.

Kewalo Basin

Ala Moana Beach

Ala Moana Park

Ala Yac Hare

Magic Island

Māmala Bay

0 ———————— 2 miles

0 ———————— 3 km

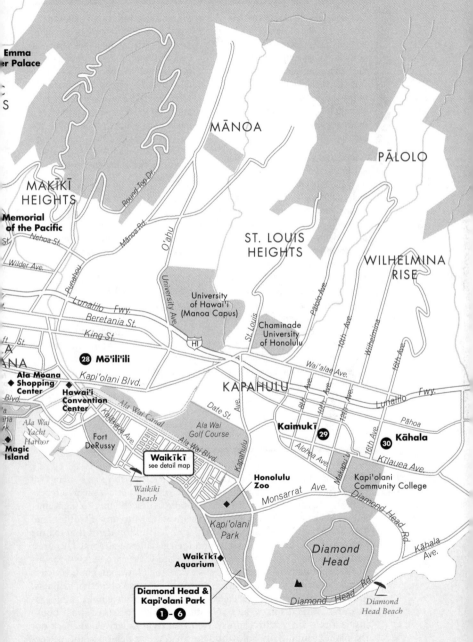

Honolulu Watershed Forest Reserve

**Emma
r Palace**

MĀNOA

PĀLOLO

MAKĪKĪ
HEIGHTS

**Memorial
of the Pacific**

Round Top Dr.

ST. LOUIS
HEIGHTS

WILHELMINA
RISE

Nehoa St.

Manoa Rd.

O'ahu

Wilder Ave.

Punahou

University Ave.

Lunalilo Fwy.
Beretania St.

University
of Hawai'i
(Manoa Capus)

St. Louis

Pālolo Ave.

King St.

H1

Chaminade
University
of Honolulu

10th Ave.

Wilhelmina

16th Ave.

28 Mō'ili'ili

Kapi'olani Blvd.

Wai'alae Ave.

KAPAHULU

Lunalilo Fwy.

**Ala Moana
♦ Shopping
Center**

Blvd.

**Hawai'i
Convention
Center**

Date St.

Ala Wai Canal

Ala Wai
Golf Course

8th Ave.

10th Ave.

12th Ave.

Pāhoa

Kaimukī **29**

30 **Kāhala**

Ala Wai
Yacht
Harbor

Kalakaua Ave.

Fort
DeRussy

Ala Wai Blvd.

Kapahulu

Alohea Ave.

Makapu'u

16th Ave.

Kīlauea Ave.

Kāhala
Ave.

**Magic
Island**

Waikīkī
Beach

Waikīkī
see detail map

**Honolulu
Zoo**

Monsarrat Ave.

Kapi'olani
Community College

Diamond Head Rd.

Kapi'olani
Park

**Diamond
Head**

**Waikīkī
Aquarium**

**Diamond Head &
Kapi'olani Park
❶-❻**

Diamond Head Rd.

Diamond
Head Beach

Honolulu's Made-Up Islands

They look like they've been there forever, but two of Honolulu's most popular parks are man-made—and years in the making, at that. And its best-known recreation area, Waikīkī, was once a marsh occupied by a network of islands. In fact, little of the shoreline between Waikīkī and downtown would be recognizable to a 19th-century Hawaiian.

Flamboyant aluminum tycoon Henry J. Kaiser pushed through a plan in the early 1960s to create a breakwater, beach, and island off beach-less Ala Moana Park with part of the land used for public recreation and part for a private hotel development. The beach was completed in 1963, but the rest of the project stalled due to public protest. For years, the coral-stewn peninsula sat deserted until the state turned it over to the City and County of Honolulu, and **Magic Island,** with its shaded picnic areas, running trails, and lagoon, finally opened in 1971. The two parks host frequent craft sales, are the staging point for numerous Waikīkī parades, and serve as crowded Honolulu's public "beach club."

Sand Island, a curved finger of land near Honolulu Harbor, was created by the federal government in the early years of the 20th century by pumping dredged material out of the harbor. In 1946 President Truman returned the land to the Territory of Hawai'i, and more than 25 years of wrangling and conflicting plans followed before a portion of the land was dedicated as a public park, which opened in 1976. It's more used by locals than tourists but offers an interesting view of the city and is the site of holiday fireworks displays.

Before the Ala Wai Canal was dredged, draining surrounding lands, **Waikīkī** was a watery marshland, home to rice farms, ducks, and secluded islands where, one popular hula song has it, lovers found private idylls. Early-20th-century society folk and Hawaiian royalty, who enjoyed sprawling summer places among the taro fields, weren't too happy about the drainage project, the decision to site the Honolulu Zoo in the area, or the growth of the tourist industry, but they soon moved out Diamond Head way to make room for the inevitable.

★ ㉕ **Bishop Museum.** Founded in 1889 by Charles R. Bishop as a memorial to his wife, Princess Bernice Pauahi Bishop, the museum began as a repository for the royal possessions of this last direct descendant of King Kamehameha the Great. Today it's the Hawai'i State Museum of Natural and Cultural History and houses more than 24.7 million items that tell the history of the Hawaiian Islands and their Pacific neighbors. The latest addition to the complex is a natural science wing with state-of-the-art interactive exhibits. Venerable but sadly aging Hawaiian Hall, which is slated for a multimillion-dollar renovation, houses Polynesian artifacts: lustrous feather capes, the skeleton of a giant sperm whale, photography and crafts displays, and an authentic, well-preserved grass house inside a two-story 19th-century Victorian style gallery. Also check out the planetarium, daily hula and Hawaiian crafts demonstrations, spe-

2

cial exhibits, and the Shop Pacifica. The building alone, with its huge Victorian turrets and immense stone walls, is worth seeing. ⊠ *1525 Bernice St., Kalihi* ☎ *808/847–3511* ⊕ *www.bishopmuseum.org* ⌖ *$14.95* ☉ *Daily 9–5.*

③⓪ Kāhala. O'ahu's wealthiest neighborhood has streets lined with multi-million-dollar homes. At intervals along tree-lined Kāhala Avenue are narrow lanes that provide public access to Kāhala's magnificent coastal beaches. Kāhala Mall is one of the island's largest indoor shopping centers. Kāhala is also the home of the private Wai'alae Golf Course, site of the annual Sony Open PGA golf tournament each January. ⊠ *East of Diamond Head.*

②⑨ Kaimukī. This is one of the few real pedestrian neighborhoods on O'ahu, with several blocks of intriguing stores and restaurants plus the quirky Movie Museum (a 17-seat theater equipped with easy chairs and playing only vintage and art films). A couple of shops offer original, hand-made fashion designs: Double Paws Wear and Montsuki. Harry's Music is an exceptional source of vintage Hawaiian recordings, sheet music, songs books, and instruments. During the holidays, Kaimukī hosts some great weekend craft fairs. Park on the street or in lots behind Wai'lae shops between 11th and 12th or 12th and Kokohead. ⊠ *West of Diamond Head.*

②⑥ National Memorial Cemetery of the Pacific (in Punchbowl Crater). Nestled in the bowl of Puowaina, or Punchbowl Crater, this 112-acre cemetery is the final resting place for more than 44,000 U.S. war veterans and family members. Among those buried here is Ernie Pyle, the famed World War II correspondent who was killed by a Japanese sniper off the northern coast of Okinawa. Puowaina, formed 75,000–100,000 years ago during a period of secondary volcanic activity, translates to "Hill of Sacrifice." Historians believe this site once served as an altar where ancient Hawaiians offered sacrifices to their gods. ■ **TIP➔ The cemetery has unfettered views of Waikīkī and Honolulu—perhaps the finest on O'ahu.** ⊠ *2177 Puowaina Dr., Nu'uanu* ☎ *808/532–3720* ⊕ *www.cem.va.gov/nchp/nmcp.htm* ⌖ *Free* ☉ *Mar.–Sept. daily 8–6:30, Oct.–Feb. daily 8–5:30.*

FUN THINGS TO DO IN HONOLULU

- Grab some green tea in Chinatown.
- Tickle a tiki at La Mariana Sailing Club bar and restaurant.
- Visit a goddess at Kuan Yin Temple.
- Bow to the throne in the only royal palace in the U.S.
- Encounter an artist at First Friday in Nu'uanu's gallery district.
- Shop 'till you drop in the funky neighborhoods of Mō'ili'ili and Kaimukī.
- Study the Hawaiian stars at Bishop Museum planetarium.
- Hum along with a Hawaiian hymn during Sunday services at Kawaiaha'o Church.
- Hang from the heavens in a parasail off the Honolulu shore.
- Eat Navy-style grub on the Mighty Mo.

28 **Mōʻiliʻili.** Don't be befuddled by the name with all its diacritical marks, just enjoy the flower and lei shops (especially Le Fleur), restaurants (Spices, Fukuya Delicatessen), and little stores such as Kuni Island Fabrics, a great source for Hawaiian quilting and other crafting materials; Siam Imports for goodies from Thailand; and Revolution Books, Honolulu's only leftist book shop. ⊠ *S. King St. between Hausten and Waiʻalae Ave.*

Pearl Harbor   See Page 47 ▶

★ **27** **Queen Emma Summer Palace.** Queen Emma and her family used this stately white home, built in 1848, as a retreat from the rigors of court life in hot and dusty Honolulu during the mid-1800s. It has an eclectic mix of European, Victorian, and Hawaiian furnishings and has excellent examples of Hawaiian quilts and koa-wood furniture as well as the queen's wedding dress and other memorabilia. ⊠ *2913 Pali Hwy.* ☎ *808/595–3167* ∰ *www.daughtersofhawaii.org* 🖃 *$5* ⊙ *Self-guided or guided tours daily 9–4.*

SOUTHEAST OʻAHU

At once historic and contemporary, serene and active, the east end of Oʻahu holds within its relatively small area remarkable variety and picture-perfect scenery of windswept cliffs and wave-dashed shores.

Driving southeast from Waikīkī on busy four-lane Kalanianaʻole Highway, you'll pass a dozen bedroom communities tucked into the valleys at the foot of the Koʻolau Range, with just fleeting glimpses of the ocean from a couple of pocket parks. Suddenly, civilization falls away, the road narrows to two lanes, and you enter the rugged coastline of Kokohead and Ka Iwi.

This is a cruel coastline: dry, wind-swept, and rocky shores, with untamed waves that are notoriously treacherous. While walking its beaches and clambering over its tumbled stones, do not turn your back on the ocean, don't venture close to wet areas where high waves occasionally reach, and heed warning signs.

At this point, you're passing through Koko Head Regional Park. On your right is the bulging remnant of a pair of volcanic craters that the Hawaiians called Kawaihoa, known today as Kokohead. To the left is Koko Crater and the area of the park that includes a hiking trail, a dryland botanical garden, a firing range, and a riding stable.

Ahead is a sinuous shoreline with scenic pull-outs and beaches to explore. Named the Ka Iwi Coast (iwi, "ee-vee", are bones—sacred to Hawaiians and full of symbolism) for the channel just offshore, this area was once home to a ranch and small fishing enclave that were destroyed by a tidal wave in the 1940s. If you attempt to swim or boogie board

Continued on page 53

USS *West Virginia* (BB48), 7 December 1941

PEARL HARBOR

December 7, 1941. Every American then alive recalls exactly what he or she was doing when the news broke that the Japanese had bombed Pearl Harbor, the catalyst that brought the United States into World War II.

Although it was clear by late 1941 that war with Japan was inevitable, no one in authority seems to have expected the attack to come in just this way, at just this time. So when the Japanese bombers swept through a gap in Oʻahu's Koʻolau Mountains in the hazy light of morning, they found the bulk of America's Pacific fleet right where they hoped it would be: docked like giant stepping stones across the calm waters of the bay named for the pearl oysters that once prospered there. More than 2,000 people died that day, including 49 civilians. A dozen ships were sunk. And on the nearby air bases, virtually every American military aircraft was destroyed or damaged. The attack was a stunning success, but it lit a fire under America, which went to war with "Remember Pearl Harbor" as its battle cry. Here, in what is still a key Pacific naval base, the attack is remembered every day by thousands of visitors, including many curious Japanese, who for years heard little WWII history in their own country. In recent years, the Memorial has been the site of reconciliation ceremonies involving Pearl Harbor veterans from both sides.

GETTING AROUND

Pearl Harbor is both a working military base and the most-visited O'ahu attraction. Three distinct destinations share a parking lot and are linked by footpath, shuttle, and ferry.

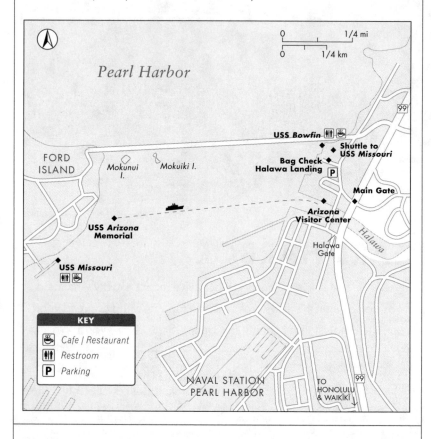

The USS *Arizona* Visitor Center is accessible from the parking lot. The *Arizona* Memorial itself is in the middle of the harbor; get tickets for the ferry ride at the Visitor center. The USS *Bowfin* is also reachable from the parking lot. The USS *Missouri* is docked at Ford Island, a restricted area of the naval base. Vehicular access is prohibited. To get there, take a shuttle bus from the station near the *Bowfin*.

ARIZONA MEMORIAL

Snugged up tight in a row of seven battleships off Ford Island, the USS *Arizona* took a direct hit that December morning, exploded, and rests still on the shallow bottom where she settled.

A visit to the *Arizona* Memorial begins prosaically—a line, a ticket that assigns you to a group and tour time, a wait filled with shopping, visiting the museum, and strolling the grounds. When your number is called, you watch a 23-minute documentary film then board the ferry to the memorial. The swooping, stark-white memorial, which straddles the wreck of the USS *Arizona,* was designed by Honolulu architect Alfred Preis to represent both the depths of the low-spirited, early days of the war, and the uplift of victory. After the carnival-like courtyard, a somber, contemplative mood descends upon visitors during the ferry ride; this is a place where 1,777 people died. Gaze at the names of the dead carved into the wall of white marble. Scatter flowers (but no leis—the string is bad for the fish). Salute the flag. Remember Pearl Harbor.

808/422–0561
www.nps.gov/usar

USS *MISSOURI* (BB63)

Together with the *Arizona* Memorial, the *Missouri's* presence in Pearl Harbor perfectly bookends America's WWII experience that began December 7, 1941, and ended on the "Mighty Mo's" starboard deck with the signing of the Terms of Surrender.

Surrender of Japan, USS *Missouri*, 2 September 1945

In the parking area behind the USS *Bowfin* Museum, board a jitney for a breezy, eight-minute ride to Ford Island and the teak decks and towering super-structure of the *Missouri,* docked for good in the very harbor from which she first went to war on January 2, 1945. The last battleship ever built, the *Missouri* famously hosted the final act of WWII, the signing of the Terms of Surrender. The commission that governs this floating museum has surrounded her with buildings tricked out in WWII style—a Canteen that serves as an orientation space for tours, a WACs and WAVEs Lounge with a flight simulator the kids will love ($5 for one person, $18 for four), Truman's Line restaurant serving Navy-style meals, and a Victory Store housing a souvenir shop and covered with period mottos ("Don't be a blabateur.").

■ TIP→ Definitely hook up with a tour guide (additional charge) or purchase an audio tour ($2)—these add a great deal to the experience.

The *Missouri* is all about numbers: 209 feet tall, six 239,000-pound guns, capable of firing up to 23 mi away. Absorb these during the tour, then stop to take advantage of the view from the decks. The Mo is a work in progress, with only a handful of her hundreds of spaces open to view.

808/423–2263 or 888/877–6477
www.ussmissouri.com

USS *BOWFIN* (SS287)

SUBMARINE MUSEUM & PARK

Launched one year to the day after the Pearl Harbor attack, the USS *Bowfin* sank 44 enemy ships during WWII and now serves as the centerpiece of a museum honoring all submariners.

 Although the *Bowfin* no less than the *Arizona* Memorial commemorates the lost, the mood here is lighter. Perhaps it's the child-like scale of the boat, a metal tube just 16 feet in diameter, packed with ladders, hatches, and other obstacles, like the naval version of a jungle gym. Perhaps it's the World War II-era music that plays in the covered patio. Or it might be the museum's touching displays—the penciled sailor's journal, the Vargas girlie posters. Aboard the boat nick-named Pearl Harbor Avenger, compartments are fitted out as though "Sparky" was away from the radio room just for a moment, and "Cooky" might be right back to his pots and pans. The museum includes many artifacts to spark family conversations, among them a vintage dive suit that looks too big for Shaquille O'Neal. A caution: The *Bowfin* could be hazardous for very young children; no one under four allowed.

808/423–1341
www.bowfin.org

CALL FOR ACTION

Pearl Harbor attractions operate with the aid of nonprofit organizations; the *Missouri* and *Bowfin* receive no government funds at all. A $34 million campaign has begun to rebuild the inadequate and aging *Arizona* Memorial Visitor's Center and create a series of mini-museums that do justice to the events that took place at Pearl Harbor. If fund-raising goes as planned, the center likely will close in 2007 during renovations.

Want to help?

Arizona **Memorial**
www.pearlharbormemorial.com, raising funds for a new visitor's center

USS *Missouri* Memorial Association
www.ussmissouri.com, membership program supports ongoing restoration

Bowfin
www.bowfin.org; no online giving, send check to USS *Bowfin*, 11 Arizona Memorial Dr., Honolulu, HI 96818

PLAN YOUR PEARL HARBOR DAY LIKE A MILITARY CAMPAIGN

DIRECTIONS

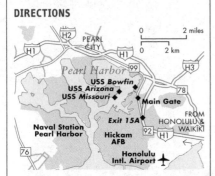

Take H1 west from Waikīkī to Exit 15A and follow signs. Or take TheBus route 20 or 47 from Waikīkī. Beware high-priced private shuttles. It's a 30-minute drive from Waikīkī.

WHAT TO BRING

Picture ID is required during periods of high alert; bring it just in case.

You'll be standing, walking, and climbing all day. Wear something with lots of pockets and a pair of good walking shoes. Carry a light jacket, sunglasses, hat, and sunscreen.

No purses, packs, or bags are allowed. Take only what fits in your pockets. Cameras are okay but without bulky bags. A private bag storage booth is near the *Arizona* Memorial parking lot. Leave nothing in your car; theft is a problem despite bicycle security patrols.

HOURS

Hours are 8 AM to 5 PM for all attractions. However, the *Arizona* Memorial starts giving out tickets on a first-come, first-served basis at 7:30 AM; the last tickets are given out at 3 PM. Spring break, summer, and holidays are busiest, and tickets sometimes run out.

TICKETS

Arizona: Free. Add $5 for museum audio tours.

Missouri: $16 adults, $8 children. Add $6 for chief's guided tour or audio tour; add $33 for in-depth, behind-the-scenes tours.

Bowfin: $10 adults, $3 children. Add $2 for audio tours. Children under 4 may go into the museum but not aboard the *Bowfin*.

KIDS

This might be the day to enroll younger kids in the hotel children's program. Preschoolers chafe at long waits, and attractions involve some hazards for toddlers. Older kids enjoy the *Bowfin* and *Missouri,* especially.

MAKING THE MOST OF YOUR TIME

Expect to spend three hours minimum— that's if you hustle and skip audio tours. The better part of a day is better.

At the *Arizona* Memorial, you'll get a ticket, be given a tour time, and then have to wait — anywhere from 15 minutes to 3 hours. Everyone has to pick up their own ticket so you can't hold places. If you've got an hour or more, skip over to the *Bowfin* to fill the time.

SUGGESTED READING

Pearl Harbor and the USS Arizona Memorial, by Richard Wisniewski. $5.95. 64-page magazine-size quick history.

Bowfin, by Edwin P. Hoyt. $14.95. Dramatic story of undersea adventure.

The Last Battleship, by Scott C. S. Stone. $11.95. Story of the Mighty Mo.

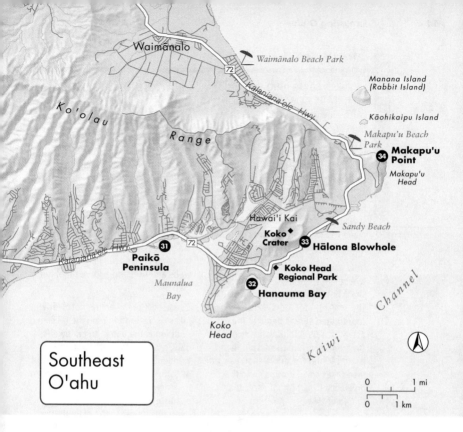

Waimānalo

Waimānalo Beach Park

Koʻolau

Range

Manana Island
(Rabbit Island)

Kāohikaipu Island

Makapuʻu Beach
Park

34 **Makapuʻu Point**

Makapuʻu Head

Hawaiʻi Kai

Koko ◆
Crater

Sandy Beach

33 **Hālona Blowhole**

31

72

Paikō Peninsula

◆ **Koko Head Regional Park**

32

Hanauma Bay

Maunalua
Bay

Koko
Head

Kaiwi Channel

Southeast
Oʻahu

0   1 mi

0   1 km

along this coast—particularly in winter—you may feel as though you've encountered a tidal wave yourself.

TIMING   Driving straight from Waikīkī to Makapuʻu Point takes from a half to a full hour, depending on traffic. There aren't a huge number of sites per se in this corner of Oʻahu, so a couple of hours should be plenty of exploring time, unless you really stop and spend time at a particular point.

33 **Hālona Blowhole.** Below a scenic turnout along the Koko Head shoreline, this oft-photographed lava tube sucks the ocean in and spits it out. Don't get too close, as conditions can get dangerous. ■ TIP➔ **Look to your right to see the tiny beach below that was used to film the wave-washed love scene in** *From Here to Eternity.* In winter this is a good spot to watch whales at play. Offshore, the islands of Molokaʻi and Lānaʻi call like distant sirens, and every once in a while Maui is visible in blue silhouette. Take your valuables with you and lock your car, because this scenic location is a hot spot for petty thieves. ✉ *Kalanianaʻole Hwy., 1 mi east of Hanauma Bay.*

32 **Hanauma Bay Nature Preserve.** The exterior wall of a volcanic crater collapsed, opening it to the sea and thereby giving birth to Oʻahu's most famous snorkeling destination. Even from the overlook, the horseshoe-

FodorsChoice
★

Shangri La

HEIRESS DORIS DUKE'S MARRIAGE AT AGE 23 to a man much older than herself didn't last. But their around-the-world honeymoon tour did leave the "Poor Little Rich Girl" with two lasting loves: Islamic art and architecture, which she first encountered on that journey; and Hawai'i, where the honeymooners made an extended stay while Doris learned to surf and made friends with Islanders who were unimpressed by her wealth.

Now visitors to her beloved Islands—where she spent most winters—can share both loves by touring her home. The sought-after tours, which are coordinated by and begin at the downtown Honolulu Academy of Arts, start with a visit to the Arts of the Islamic World Gallery. A short van ride then takes small groups on to the house itself, just on the far side of Diamond Head.

In 1936 Duke bought five acres at Black Point, down the coast from Waikīkī, and began to build and furnish the first home that would be all her own. She called it Shangri La. For more than 50 years, the home was a work always in progress as Duke traveled the world, buying furnishings and artifacts, picking up ideas for her Mughul garden, for the Playhouse in the style of an Irani pavilion, and for the water terraces and tropical gardens. When she died in 1993, Duke left instructions that her home was to become a center for the study of

Islamic art, open to the public for tours.

To walk through the house and its gardens—which have remained much as Duke left them with only some minor conservation-oriented changes—is to experience the personal style of someone who saw everything as raw material for her art.

With her trusted houseman, Jin de Silva, she literally built the elaborate Turkish or Damascus Room, trimming tiles and painted panels to fit the walls and building a fountain of her own design.

One aspect of the home that clearly takes its inspiration from the Muslim tradition is the entry: an anonymous gate, a blank white wall and a wooden door—19th century from Egypt or Syria—which bids you "Enter herein in peace and security" in Arabic characters. Inside, tiles glow, fountains tinkle, shafts of light illuminate artworks through arches and high windows. This was her private world, entered only by trusted friends.

Tickets are $25; children under 12 are not admitted. Tours are available Wednesday through Saturday by reservation only. First tour is 8:30 AM, last tour 1:30 PM; tour takes 2½ hours. All tours begin at the Academy of Arts, 900 S. Beretania. To arrange for tickets, go to www.honoluluacademy. org or call 808/532-3853.

shape bay is a beauty, and you can easily see the reefs through the clear aqua waters. The wide beach is a great place for sunbathing and picnics. This is a marine conservation district, and regulations prohibit feeding the fish. Visitors are required to go through the Bay's Education Center before trekking down to the Bay. The center provides a cultural history of the area and exhibits about the importance of protecting its marine life. Check out the "Today at the Bay" exhibit for up-to-date information on daily tides, ocean safety warnings, and event activities. Food concessions and equipment rentals are also on-site. ■ TIP→ Come early to get parking, as the number of visitors allowed per day is limited. Also note that the bay is best in the early hours before the waters are churned up. Call for current conditions. Weather permitting, Hanauma Bay by Starlight events are held on the second Saturday of every month, extending the opening hours to 10 PM. ⊠ *7455 Kalaniana'ole Hwy.* ☎ *808/396–4229* ✉*Donation $5; parking $1; mask, snorkel, and fins rental $8; tram from parking lot down to beach $1.50 round-trip* ☾ *Wed.–Mon. 6–6.*

34 **Makapu'u Point.** This spot has breathtaking views of the ocean, mountains, and the windward islands. The point of land jutting out in the distance is **Mōkapu Peninsula,** site of a U.S. Marine base. The spired mountain peak is **Mt. Olomana.** In front of you on the long pier is part of the **Makai Undersea Test Range,** a research facility that's closed to the public. Offshore is **Manana Island (Rabbit Island),** a picturesque cay said to resemble a swimming bunny with its ears pulled back. Ironically enough, Manana Island was once overrun with rabbits, thanks to a rancher who let a few hares run wild on the land. They were eradicated in 1994 by biologists who grew concerned that the rabbits were destroying the island's native plants.

Nestled in the cliff face is the **Makapu'u Lighthouse,** which became operational in 1909 and has the largest lighthouse lens in America. The lighthouse is closed to the public, but near the Makapu'u Point turnout you can find the start of a mile-long paved road (closed to traffic). Hike up to the top of the 647-foot bluff for a closer view of the lighthouse and, in winter, a great whale-watching vantage point. ⊠ *Kalaniana'ole Hwy., turnout above Makapu'u Beach.*

31 **Paikō Peninsula.** This slim spit is reached by a narrow residential road that dead-ends at the Paikō Lagoon State Reserve, which is off-limits to the public. However, in Hawai'i, all beaches are public to the high-water line, and there's a beach access pathway just a few houses before the road's end. Turn left when you get to the beach and find your spot near where the houses end. Secluded within the confines of the bay, private and quiet, this is a lovely place to spend a morning or afternoon swimming, snorkeling, reading, and dozing. ⊠ *Kalaniana'ole Hwy., just past Niu Valley, on the right, on Paikō Dr.*

WINDWARD O'AHU

To look at Honolulu's topsy-turvy urban sprawl, you would never suspect the Windward side existed. It's a secret Oahuans like to keep, so they can watch the look of awe on the faces of their guests when the car emerges from the tunnels through the mountains and they gaze for the first time on the panorama of turquoise bays and emerald valleys watched over by the knife-edged Ko'olau ridges. Jaws literally drop. Every time. And this just a 15-minute drive from downtown.

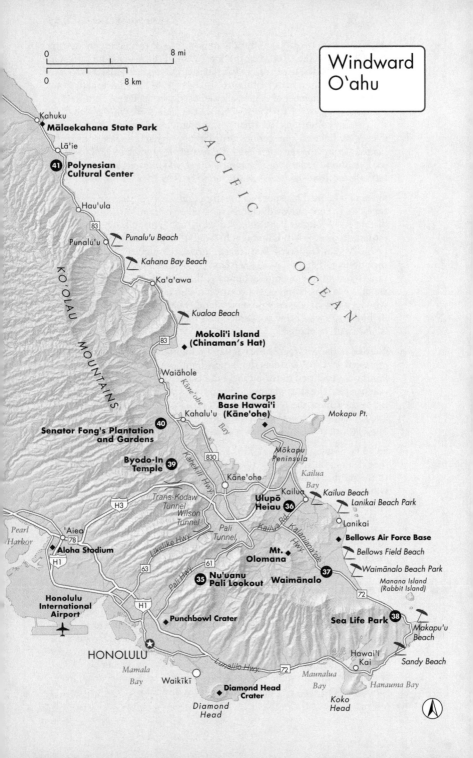

Drive-phobic Honolulans tend to pack food and water when they have to trek to "the other side"—just the kind of thinking that Windward siders, who know what a good thing they have, like to encourage.

It is on this side of the island that many Native Hawaiians live. Evidence of traditional lifestyles is abundant in crumbling fish ponds, rock platforms that once were altars, taro patches still being worked, and throw-net fishermen posed stock-still above the water (though today, they're invariably wearing polarized sunglasses, the better to spot the fish).

Here, the pace is slower, more oriented toward nature. Beach-going, hiking, diving, surfing, and boating are the draw, along with a visit to the Polynesian Cultural Center, poking through little shops and wayside stores. Many vacation rentals and bed-and-breakfast operations can be found on this side of the island, offering a tantalizing taste of real island life.

TIMING You can easily spend an entire day exploring Windward Oʻahu—spending the morning at a botanical park or beach in Kailua or Kāneʻohe, having lunch at one of the small local restaurants in the area—or you can just breeze on through, nodding at the sights on your way to the North Shore. Waikīkī to Windward is a drive of less than half an hour; to the North Shore via Kamehameha Highway along the Windward Coast is one hour minimum.

Top Attractions

㊴ Byodo-In Temple. Tucked away in the back of the Valley of the Temples cemetery is a replica of the 11th-century Temple at Uji in Japan. A 2-ton carved wooden statue of the Buddha presides inside the main temple building. Next to the temple building are a meditation house and gardens set dramatically against the sheer, green cliffs of the Koʻolau Mountains. You can ring the 5-foot, 3-ton brass bell for good luck and feed some 10,000 carp that inhabit the garden's 2-acre pond. ⊠ *47-200 Kahekili Hwy., Kāneʻohe* ☎ *808/239–8811* ✉ *$2* ☉ *Daily 8:30–4:30.*

★ **Kailua Beaches.** Ready for a beach break? Head straight on Kailua Road to the 35-acre, 2.5-mile long **Kailua Beach Park,** which many people consider the best on the island. South of the Kailua Beach is **Lanikai,** originally a summer beach house community for Oʻahu's wealthy; the beach here (there are public access trails) is narrow but less used. Both beaches have won Best Beach awards. Take Kailua Road to S. Kalaheo, turn right and continue as the road veers left, cross the bridge and enter the park on the left. To get to Lanikai, continue on as S. Kalaheo becomes Kawailoa, turn left at the dead end and enter the Aʻalapapa/Mokulua Drive loop. Park on the Mokulua and look for beach access. ⊠ *Kawailoa Rd.*

NEED A BREAK? Generations of children have purchased their beach snacks and sodas at **Kalapawai Market** (⊠ 306 S. Kalāheo Ave.), near Kailua Beach. A windward landmark since 1932, the green-and-white market has distinctive charm. It's a good source for your carryout lunch, since there's no concession stand at the beach.

㉟ Nuʻuanu Pali Lookout. This panoramic perch looks out to windward Oʻahu. It was in this region that King Kamehameha I drove defending

Oʻahu's Offshore Islands

OFFSHORE ISLANDS ARE STRUNG along Oʻahu's Windward side and North Shore—shapes that range from alluring low crescents of half-sunk calderas to the brooding 361-foot volcanic cone called Manana (Rabbit Island).

They seem to promise fulfillment of a dream: a deserted island, just you, the wind, and the waves. But before heading for the kayak rental shop, be aware:

Approaching or landing on these islands can be extremely hazardous. Swift-moving tides swirl about their rocky shores. Most are unreachable except by kayak. Only the strong and experienced should venture outside of protected bays, except on guide-led excursions. Check weather and tides and seek guidance from lifeguards or those who know the area. Kayakers might consult Hui Waʻ Kaukahi kayaking club; www.huiwaa.org.

Many of the islands are bird sanctuaries, where landings are restricted or prohibited. If landings are allowed, remain on or close to the beach, and tread carefully so as not to disturb nesting birds. Access to two of the islands requires permission: due to increased post 9/11 security, only residents and guests, and people on guided tours, have access to Ford Island in Pearl Harbor. And Moku O Loʻe (Coconut Island), off Kāneʻohe, which is home to the research labs of the Hawaiʻi Institute of Marine Biology, is open only to visiting researchers and students sponsored by faculty. No landings are allowed on the bird sanctuaries of Popoʻia (Flat Island) off Kailua, or Manana (Rabbit Island), off Makapuʻu.

Some popular spots that can be visited:

The Moku Lua Islets, popularly known as **"The Mokes,"** are 4 mi off Kailua Beach Park. Arguably Oʻahu's most popular kayaking destination, the Mokes have a sandy pullout, grassy area, and protected bays for swimming.

Ahu O Laka Islet, a.k.a. **"The Sandbar,"** a few hundred yards off Heʻeia Pier in Kāneʻohe Bay, is a shallow sand islet visible only at low tide. On weekends and holidays, dozens of boaters, rafters, kayakers, canoeists, and even swimmers congregate here, bringing hibachis, coolers, beach chairs—the works.

Kapapa Island, 2.5 miles off Heʻeia Pier in Kāneʻohe Bay, can be reached by kayak or canoe. Enjoy the gorgeous views, sandy beach, and grassy area; stay away from ironwood forest where wedgetailed shearwaters nest.

Moku ʻAuia (Goat Island), is just offshore at Mālaekahana State Recreation Area. This longish stretch of land offers an exciting, wind-swept vantage point and some hidden beaches. However, it is separated from the park by a few yards of powerful surf, swirling in from both sides. Visit in groups. Do not attempt to walk across except at low tide (and get back before the tide changes), and wear reef shoes to traverse rocks and coral. Not recommended at all between September and April.

(*top*) View of Windward Oʻahu from the Nuʻuanu Pali Lookout. (*bottom*) Kayaking in Kāneʻohe Bay.

(*top*) Sunrise over Manana Island (Rabbit Island) off Makapuʻu Point. (*bottom*) Surf lesson on Waikīkī Beach.

(*top*) ʻIolani Palace in downtown Honolulu. (*bottom*) Aerial view of Honolulu and Waikīkī, looking east to Diamond Head.

Aerial view of the Koʻolau Range in Windward Oʻahu.
(*opposite page, top*) Lanikai Beach in Windward Oʻahu. (*opposite page, bottom*) Leis.

(*top*) Surfing the Banzai Pipeline. (*bottom left*) Chinese New Year celebrations in downtown Honolulu. (*bottom right*) Keiki hula dancers from Hālau Hula O Hōkūlani in Kapiʻolani Park.

(*top*) Relaxing with a view of Waikīkī and Diamond Head. (*bottom*) USS *Arizona* Memorial in Pearl Harbor.

Waikīkī Beach.

forces over the edges of the 1,000-foot-high cliffs, thus winning the decisive battle for control of Oʻahu. From here you can see views that stretch from Kāneʻohe Bay to Mokuliʻi (Chinaman's Hat), a small island off the coast, and beyond. Temperatures at the summit are several degrees cooler than in warm Waikīkī, so bring a jacket along. And hang on tight to any loose possessions; it gets extremely windy at the lookout. Lock your car; break-ins have occurred here. ⊠ *Top of Pali Hwy.* ☉ *Daily 9–4.*

Offshore Islands and Rocks. As you drive the Windward and North Shores along Kamehameha Highway, you'll note a number of interesting geological features. At Kualoa look to the ocean and gaze at the uniquely shaped little island of **Mokoliʻi** (little lizard), a 206-foot-high sea stack also known as Chinaman's Hat. According to Hawaiian legend, the goddess Hiʻiaka, sister of Pele, slew the dragon Mokoliʻi and flung its tail into the sea, forming the distinct islet. Other dragon body parts—in the form of rocks, of course—were scattered along the base of nearby Kualoa Ridge. In Lāʻie, if you turn right on Anemoku Street, and right again on Naupaka, you come to a scenic lookout where you can see a group of islets, dramatically washed in by the waves.

🐚 ㊶ **Polynesian Cultural Center.** Re-created, individual villages showcase the lifestyles and traditions of Hawaiʻi, Tahiti, Samoa, Fiji, the Marquesas Islands, New Zealand, and Tonga. This 45-acre center, 35 mi from Waikīkī, was founded in 1963 by the Church of Jesus Christ of Latter-day Saints. It houses restaurants, hosts lūʻaus, and demonstrates cultural traditions such as tribal tattooing, fire dancing, and ancient customs and ceremonies. The expansive open-air shopping village carries Polynesian handicrafts. If you're staying in Honolulu, see the center as part of a van tour so you won't have to drive home late at night after the two-hour evening show. Various packages are available, from basic admission to an all-inclusive deal. Every May, the PCC hosts the World Fire Knife Dance Competition, an event that draws the top fire knife dance performers from around the world. ⊠ *55-370 Kamehameha Hwy., Lāʻie* ☏ *808/293–3333 or 800/367–7060* ⊕ *www.polynesia.com* ☝ *$50–$218* ☉ *Mon.–Sat. 12:30–9:30. Islands close at 6:30.*

㊵ **Senator Fong's Plantation and Gardens.** The one-time estate of the late Hiram Fong, the first Asian-American to be elected to Congress, this 700-acre garden is now open for tours. Twice-daily one-mile (10:30 AM and 1 PM), one-hour walking tours explore the park's five lush valleys, each named for a U.S. president that Fong served under during his 17-year tenure in the Senate. The visitor center has a snack bar and gift shop. ⊠ *47-285 Pūlama Rd., off Kahekili Hwy., 2 mi north of Byodo-In Temple, Kahaluʻu* ☏ *808/239–6775* ⊕ *www.fonggarden.net* ☝ *$14.50* ☉ *Daily 10 AM–2 PM.*

Windward Villages. Tiny villages—generally consisting of a sign, store, a beach park, possibly a post office, and not much more—are strung along Kamehameha Highway on the Windward side. Each has something to offer. In **Waiahole,** look for fruit stands and an ancient grocery store. In **Kaʻaʻawa,** there's a lunch spot and convenience store/gas station. In **Punaluʻu,** stop at the gallery of fanciful landscape artist Lance

Fairly and the woodworking shop, Kahaunani Woods & Crafts, plus venerable Kaya Store or the Shrimp Shack. Kim Taylor Reece's photo studio, featuring haunting portraits of hula dancers, is between Punalu'u and Hau'ula. **Hau'ula** has Ching Store, now a clothing shop where sarongs wave like banners and, at Ha'ula Kai Shopping Center, Tamura Market, with excellent seafood and the last liquor before Mormon-dominated Lā'ie.

Also Worth Seeing

Sea Life Park. Dolphins leap and spin, penguins frolic, and a killer whale performs impressive tricks at this marine-life attraction 15 mi from Waikīkī at scenic Makapu'u Point. In addition to a 300,000-gallon Hawaiian reef aquarium, there are the Pacific Whaling Museum, the Hawaiian Monk Seal Care Center, and a breeding sanctuary for Hawai'i's endangered *Honu* sea turtle. There are several interactive activities such as a stingray encounter, an underwater photo safari, and a "Splash University" dolphin-training session (⇨ Chapter 4, Water Activities & Tours). Inquire about the park's behind-the-scenes tour for a glimpse of dolphin-training areas and the seabird rehabilitation center. ⊠ *41-202 Kalaniana'ole Hwy., Waimānalo* ☎ *808/259–7933 or 886/365–7446* ⊕ *www.sealifepark.com* ✎ *$26* ⊙ *Daily 9:30–5.*

Ulupō Heiau. Though they may look like piles of rocks to the uninitiated, *heiau* are sacred stone platforms for the worship of the gods and date from ancient times. *Ulupō* means "night inspiration," referring to the legendary *Menehune,* a mythical race of diminutive people who are said to have built the heiau under the cloak of darkness. ⊠ *Behind YMCA at Kalaniana'ole Hwy. and Kailua Rd.*

Waimānalo. This modest little seaside town flanked by chiseled cliffs is worth a visit. Its biggest draws are its beautiful beaches, offering glorious views to the windward side. **Bellows Beach** is great for swimming and bodysurfing, and **Waimānalo Beach Park** is also safe for swimming. Down the side roads, as you head mauka, are little farms that grow a variety of fruits and flowers. Toward the back of the valley are small ranches with grazing horses. ■ **TIP→ If you see any trucks selling corn and you're staying at a place where you can cook it, be sure to get some in Waimānalo. It may be the sweetest you'll ever eat, and the price is the lowest on O'ahu.** ⊠ *Kalaniana'ole Hwy.*

THE NORTH SHORE

An hour from town and a world away in atmosphere, O'ahu's North Shore, roughly from Kahuku Point to Ka'ena Point, is about small farms and big waves, tourist traps, and other-worldly landscapes. Parks and beaches, roadside fruit stands and shrimp shacks, a rare shop full of Hawaiian and Asian collectibles, a bird sanctuary, and a valley preserve offer a dozen reasons to stop between the one-time plantation town of Kahuku and the surf mecca of Hale'iwa.

Hale'iwa has had many lives, from resort getaway in the 1900s to plantation town through the 20th century to its life today as a surf and tourist

Continued on page 65

Imagine picking your seat for free at the Super Bowl or wandering the grounds of Augusta National at no cost during The Masters, and you glimpse the opportunity you have when attending the Vans Triple Crown of Surfing on the North Shore.

NORTH SHORE SURFING & THE TRIPLE CROWN

10-FOOT WAVES.
10,000 FANS.
TOP 50 SURFERS.

Long considered the best stretch of surf breaks on Earth, the North Shore surf area encompasses 6 mi of coastline on the northwestern tip of O'ahu from Hale'iwa to Sunset Beach. There are over 20 major breaks within these 6 mi. Winter storms in the North Pacific send huge swells southward which don't break for thousands of miles until they hit the shallow reef of O'ahu's remote North Shore. This creates optimum surfing all winter long and was the inspiration for having surf competitions here each holiday season.

Every November and December the top 50 surfers in world rankings descend on "The Country" to decide who is the best all-around surfer in the world. Each of the three invitation-only contests that make up the Triple Crown has its own winner; competitors also win points based on the final standings. The surfer who excels in all three contests, racking up the most points overall, wins the Vans Triple Crown title. The first contest is held at **Hale'iwa Beach,** the second at **Sunset Beach.** The season reaches its crescendo at the most famous surf break in the world, the **Banzai Pipeline.**

The best part is the cost to attend the events—nothing; your seat for the show—wherever you set down your beach towel. Just park your car, grab your stuff, and watch the best surfers in the world tame the best waves in the world.

The only surfing I understand involves a mouse.

The contests were created not only to fashion an overall champion, but to attract the casual fan to the sport. Announcers explain each ride over the loudspeakers, discussing the nuances and values being weighed by the judges. A scoreboard displays points and standings during the four days of each event.

If this still seems incomprehensible to you, the action on the beach can also be exciting as some of the most beautiful people in the world are attracted to these contests.

For more information, see www.triplecrownofsurfing.com

What should I bring?

Pack for a day at the Triple Crown the way you would for any day at the beach—sun block, beach towel, bottled water, and if you want something other than snacks, food.

These contests are held in rural neighborhoods (read: few stores), so pack anything you might need during the day. Also, binoculars are suggested, especially for the contest at Sunset. The pros will be riding huge outside ocean swells, and it can be hard to follow from the beach without binoculars. Hale'iwa's breaks and Pipeline are considerably closer to shore, but binoculars will let you see the intensity on the contestants' faces.

Hale'iwa Ali'i Beach Park
Vans Triple Crown Contest #1: OP Pro Hawaii

The Triple Crown gets underway with high-performance waves (and the know-how to ride them) at Hale'iwa. Though lesser known than the other two breaks of the Triple Crown, it is the perfect wave for showing off: the contest here is full of sharp cutbacks (twisting the board dramatically off the top or bottom of the wave), occasional barrel rides, and a crescendo of floaters (balancing the board on the top of the cresting wave) before the wave is destroyed on the shallow tabletop reef called the Toilet Bowl. The rider who can pull off the most tricks will win this leg, evening the playing field for the other two contests, where knowledge of the break is the key. Also, the beach park is walking distance from historic Hale'iwa town, a mecca to surfers worldwide who make their pilgrimage here every winter to ride the waves. Even if you are not a fan, immersing yourself in their culture will make you one by nightfall.

Sunset Beach
Vans Triple Crown Contest #2: O'Neill World Cup of Surfing

At Sunset, the most guts and bravado win the day. The competition is held when the swell is at 8 to 12 feet and from the northwest. Sunset gets the heaviest surf because it is the exposed point on the northern tip of O'ahu. Surfers describe the waves here as "moving mountains." The choice of waves is the key to this contest as only the perfect one will give the competitor a ride through the jigsaw-puzzle outer reef, which can kill a perfect wave instantly, all the way into the inner reef. Big bottom turns (riding all the way down the face of the wave before turning dramatically back onto the wave) and slipping into a super thick tube (slowing down to let the wave catch you and riding inside its vortex) are considered necessary to carry the day.

Banzai Pipeline
Vans Triple Crown Contest #3: Rip Curl Pipeline Masters

It is breathtaking to watch the best surfers in the world disappear into a gaping maw of whitewash for a few seconds only to emerge from the other side unscathed. Surfing the Pipeline showcases their ability to specialize in surfing, to withstand the power and fury of a 10-foot wave from within its hollow tube.

How does the wave become hollow in the first place? When the deep ocean floor ascends steeply to the shore, the waves that meet it will pitch over themselves sharply, rather than rolling. This pitching causes a tube to form, and in most places in the world that tube is a mere couple of feet in diameter. In the case of Pipeline, however, its unique, extremely shallow

■ **TIP** ➜ The Banzai Pipeline is a surf break, not a beach. The best place to catch a glimpse of the break is from 'Ehukai Beach.

reef causes the swells to open into 10-foot-high moving hallways that surfers can pass through. Only problem: a single slip puts them right into the raggedly sharp coral heads that caused the wave to pitch in the first place. Broken arms and boards are the rule rather than the exception for those who dare to ride and fail.

When Are the Contests?

The first contests at Hale'iwa begin the second week of November, and the Triple Crown finishes up right before Christmas.

Surfing, more so than any other sport, relies on Mother Nature to allow competition. Each contest in the Triple Crown requires only four days of competition, but each is given a window of twelve days. Contest officials decide by 7 AM of each day whether the contest will be held or not, and they release the information to radio stations and via a hotline (whose number changes each year, unfortunately). By 7:15, you will know if it is on or not. Consult the local paper's sports section for the hotline number or listen to the radio announcement. The contests run from 8:30 to 4:30, featuring half-hour heats with four to six surfers each.

If big crowds bother you, go early on in the contests, within the first two days of each one. While the finale of the Pipeline Masters may draw about 10,000 fans, the earlier days have the same world class surfers with less than a thousand fans.

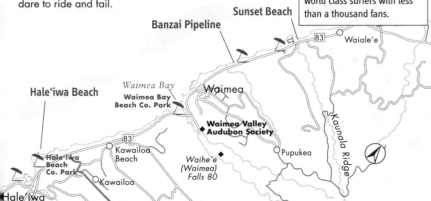

How Do I Get There?

If you hate dealing with parking and traffic, take TheBus. It will transport you from Waikīkī to the contest sites in an hour for two bucks and no hassle.

If you must drive, watch the news the night before. If they are expecting big waves that night, there is a very good chance the contest will be on in the morning. Leave by 6 AM to beat the crowd. When everybody else gets the news at 7:15 AM that the show is on, you will be parking your car and taking a snooze on the beach waiting for the surfing to commence.

Parking is limited so be prepared to park alongside Kamehameha Highway and trek it in.

But I'm not coming until Valentine's Day.

There doesn't need to be a contest underway for you to enjoy these spots from a spectator's perspective. The North Shore surf season begins in October and concludes at the end of March. Only the best can survive the wave at Pipeline. You may not be watching Kelly Slater or Andy Irons ripping, but, if the waves are up, you will still see surfing that will blow your mind. Also, there are surf contests year-round on all shores of O'ahu, so check the papers to see what is going on during your stay. A few other events to be on the lookout for:

Buffalo's Annual Big Board Surfing Classic

Generally held in March at legendary waterman "Buffalo" Keaulana's home beach of Mākaha, this is the Harlem Globetrotters of surfing contests. You'll see tandem riding, headstands, and outrigger canoe surfing. The contest is more about making the crowds cheer than beating your competitors, which makes it very accessible for the casual fan.

Converse Hawaiian Open

During the summer months, the waves switch to the south shore, where there are surf contests of one type or another each week. The Open is one of the biggest and is a part of the US Professional Longboard Surfing Championships. The best shoot it out every August on the waves Duke Kahanamoku made famous at Queen's Beach in Waikīkī.

Quiksilver in Memory of Eddie Aikau Big Wave Invitational

The granddaddy of them all is a one-day, winner-take-all contest in 25-foot surf at Waimea Bay. Because of the need for huge waves, it can be held only when there's a perfect storm. That could be at any time in the winter months, and there have even been a few years when it didn't happen at all. When Mother Nature does comply, however, it is not to be missed. You can hear the waves from the road, even before you can see the beach or the break.

magnet, offering fashion boutiques, surf shops, restaurants, and the best grilled mahimahi sandwich on the North Shore at Kua 'Aina Sandwich.

Beyond Hale'iwa is the tiny village of Waialua, a string of beach parks, an airfield where gliders, hang-gliders, and parachutists play, and, at the end of the road, Ka'ena Point State Recreation Area, which offers a brisk hike, striking views and whale-watching in season.

TIMING Pack wisely for a day's North Shore excursion: swim and snorkel gear, light jacket and hat (the weather is mercurial, especially in winter), sunscreen and sunglasses, bottled water and snacks, towels and a picnic blanket, and both sandals and close-toed shoes for hiking. A small cooler is nice; you may want to pick up some fruit or fresh corn. As always, leave valuables in the hotel safe and lock the car whenever you leave it.

From Waikīkī, the quickest route to the North Shore is H1 east to H2 north and then the Kamehameha Highway past Wahiawa'; you'll hit Hale'iwa in just less than an hour. The Windward route (H1 east, H3 through the mountains, and Kamehameha Highway north) takes at least 90 minutes to Halēiwa.

Top Attractions

44 **Hale'iwa.** During the 1920s this seaside hamlet boasted a posh seaside hotel at the end of a railroad line (both long gone). During the 1960s, hippies gathered here, followed by surfers from around the world. Today Hale'iwa is a fun mix, with old general stores and contemporary boutiques, galleries, and eateries. Be sure to stop in at **Lili'uokalani Protestant Church,** founded by missionaries in the 1830s. It's fronted by a large, stone archway built in 1910 and covered with night-blooming cereus. ⌧ *Follow H–1 west from Honolulu to H–2 north, exit at Wahiawā, follow Kamehameha Hwy. 6 mi, turn left at signaled intersection, then right into Hale'iwa* ⊕ *www.haleiwamainstreet.com.*

▪ NEED A BREAK?

For a real slice of Hale'iwa life, stop at **Matsumoto's** (⌧ 66-087 Kamehameha Hwy. ⊕ www.matsumotoshaveice.com), a family-run business in a building dating from 1910, for shave ice in every flavor imaginable. For something different, order a shave ice with *adzuki* beans—the red beans are boiled until soft, mixed with sugar, and then placed in the cone with the ice on top.

46 **Ka'ena Point State Recreation Area.** The name means "the heat" and, indeed, this windy, barren coast lacks both shade and fresh water (or any man-made amenities). Pack water, wear sturdy close-toed shoes, don sunscreen and a hat, and lock the car.

WAVING IN THE WIND

The North Shore is sarong territory. As you drive along Kamehameha Highway, you'll see squares of colorful fabric flapping in the breeze, drawing your attention to roadside shops. You can pay anything from $5 to $25 for a sarong (pa'u in Hawaiian, pareu in Tahitian), but the best prices are here, far from town. Sarongs come in handy as beach cover-ups, bathrobes, evening shawls, skirts, scarves, and even picnic blankets. Along with a bikini and some rubber slippers, they are standard beachgirl wear.

WHAT DOES IT MEAN?	
T-shirts and bumper stickers common in O'ahu may stump you. Here's a guide: ■ Eddie Would Go: Inspirational reference to big wave surfer Eddie Aikau, who lost his life attempting to save those aboard a swamped voyaging canoe. ■ Wala'au: Gossip. The name of a popular Kaua'i radio show.	■ Kau Inoa: Put or place your name. Urges Hawaiians to sign up to help organize a Native Hawaiian governing entity. ■ What part of a'ole don't you understand?: A'ole means "no." ■ If can, can; if no can, no can: Pidgin for "whatever." ■ Got koko?: Got blood, meaning, are you Hawaiian?

The hike is along a rutted dirt road, mostly flat and three miles long, ending in a rocky, sandy headland. It is here that Hawaiians believed the souls of the dead met with their family gods, and, if judged worthy to enter the afterlife, leapt off into eternal darkness at Leinaaka'uane, just south of the point. In summer and at low tide, the small coves offer bountiful shelling; in winter, don't venture near the water. Rare native plants dot the landscape. November through March, watch for humpbacks, spouting and breaching. Binoculars and a camera are highly recommended. ⊠ *North end of Kamehameha Hwy.*

★ ☺ ㊷ **Waimea Valley Audubon Center.** Waimea may get lots of press for the giant winter waves in the bay, but the valley itself is a newsmaker and an ecological treasure in its own right. The National Audubon Society is working to conserve and restore the natural habitat. Follow the Kamananui Stream up the valley through the 1,800 acres of gardens. The botanical collections here include over 5,000 species of tropical flora, including a superb gathering of Polynesian plants. It's the best place on the island to see native species, such as the endangered Hawaiian moorhen. You can also see the remains of the Hale O Lono heiau along with other ancient archaeological sites; evidence suggests that the area was an important spiritual center. At the back of the valley, **Waihī Falls** plunges 45 feet into a swimming pond. ■ TIP➜ **Bring your suit—a swim is the perfect way to end your hike. There's a lifeguard and changing room. Be sure to bring mosquito repellent, too; it gets buggy.** ⊠ *59-864 Kamehameha Hwy., Hale'iwa* ☎ *808/638-9199* ⊕ *www.audubon.org* ⊠ *$8, parking $2* ☾ *Daily 9:30–5.*

NEED A BREAK? The chocolate haupia pie at **Ted's Bakery** (⊠ 59-024 Kamehameha Hwy., near Sunset Beach ☎ 808/638-8207) is legendary. Stop in for a take-out pie or for a quick plate lunch or sandwich.

Also Worth Seeing

㊺ **North Shore Surf and Cultural Museum.** Shop owner and curator Stephen Gould displays more than 30 vintage surfboards dating back to the 1930s, a shrine dedicated to legendary surfer Duke Kahanamoku, video presentations, surf memorabilia, and even a motorized surfboard that served as the forerunner to the Jet Ski. Donations accepted. ✉ *66-250 Kamehameha Hwy., Haleʻiwa* ☎ *808/637–8888* ⏱ *Wed.–Mon. 11–5.*

㊸ Puʻuomahuka Heiau. Worth a stop for its spectacular views from a bluff high above the ocean overlooking Waimea Bay, this sacred spot was once the site of human sacrifices. It's now on the National Register of Historic Places. ✉ *½ mi north of Waimea Bay on Rte. 83, turn right on Pūpūkea Rd. and drive 1 mi uphill.*

CENTRAL AND WEST (LEEWARD) OʻAHU

Oʻahu's central plain is a patchwork of old towns and new residential developments, military bases, farms, ranches, and shopping malls, with a few visit-worthy attractions and historic sites scattered about. Central Oʻahu encompasses the Moanalua Valley, residential Pearl City, and the old plantation town of Wahiawā, on the uplands half-way to the North Shore. Sights are reached by the H1 and H2 freeways.

West (or Leeward) Oʻahu has the island's fledgling "second city"—the planned community of Kapolei, where the government hopes to attract enough jobs to lighten inbound traffic to downtown Honolulu—then continues on past a far-flung resort to the Hawaiian communities of Nānākuli and Waiʻanae, to the beach and the end of the road at Keaweʻula, a.k.a. Yokohama Bay. West Oʻahu begins at folksy Waipahu and continues past Makakilo and Kapolei on H1 and Highway 93, Farrington Highway.

A couple of cautions as you head to the leeward side: Highway 93 is a narrow, winding two-lane notorious for accidents. There's an abrupt transition from freeway to highway at Kapolei, and by the time you reach Nānākuli, it's a country road, so slow down. Car break-ins and beach thefts are common so have a care.

TIMING If you've got to leave one part of Oʻahu for the next trip, the West coast is probably the one. It's a longish drive by island standards: 45 minutes to Kapolei from Waikīkī and 90 minutes to Waiʻanae. The attraction most worth the trek is Hawaii's Plantation Village in Waipahu, about a half hour out of town; it's a living history museum built from actual homes of turn-of-the-century plantation workers.

Central Oʻahu

 ㊼ Dole Plantation. Celebrate Hawaiʻi's famous golden fruit at this promotional, tourist-oriented center with exhibits, a huge gift shop, a snack

FUN THINGS TO DO AROUND OʻAHU

- Loop a mountain trail high above the city.
- Play Hawaiian checkers at the Paradise Cove lūʻau.
- Walk to the ends of the earth at Kaʻena Point.
- Watch winter's house-size waves on the North Shore.
- Kayak to Kapapa off the Kualoa shore.
- Lose yourself in a tropical maze at Dole Plantation.
- Pick up a papaya at a roadside stand.
- Let the wind whip your cares away on Nuʻuanu Pali Overlook.

O'AHU SIGHTSEEING TOURS

Guided tours are convenient; you don't have to worry about finding a parking spot or getting admission tickets. You'll likely gain insights that you wouldn't get on your own. Most of the tour guides have taken special Hawaiiana classes in history and lore, and many are certified by the state of Hawai'i. On the other hand, you won't have the freedom to proceed at your own pace, nor will you have the ability to take a detour trip if something else catches your attention.

BUS & VAN TOURS

■ TIP➔ Ask exactly what the tour includes in the way of actual get-off-the-bus stops and window sights.

Polynesian Adventure Tours. ☎ 808/833-3000 ⊕ www.polyad. com.

Polynesian Hospitality. ☎ 808/526-3565 ⊕ www.kobay.com.

Roberts Hawai'i. ☎ 808/539-9400 ⊕ www.robertshawaii.com.

THEME TOURS
Culinary Tour of Chinatown. Anthony Chang leads tours of noodle shops, dim sum parlors, food courts, bakers, and other food vendors. ☎ 808/533-3181.

E Noa Tours. Certified tour guides conduct Circle Island, Pearl Harbor, and shopping tours. ☎ 808/591-2561 ⊕ www.enoa.com.

Hawaiian Islands Eco-tours, Ltd.'s. Experienced guides take nature lovers and hikers on limited-access trails for tours ranging from hidden waterfalls to bird-watching. ☎ 808/236-7766.

Home of the Brave and Top Gun Tours. Perfect for military-history buffs. Narrated tours visit O'ahu's military bases and the National Memorial Cemetery of the Pacific. ☎ 808/396-8112 ⊕ www. pearlharborhq.com.

Matthew Gray's Hawaii Food Tours. Three different restaurant tour itineraries include samplings, meals, and discussion of Hawai'i foodways. ☎ 808/926-3663 ⊕ www.hawaiifoodtours.com.

Polynesian Cultural Center. An advantage of this tour is that you don't have to drive yourself back to Waikīkī after dark if you take in the evening show. ☎ 808/293-3333 or 808/923-1861 ⊕ www.polynesia. com.

WALKING TOURS
American Institute of Architects (AIA) Downtown Walking Tour. See Downtown Honolulu from an architectural perspective. ✉ American Institute of Architects, 119 Merchant St., #402, Downtown Honolulu ☎ 808/545-4242.

Chinatown Walking Tour. Meet at the Chinese Chamber of Commerce for a fascinating peek into herbal shops, an acupuncturist's office, and open-air markets. ✉ Chinese Chamber of Commerce ☎ 808/533-3181.

Hawai'i Geographic Society. Downtown Honolulu historic temple and archaeology walking tours are available. ☎ 808/538-3952.

Honolulu Time Walks. Costumed narrators explore the mysteries of Honolulu—its haunts, historic neighborhoods, and colorful history. ☎ 808/943-0371.

concession, educational displays, and the world's largest maze. Take a self-guided Garden Tour or hop aboard the Pineapple Express for a 20-minute train tour to learn a bit about life on a pineapple plantation. Kids love the 1.7-mi Pineapple Garden Maze, made up of 11,000 tropical plants and trees. This is about a 40-minute drive from Waikīkī, a suitable stop on the way to or from the North Shore. ⊠ *64-1550 Kamehameha Hwy.* ☎ *808/621–8408* ⊕ *www.dole-plantation.com* ⊠ *Pavilion free, maze $5, train $7.50* ⊙ *Daily 9–5:30; last train tour starts at 5.*

48 Kūkaniloko Birthstone State Monument. In the cool uplands of Wahiawā is haunting Kūkaniloko, where noble chieftesses went to give birth to high-ranking children. One of the most significant cultural sites on the island, the lava rock stones here were believed to possess the power to ease the labor pains of childbirth. The site is marked by approximately 180 stones covering about a half-acre. It's about a 40–45 minute drive from Waikīkī. ⊠ *North side of Wahiawā town, intersection of Kamehameha Hwy. and Whitmore Ave.*

49 Moanalua Gardens. This lovely park is the site of the internationally acclaimed Prince Lot Hula Festival on the third weekend in July. Throughout the year, the Moanalui Gardens Foundation sponsors 3-mi guided walks into Kamananui Valley, usually on Sunday; call for specific times. Self-guided tour booklets ($5) are also available from the Moanalua Gardens Foundation office. To reach Moanalua Gardens, take the Moanalua Freeway westbound (78). Take the Tripler exit, then take a right on Mahiole Street. Pineapple Place is right after Moanalua Elementary School. ⊠ *1352 Pineapple Pl., Honolulu* ☎ *808/833–1944* ⊕ *www.mgf-hawaii. com* ⊠ *Free, guided hikes $5* ⊙ *Weekdays 8–4:30.*

West Oʻahu

51 Hawaiian Waters Adventure Park. This 25-acre family attraction offers water slides, water cannons, waterfalls, and even a beach volleyball court. It's off H-1 at Exit 1. ⊠ *400 Farrington Hwy., Kapolei* ☎ *808/674–9283* ⊕ *www.hawaiianwaters.com* ⊠ *$35* ⊙ *Hours vary, call ahead to confirm.*

50 Hawaiʻi's Plantation Village. Starting in the 1800s, immigrants seeking work on the sugar plantations came to these islands like so many waves against the shore. Tour authentically furnished buildings, both original and replicated, that re-create and pay tribute to the plantation era. See a Chinese social hall; a Japanese shrine, sumo ring, and saimin stand; a dental office; and historic homes at this living museum 30 minutes from Downtown Honolulu. ⊠ *Waipahu Cultural Gardens Park, 94-695 Waipahu St., Waipahu* ☎ *808/677–0110* ⊕ *www.hawaiiplantationvillage. org* ⊠ *$10* ⊙ *Mon.–Sat. 10–3, with guided tours on the hr.*

55 Keawaʻula Beach (Yokohama Bay). The last sandy beach and, indeed, the last stop on Farrington Highway, is both a surfing beach and a sunbathing spot far, far from the madding crowd. Just down the road is the western end of the undeveloped Kaʻena Point State Recreation Area; you can hike to Kaʻena Point from here, but it's a rugged trek (⇨ Chapter 5, Golf, Hiking & Other Outdoor Activities). ⊠ *End of Farrington Hwy., Waiaʻanae.*

SNAP! CRACKLE! POP!

Influenced by a large Chinese population, Islanders are just crazy about fireworks.

- Free Friday fireworks off the Hilton Hawaiian Village are visible all along the Honolulu shoreline: 7:30 PM October to March; 8 PM April to September.

- Fourth of July displays light up the skies off Magic Island in Honolulu, at Kailua Beach, and at Pearl Harbor, Schofield Barracks, and Kāne'ohe Marine base.

- Entire neighborhoods are wreathed in smoke on New Year's Eve, as families scare away bad luck with firecrackers. Midnight fireworks are at Sand Island, on a barge off Waikīkī, and usually in a couple of other spots.

- On Chinese New Year (January or February), Chinatown is alive with crackling 1,000-firecracker strings and lions dancing through businesses to munch money gifts handed out by store owners and patrons.

52 **Ko Olina.** The Ko Olina resort—golf course, hotels, gated residences—offers a number of amenities for visitors, including the challenging (and pricy) Ted Robinson–designed golf course, a couple of nice, sit-down lunch spots (Roy's Ko Olina at the golf course and the Naupaka Terrace at the JW Marriott Ko Olina Resort & Spa), and a couple of open-to-the-public man-made swimming lagoons surrounded by lush lawns with changing and bathroom facilities. ⊠ *Farrington Highway at Ali'inui Dr.*

54 **Mākaha Beach Park.** Famous as a surfing and boogie-boarding park, Mākaha hosts an annual surf meet and draws many scuba divers in summer, when the waves are calm, to explore underwater caverns and ledges. It's popular with families year-round but, in winter, watch for rip tides and currents; Mākaha means "fierce," and there's a reason for that. ⊠ *84-369 Farrington Hwy., Waia'anae.*

53 **Pōkai Bay Beach Park.** This gorgeous swimming and snorkeling beach is protected by a long breakwater left over from a now-defunct boat harbor. The beach's entire length is sand and a close-in reef creates smallish waves perfect for novice surfers. ⊠ *85-027 Wai'anae Valley Rd., off Farrington Hwy., Waia'anae.*

Beaches

Waikīkī Beach

WORD OF MOUTH

"Lanikai Beach was awesome—a perfect spot for a post-pancake nap and the newest addition to my favorite beach list. Water is perfectly calm and pleasant for dipping/floating."

—bogart04

"Another good beach for families is San Souci beach at the opposite end of Waikīkī . . . Clean sand, gentle waves, decent parking, grass and trees above the sandy area, and snack bar in the New Otani Hotel."

—lcuy

By Chad Pata

TROPICAL SUN MIXED WITH COOLING TRADE WINDS and pristine waters make Oʻahu's shores a literal heaven on Earth. But contrary to many assumptions, the island is not one big beach. There are miles and miles of coastline without a grain of sand, so you need to know where you are going to fully enjoy the Hawaiian experience.

Many of the island's southern and eastern coasts are protected by inner reefs. The reefs provide still coastline water but not much as far as sand is concerned. However, where there are beaches on the south and east shores, they are mind-blowing. In West Oʻahu and on the North Shore you can find the wide expanses of sand you would expect for enjoying the sunset. Sandy bottoms and outside reefs make the water an adventure in the winter months. Most visitors assume the seasons don't change a thing in the Islands, and they would be right—except for the waves, which are big on the south shore in summer and placid in winter. It's exactly the opposite on the north side where winter storms bring in huge waves, but the ocean goes to glass come May and June.

We start on the famed Waikīkī Beach and then work our way counterclockwise around the island to the epic waves of the North Shore. In the final section we head west, where the populations dwindle and the beauty expands.

WAIKĪKĪ

The 2½-mi strand called Waikīkī Beach extends from Hilton Hawaiian Village on one end to Kapiʻolani Park and Diamond Head on the other. Although it's one contiguous piece of beach, it's as varied as the people that inhabit the Islands. Whether you're an old-timer looking to enjoy the action from the shade or a sports nut wanting to do it all, you can find every beach activity here without ever jumping in the rental car.

■ TIP➜ **If you're staying outside the area, our best advice is to park at either end of the beach and walk in.** Plentiful parking exists on the west end at the Ala Wai Marina, where there are myriad free spots on the beach as well as metered stalls around the harbor. For parking on the east end, Kapiʻolani Park and the Honolulu Zoo both have metered parking for $1 an hour—more affordable than the $10 per hour the resorts want.

We highlight the differences in this famous beach from west to east, letting you know not only where you may want to sunbathe but why.

Ⓒ **Duke Kahanamoku Beach.** Named for Hawaiʻi's famous Olympic swimming champion, Duke Kahanamoku, this is a hard-packed beach with the only shade trees on the sand in Waikīkī. It's great for families with young children because of the shade and the calmest waters in Waikīkī, thanks to a rock wall that creates a semiprotected cove. The ocean clarity here is not as brilliant as most of Waikīkī because of the stillness of the surf, but it's a small price to pay for peace of mind about youngsters. ⌂ *In front of Hilton Hawaiian Village Beach Resort and Spa* ⌂ *Toilets, showers, food concession.*

Ⓒ **Fort DeRussy Beach Park.** Even before you take the two newly refurbished beach parks into account, this is one of the finest beaches on the south

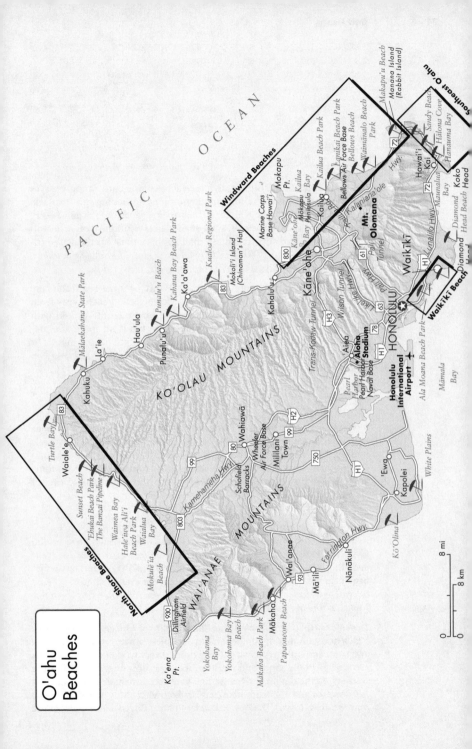

O'ahu
Beaches

PACIFIC OCEAN

North Shore Beaches

Turtle Bay
Waiale'e
Sunset Beach
'Ehukai Beach Park
The Banzai Pipeline
Waimea Bay
Hale'iwa Ali'i Beach Park
Waialua Bay
Mokulē'ia Beach

Kahuku
La'ie
Hau'ula
Punalu'u
Kahana Bay Beach Park
Ka'a'awa
Punalu'u Beach
Mālaekahana State Park

Ka'ena Pt.
Dillingham Airfield
Mokulē'ia Beach
Mākaha Beach Park
Papaoneone Beach
Yokohama Bay Beach
Yokohama Bay
Mākaha
Wai'anae
Mā'ili
Nānākuli
Kō 'Olina
'Ewa
Kapolei
White Plains

WAI'ANAE MOUNTAINS

KO'OLAU MOUNTAINS

Kualoa Regional Park
Mokoli'i Island (Chinaman's Hat)
Kahalu'u
Kāne'ohe

Wahiawā
Wheeler Air Force Base
Schofield Barracks
Mililani Town

Windward Beaches

Marine Corps Base Hawai'i
Mokapu Pt.
Kāne'ohe Bay
Kailua Bay
Mōkapu Peninsula
Kailua Beach Park
Lanikai Beach Park
Bellows Air Force Base
Lanikai Beach
Bellows Beach
Waimānalo Beach Park
Makapu'u Beach
Manana Island (Rabbit Island)

Mt. Olomana
Pali Hwy.
Pali Tunnel
Wilson Tunnel
Trans-Ko'olau Tunnel
Kalaniana'ole Hwy.
Likelike Hwy.

'Aiea
Aloha Stadium
Pearl Harbor
Pearl Harbor Naval Base
Honolulu International Airport
HONOLULU
Waikīkī
Ala Moana Beach Park
Māmala Bay
Waikīkī Beach

Hawai'i Kai
Maunalua Bay
Koko Head
Diamond Head Beach Park
Diamond Head
Hālona Cove
Sandy Beach
Hanauma Bay

Southeast O'ahu

Kamehameha Hwy.

0   8 mi
0   8 km

BEACHES KEY

🚻	Restroom
🚿	Shower
🏄	Surfing
🤿	Snorkel/Scuba
👶	Good for kids
P	Parking

side of Oʻahu. Wide, soft, ultrawhite beaches with gently lapping waves make it a family favorite for running/jumping/frolicking fun (this also happens to be where the NFL holds their rookie sand football game every year). Add to that the new, heavily-shaded grass grilling area, sand volleyball courts, and aquatic rentals, making this a must for the active visitor. ☒ *In front of Fort DeRussy and Hale Koa Hotel � Lifeguard, toilets, showers, food concession, picnic tables, grills, playground.*

Gray's Beach. A little lodging house called Gray's-by-the-Sea stood here in the 1920s; now it's a gathering place for eclectic beach types from sailing pioneers like George Parsons to the bird men of Waikīkī with their colorful parrots for rent. The tides often put sand space at a premium, but if you want a look back into old Waikīkī, have a mai tai at the Shorebird and check out a time gone by. ☒ *In front of Halekūlani � Lifeguard, toilets, showers, food concession.*

Kahaloa and Ulukou Beaches. The beach widens back out here, creating the "it" spot for the bikini crowd. Beautiful bodies abound, as do activities. ■ TIP→ This is where you find most of the sailing catamaran charters for a spectacular sail out to Diamond Head or surfboard and outrigger canoe rentals for a ride on "Hawaiʻi's Malibu" at Canoe's surf break. Great music and outdoor dancing beckon the sand-bound visitor to Duke's Bar and Grill, where shirt and shoes not only aren't required, they're discouraged. ☒ *In front of Royal Hawaiian Hotel and Sheraton Moana Surfrider � Lifeguard, toilets, showers, food concession.*

☪ **Kūhiō Beach Park.** Due to recent renovations, this beach has seen a renaissance. Now bordered by a landscaped boardwalk, it's great for romantic walks any time of day. Check out the Kūhiō Beach hula mound nightly at 6:30 for free hula and Hawaiian-music performances; weekends there's a torch-lighting ceremony at sunset. ■ TIP→ Surf lessons for beginners are available from the beach center here every half hour. ☒ *Past Sheraton Moana Surfrider Hotel to Kapahulu Ave. pier � Lifeguard, toilets, showers, food concession.*

☪ **Queen's Surf.** So named as it was once the site of Queen Liliʻuokalani's beach house. A mix of families and gay couples gathers here, and it seems as if someone is always playing a steel drum. Every weekend movie screens are set up on the sand, and major motion pictures are shown after the sun sets. In the daytime, there are banyan trees for shade and volleyball nets for pros and amateurs alike (this is where Misty May and Kerri Walsh play while in town). ■ TIP→ The water fronting Queen's Surf is an aquatic

SURF WITH THE WHOLE FAMILY

For simple, cheap fun in Waikīkī, outrigger canoes are often overlooked. Everyone is clamouring to learn to surf or to go for a sail, but no one notices the long, funny-looking boats in front of Duke's that allow you to do both for much cheaper. At $10 for three rides, the price hasn't changed in a decade, and the thrill hasn't changed in centuries. You can get a paddle, but no one expects you to use it—the beach boys negotiate you in and out of the break as they have been doing all their lives. If you think taking off on a wave on a 10-foot board is a rush, wait until your whole family takes off on one in a 30-foot boat!

preserve, providing the best snorkeling in Waikīkī. ⊠ *Across from entrance to Honolulu Zoo* ⚐ *Lifeguard, toilets, showers, picnic tables, grills.*

Sans Souci. Nicknamed Dig-Me Beach because of its outlandish display of skimpy bathing suits, this small rectangle of sand is nonetheless a good sunning spot for all ages. Children enjoy its shallow, safe waters that are protected by the walls of the historic Natatorium, an Olympic-size saltwater swimming arena. Serious swimmers and triathletes also swim in the channel here, beyond the reef. Sans Souci is favored by locals wanting to avoid the crowds while still enjoying the convenience of Waikīkī. ⊠ *Across from Kapiʻolani Park, between New Otani Kaimana Beach Hotel and Waikīkī War Memorial Natatorium* ⚐ *Lifeguard, toilets, showers, picnic tables.*

Diamond Head Beach. You have to like hiking to like Diamond Head Beach. This beautiful, remote spot is at the base of Diamond Head crater. The beach is just a small strip of sand with lots of coral in the water. This said, the natural views looking out from the point are breathtaking, and it's amazing to watch the windsurfers skimming along, driven by the gusts off the point. From the parking area, look for an opening in the wall where an unpaved trail leads down to the beach. Even for the un-adventurous, a stop at the lookout point is well worth the time. ⊠ *At base of Diamond Head. Park at the crest of Diamond Head Rd. and walk down* ⚐ *Showers, parking lot.*

HONOLULU

The city of Honolulu only has one beach, the monstrous Ala Moana. It hosts everything from Dragon Boat competitions to the Aloha State Games.

Ala Moana Beach Park. Ala Moana has a protective reef, which makes it ostensibly a ½-mi wide saltwater swimming pool. After Waikīkī, this is the most popular beach among visitors. To the Waikīkī side is a peninsula called Magic Island, with shady trees and paved sidewalks ideal for jogging. Ala Moana also has playing fields, tennis courts, and a couple of small ponds for sailing toy boats. This beach is for everyone, but only in the daytime. It's a high-crime area after dark. ⊠ *Honolulu, near Ala Moana Shopping Center and Ala Moana Blvd. From Waikīkī take Bus 8 to shopping center and cross Ala Moana Blvd.* ⚲ *Lifeguard, toilets, showers, food concession, picnic tables, grills, parking lot.*

SOUTHEAST O'AHU

Much of Southeast O'ahu is surrounded by reef, making most of the coast uninviting to swimmers, but the spots where the reef opens up are true gems. The drive along this side of the island is amazing with its sheer lava-rock walls on one side and deep-blue ocean on the other. There are plenty of restaurants in the suburb of Hawai'i Kai, so you can make a day of it, knowing that food isn't far away. Beaches are listed from south to north.

Hanauma Bay Nature Preserve. Picture this as the world's biggest open-air aquarium. You go here to see fish, and fish you'll see. Due to their exposure to thousands of visitors every week, these fish are more like family pets than the skittish marine life you might expect. An old volcanic crater has created a haven from the waves where the coral has thrived. There's an educational center where you must watch a nine-minute video about the nature preserve before being allowed down to the bay. ■ **TIP➔ The bay is best early in the morning (around 7), before the crowds arrive; it can be difficult to park later in the day.** No smoking is allowed, and the beach is closed on Tuesday. **Hanauma Bay Dive Tours** (☎ 808/256–8956), runs snorkeling, snuba, and scuba tours to Hanauma Bay with transportation from Waikīkī hotels. ⊠ *7455 Kalaniana'ole Hwy.* ☎ *808/396–4229* ⚲ *Lifeguard, toilets, showers, food concession, picnic tables, parking lot* ▧ *Donation $5; parking $1; mask, snorkel, and fins rental $8; tram from parking lot down to beach $1.50* ☉ *Wed.–Mon. 6–7.*

Hālona Cove. Also known as "From Here to Eternity Beach" and "Pounders," this little beauty is never crowded due to the short treacherous climb down to the sand. But for the intrepid, what a treat this spot can be. It's in a break in the ocean cliffs, with the surrounding crags providing protection from the wind. Open–ocean waves roll up on the beach (thus the second nickname), but, unlike Sandy's, a gently sloping sand bottom takes much of the punch out of them before they hit the

BEACHES KEY

🚻	Restroom
🚿	Shower
🏄	Surfing
🤿	Snorkel/Scuba
👶	Good for kids
P	Parking

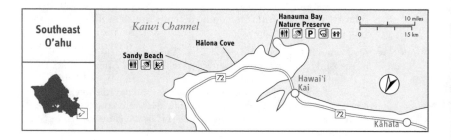

BEACH SAFETY

Yes, the beaches are beautiful, but always be cognizant of the fact you are on a little rock in the middle of the Pacific Ocean. The current and waves will be stronger and bigger than any you may have experienced. Riptides can take you on a ride they call the "Moloka'i Express"—only problem is that it doesn't take you to the island of Moloka'i but rather out into the South Pacific.

Never swim alone. It is hard for even the most attentive lifeguards

to keep their eyes on everyone at once, but a partner can gain their attention if you should run into trouble. There are many safe spots, but always pay attention to the posted signs. The lifeguards change the signs daily, so the warnings are always applicable to the day's conditions. If you have any doubts, ask a lifeguard for their assessment. They're professionals and can give you competent advice.

shore. Use caution here: it is mellow inside the cove but dangerous once you get outside of it. Turtles frequent the small cove, seeking respite from the otherwise blustery coast. It's great for packing a lunch and holing up for the day. ⊠ *Below Hālona Blow Hole Lookout parking lot* ⚲ *No facilities.*

★ **Sandy Beach.** Probably the most popular beach with locals on this side of O'ahu, the broad, sloping beach is covered with sunbathers there to watch **the Show** and soak up rays. The Show is a shore break that's like no other in the Islands. Monster ocean swells rolling into the beach combined with the sudden rise in the ocean floor causes waves to jack up and crash magnificently on the shore. Young and old brave this danger to get some of the biggest barrels you can find for bodysurfing, but always keeping in mind the beach's other nickname, "Break Neck Beach." Use extreme caution when swimming here, but feel free to kick back and watch the drama unfold from the comfort of your beach chair. ⊠ *Makai of Kalaniana'ole Hwy., 2 mi east of Hanauma Bay* ⚲ *Lifeguard, toilets, showers, picnic tables.*

WINDWARD O'AHU

The Windward side lives up to its name with ideal spots for windsurfing and kiteboarding, or for the more intrepid, hang gliding. For the most part the waves are mellow, and the bottoms are all sand—making for nice spots to visit with younger kids. The only drawback is that this side does tend to get more rain. But, as beautiful as the vistas are, a little sprinkling of "pineapple juice" shouldn't dampen your experience; plus it turns on the waterfalls that cascade down the Ko'olaus. Beaches are listed from north to south.

Fodor's Choice **Makapu'u Beach.** A magnificent beach protected by Makapu'u Point wel★ comes you to the Windward side. Hang gliders circle above the beach,

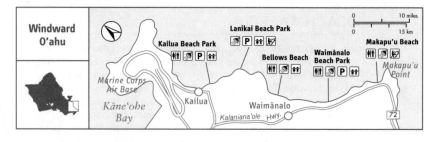

BEACHES KEY

♦♦	Restroom
⑤	Shower
ⓚ	Surfing
ⓖ	Snorkel/Scuba
♦♦	Good for kids
Ⓟ	Parking

and the water is filled with body boarders. Just off the coast you can see Bird Island, a sanctuary for aquatic fowl, jutting out of the blue. The currents can be heavy, so check with a lifeguard if you're unsure of safety. Before you leave, take the prettiest (and coldest) outdoor shower available on the island. Being surrounded by tropical flowers and foliage while you rinse off that sand will be a memory you will cherish from this side of the rock. ⊠ *Across from Sea Life Park on Kalaniana'ole Hwy., 2 mi south of Waimānalo* ⚬ *Lifeguard, toilets, showers, picnic tables, grills.*

ⓒ **Waimānalo Beach Park.** This is a "local" beach, busy with picnicking families and active sports fields. Treat the beach with respect (read: don't litter) and lock your car. This beach is one of the island's most beautiful. Expect a wide stretch of sand; turquoise, emerald, and deep-blue seas; and gentle shore breaking waves that are fun for all ages to play in. ⊠ *South of Waimānalo town, look for signs on Kalaniana'ole Hwy.* ⚬ *Lifeguard, toilets, showers, picnic tables.*

Bellows Beach. Bellows is the same exact beach as Waimānalo, but it's under the auspices of the military, making it more friendly for visitors. The park area is excellent for camping, and ironwood trees provide plenty of shade. There's no food concession, but McDonald's and other takeout fare is right outside the entrance gate. ⊠ *Entrance on Kalaniana'ole Hwy., near Waimānalo town center* ⚬ *Lifeguard, toilets, showers, picnic tables, grills.*

★ **Lanikai Beach Park.** Think of the beaches you see in commercials: peaceful blue waters, perfectly soft sand, families and dogs frolicking mindlessly. It's an ideal spot for camping out with a book. Plenty of action from wind- and kite surfers will keep non-readers occupied. ⊠ *Past Kailua Beach Park; street parking on Mokulua Dr. for various public–access points to beach* ⚬ *Lifeguard, showers.*

Fodor's Choice **Kailua Beach Park.** This is like a big Lanikai Beach, but a little windier
★ and a little wider. It's a better spot for a full day at the beach, though. A line of palms provides shade on the sand, and a huge park has picnic pavilions where you can escape the heat or feed the hordes. ■ **TIP→ This is the "it" spot if you're looking to try your hand at windsurfing.** ⊠ *Near Kailua town, turn right on Kailua Rd. at market, cross bridge, then turn left into beach parking lot* ⚬ *Lifeguard, toilets, showers, picnic tables, grills, playground, parking lot.*

Kualoa Regional Park. Grassy expanses border a long, narrow stretch of beach with spectacular views of Kāneʻohe Bay and the Koʻolau Mountains, making Kualoa one of the island's most beautiful picnic, camping, and beach areas. Dominating the view is an islet called Mokoliʻi, better known as Chinaman's Hat, which rises 206 feet above the water. You can swim in the shallow areas year-round. ■ TIP→ **The one drawback is that it's usually windy, but the wide open spaces are ideal for kite flying.** ⊠ *North of Waiāhole, on Kamehameha Hwy.* ⚿ *Lifeguard, toilets, showers, picnic tables, grills.*

3

☃ **Kahana Bay Beach Park.** Local parents often bring their children here to wade in safety in the very shallow, protected waters. This pretty beach cove has a long sand strip that is great for walking and a cool, shady grove of tall ironwood and pandanus trees that is ideal for a picnic. An ancient Hawaiian fishpond, which was in use until the '20s, is visible nearby. The water here is not generally a clear blue due to the run-off from the heavy rains in the valley. ⊠ *North of Kualoa Park on Kamehameha Hwy.* ⚿ *Lifeguard, toilets, showers, picnic tables.*

Punaluʻu Beach Park. If you're making a circle of the island, this is a great stopping point to jump out of your car and stretch your legs. It's easy, because the sand literally comes up to your parked car, and nice, because there is a sandy bottom and mostly calm conditions. Plus there are full facilities and lots of shade trees. Often overlooked, and often overcast, Punaluʻu can afford you a moment of solitude and fresh air before you get back to your sightseeing. ⊠ *In Punaluʻu, on Hwy. 83* ⚿ *Toilets, showers, picnic tables.*

Mālaekahana Beach Park. The big attraction here is tiny Goat Island, a bird sanctuary just offshore. At low tide the water is shallow enough—never more than waist high—so that you can wade out to it. Wear sneakers so you don't cut yourself on the coral. The beach itself is fairly narrow but long enough for a 20-minute stroll, one-way. The waves are never too big, and sometimes they're just right for the beginning bodysurfer. Note that the entrance gates are easy to miss because you can't see the beach from the road. Families love to camp in the groves of ironwood trees at Mālaekahana State Park. Cabins are also available here, making a perfect rural getaway. ⊠ *Entrance gates are ½ mi north of Lāʻie on Kamehameha Hwy.* ⚿ *Toilets, showers, picnic tables, grills.*

NORTH SHORE

"North Shore, where the waves are mean, just like a washing machine" sing the Kaʻau Crater Boys about this legendary side of the island. And in winter they are absolutely right. At times the waves overtake the road, stranding tourists and locals alike. When the surf is up, there will even be signs on the beach telling you how far to stay back so that you aren't swept out to sea. The most prestigious big-wave contest in the world, "The Eddie Aikau," is held at Waimea Bay on waves the size of a six-story building. The Triple Crown of Surfing (⇨ *See* North Shore Surfing and the Triple Crown *in* Chapter 2) roams across three beaches in the winter months.

All this changes come summer when this tiger turns into a kitty with water smooth enough to water ski on and ideal for snorkeling. The fierce Banzai Pipeline surf break becomes a great dive area, allowing you to explore the deadly coral heads that have claimed so many on the ultra-hollow tubes that are created here in winter. But even with the monster surf subsided, this is still a time for caution. Lifeguards become more scarce, and currents don't go away just because the waves do.

This all being said, it's a place like no other on earth and must be explored. From the turtles at Mokule'ia to the tunnels at Shark's Cove, you could spend your whole trip on this side and not be disappointed. Beaches are listed from east to west.

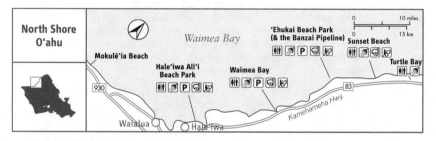

North Shore O'ahu

Mokulē'ia Beach

Hale'iwa Ali'i Beach Park

Waimea Bay

Waimea Bay

'Ehukai Beach Park (& the Banzai Pipeline) Sunset Beach

Turtle Bay

Kamehameha Hwy.

Waialua   Hale'iwa

BEACHES KEY

🚻	Restroom
🚿	Shower
🏄	Surfing
🤿	Snorkel/Scuba
🧒	Good for kids
P	Parking

Turtle Bay. Now known more for its resort than its magnificent beach, Turtle Bay is mostly passed over on the way to the more known beaches of Sunset and Waimea. But for the average visitor with the average swimming capabilities, this is the place to be on the North Shore. The crescent-shape beach is protected by a huge sea wall. You can see and hear the fury of the northern swell, while blissfully floating in cool, calm waters. The convenience of this spot is also hard to pass up—there is a concession selling sandwiches and sunblock right on the beach. ⊠ *4 mi north of Kahuku on Kamehameha Hwy. Turn into the resort and let the guard know where you are going; they offer free parking to beach guests.* ⛱ *Toilets, showers, concessions, picnic tables.*

★ **Sunset Beach.** The beach is broad, the sand is soft, the summer waves are gentle, and the winter surf is crashing. Many love searching this shore for the puka shells that adorn the necklaces you see everywhere. ■ **TIP→ Use caution in the water; at times the current can come ripping around the point.** Carryout truck stands selling shave ice, plate lunches, and sodas usually line the adjacent highway. ⊠ *1 mi north of 'Ehukai Beach Park on Kamehameha Hwy.* ⛱ *Lifeguard, toilets, showers, picnic tables.*

'Ehukai Beach Park & the Banzai Pipeline. What sets 'Ehukai apart is the view of the famous **Banzai Pipeline,** where the winter waves curl into magnificent tubes, making it an experienced wave-rider's dream. It's also an inexperienced swimmer's nightmare; spring and summer waves are more accommodating to the average swimmer. Except when the surf contests are going on, there's no reason to stay on the central strip. Travel either way on the beach, and the conditions remain the same. But the population thins out, leaving you with a magnificent stretch of sand all to yourself. ⊠ *Small parking lot borders Kamehameha Hwy. 1 mi north of Foodland at Pūpūkea* ♿ *Lifeguard, toilets, showers, parking lot.*

Fodor'sChoice
★ **Waimea Bay.** Made popular in that old Beach Boys song "Surfin' U.S.A.," Waimea Bay is a slice of big-wave heaven, home to king-size 25- to 30-foot winter waves. Summer is the time to swim and snorkel in the calm waters. The shore break is great for novice bodysurfers. Due to its popularity, the postage-stamp parking lot is quickly filled, but everyone parks along the side of the road and walks in. ■ **TIP→ Use some caution as currents can get out of hand.** ⊠ *Across from Waimea Valley, 3 mi north of Hale'iwa on Kamehameha Hwy.* ♿ *Lifeguard, toilets, showers, picnic tables, parking lot.*

> ## GOT A GOZA?
>
> For sun bathing, buy a *goza*, a Japanese beach mat. Everyone knows the frustration of getting out of the ocean and laying down on your beach towel, only to have it quickly become a 20-pound, sand-caked nuisance. The straw gozas keep the sand off your bum without absorbing all the water a towel would, giving you a cool, comfortable place to recline on the beach. Weighing just ounces and costing just pennies, it will be the best thing you buy on your trip.

Hale'iwa Ali'i Beach Park. The winter waves are impressive here, but in summer the ocean is like a lake, ideal for family swimming. The beach itself is big and often full of locals. Its broad lawn off the highway invites volleyball and Frisbee games and groups of barbecuers. This is also the opening break for the Triple Crown of Surfing, and the grass is often filled with art festivals or carnivals. ⊠ *North of Hale'iwa town center and past harbor on Kamehameha Hwy.* ♿ *Lifeguard, toilets, showers, picnic tables.*

Mokulē'ia Beach Park. There is a reason why the producers of the TV show *Lost* chose this beach for their set. On the remote northwest point of the island, it is about 10 mi from the closest store or public restroom; you could spend a day here and not see another living soul. And that is precisely its beauty—all the joy of being stranded on a deserted island without the trauma of the plane crash. The beach is wide and white, the waters bright blue (but a little choppy) and full of sea turtles and other marine life. Mokulē'ia is a great secret find, just remember to pack supplies and use caution as there are no lifeguards. ⊠ *East of Hale'iwa town center, across from Dillingham Airfield.* ♿ *No facilities.*

WEST (LEEWARD) O'AHU

The North Shore may be known as "Country," but the West side is truly the rural area on O'ahu. There are commuters from this side to Honolulu, but many are born, live, and die on this side with scarcely a trip to town. For the most part, there's less hostility and more curiosity toward outsiders. Occasional problems have flared up, mostly due to drug abuse that has ravaged the fringes of the island. But the problems have generally been car break-ins, not violence. So, in short, lock your car, don't bring valuables, and enjoy the amazing beaches.

The beaches on the west side are expansive and empty. Most Oʻahu residents and tourists don't make it to this side simply because of the drive; in traffic it can take almost 90 minutes to make it to Kaʻena Point from Downtown Honolulu. But you'll be hard pressed to find a better sunset anywhere. Beaches are listed here in a south to north direction, starting from just west of Honolulu.

FodorsChoice
★ **White Plains.** Concealed from the public eye for many years as part of the Barbers Point Naval Air Station, this beach is reminiscent of Waikīkī but without the condos and the crowds. It is a long, sloping beach with numerous surf breaks, but it is

> ### BEWARE THE BURN
>
> It's the tradewinds that get you. It just feels so cool and refreshing out there on the beach that there is no way you can be getting burned, right? Wrong. Due to Oʻahu's proximity to the equator, the sun will scorch you here quicker than it ever would back home. Even a short time in the sun can lead to long nights of aloe and cold showers. Use sunblock early and often. The SPF you choose is your own, but we suggest nothing lower than 30 if you plan to spend more than an hour in the sun.

also mild enough at shore for older children to play freely. It has views of Pearl Harbor and, over that, Diamond Head. Although the sand lives up to its name, the real joy of this beach comes from its history as part of a military property for the better part of a century. Expansive parking, great restroom facilities, and numerous tree-covered BBQ areas make it a great day-trip spot. As a bonus, a Hawaiian monk seal takes up residence here several months out of the year (seals are rarely seen anywhere in the Islands). ⊠ *Take the Makakilo exit off H1 West, turn left. Follow it into the base gates, make a left. Follow the blue signs to the beach.* ⚲ *Lifeguard, toilets, showers, picnic tables.*

★ ☺ **Kō ʻOlina.** ■ TIP→ **This is the best spot on the Island if you have small kids.** The resort commissioned a series of four man-made lagoons, but, as they have to provide public beach access, you are the winner. Huge rock walls protect the lagoons, making them into perfect spots for the kids to get their first taste of the ocean without getting bowled over. The large expanses of seashore grass and hala trees that surround the semi-circle beaches are made-to-order for naptime. And, if walks are in order, there is a 1½-mi jogging track connecting the lagoons. Keep in mind that, due to its perfection for keikis, Kō ʻOlina is popular. The parking lot fills up quickly when school is out and on weekends, so try to get there before 10 AM. The biggest parking lot is at the farthest lagoon from the entrance. ⊠ *23 mi west of Honolulu. Take Kō ʻOlina exit off H1 West and proceed to guard shack.* ⚲ *Toilets, showers, concessions.*

Papaoneone Beach. You have to do a little exploring to find Pamaoneone Beach, which is tucked away behind three condos. Duck through a wide, easy-to-spot hole in the fence, and you find an extremely wide, sloping beach that always seems to be empty. The waters are that eerie blue that seems to only be found on the West side. The waves can get high here (it faces the same direction as the famed Mākaha Beach), but, for the most part, the shore break makes for great easy rides on your boogie board or belly. The only downside is that, with the exception of a shower, all the facilities are for the condos, so it's just you and the big blue. ✉ *In Mākaha, just across from Jade St.* ⚑ *Showers.*

Mākaha Beach Park. This beach provides a slice of local life most visitors don't see. Families string up tarps for the day, fire up hibachis, set up lawn chairs, get out the fishing gear, and strum 'ukuleles while they "talk story" (chat). Legendary waterman Buffalo Kaeulana can be found in the shade of the palms playing with his grandkids and spinning yarns of yesteryear. In these waters Buffalo not only invented some of the most outrageous methods of surfing, but also raised his world champion son Rusty. He also made Mākaha the home of the world's first international surf meet in 1954 and still hosts his Big Board Surfing Classic. The swimming is generally decent in summer, but avoid the big winter waves. With its long, slow-building waves, it's a great spot to try out long boarding. ✉ *1½ hrs west of Honolulu on H–1 Fwy. then Farrington Hwy.* ⚑ *Lifeguard, toilets, showers, picnic tables, grills.*

Yokohama Bay. You'll be one of the few outsiders at this Wai'anae Coast beach at the very end of the road. If not for the little strip of paved road, you'd feel like you're on a deserted isle. No stores, no houses, just a huge sloping stretch of beach and some of the darkest blue water off the island. Locals come here to fish and swim in waters that are calm enough for children in summer. Early morning brings with it spinner dolphins by the dozens just offshore. Though Makua Beach up the road is the best spot to see these animals, it's not nearly as beautiful or sandy as "Yokes." ✉ *Northern end of Farrington Hwy., about 7 mi north of Mākaha* ⚑ *Toilets, showers.*

Water Activities & Tours

WORD OF MOUTH

"Just wanted to add a comment about Shark's Cove . . . Excellent snorkeling! Saw an amazing array of fish and the butt of a big sea turtle as he swam behind a rock."

–Sandra_E

". . . taking a sailing cruise out of Waikīkī and viewing the island from the water. [It was] so amazing to see a big city coming out of the water with the mountains and clouds in the background!"

–dreamathers

By Chad Pata   **THERE'S MORE TO THE BEACH** than just lying on it. O'ahu is rife with every type of activity you can imagine. Most of the activities are offered in Waikīkī, right off the beach.

On the sand in front of your hotel, the sights and sounds of what is available will overwhelm you. Rainbow-colored parachutes dot the horizon as parasailers improve their vantage point on paradise. The blowing of conch shells announces the arrival of the beach catamarans that sail around Diamond Head Crater. Meanwhile, the white caps of Waikīkī are being sliced by all manner of craft, from brilliant red outrigger canoes to darting white surf boards. Enjoy observing the flurry of activity for a moment, then jump right in.

As with all sports, listen to the outfitter's advice—they're not just saying it for fun. Caution is always the best bet when dealing with "mother" ocean. She plays for keeps and forgives no indiscretions. That being said, she offers more entertainment than you can fit into a lifetime, much less a vacation. So try something new and enjoy.

A rule of thumb is that the ocean is much more wily and unpredictable on the north- and west-facing shores, but that's also why those sides have the most famous waves on Earth. So plan your activity side according to your skill level.

BOAT TOURS & CHARTERS

Hawai'i Nautical. It's a little out of the way, but the experiences with this local company are worth the drive. Catamaran cruises lead to snorkeling with dolphins, gourmet dinner cruises head out of beautiful Kō'Ōlina harbor, and sailing lessons are available on a 20-foot sailboat and a 50-foot cat. If you're driving out from Waikīkī, you may want to make a day of it, with sailing in the morning then 18 holes on the gorgeous resort course in the afternoon. Two-hour cruise rates with snacks and two drinks begin at $65 per person. ⊠ *Kō'Ōlina Harbor, Kō'Ōlina Marriot Resort, Kapolei* ☎ *808/234–7245.*

Fodor'sChoice
★   **Hawai'i Sailing Adventures.** Looking to escape the "cattle-maran" experience? Then this charter, with its goal of exclusivity and the largest private sailing yacht in the Islands, is for you. They have capacity for up to 50 guests but prefer smaller crowds, and they specialize in dinners catered to your specs. When you want a sail for a romantic occasion or a family reunion unfettered by crowds of people you don't know, try their yacht *Emeraude* and ask for Captain Roger. Two-hour dinner cruise rates with unlimited super well drinks (drinks made with premium liquors like Tanqueray Ten, Grey Goose) begin at $119 per person. ⊠ *Kewalo Basin, Slip S, Honolulu* ☎ *808/596–9696.*

Paradise Cruises. One-stop shopping for specialty cruises. Offerings run the gamut from day cruises around Diamond Head with snorkeling, kayaking, and windsurfing to fine dining night cruises with lobster and live entertainment to winter whale-watching cruises. You can learn lei-making or coconut frond–weaving, or you can take a 'ukulele or hula lesson. They also offer seminars on Hawaiian history and culture, and there are artifact displays onboard the boat. Two-hour dinner cruise rates begin at $139 per person. ⊠ *Pier 5, Honolulu Harbor, Honolulu* ☎ *808/ 983–7700.*

Sashimi Fun Fishing. A combination trip suits those who aren't quite ready to troll for big game in the open–ocean swells. Sashimi Fun Fishing runs a dinner cruise with fishing and music. They keep close enough to shore that you can still see O'ahu and jig for a variety of reef fish. The cruise includes a local barbecue dinner, and you can also cook what you catch. The four-hour dinner cruise rates with hotel transportation begin at $63 per person. ☎ *808/955–3474.*

Tradewind Charters. Tradewind specializes in everything from weddings to funerals. They offer half-day private-charter tours for sailing, snorkeling, and whale-watching. Traveling on these luxury yachts not only gets you away from the crowds but also gives you the opportunity to "take the helm" if you wish. The cruise includes snorkeling at an exclusive anchorage as well as hands-on snorkeling and sailing instruction. Charter prices are approximately $495 for up to six passengers. ⊠ *796 Kalanipuu St., Honolulu* ☎ *800/829–4899* ⊕ *www. tradewindcharters.com.*

BOOGIE BOARDING & BODYSURFING

Boogie boarding (or sponging) has become a popular alternative to surfing for a couple of reasons. First, the start-up cost is much less—a usable board can be purchased for $30 to $40 or can be rented on the beach for $5 an hour. Second, it's a whole lot easier to ride a boogie board than to tame a surfboard. For beginner boogie boarding all you must do is paddle out to the waves, turn toward the beach, and kick like crazy when the wave comes.

Most grocery and convenience stores sell boogie boards. Though the boards do not rival what the pros use, you won't notice a difference in their handling on smaller waves.

■ TIP→ Another small investment you'll want to make is surf fins. These smaller, sturdier versions of dive fins sell for $25–$35 at surf and dive stores, sporting-goods stores, or even Wal-Mart. Most beach stands do not rent fins with the boards. Though they are not necessary for boogie boarding, fins do give you a tremendous advantage when you are paddling into waves. If you plan to go out in bigger surf, we would also advise you to get fin leashes to prevent loss. For bodysurfing, you definitely want to invest in fins. Check out the same spots as for boogie boarding.

LOOK FIRST

With all ocean activities, check out your environment before entering the water. Are there rocks in the surf zone? Which way is the current pulling? Where are the closest lifeguard stands? It's always a good idea to spend at least 15 minutes on the beach watching the break you intend to surf. This allows you not only to check for dangerous areas and the size of the surf but also to see what spot is breaking cleanest and will therefore be the most fun.

If the direction of the current or dangers of the break are not readily apparent to you, don't hesitate to ask a lifeguard for advice.

Best Spots

Boogie boarding and bodysurfing can be done anywhere there are waves, but, due to a paddling advantage surfers have over spongers, it's usually more fun to go to exclusively boogie-boarding spots.

Kūhiō Beach Park (⊠ Waikīkī, past Sheraton Moana Surfrider Hotel to Kapahulu Ave. pier) is an easy spot for the first timer to check out the action. Try **The Wall,** a break so named for the breakwall in front of the beach. It's a little crowded with kids, but it's close enough to shore to keep you at ease. There are dozens of breaks in Waikīkī, but the Wall is the only one solely occupied by spongers. Start out here to get the hang of it before venturing out to **Canoes** or **Kaiser Bowl's.**

Makapuʻu Beach (⊠ Across from Sea Life Park, 2 mi south of Waimānalo on Kalanianaʻole Hwy.) on the Windward side is a sponger's dream beach with its extended waves and isolation from surfers. If you're a little more timid, go to the far end of the beach to **Keiki's,** where the waves are mellowed by Makapuʻu Point, for an easier, if less thrilling, ride. Although the main break at Makapuʻu is much less dangerous than Sandy's, check out the ocean floor—the sands are always shifting, sometimes exposing coral heads and rocks. Also always check the currents, they can get strong. But for the most part, this is the ideal beach for both boogie boarding and bodysurfing.

★ The best spot on the island for advanced boogie boarding is **Sandy Beach** (⊠ 2 mi east of Hanauma Bay on Kalanianaʻole Hwy.) on the Windward side. It's a short wave that goes right and left, but the barrels here are unparalleled for pure sponging. The ride is intense and breaks so sharply that you actually see the wave suck the bottom dry before it crashes on to it. That's the reason it's also called "Break Neck Beach." It's awesome for the advanced, but know its danger before enjoying the ride.

Equipment Rentals

There are more than 30 rental spots on Waikīkī Beach, all offering basically the same prices. But if you plan to boogie board for more than just an hour, we would suggest buying a board for $20 to $30 at an ABC convenience store and giving it to a kid when you're preparing to end your vacation. It will be more cost-effective for you and will imbue you with the aloha spirit while making a kid's day.

DEEP-SEA FISHING

The joy of fishing in Hawaiʻi is that there isn't really a season; it's good year-round. Sure, the bigger yellowfin tuna (ʻahi) are generally caught in summer, and the coveted spearfish are more frequent in winter, but you can still catch them any day of the year. You can also find dolphin fish (mahimahi), wahoo (ono), skip jacks, and the king—Pacific blue marlin—ripe for the picking on any given day.

When choosing a fishing boat in the Islands, keep in mind the immensity of the surrounding ocean. Look for the older, grizzled captains who have been trolling these waters for half a century. All the fancy gizmos in the world can't match an old tar's knowledge of the waters.

> **TIP**
>
> Trying to get out on the cheap with half-day excursions can be a way to cut costs, but we suggest the full charter. It dramatically improves your odds of catching something, and that after all is why you're out there.

The general rule for the catch is an even split with the crew. Unfortunately, there are no "freeze-and-ship" providers in the state, so, unless you plan to eat the fish while you're here, you'll probably want to leave it with the boat. Most boats do offer mounting services for trophy fish; ask your captain.

Besides the gift of fish, a gratuity of 10% to 20% is standard. It's up to the fisherman; use your own discretion depending on how you felt about the overall experience.

Boats & Charters

Inter-Island Sportfishing. The oldest-running sportfishing company on O'ahu also boasts the largest landed Blue Marlin—more than 1,200 pounds. With two smaller boats and the 53-foot *Maggie Joe* (which can hold up to 25), they can manage any small party with air-conditioned cabins and cutting-edge fishing equipment. They also work with Grey's Taxidermy, the world's largest marine taxidermist, to mount the monster you reel in. Half-day exclusive charter rates for groups of six begin at $700. ☎ *808/591–8888* ⊕ *www.fish-hawaii.com.*

Magic Sportfishing. The awards Magic has garnered are too many to mention here, but we can tell you their magnificent 50-foot *Pacifica* fishing yacht is built for comfort, fishing, or otherwise. Unfortunately, Magic can accommodate only up to six. Full-day exclusive charter rates for groups of six begin at $950. ☎ *808/596–2998.*

Monkey Biz. If you want a more intimate experience with a smaller company, the apes of the sea may be what you are looking for. Known for their reliable boats and friendly crews, these six-man charters can make your Hawai'ian fishing experience a happy one. Half-day exclusive charter rates for groups of six begin at $650. ☎ *808/591–2520* ⊕ *www. monkeybizsportfishing.com.*

DOLPHIN ENCOUNTERS

Pods of dolphins surround the Islands, and spotting them can be as easy as just getting yourself out in the ocean. They are wild animals, of course, and do not follow a schedule, but a catamaran sail off Waikīkī will usually net you a spotting. Dolphins also generally make appearances shortly after sunrise on the West Shore and can be clearly observed from beaches like Makua and Mākaha. And while they won't have the peppy music of Sea World in the background, their jumping and spinning is even more awe-inspiring when you realize they are just doing it for fun rather than for a reward.

Dolphin Quest at the Kāhala. This worldwide dolphin encounter group now has a O'ahu location in the Kāhala. Trained Atlantic bottlenose dolphins hold court in an enclosed lagoon at the center of the hotel. The Kid's Quest for Knowledge ($175) is a two-hour, in-the-water session of feeding and interacting with sting rays, dolphins, and sea turtles. The adult session is only an hour, but it involves in-the-water interaction as well as education for $250. ✉ *The Kāhala, 5000 Kāhala Ave., Kāhala* ☎ *808/739–8918* ⊕ *www.dolphinquest.org.*

★ **Sea Life Park.** Dolphins are just one of the attractions at this outdoor marine life park. Seals, sting rays, and Hawaiian sea turtles are also in residence. Rates for the 45-minute interaction sessions with their Atlantic bottlenose dolphins in the salt water lagoon begin at $140. The in-the-water action includes belly rides along the surface as you hold onto a dolphin's pectoral fin. Not as ritzy as the Kāhala, but it may be more feasible for the everyman budget. ✉ *41-202 Kalaniana'ole Hwy., Waimānalo* ☎ *808/259–7933 or 886/365–7446.*

Fodor'sChoice **Wild Side Speciality Tours.** This west-side charter follows the wild spin-
★ ner dolphins that make their home off of Makua Beach. Marine biologists conduct the tours, adding a depth of knowledge not found with boat captains and dive masters. The biologists also evaluate the dolphins' mood; when the animals are playful and open to interaction, you are allowed to jump in and snorkel with them. If the dolphins seem strained or agitated, then you watch from the boat. There are no guarantees as these are wild animals. Wild Side offers morning, afternoon, and evening sails with meals on their 42-foot catamaran with a maximum load of only 16. Rates for the four-hour sail begin at $95 per person. ✉ *Wai'anae Boat Harbor, Slip A-11* ☎ *808/306–7273* ⊕ *www.sailhawaii.com.*

JET SKIING, WAKEBOARDING & WATERSKIING

Aloha Parasail/Jet Ski. Jet ski in the immense Ke'ehi Lagoon as planes from Honolulu International take off and land right above you. After an instructional safety course, you can try your hand at navigating their buoyed course. They provide free pickup and drop-off from Waikīkī. The Waverunners run about $40 per person for 45 minutes of riding time. ☎ *808/521–2446.*

Hawai'i Sports Wakeboard and Water Ski Center. Hawai'i Sports turns Maunalua Bay into an action water park with activities for all ages. While dad's learning to wakeboard, the kids can hang on for dear life on bumper tubes, and mom can finally get some peace parasailing over the bay with views going to Diamond Head and beyond. There are also banana boats that will ride six, Jet Skis for two, and scuba missions. Half-hour jet ski rental rates begin at $49 per person, and package deals are available. ✉ *Koko Marina Shopping Center, 7192*

Kalaniana'ole Hwy., Hawai'i Kai ☎ *808/395–3773* ⊕ *www. hawaiiwatersportscenter.com.*

KAYAKING

Kayaking is quickly becoming a top choice for visitors to the Islands. Kayaking alone or with a partner on the open ocean provides a vantage point not afforded by swimming and surfing. Even amateurs can travel long distances and keep a lookout on what's going on around them.

This ability to travel long distances can also get you into trouble. ■ **TIP→ Experts agree that rookies should stay on the Windward side.** Their reasoning is simple: if you tire, break or lose an oar, or just plain pass out, the onshore winds will eventually blow you back to the beach. The same cannot be said for the offshore breezes of the North Shore and West O'ahu.

Kayaks are specialized: some are better suited for riding waves while others are designed for traveling long distances. Your outfitter can address your needs depending on your activities. Expressing your plans with your outfitter can lead to a more enjoyable experience.

Best Spots

★ The hands-down winner for kayaking is **Lanikai Beach** (⊠ Past Kailua Beach Park; street parking on Mokulua Drive for various public-access points to beach) on the Windward side. This is perfect amateur territory with its still waters and onshore winds. If you're feeling more adventurous, it's a short paddle out to the Mokes. This pair of islands off the coast has beaches, surf breaks on the reef, and great picnicking areas. Due to the distance from shore (about a mile), the Mokes usually afford privacy from all but the intrepid kayakers. Lanikai is great year-round, and most kayak-rental companies have a store right up the street in Kailua.

For something a little different try **Kahana River** (⊠ Empties into Kahana Bay, 8 mi east of Kāne'ohe), also on the Windward side. The river may not have the blue water of the ocean, but the Ko'olau Mountains, with waterfalls aplenty when it's raining, are magnificent in the background. It's a short jaunt, about 2 mi round-trip, but it is packed with rain-forest foliage and the other rain-forest denizen, mosquitos. Bring some repellent and enjoy this light workout.

If you want to try your hand at surfing kayaks, **Bellows Beach** (⊠ Near Waimānalo town center, entrance on Kalaniana'ole Hwy.) on the Windward side and **Mokulē'ia Beach** (⊠ Across from Dillingham Airfield)

THE MOKES

"The Mokes," the two islands off Lanikai Beach, are a perfect kayaking destination. Both islands have little beach areas, and you will feel a little like Robinson Crusoe on a weekday, so long as you don't look at the multimillion dollar homes looming on the hillsides of Lanikai. There are guided tours, which pretty much consist of simply escorting you out to the islands. But, as the water between the Mokes and Lanikai is calm and as it would be impossible to miss them, spend your money on suntan oil and snacks instead and enjoy the paddle.

on the North Shore are two great spots. Hard-to-reach breaks, the ones that surfers exhaust themselves trying to reach, are easily accessed by kayak. The buoyancy of the kayak also allows you to catch the wave earlier and get out in front of the white wash. One reminder on these spots: if you're a little green, stick to Bellows with those onshore winds. Generally speaking, you don't want to be catching waves where surfers are; in Waikīkī, however, pretty much anything goes.

Equipment Rentals & Tours

Go Bananas. Staffers make sure that you rent the appropriate kayak for your abilities, and they also outfit the rental car with soft racks to transport the boat to the beach. The store also carries clothing and kayaking accessories. Full-day rates begin at $30 for single kayaks, and $42 for doubles. ✉ *799 Kapahulu Ave., Honolulu* ☎ *808/737–9514.*

Prime Time Sports. This is one of many stands renting kayaks right on Waikīkī beach. The prices among the different stands are pretty much the same. The convenience of Prime Time's central location is their primary drawing card. Hourly rates begin at $10 for single kayaks, and $20 for doubles. ✉ *Fort DeRussy Beach, Waikīkī* ☎ *808/949–8952.*

Surf 'N Sea. This outfitter is located right on the beach, so you don't have to worry about transporting your boat—just rent it and start paddling. They also offer everything from paddleboats to windsurfing lessons. Keep in mind that their yellow boats are great in summer when the ocean turns peaceful, but winter on the North Shore is hazardous for even the hard-core fan. From spring to fall, however, kayaks are great for getting to outside reef–snorkeling spots or surfing the reduced waves. Full-day rates begin at $35 for single kayaks. ✉ *62-595 Kamehameha Hwy., North Shore* ☎ *808/637–9887.*

Twogood Kayaks Hawaiʻi. The one-stop shopping outfitter for kayaks on the Windward side offers rentals, lessons, guided kayak tours, and even weeklong camps if you want to immerse yourself in the sport. Guides are trained in history, geology, and birdlife of the area. Kayak a full day with a guide for $89; this includes lunch, snorkeling gear, and transportation from Waikīkī. Although their rental prices are about $10 more than average, they do deliver the boats to the water for you and give you a crash course in ocean safety. It's a small price to pay for the convenience and for peace of mind when entering new waters. Full-day rates begin at $49 for single kayaks, and $59 for doubles. ✉ *345 Hahani St., Kailua* ☎ *808/262–5656* ⊕ *www.twogoodkayaks.com.*

KITEBOARDING

⇨ *See* Windsurfing & Kiteboarding

PARASAILING

Parasailing is the training-wheels approach to extreme sports—you think you want to try something crazy, but you're not ready to step out of an airplane quite yet. Generally you fly about 500 feet off the water, enjoying a bird's-eye view of everything, while also enjoying the silence that envelops you at that height. As we said, it's a nice alternative to leaping from planes that still gets you seeing the sights.

Hawai'i X–Treme Parasailing. Reputed to be the highest parasail ride on O'ahu, rides here actually pull people as high as 1,200 feet for 15 minutes. They offer pickups from Waikīkī, making it convenient to try this combo of water skiing and parachuting. Rates run from $38 to $69 and reservations can be made online. ⊠ *Kewalo Basin Harbor, Honolulu* ☎ *808/330–8308.*

SAILING

For a sailing experience in O'ahu, you need go no farther than the beach in front of your hotel in Waikīkī. Strung along the sand are seven beach catamarans that will provide you with one-hour rides during the day and 90-minute sunset sails. Pricewise look for $12 to $15 for day sails and $15 to $20 for sunset rides. ■ **TIP➔ They all have their little perks and they're known for bargaining so feel free to haggle, especially with the smaller boats.** Some provide drinks for free, some charge for them, and some let you pack your own, so keep that in mind when pricing the ride.

If you would like a fancier ride, ⇨ *see* Boat Tours & Charters.

Mai'Tai Catamaran. Taking off from in front of the Sheraton Hotel, this cat is the fastest and sleekest on the beach. If you have a need for speed and enjoy a little more upscale experience, this is the boat for you. ☎ *808/ 922–5665.*

Na Hoku II Catamaran. The diametric opposite of Mai'Tai, this is the Animal House of catamarans with reggae music and cheap booze. Their motto is "Cheap drinks, Easy Crew." They're beached right out in front of Duke's Barefoot Bar at the Outrigger Waikīkī Hotel and sail five times daily. ☎ *808/239–3900* ⊕ *www.nahokuii.com.*

SCUBA DIVING

All the great stuff to do atop the water sometimes leads us to forget the real beauty beneath the surface. Although snorkeling and snuba (more on that later) do give you access to this world, nothing gives you the freedom of scuba.

The diving on O'ahu is comparable with any you might do in the tropics, but its uniqueness comes from the isolated environment of the Islands. There are literally hundreds of species of fish and marine life that you can only find in this chain. Adding to the singularity of diving off O'ahu is the human history of the region. Military activities and tragedies of the 20th century filled the waters surrounding O'ahu with wreckage that the ocean creatures have since turned into their homes.

Although instructors certified to license you in scuba are plentiful in the Islands, we suggest that you get your PADI certification before coming as a week of classes may be a bit of a commitment on a short vacation.

■ **TIP→** You can go on introductory dives without the certification, but the best dives require it.

Best Spots

Hanauma Bay (⊠ 7455 Kalaniana'ole Hwy.) is an underwater state park and a popular dive site in Southeast O'ahu. The shallow inner reef of this volcanic crater bay is filled with snorkelers, but its floor gradually drops from 10 to 70 feet at the outer reef where the big fish prefer the lighter traffic. It's quite a trek down into the crater and out to the water so you may want to consider a dive tour company to do your heavy lifting. Expect to see butterfly fish, goatfish, parrot fish, surgeonfish, and sea turtles.

The *Mahi Wai'anae,* a 165-foot minesweeper, was sunk in 1982 in the waters just south of Wai'anae on O'ahu's leeward coast to create an artificial reef. It's intact and penetrable, but you'll need a boat to access it. In the front resides an ancient moray eel who is so mellowed that you can pet his barnacled head without fearing for your hand's safety. Goatfish, tame lemon-butterfly fish, and blue-striped snapper hang out here, but the real stars are the patrols of spotted eagle rays that are always cruising by. It can be a longer dive as it's only 90 feet to the hull.

East of Diamond Head, **Maunalua Bay** has several boat-access sites, including Turtle Canyon, with lava-flow ridges and sandy canyons teeming with green sea turtles of all sizes; *Kāhala Barge,* a penetrable, 200-foot sunken vessel; Big Eel Reef, with many varieties of moray eels; and Fantasy Reef, a series of lava ledges and archways populated with barracuda and eels. There's also the sunken Corsair. It doesn't boast much for sea life, but there's something about sitting in the cockpit of a plane 100 feet below the surface of the ocean.

Just off Diamond Head, a collection of volcanic boulders creates a series of caves known as **Hundred Foot Hole.** Once a fishing ground reserved for royalty, it now serves as a great spot for everyone to get Hawaiian lobsters. A dive light is a good idea here because much of the area is shaded, and you don't want to miss such sea life as octopus, manta rays, and white-tip sharks. It is shore accessible.

Fodor's Choice
★ The best shore dive on O'ahu is **Shark's Cove** (⊠ Across from Foodland in Pūpūkea) on the North Shore, but unfortunately it's only accessible during the summer months. Novices can drift along the outer wall, watching everything from turtles to eels. Veterans can explore the numerous lava tubes and tunnels where diffused sunlight from above creates a dreamlike effect in spacious caverns. It's 10- to 45-feet deep, ready-made for shore diving with a parking lot right next to the dive spot. **Three Tables** is just west of Shark's Cove, enabling you to have a second dive without moving your car or being redundant. Follow the three perpendicular rocks that break the surface out to this dive site, where you can find a variety of parrot fish and octopus, plus occasional shark and ray sightings at depths of 30 to 50 feet. It's not as exciting as Shark's Cove, but it is more accessible for the novice diver. Be cautious the later in the year you go to either of these sights; the waves pick up strength in fall, and the reef can be turned into a washboard for you and your gear. Both are null and void during the winter surf sessions.

Charters, Lessons & Equipment

Captain Bruce's Hawai'i. Captain Bruce's focuses on the west and east shores, covering the *Mahi* and the Corsair. This full-service company has refresher and introductory dives as well as more advanced drift and night dives. No equipment is needed; they provide it all. Most importantly, this is the only boat on O'ahu that offers hot showers onboard. Two-tank boat dive rates begin at $110 per person. ☎ *808/373–3590 or 800/535–2487* ⊕ *www.captainbruce.com.*

Hanauma Bay Dive Tours. You can guess the specialty here. They offer introductory dives in the federally protected reserve for those aged 12 and above, with snuba available to 8 years old and up. The charge is $89 for the day plus a $5 fee for park entry. ☎ *808/256–8956.*

4

Reeftrekkers. The owners of the slickest dive Web site in Hawai'i are also the *Scuba Diving* Reader's Choice winners for the past four years. Using the dive descriptions and price quotes on their Web site, you can plan your excursions before ever setting foot on the island. Two-tank boat dive rates begin at $95 per person. ☎ *808/943–0588* ⊕ *www.reeftrekkers.com.*

Surf-N-Sea. The North Shore headquarters for all things water-related is great for diving that side as well. There is one interesting perk—the cameraman can shoot a video of you diving. It's hard to see facial expressions under the water, but it still might be fun for those that need documentation of all they do. Two-tank boat dive rates begin at $110 per person. ☎ *808/637–3337* ⊕ *www.surfnsea.com.*

SNORKELING

One advantage that snorkeling has over scuba is that you never run out of air. That and the fact that anyone who can swim can also snorkel without any formal training. A favorite pastime in Hawai'i, snorkeling can be done anywhere there's enough water to stick your face in it. Each spot will have its great days depending on the weather and time of year, so consult with the purveyor of your gear for tips on where the best viewing is that day. Keep in mind that the North Shore should only be attempted when the waves are calm, namely in the summertime.

■ TIP➔ **Think of buying a mask and snorkel as a prerequisite for your trip— they make any beach experience better.** Just make sure you put plenty of sunblock on your back because once you start gazing below, your head may not come back up for hours.

Best Spots

As Waimea Bay is to surfing, **Hanauma Bay** (✉ 7455 Kalaniana'ole Hwy.) in Southeast O'ahu is to snorkeling. By midday it can look like the mall at Christmas with all the bodies, but, with over a half million fish to observe, there's plenty to go around. Due to the protection of the narrow mouth of the cove and the prodigious reef, you will be hard pressed to find a place you will feel safer while snorkeling.

Right on the edge of Waikīkī, **Queen's Surf** is a marine reserve located between the break wall and the Queen's pier. It's not as stocked full of

Continued on page 98

SNORKELING IN HAWAI'I

The waters surrounding the Hawaiian Islands are filled with life—from giant manta rays cruising off the Big Island's Kona Coast to humpback whales giving birth in Maui's Mā'alaea Bay. Dip your head beneath the surface to experience a spectacularly colorful world: pairs of milletseed butterfly fish dart back and forth, red-lipped parrot fish snack on coral algae, and spotted eagle rays flap past like silent spaceships. Sea turtles bask at the surface while tiny wrasses give them the equivalent of a shave and a haircut. The water quality is typically outstanding; many sites afford 30 foot-plus visibility. On snorkel cruises, you can often stare from the boat rail right down to the bottom.

Certainly few destinations are as accommodating to every level of snorkeler as Hawai'i. Beginners can tromp in from sandy beaches while more advanced divers descend to shipwrecks, reefs, craters, and sea arches just offshore. Because of Hawai'i's extreme isolation, the island chain has fewer fish species than Fiji or the Caribbean—but many of the fish that are here exist nowhere else. The Hawaiian waters are home to the highest percentage of endemic fish in the world.

The key to enjoying the underwater world is slowing down. Look carefully. Listen. You might hear the strange crackling sound of shrimp tunneling through coral, or you may hear whales singing to one another during winter. A shy octopus may drift along the ocean's floor beneath you. If you're hooked, pick up a waterproof fishkey from Long's Drugs. You can brag later that you've looked the Hawaiian turkeyfish in the eye.

Picasso Triggerfish	Milletseed Butterfly Fish*	Yellow Tang
Moorish Idol	Hawaiian Whitespotted Toby*	Saddleback Wrasse*
Red-lipped Parrot Fish	Hawaiian Turkeyfish*	Zebra Moray Eel
Stocky Hawkfish	Green Sea Turtle	Spotted Eagle Ray

*endemic to Hawai'i

POLYNESIA'S FIRST CELESTIAL NAVIGATORS: HONU

Honu is the Hawaiian name for two native sea turtles, the hawksbill and the green sea turtle. Little is known about these dinosaur-age marine reptiles, though snorkelers regularly see them foraging for *limu* (seaweed) and the occasional jellyfish in Hawaiian waters. Most female honu nest in the uninhabited Northwestern Hawaiian Islands, but a few sociable ladies nest on Maui beaches. Scientists suspect that they navigate the seas via magnetism—sensing the earth's poles. Amazingly, they will journey up to 800 miles to nest—it's believed that they return to their own birth sites. After about 60 days of incubation, nestlings emerge from the sand at night and find their way back to the sea by the light of the stars.

fish as Hanauma, but it has its share of colorful reef fish and the occasional sea turtle just yards from shore. It's a great spot for an escape if you're stuck in Waikīkī and have grown weary of watching the surfers.

Fodor'sChoice Great shallows right off the shore
★ with huge reef protection make **Shark's Cove** (⊠ Across from Foodland in Pūpūkea) on the North Shore a great spot for youngsters in the summertime. You can find a plethora of critters from crabs to octopus, in waist-deep or shallower water. The only caveat is that once the winter swell comes, this becomes a human pinball game rather than a peaceful observation spot. Summer only.

> **SHARK!**
>
> "You go in the cage, cage goes in the water, you go in the water, shark's in the water . . ." You remember this line from *Jaws*, and now you get to play the role of Richard Dreyfus, as **North Shore Shark Adventures** provides you with an interactive experience out of your worst nightmare. The tour allows you to swim and snorkel in a cage as dozens of sharks lurk just feet from you in the open ocean off the North Shore, and all for just $120. ☎ *808/228–5900* ⊕ *sharktourshawaii.com.*

Directly across from the electric plant outside of Kō'Ōlina resort, **Electric Beach** (⊠ 1 mi west of Kō'Ōlina) in West O'ahu has become a haven for tropical fish. The expulsion of hot water from the plant warms the ocean water, attracting all kinds of wildlife. Although the visibility is not always the best, the crowds are thin, and the fish are guaranteed. Just park next to the old train tracks and enjoy this secret spot.

Equipment Rental

Hanauma Bay Rental Stand. You can get masks, fins, and snorkels right at the park. ☎ *808/395–4725.*

Snorkel Bob's. We suggest buying your gear, unless it's going to be a one-day affair. Either way, Snorkel Bob's has all the stuff you'll need (and a bunch of stuff you don't) to make your water adventures enjoyable. Also feel free to ask the staff about the good spots at the moment, as the best spots can vary with weather and seasons. ⊠ *700 Kapahulu Ave.* ☎ *808/ 735–7944.*

Snorkel Sails

Hanauma Bay Snorkeling Excursions. For those who are a little more timid about entering these waters, this outfitter provides a tour with a guide to help alleviate your fears. They'll even pick you up in Waikīkī and provide you with equipment and knowledge for around $30. ☎ *808/ 373–5060.*

Kahala Kai. The *Kahala Kai* sails out of Kewalo Basin in Honolulu–very convenient if you have other plans in town. Take a two-hour sail out to sea turtle breeding grounds where 50-foot-plus visability makes for great snorkeling with loads of sea life from turtles and reef fish to dolphins, and, in the wintertime, whales. Rates for a two-hour sail, all equipment included, begin at $45 per person; ask for Captain Roger. ☎ *808/ 227–3556.*

Ko Olina Kat. The dock in Ko Olina harbor is a little more out of the way, but this is a much more luxurious option than the town snorkel cruises. Three-hour tours of the west side of Oʻahu are punctuated with stops for observing dolphins from the boat and a snorkel spot well populated with fish. All gear, snacks, sandwiches, and two alcoholic beverages make for a more complete experience, but also a pricier one (starting at $99.50 per person). ☎ *808/234–7145.*

SNUBA

Snuba, the marriage of scuba and snorkeling, gives the nondiving set their first glimpse of the freedom of scuba. Snuba utilizes a raft with a standard airtank on it and a 20-foot air hose that hooks up to a regulator. Once attached to the hose, you can swim, unfettered by heavy tanks and weights, up to 15 feet down to chase fish and examine reef for as long as you fancy. If you ever get scared or need a rest, the raft is right there, ready to support you. Kids eight years and older can use the equipment. It can be pricey, but, then again, how much is it worth to be able to sit face to face with a 6-foot-long sea turtle and not have to rush to the surface to get another breath? At **Hanauma Bay Snuba Dive** (☎808/256–8956), a three-hour outing (with 45 minutes in the water), costs $87.

SUBMARINE TOURS

★ *Atlantis* **Submarines.** This is the underwater venture for the unadventurous. Not fond of swimming but want to see what you have been missing? Board this 64-passenger vessel for a ride down past ship wrecks, turtle breeding grounds, and coral reefs galore. Unlike a trip to the aquarium, this gives you a chance to see nature at work without the limitations of mankind. The tours, which leave from the pier at the Hilton Hawaiian Village, are available in several languages and run from $69 to $115. ⊠ *Hilton Hawaiian Village Beach Resort and Spa, 2005 Kālia Rd., Waikīkī, 96815* ☎ *808/973–1296.*

SURFING

Perhaps no word is more associated with Hawaiʻi than surfing. Every year the best of the best gather here to have their Super Bowl: Vans Triple Crown of Surfing (⇨ *See* North Shore Surfing and the Triple Crown *in* Chapter 2). The pros dominate the waves for a month, but the rest of the year belongs to people like us, just trying to have fun and get a little exercise.

Oʻahu is unique because it has so many famous spots: Banzai Pipeline, Waimea Bay, Kaiser Bowls, and Sunset Beach resonate in young surfers' hearts the world over. The reknown of these spots comes with a price: competition for those waves. The aloha spirit lives in many places but not on premium waves. ■ **TIP→ If you're coming to visit and want to surf these world-famous breaks, you need to go out with a healthy dose of respect and patience.** As long as you follow the rules of the road and concede waves to local riders, you should not have problems. Just remember

---

SURF SMART

A few things to remember when surfing in O'ahu:

• The waves switch with the seasons—they're big in the south in summer, and they loom large in the north in winter. If you're not experienced, it's best to go where the waves are small. There will be fewer crowds, and your chances of injury dramatically decrease.

• Always wear a leash. It may not look the coolest, but when your board gets swept away from you and you're swimming a half mile after it, you'll remember this advice.

• Watch where you're going. Take a few minutes and watch the surf from the shore. Observe how big it is, where it's breaking, and how quickly the sets are coming. This knowledge will allow you to get in and out more easily and to spend more time riding waves and less time paddling.

---

that locals view these waves as their property, and everything should be all right.

If you're nervous and don't want to run the risk of a confrontation, try some of the alternate spots listed below. They may not have the name recognition, but the waves can be just as great.

Best Spots

In Waikīkī, try getting out to **Populars**, a break at **Ulukou Beach** (⊠ Waikīkī, in front of Royal Hawaiian Hotel). Nice and easy, Populars never breaks too hard and is friendly to both the rookie and the veteran. The only downside here is the half-mile paddle out to the break, but no one ever said it was going to be easy, plus the long pull keeps it from getting over-crowded.

White Plains Beach (⊠ In former Kalaeloa Military Installation) is a spot where trouble will not find you. Known among locals as "mini-Waikīkī," it breaks in numerous spots, preventing the logjam that happens with many of O'ahu's more popular breaks. As part of a military base in West O'ahu, the beach was closed to the public until a couple of years ago. It's now occupied by mostly novice to intermediate surfers, so egos are at a minimum, though you do have to keep a lookout for loose boards.

If you like to ride waves in all kinds of craft, try **Mākaha Beach** (⊠ 1½ hrs west of Honolulu on H1 Fwy. and Farrington Hwy.). It has inter-minable rights that allow riders to perform all manner of stunts: from six-man canoes with everyone doing headstands to bully boards (over-size boogie boards) with dad's whole family riding with him. Mainly known as a long-boarding spot, it's predominantly local but not overly aggres-sive to the respectful outsider. The only downside is that it's way out on the West shore. Use caution in the wintertime as the surf can get huge.

Finally, if you really need to go somewhere people have heard of, your safest bet on the North Shore is **Sunset Beach** (⊠ 1 mi north of 'Ehukai Beach Park on Kamehameha Hwy.). There are several breaks here including **Kammie's** on the west side of the strip and **Sunset Point,** which is inside of the main Sunset break. Both of these tend to be smaller and safer rides for the less experienced. For the daring, Sunset is part of the Triple Crown for a reason. Thick waves and long rides await, but you're going to want to have a thick board and a thicker skull. The main break is very local, so mind your Ps and Qs.

Surf Shops

C&K Beach Service. To rent a board in Waikīkī, visit the beach fronting the Hilton Hawaiian Village. Rentals cost $10 to $15 per hour, depending on the size of the board, and $18 for two hours. Small group lessons are $50 per hour with board, and trainers promise to have you riding the waves by lesson's end. ☎ *No phone.*

★ **Surf 'N Sea.** This is the Wal-Mart of water for the North Shore. Rent a short board for $5 an hour or a long board for $7 an hour ($24 and $30 for full-day rentals). Lessons cost $69 for two hours. Depending on how you want to attack your waves, you can also rent boogie boards or kayaks. ✉ *62-595 Kamehameha Hwy.* ☎ *808/637–9887* ⊕ *www. surfnsea.com.*

Surfing Lessons

Hans Hedemann Surf Hawaii. Hans Hedemann spent 17 years on the professional surfer World Tour circuit. He and his staff offer surfing and bodysurfing instruction, four-day intensive surf camps on the North Shore and in Waikīkī, and fine-tuning courses with Hans himself. One-hour group lesson rates begin at $50 per person, $115 per person for a private lesson. ☎ *808/924–7778* ⊕ *www.hhsurf.com.*

☯ **Hawaiian Fire, Inc.** Off-duty Honolulu firefighters—and some of Hawai'i's most knowledgeable water-safety experts—man the boards at one of Hawai'i's hottest new surfing schools. Lessons include equipment, safety and surfing instruction, and two hours of surfing time (with lunch break) at a secluded beach near Barbers Point. Transportation is available from Waikīkī. Two-hour group lesson rates begin at $97 per person, $139 per person for a private lesson. ☎ *808/737–3473 or 888/955– 7873* ⊕ *www.hawaiianfire.com.*

North Shore Eco-Surf Tours. The only prerequisites here are "the ability to swim and the desire to surf." North Shore Eco-Surf has a more relaxed view of lessons, saying that the instruction will last somewhere between 90 minutes and four hours. The group rate begins at $65 per person, $120 for a private lesson. ☎ *808/638–9503* ⊕ *www.ecosurf-hawaii.com.*

WHALE-WATCHING

November is marked by the arrival of snow in most of America, but in Hawai'i it marks the return of the humpback whale. These migrating behemoths move south from their North Pacific homes during the winter months for courtship and child birth and what a display they conduct. Watching males and females alike throwing themselves out of the ocean and into the sunset awes even the saltiest of sailors. Newborn calves riding gently next to their two-ton mothers will stir you to your core. These gentle giants can be seen from the shore as they make quite a splash, but there is nothing like having your boat rocking beneath you in the wake of a whale's breach.

Hawai'i Sailing Adventures and Hawai'i Nautical (⇨ *See* Boat Tours & Charters) both run whale-watching charters during the winter months. At Hawai'i Sailing Adventures, two-hour whale-watching cruise rates with dinner start at $119. At Hawai'i Nautical, three-hour whale-watching cruise rates with snacks start at $100.

★ **Wild Side Specialty Tours.** Boasting a marine biologist crew, this west-side tour boat takes you to undisturbed snorkeling areas. Along the way you can view dolphins, turtles, and, in winter, whales. The tours leave early (7 AM) to catch the wildlife still active, so it's important to plan ahead as they're an hour outside Honolulu. Four-hour whale-watching cruise rates with continental breakfast start at $95. ⊠ *Wai'anae Boat Harbor, Slip A11, Wai'anae Boat Harbor* ☎ *808/306–7273.*

WINDSURFING & KITEBOARDING

Those who call windsurfing and kiteboarding cheating because they require no paddling have never tried hanging on to a sail or kite. It will turn your arms to spaghetti quicker than paddling ever could, and the speeds you generate . . . well, there's a reason why these are considered extreme sports.

Windsurfing was born here in the Islands. For amateurs, the Windward side is best because the onshore breezes will bring you back to land even if you don't know what you're doing. The new sport of kite surfing is tougher but more exhilarating as the kite will sometimes take you in the air for hundreds of feet. We suggest only those in top shape try the kites, but windsurfing is fun for all ages.

Equipment Rentals & Lessons

Kailua Sailboard and Kayaks Company. The appeal here is that they offer both beginner and high-performance gear. They also give lessons, either at $69 for a three-hour group lesson or $35 for a one-hour individual lesson (you must rent a board half-day at $39). ■ TIP➜ Since both options are around the same price, we suggest the one-hour individual lesson; then you have the rest of the day to practice what they preach. ⊠ *130 Kailua Rd., Kailua* ☎ *808/262–2555.*

Naish Hawai'i. If you like to learn from the best, try out world-champion Robby Naish and his family services. Not only do they build and sell boards, rent equipment, provide accommodation referrals, but they also offer their windsurfing and kiteboarding expertise. A four-hour package, including 90 minutes

> ## ON THE SIDELINES
>
> Watch the pros jump and spin on the waves during July's **Pan Am Hawaiian Windsurfing World Cup** (☎ 808/734–6999) off Kailua Beach. August's **Wahine Classic** (☎ 808/521–4322), held off Diamond Head point, features the world's best female boardsailors.

of instruction and a four-hour board rental, costs $55. ✉ *155A Hamakua Dr., Kailua* ☎ *808/261–6067* ⊕ *www.naish.com.*

★ **Surf 'N Sea.** Once again, this is where you want to go for the North Shore experience, but please limit it to summer. Windsurfing gear here rents for $12 per hour. A two-hour package, including lesson and rentals, costs $89. ✉ *7192 Kalaniana'ole Hwy., Hale'iwa* ☎ *808/637–9887.*

4

Golf, Hiking & Outdoor Activities

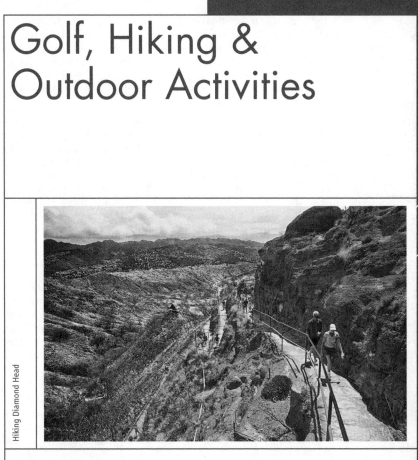

Hiking Diamond Head

WORD OF MOUTH

"Diamond Head was a great hike, not too crowded, and really somewhat windy toward the top. Showers were on and off, [creating] very gorgeous views of the lighthouse on the coast and Waikīkī. There were rainbows galore."

—makai1

"We played the Ko Olina golf course, which was fairly easy and beautiful—lots of waterfalls, ponds, and swans."

—dolciani

By Chad Pata
& Don
Chapman

ALTHOUGH MUCH IS WRITTEN about the water surrounding this little rock known as Oʻahu, there is as much to be said for the rock itself. It's a wonder of nature, thrust from the ocean floor a hundred millennia ago by a volcanic hot spot that is still spitting out islands today. It is the most remote island chain on earth, and there are creatures and plants that can be seen here and nowhere else. And there are dozens of ways for you to check it all out.

From the air you can peer down into nooks and crannies in the mountains—places that cars cannot reach and that hikers don't dare. Whether flitting here and there amidst a helicopter's rush and roar, or sailing by in the silence of a glider's reverie, you glimpse sights that few have experienced. Or if you would rather, take a step back in time and take off from the waters of Keʻehi Lagoon in a World War II–era seaplane. Follow the flight path flown by the Japanese Zeros as they attempted to destroy Pearl Harbor and the American spirit. On the North Shore, you can even throw yourself from an airplane and check out the unique reef formations as you hurtle toward earth at 120 mph.

Would you prefer the ground tour, where gravity and you are no longer at odds? Oʻahu is covered in hikes that vary from tropical rain forest to arid desert. Even when in the bustling city of Honolulu, you are but ten minutes from hidden waterfalls and bamboo forests. Out west you can wander a dusty path that has long since given up its ability to accommodate cars but is perfect for hikers. You can splash in tidal pools, admire sea arches, and gape at caves opened by the rock slides that closed the road. You can camp out for free on most of these treks and beaches. You might end up swearing that being homeless in Hawaiʻi is better than living in the houses back home.

If a little less rugged and less vigorous exploration is more your style, how about letting horses or SUVs do your dirty work? You can ride them on the beaches and in the valleys, checking out ancient holy sites, movie sets, and brilliant vistas. Less sweat and more ground covered, but both are still a little stinky.

Finally, there is the ancient sport of Scotland. Why merely hike into the rain forest when you can slice a 280-yard drive through it and then hunt for your Titleist in the bushy leaves instead? Almost 40 courses cover this tiny expanse, ranging from the target jungle golf of Luana Hills to the pro-style links of Turtle Bay. There is no offseason in the tropics, and no one here knows your real handicap.

AERIAL TOURS

An aerial tour of the Islands opens up a world of perspective. Looking down from the sky at the outline of the USS *Arizona* where it lays in its final resting place below the waters of Pearl Harbor or getting a glimpse of how Mother Nature carved a vast expanse of volcanic crater are the kind of views only seen by an "eye in the sky." If you go, don't forget your camera.

★ **Island Seaplane Service.** Harking back to the days of the earliest air visitors to Hawai'i, the seaplane has always had a special spot in island lore. The only seaplane service still operating in Hawai'i takes off from Ke'ehi Lagoon. Flight options are either a half-hour south and eastern O'ahu shoreline tour or an hour island circle tour. The *Pan Am Clipper* may be gone, but you can revisit the experience for $99 to $179. ⊠ *85 Lagoon Dr., Honolulu* ☎ *808/836–6273.*

Makani Kai Helicopters. This may be the best way to now see the infamous and now closed Sacred Falls park, where a rock slide killed 20 people and injured dozens more; Makani Kai dips their helicopter down to show you one of Hawai'i's former favorite hikes. There's also a Waikīkī by Night excursion that soars by the breathtaking Honolulu city lights. Half-hour tour rates begin at $109 per person, and customized charters are available starting at $550 per hour. ⊠ *110 Kapalulu Pl., Honolulu* ☎ *808/834–5813* ⊕ *www.makanikai.com.*

★ **The Original Glider Rides.** "Mr. Bill" has been offering piloted glider (sailplane) rides over the northwest end of O'ahu's North Shore since 1970. These are piloted scenic rides for one or two passengers in sleek, bubble-top, motorless aircraft. You'll get aerial views of mountains, shoreline, coral pools, windsurfing sails, and, in winter, humpback whales. Reservations are recommended; 10-, 15-, 20-, and 30-minute flights leave every 20 minutes daily 10–5. The charge for one passenger is $59–$139, depending on the length of the flight; two people fly for $138–$238. ⊠ *Dillingham Airfield, Mokulē'ia* ☎ *808/677–3404.*

BIKING

O'ahu's coastal roads are flat, well paved, and unfortunately, awash in vehicular traffic. Frankly, biking is no fun in either Waikīkī or Honolulu, but things are a bit better outside the city. ■ **TIP→ Be sure to take along a nylon jacket for the frequent showers on the windward side and remember that Hawai'i is "paradise after the fall": lock up your bike.**

Honolulu City and County Bike Coordinator (☎ 808/527–5044) can answer all your biking questions concerning trails, permits, and state laws.

Best Spots

Biking the North Shore may sound like a great idea, but the two-lane road is narrow and traffic-heavy. We suggest you try the **West Kaunala Trail** (⊠ End of Pūpūkea Rd. This road is next to Foodland, the only grocery store on North Shore). It's a little tricky at times, but with the rain forest surroundings and beautiful ocean vistas you'll hardly notice your legs burning on the steep ascent at the end. It's about 5.5 mi round-trip. Bring water because there's none on the trail unless it comes from the sky.

If going up a mountain is not your idea of mountain biking, then perhaps **Ka'ena Point Trail** (⊠ West O'ahu, end of Farrington Hwy.) is better suited to your needs. A longer ride (10 mi), but much flatter, takes you oceanside around the westernmost point on the Island. You pass sea arches and a mini-blowhole then finish up with some motocross jumps right before you turn around. There's no water on this ride either, but at least at the end you have the Yokohama beach showers to cool you off.

Fodor'sChoice Our favorite ride is in central O'ahu
★ on the **'Aiea Loop Trail** (⊠ Central O'ahu, just past Kea'iwa Heiau State Park, at end of 'Aiea Heights Dr.). There's a little bit of everything you expect to find in Hawai'i—wild pigs crossing your path, an ancient Hawaiian *heiau* (holy ground), and the remains of a World War II crashed airplane. Campsites and picnic tables are available along the way and, if you need a snack, strawberry guava trees abound. Enjoy the foliage change from bamboo to Norfolk pine in your climb along this 4.5-mi track.

> **MOTORSPORTS**
>
> Gear heads needn't leave their passion behind when they visit O'ahu. If it has wheels they race it at the Hawai'i Motorsports Center. They have a dirtbike track, go-carts, a drag strip, and even an Indy car road course. On weekends, amateurs come out to race their suped-up Hondas against each other, but even during the week the park is rarely quiet. If speed is what you crave, check out their website (www. hawaiiracewaypark.com) for events or racing classes during your stay.

Bike Shops & Clubs

Blue Sky Rentals & Sports Center. Known more for motorcycles than for man-powered bikes, Blue Sky does have bicycles for $18 per day (from 8 to 6), $26 for 24 hours, and $75 per week—a $100 deposit is required for weekly rentals. The prices include a bike, a helmet, a lock, and a water bottle. ⊠ *1920 Ala Moana Blvd., across from Hilton Hawaiian Village, Waikīkī, Honolulu* ☎ *808/947–0101.*

Boca Hawai'i LLC. This is your first stop if you want to do intense riding. The triathlon shop, owned and operated by top athletes, has full-suspension Trek 4500s for $35 a day with a two-day minimum ($25 for each additional day). Call ahead and reserve a bike as supplies are limited. ⊠ *330 Cooke St., next to Bike Factory, Kaka'ako, Honolulu* ☎ *808/591–9839.*

Hawai'i Bicycling League. Not much for riding by yourself? Visit this shop online, and you can get connected with rides and contests. ✆ *Box 4403, Honolulu 96813* ☎ *808/735–5756* ⊕ *www.bikehawaii.com.*

CAMPING

Camping has always been the choice of cost-conscious travelers who want to be vacationing for a while without spending a lot of money. But now, with the growth of ecotourism and the skyrocketing cost of gas, it has become more popular than ever. Whatever your reasons for getting back to nature, O'ahu has plenty to offer year-round.

■ **TIP→** Camping here is not as highly organized as it is on the Mainland: expect few marked sites, scarce electrical outlets, and nary a ranger station. What you find instead are unblemished spots in the woods and on the beach. With price tags ranging from free to $5, it's hard to complain about the lack of amenities.

State Parks

There are four state recreation areas at which you can camp, one in the mountains and three on the beach. All state parks require 30 days advance notice and a $5 fee a day. To obtain a camping permit as well as rules and regulations for state parks, write to the **Department of Land and Natural Resources, State Parks Division** (🖃 Box 621, Honolulu 96809 ☎ 808/587–0300 ⊕ www.state.hi.us/dlnr/dsp).

Keaīwa Heiau State Recreation Area (🖃 End of ʻAiea Heights Rd. ☎ 808/ 483–2511), the mountain option, consists of nearly 400 acres of forests and hiking trails in the foothills of the Koʻolaus. The park is centered around an ancient Hawaiian holy site, known as a heiau, that is believed to be the site of many healings. Proper respect is asked of campers in the area.

Of the beach sites, **Kahana Valley State Park** (🖃 Kamehameha Hwy. near Kahana Bay) is the choice for a true Hawaiian experience. You camp alongside a beautiful Windward bay, a short walk away from the Huilua Fishpond, a national historic landmark. There are rain forest hikes chock-full of local fruit trees, a public hunting area for pigs, and a coconut grove for picnicking. The water is suitable for swimming and body surfing, though it's a little cloudy for snorkeling. Camping here gives you a true taste of old Hawaiʻi, as they lived it.

County Campsites

As for the county spots, there are 15 currently available and they all do require a permit. The good news is that the permits are free and are easy to acquire. Contact the **Department of Parks and Recreation** (🖃 650 S. King St., Honolulu 96707 ☎ 808/523–4525), or any of the satellite city halls (Ala Moana Mall, Fort St. Mall, and Kapolei Hale), for permits and rules and regulations.

Fodor'sChoice
★
For beach camping we suggest Bellows and Kualoa. **Bellows Field Beach Park** (🖃 220 Tinker Rd. ☎ 808/259–8080) has the superior beach as well as excellent cover in the grove of ironwood trees. The Windward beach is over 3 mi long, and both pole fishing and campfires in designated areas are allowed here. You can feel secure with the kids as there are lifeguards and public phones. The only downside is that camping is only permitted on the weekends.

The beach at **Kualoa Regional Park** (🖃 49-479 Kamehameha Hwy. ☎ 808/237–8525) isn't the magnificent giant that Bellows is, but the vistas are both magnificent and historic. Near Chinaman's Hat (Mokoliʻi Island) at the northern end of Kāneʻohe Bay, the park is listed on the National Registry of Historic Places due to its significance to the Hawaiians. The park is expansive, with large grassy areas, picnic tables, and comfort stations. Although the beach is just a bit of a sandy strip, the swimming and snorkeling are excellent.

Camping is not just all about the beach, however. Nestled in the foothills of the Koʻolaus is the serene **Hoomaluhia Botanical Garden** (🖃 End of Lu-

luku Rd. in Kāne'ohe ☎ 808/233–7323). The 400-acre preserve has catch-and-release fishing, extensive hiking trails, and a large selection of tropical shrubs and trees. There are five fire circles. Though it is a beautiful area, they do caution campers to be prepared for rain, mud, and mosquitoes.

Camping Indoors

If tent camping sounds a little too rugged, consider cabin camping on the beach. These spots do not offer the amenities of the island's hotels and resorts, but they do provide oceanfront rooms for those on smaller budgets.

★ Starting with the least expensive is **The Friends of Malaekahana** (⊠ 56-335 Kamehameha Hwy. ☎ 808/293–1736) just outside the North Shore's Laie. The complex is a series of oceanfront cottages built 60 years ago, taken over by the state, and now run by The Friends as a private venture in what they call "indoor camping." Over a half century of North Shore winters has dilapidated the cabins to mere shells of their former quaintness. But, at $66 a night for a cabin that sleeps ten, it is easy to see why it's almost impossible to get one during the summer. In the wintertime you can usually secure one for weekday rentals. ■ TIP→ **Remember to bring everything that you would bring for camping, because they mean it when they say "indoor camping."** But sunrise from your lanai (albeit a lanai that leans at an angle) is not to be had anywhere else for this price.

For a little step up there is the YMCA's **Camp Erdman** (⊠ 69-385 Farrington Hwy. ☎ 808/637–4615), also on the North Shore. It is a youth camp, but they almost always have extra cabins available for the public. The cabins are in much better condition than Malaekahana, and they offer nicer facilities, including volleyball and basketball, and serve hot meals. The beach is nearly deserted, and there is an amazing ropes course for those without a fear of heights. Though $134 a person for three nights seems a bit steep for camping, keep in mind that the fee also covers nine meals. Just try to eat in Waikīkī for three days on such a small amount!

Finally, if you have a big group to house, there is **Camp Mokulē'ia** (⊠ 68-729 Farrington Hwy. ☎ 808/637–6241). This privately-run operation has wide-open beach space, a monstrous fire pit, and camp sites that can accommodate 30. While the camp sites are a bargain at $10 a night, the cabins are a bit pricey unless you have a troop. Their studio cottages are $90 a night, but the 14-bed cottages are only $170. Located just up the road from Camp Erdman, they offer fewer kids and more privacy, but you are on your own as far as cooking is concerned.

Rentals

Bike Shop. You can rent everything from tents to backpacks here. ⊠ *1149 S. King St., Mō'ili'ili* ☎ *808/595–0588* ⊕ *www.bikeshophawaii.com.*

GOLF

Unlike the Neighbor Islands, the majority of O'ahu's golf courses are not associated with hotels and resorts. In fact, of the island's three-dozen-

TIPS FOR THE GREEN

Before you head out to the first tee, there are a few things you should know about golf in Hawai'i:

• All resort courses and many daily fee courses provide rental clubs. In many cases, they're the latest lines from Titleist, Ping, Callaway, and the like. This is true for both men and women, as well as lefthanders, which means you don't have to schlepp clubs across the Pacific.

• Most courses offer deals varying from twilight discount rates to frequent visitor's discounts, even for tourists. Ask questions when calling pro shops, don't just accept their first quotes; deals abound if you persist.

• Pro shops at most courses are well-stocked with balls, tees, and other accoutrements, so even if you bring your own bag, it needn't weigh a ton.

• Come spikeless—very few Hawai'i courses still permit metal spikes.

• Sunscreen. Buy it, apply it (minimum 30 SPF). The subtropical rays of the sun are intense, even in December.

• Resort courses, in particular, offer more than the usual three sets of tees, sometimes four or five. So bite off as much or as little challenge as you like. Tee it up from the tips and you'll end up playing a few 600-yard par-5s and see a few 250-yard forced carries.

• In theory, you can play golf in Hawai'i 365 days a year. But there's a reason the Hawaiian islands are so green. Better to bring an umbrella and light jacket and not use them than to not bring them and get soaked.

• Unless you play a muni or certain daily fee courses, plan on taking a cart. Riding carts are mandatory at most courses and are included in the green fees.

plus courses, only five are tied to lodging and none of them are in the tourist hub of Waikīkī.

Green Fees: Green fees listed here are the highest course rates per round on weekdays/weekends for U.S. residents. (Some courses charge non-U.S. residents higher prices.) Discounts are often available for resort guests and for those who book tee times on the Web. Twilight fees are usually offered, call individual courses for information.

Waikīkī

Ala Wai Municipal Golf Course. Just across the Ala Wai Canal from Waikīkī, Ala Wai is said to host more rounds than any other U.S. course. Not that it's a great course, just really convenient, being Honolulu's only public "city course." Although residents can obtain a city golf card that allows automated tee times over the phone, the best bet for a visitor is to show up and expect a minimum hour's wait. The course itself is flat. Robin Nelson did some redesign work in the 1990s, adding mounding, trees, and a lake. The Ala Wai Canal comes into play on several holes on the back nine, including the treacherous 18th. ⊠ *404*

Kapahulu Ave., Waikīkī ☎ *808/733–7387, 808/739–1900 golf shop* 🏌 *18 holes. 5861 yds. Par 70. Green Fee: $42* ☞ *Facilities: Driving range, putting green, golf carts, pull carts, rental clubs, pro shop, lessons, restaurant, bar.*

Honolulu

Moanalua Country Club. Said to be (but not without dispute) the oldest golf club west of the Rockies, this 9-holer is private but allows public play except on weekend and holiday mornings. It's a bit quirky, but the final two holes, a par-3 off a cliff to a smallish tree-rimmed green and a par-4 with an approach to a green set snugly between stream and jungle, are classic. ✉ *1250 Ala Aolani St.* ☎ *808/839–2411* 🏌 *9 holes. 3062 yds. Par 36. Green Fee: $31.50* ☞ *Facilities: Putting green, golf carts, rental clubs, restaurant, bar.*

Southeast Oʻahu

Hawaiʻi Kai Golf Course. The **Championship Golf Course** (William F. Bell, 1973) winds through a Honolulu suburb at the foot of Koko Crater. Homes (and the liability of a broken window) come into play on many holes, but that is offset by views of the nearby Pacific and a crafty routing of holes. With several lakes, lots of trees, and bunkers in all the wrong places, Hawaiʻi Kai really is a "championship" golf course, especially when the trade winds howl. The **Executive Course** (1962), a par-55 track, is the first of only three courses in Hawaiʻi built by Robert Trent Jones Sr. Although a few changes have been made to his original design, you can find the usual Jones attributes, including raised greens and lots of risk-reward options. ✉ *8902 Kalanianaʻole Hwy., Hawaiʻi Kai* ☎ *808/ 395–2358* ⊕ *www.hawaiikaigolf.com* 🏌 *Championship Course: 18 holes. 6222 yds. Par 72. Green Fee: $80/$90. Executive Course: 18 holes. 2223 yds. Par 55. Green Fee: $37/$42* ☞ *Facilities: Driving range, putting green, golf carts, pull carts, rental clubs, pro shop, lessons, restaurant, bar.*

Windward Oʻahu

Bayview Golf Links. Robin Nelson created a terrific 18-hole par-60 executive course. Unfortunately, maintenance issues—no sand in the sand traps, for example—have diminished what ought to be a great little track. Still, with up-close mountain and ocean views, and Nelson's design, it's a bargain. ✉ *45-285 Kāneʻohe Bay Dr., Kāneʻohe* ☎ *808/247–0451* 🏌 *18 holes. 3269 yds. Par 60. Green Fee: $40* ☞ *Facilities: Driving range, putting green, golf carts, pull carts, restaurant, bar.*

Kahuku Municipal Golf Course. The only true links course in Hawaiʻi, this 9-hole muni is not for everyone. Maintenance is an on-going issue, and in summer it can look a bit like the Serengeti. It's walking-only (a few pull-carts are available for rent); there's no pro shop, just a starter who sells lost-and-found balls; and the 19th hole is a soda machine and a covered picnic bench. And yet . . . the course stretches out along the blue Pacific where surf crashes on the shore, the turf underfoot is spongy, sea mist drifts across the links, and wildflowers bloom in the rough. ✉ *56-501 Kamehameha Hwy., Kahuku* ☎ *808/293–5842* ✠ *9 holes. 2699 yds. Par 35. Green Fee: $42* ☞ *Facilities: Putting green, pull carts.*

Koʻolau Golf Club. Koʻolau Golf Club is marketed as the toughest golf course in Hawaiʻi and one of the most challenging in the country. Dick Nugent and Jack Tuthill (1992) routed 10 holes over jungle ravines that require at least a 110-yard carry. The par-4 18th may be the most difficult closing hole in golf. The tee shot from the regular tees must carry 200 yards of ravine, 250 from the blue tees. The approach shot is back across the ravine, 200 yards to a well-bunkered green. Set at the windward base of the Koʻolau Mountains, the course is as much beauty as beast. Kāneʻohe Bay is visible from most holes, orchids and yellow ginger bloom, the shama thrush (Hawaiʻi's best singer since Don Ho) chirrups, and waterfalls flute down the sheer, green mountains above. ✉ *45-550 Kionaole Rd., Kāneʻohe* ☎ *808/236–4653* ⊕ *www. koolaugolfclub.com* ✠ *18 holes. 7310 yds. Par 72. Green Fee: $135* ☞ *Facilities: Driving range, putting green, golf carts, rental clubs, pro shop, golf academy, restaurant, bar.*

Fodor'sChoice **Luana Hills Country Club.** In the cool, lush Maunawili Valley, Pete and
★ Perry Dye created what can only be called target jungle golf. In other words, the rough is usually dense jungle, and you may not hit driver on three of the four par-5s, or several par-4s, including the perilous 18th that plays off a cliff to a narrow green protected by a creek. Mt. Olomana's twin peaks tower over Luana Hills. ■ **TIP→ The back nine wanders deep into the valley, and includes an island green (par-3 11th) and perhaps the loveliest inland hole in Hawaiʻi (par-4 12th).** ✉ *770 Auloa Rd., Kailua* ☎ *808/262–2139* ⊕ *www.luanahills.com* ✠ *18 holes. 6164 yds. Par 72. Green Fee: $125* ☞ *Facilities: Driving range, putting green, golf carts, rental clubs, pro shop, restaurant, bar.*

★ **Olomana Golf Links.** Bob and Robert L. Baldock are the architects of record for this layout, but so much has changed since it opened in 1969 that they would recognize little of it. A turf specialist was brought in to improve fairways and greens, tees were rebuilt, new bunkers added, and mangroves cut back to make better use of natural wetlands. But what really puts Olomana on the map is that this is where wunderkind Michelle Wie learned the game. ✉ *41-1801 Kalanianaole Hwy., Waimānalo* ☎ *808/259–7926* ⊕ *www.olomanagolflinks.com* ✠ *18 holes. 6326 yds. Par 72. Green Fee: $80* ☞ *Facilities: Driving range, putting green, golf carts, pull carts, rental clubs, pro shop, lessons, restaurant, bar.*

North Shore

Turtle Bay Resort & Spa. When the Lazarus of golf courses, the **Fazio Course** at Turtle Bay (George Fazio, 1971), rose from the dead in 2002, Turtle Bay on Oʻahu's rugged North Shore became a premier golf destination. Two holes had been plowed under when the Palmer Course at Turtle Bay (Arnold Palmer and Ed Seay, 1992) was built, while the other seven lay fallow, and the front nine remained open. Then new owners came

SAVING THE BEST FOR LAST

AMONG GOLF'S GREAT TRADITIONS is the 19th Hole. No matter how the first 18 go, the 19th is sure to offer comfort and cheer, not to mention a chilled beverage.

Honey's at Ko'olau is named for Don Ho's mother's original Honey's in Kāne'ohe, where the crooner got his start. Good fare and great views of the verdant Ko'olau Mountains. Nearby at Olomana, the 19th hole overlooks the course, serves good local fare, and on Friday afternoons a Hawaiian ladies club gathers after their weekly tournament to enjoy a beverage or two, sing four-part harmony, play 'ukuleles, and dance hula. At Turtle Bay, the 19th hole is bright, airy, and serves excellent food. Affiliated as it is with the Hawai'i Prince Hotel, and with a view across a large lake toward the course, the Hawai'i Prince's 19th is a nice place to linger. O'ahu's best—and perhaps the state's best—is at Kō'Ōlina, where the open-air bar is perched at the top of a waterfall that cascades down past the 18th green. Food from the adjacent restaurant, Niblicks, is by renowned chef Roy Yamaguchi.

Cheers!

along and re-created holes 13 and 14 using Fazio's original plans, and the Fazio became whole again. It's a terrific track with 90 bunkers. The gem at Turtle Bay, though, is the **Palmer Course.** The front nine is mostly open as it skirts Punaho'olapa Marsh, a nature sanctuary, while the back nine plunges into the wetlands and winds along the coast. The short par-4 17th runs along the rocky shore, with a diabolical string of bunkers cutting diagonally across the fairway from tee to green. ⊠ 57-049 Kuilima Dr., Kahuku ☎ 808/293–8574 ⊕ www.turtlebayresort.com ⅃. Fazio Course: 18 holes. 6535 yds. Par 72. Green Fee: $155. Palmer Course: 18 holes. 7199 yds. Par 72. Green Fee: $165 ☞ Facilities: Driving range, putting green, golf carts, rental clubs, pro shop, lessons, restaurant, bar.

Kapolei & Central O'ahu

★ **Coral Creek Golf Course.** On the 'Ewa Plain, 4 mi inland, Coral Creek is cut from ancient coral—left from when this area was still under water. Robin Nelson (1999) does some of his best work in making use of the coral, and of some dynamite, blasting out portions to create dramatic lakes and tee and green sites. They could just as easily call it Coral Cliffs, because of the 30- to 40-foot cliffs Nelson created. They include the par-3 10th green's grotto and waterfall, and the vertical drop-off on the right side of the par-4 18th green. An ancient creek meanders across the course, but there's not much water, just enough to be a babbling nuisance. ⊠ 91-1111 Geiger Rd., 'Ewa Beach ☎ 808/441–4653 ⊕ www.coralcreekgolfhawaii.com ⅃. 18 holes. 6818 yds. Par 72. Green Fee: $130 ☞ Facilities: Driving range, putting green, golf carts, rental clubs, pro shop, lessons, restaurant, bar.

Hawai'i Country Club. Also known as Kunia, but not to be confused with Royal Kunia a few miles away, this course is in the middle of sugarcane fields and dates to plantation times. Several par-4s are driveable, including the 9th and 18th holes. This is a fun course, but a bit rough around the edges. ⊠ *94-1211 Kunia Rd., Wahiawā* ☎ *808/621–5654* ⊕ *www.hawaiicc.com* ⅄ *18 holes. 5910 yds. Par 72. Green Fee: $53/$63* ☞ *Facilities: Driving range, putting green, rental clubs, pro shop, restaurant, bar.*

Hawai'i Prince Golf Course. Affiliated with the Hawai'i Prince Hotel in Waikīkī, the Hawai'i Prince Golf Course (not to be confused with the Prince Course at Princeville, Kaua'i) has a links feel to it, and it is popular with local charity fund-raiser golf tournaments. Arnold Palmer and Ed Seay (1991) took what had been flat, featureless sugarcane fields and sculpted 27 challenging, varied holes. Mounding breaks up the landscape, as do 10 lakes. Water comes into play on six holes of the A course, three of B, and seven of C. The most difficult combination is A and C (A and B from the forward tees). ⊠ *91-1200 Fort Weaver Rd., 'Ewa Beach* ☎ *808/944–4567* ⊕ *www.princeresortshawaii.com* ⅄ *A Course: 9 holes. 3138 yds. Par 36. B Course: 9 holes. 3099 yds. Par 36. C Course: 9 holes. 3076 yds. Par 36. Green Fee: $140* ☞ *Facilities: Driving range, putting green, golf carts, pull carts, rental clubs, pro shop, golf academy/lessons, restaurant, bar.*

Kapolei Golf Course. This is a Ted Robinson water wonderland with waterfalls and four lakes—three so big they have names—coming into play on 10 holes. Set on rolling terrain, Kapolei is a serious golf course, especially when the wind blows. ⊠ *91-701 Farrington Hwy., Kapolei* ☎ *808/674–2227* ⅄ *18 holes. 7001 yds. Par 72. Green Fee: $130/$140* ☞ *Facilities: Driving range, putting green, golf carts, rental clubs, pro shop, lessons, restaurant, bar.*

Mililani Golf Course. Located on O'ahu's central plain, Mililani is usually a few degrees cooler than downtown, 25 minutes away. The eucalyptus trees through which the course plays add to the cool factor and stands of Norfolk pines give Mililani a "mainland course" feel. Bob and Robert L. Baldock (1966) make good use of an old irrigation ditch reminiscent of a Scottish burn. ⊠ *95-176 Kuahelani Ave., Mililani* ☎ *808/ 623–2222* ⊕ *www.mililanigolf.com* ⅄ *18 holes. 6455 yds. Par 72. Green Fee: $95* ☞ *Facilities: Driving range, putting green, golf carts, rental clubs, pro shop, lessons, restaurant, bar.*

New 'Ewa Beach Golf Club. A private course open to the public, New 'Ewa is one of the delightful products of the too brief collaboration of Robin Nelson and Rodney Wright (1992). Trees are very much part of the character here, but there are also elements of links golf, such as a double green shared by the 2nd and 16th holes. ⊠ *91-050 Fort Weaver Rd., 'Ewa Beach* ☎ *808/689–8351* ⅄ *18 holes. 6124 yds. Par 72. Green Fee: $65* ☞ *Facilities: Putting green, golf carts, rental clubs, pro shop, restaurant.*

Pearl Harbor Country Club. Carved in the hillside high above Pearl Harbor, the 18 holes here are really two courses. The front nine rambles out along gently sloping terrain, while the back nine zig-zags up and down a steeper portion of the slope as it rises into the Koʻolau Mountains. ■ TIP→ **The views of Pearl Harbor are breathtaking.** ⊠ *98-535 Kaonohi St., ʻAiea* ☎ *808/487–3802* ⊕ *www.pearlcc.com* ⅂. *18 holes. 6230 yds. Par 72. Green Fee: $100/$110* ⌑ *Facilities: Driving range, putting green, golf carts, rental clubs, pro shop, lessons, restaurant, bar.*

Royal Kunia Country Club. At one time the PGA Tour considered buying Royal Kunia Country Club and hosting the Sony Open there. It's that good. ■ TIP→ **Every hole offers fabulous views from Diamond Head to Pearl Harbor to the nearby Waiʻanae Mountains.** Robin Nelson's eye for natural sight lines and dexterity with water features adds to the visual pleasure. ⊠ *94-1509 Anonui St., Waipahu* ☎ *808/688–9222* ⊕ *www. royalkuniacc.com* ⅂. *18 holes. 7007 yds. Par 72. Green Fee: $110/$120* ⌑ *Facilities: Driving range, putting green, golf carts, rental clubs, pro shop, restaurant.*

Waikele Golf Course. Outlet stores are not the only bargain at Waikele. The adjacent golf course is a daily fee course that offers a private club-like atmosphere and a terrific Ted Robinson (1992) layout. The target off the tee is Diamond Head, with Pearl Harbor to the right. Robinson's water features are less distinctive here, but define the short par-4 4th hole, with a lake running down the left side of the fairway and guarding the green; and the par-3 17th, which plays across a lake. The par-4 18th is a terrific closing hole, with a lake lurking on the right side of the green. At this writing, the course was closed for renovations but scheduled to be open by early 2007. ⊠ *94-200 Paioa Pl., Waipahu* ☎ *808/ 676–9000* ⊕ *www.golfwaikele.com* ⅂. *18 holes. 6261 yds. Par 72. Green Fee: $125* ⌑ *Facilities: Driving range, putting green, golf carts, rental clubs, pro shop, lessons, restaurant, bar.*

West Loch Municipal Golf Course. The best of Honolulu's municipal courses, this Robin Nelson (1991) design plays along Pearl Harbor's West Loch. In the process of building the course wetlands were actually expanded, increasing bird habitat. ⊠ *91-1126 Okupe St., ʻEwa Beach* ☎ *808/675–6076* ⅂. *18 holes. 6335 yds. Par 72. Green Fee: $42* ⌑ *Facilities: Driving range, putting green, golf carts, rental clubs, restaurant.*

West Oʻahu

Kōʻōlina Golf Club. Hawaiʻi's golden age of golf-course architecture came to Oʻahu when Kōʻōlina Golf Club opened in 1989. Ted Robinson, king of the water features, went splash-happy here, creating nine lakes that come into play on eight holes, including the par-3 12th, where you reach the tee by driving behind a Disney-like waterfall. Tactically, though, the most dramatic is the par-4 18th, where the approach is a minimum 120 yards across a lake to a two-tiered green guarded on the left by a cascading waterfall. Today, KōʻŌlina, affiliated with the adjacent ʻIhilani Resort and Spa (guests receive discounted rates), has matured into one of Hawaiʻi's top courses. You can niggle about routing issues—the first three holes play into the trade winds (and the morning sun), and two consecutive par-5s on the back nine play into the trades—but Robinson does enough solid design to make those of passing concern. ✉ *92-1220 Ali'inui Dr., Kapolei* ☎ *808/676–5300* ⊕ *www.koolinagolf.com* ⅃ *18 holes. 6867 yds. Par 72. Green Fee: $160* ☞ *Facilities: Driving range, putting green, golf carts, rental clubs, pro shop, golf academy, restaurant, bar.*

★ **Mākaha Resort Golf Club.** Known locally as Mākaha West, this William F. Bell classic design (1969) remains one of the island's true gems, and a serious golf course where subtle elevation changes, if not duly noted, can significantly affect scores. The back nine plays up into Mākaha Valley. Roving peacocks make Mākaha West one of the island's most colorful layouts. ✉ *84-626 Mākaha Valley Rd., Wai'anae* ☎ *808/695–7519* ⊕ *www.makaharesort.com* ⅃ *18 holes. 7077 yds. Par 72. Green Fee: $110* ☞ *Facilities: Driving range, putting green, golf carts, rental clubs, pro shop, lessons, restaurant, bar.*

Mākaha Valley Country Club. This course (William F. Bell, 1968), known locally as Mākaha East, is indeed a valley course, taking great advantage of the steep valley walls and natural terrain. It's shorter than the nearby West course, but offers plenty of challenge from the back tees. The double-dogleg, downhill-uphill, par-5 18th is a doozy of a closer. ✉ *84-627 Mākaha Valley Rd., Wai'anae* ☎ *808/695–9578* ⊕ *www.makahavalleyccc. com* ⅃ *18 holes. 6091 yds. Par 71. Green Fee: $55* ☞ *Facilities: Driving range, putting green, golf carts, rental clubs, pro shop, restaurant, bar.*

Municipal Golf Courses

We don't have room to mention every muni on O'ahu, so here are three more you may want to consider. Your best bet for a tee time is to call the day-of and inquire about walk-on availability. Green fees are standard at city courses, $42 walking rate, riding cart $8 per person, pull carts $4.

'Ewa Villages Golf Course Municipal. ✉ *91-1760 Park Row St., 'Ewa Beach* ☎ *808/681–0220* ⅃ *18 holes. 6455yds. Par 73.*

Pali Golf Course Municipal. ✉ *45-050 Kamehameha Hwy., Kāne'ohe* ☎ *808/266–7612* ⅃ *18 holes. 6524 yds. Par 72.*

Ted Makalena Golf Course Municipal. ✉ *93-059 Waipio Pt. Access Rd., Waipahu* ☎ *808/675–6052* ⅃ *18 holes. 5946 yds. Par 71.*

HIKING

The trails of O'ahu cover a full spectrum of environments: desert walks through cactus, slippery paths through bamboo-filled rain forest, and scrambling rock climbs up ancient volcanic calderas. The only thing you won't find is an overnighter as even the longest of hikes won't take you more than half a day. In addition to being short in length, many of the prime hikes are within 10 minutes of downtown Waikīkī, meaning that you won't have to spend your whole day getting back to nature.

For a free O'ahu recreation map that outlines the island's 33 major trails, contact the **Hawai'i State Department of Land and Natural Resources** (⌂ 1151 Punchbowl St., Room 130, Honolulu 96813 ☎ 808/587–0300 ⊕ www.hawaii.gov). Contact the City and County of Honolulu's

5

TIPS FOR THE TRAIL

There are a couple things to remember when hiking here in the Islands, things that you may not run into at home:

• When hiking the waterfall and rain forest trails, use insect repellent. The dampness draws huge swarms of blood suckers that can ruin a walk in the woods real quick.

• Volcanic rock is very porous and therefore likely to be loose. Rock climbing is strongly discouraged as you never know which little ledge is going to go.

• Always let someone know where you are going and never hike alone. The foliage gets very dense, and, as little as the island is, many hikers have gotten lost for a week or longer.

Trails and Access Manager (☎ 808/973–9782) for a free hiking-safety guide. Ask for a copy of "Hiking on O'ahu: The Official Guide."

Best Spots

Every vacation has requirements that must be fulfilled so that when your neighbors ask, you can say, "Yeah, did it." **Diamond Head Crater** is high on that list of things to do on O'ahu. It's a hike easy enough that even grandma can do it, as long as she takes a water bottle because it's hot and dry. Only a mile up, a clearly marked trail with handrails scales the inside of this extinct volcano. At the top, the fabled 99 steps take you up to the pill box overlooking the Pacific Ocean and Honolulu. It's a breathtaking view and a lot cheaper than taking a helicopter ride for the same photo op. ✛ *Diamond Head Rd. at 18th Ave. Enter on east of crater; there's limited parking inside, most park on street and walk in.*

Fodor'sChoice Travel up into the valley beyond Honolulu to make the **Mānoa Falls** hike.
★ Though only a mile long, this path passes through so many different ecosystems that you feel as if you're in an arboretum. Walk among the elephant ear ape plants, ruddy fir trees, and a bamboo forest straight out of China. At the top is a 150-foot falls with a small pool not quite suited for swimming but good for wading. This hike is more about the journey than the destination. Make sure you bring some mosquito repellent because they grow 'em big up here. ✛ *Behind Mānoa Valley in Paradise Park. Take West Mānoa Rd. to end, park on side of road, and follow trail signs in.*

★ Need more waterfall action that you can actually swim? Then **Maunawili Falls** is your trip. In fact, even if you don't want to get wet, you're going to have to cross Maunawili Stream several times to get to the falls. Along the mile and a half trek enjoy the ginger, vines, and heleconia before greeting fern-shrouded falls that are made for swimming. The water is not the clearest, but it's cool and refreshing after battling the bugs to get here. ✛ *Take Pali Hwy., Rte. 61, from Honolulu through the tunnels, take 3rd right onto Auloa Rd., then take left fork immediately. At dead end, climb over vehicle gate for trailhead.*

For the less adventurous hiker and anyone looking for a great view, there is the **Makapuʻu Lighthouse Trail.** The paved trail runs up the side of Makapuʻu Point in southeast Oʻahu. Early on, the trail is surrounded by lava rock, but, as you ascend, foliage—the tiny white koa haole flower and the cream-tinged spikes of the kiawe—begins taking over the barren rock. Once atop the point, you begin to understand how alone these Islands are in the Pacific. The easternmost tip of Oʻahu, this is where the island divides the sea, giving you a spectacular view of the cobalt ocean meeting the land in a cacophony of white caps. To the south are several tide pools and the lighthouse. The eastern view looks down upon Rabbit and Kāohikaipu Islands, two bird sanctuaries just off the coast. The 2-mi round-trip hike is a great break on a circle-island trip. ⊹ *Take Kalanianaʻole Hwy. to the base of Makapuʻu Pt. Look for the asphalt strip snaking up the mountain.*

> ## PAINTBALL
>
> For the more aggressive among you, there is Hawaii All-Star Paintball Games where you can do Jackson Pollack–style battle for $30 for an all-day rental. They have three different battlefields and they separate groups into skill levels. The course is right next to the airport and tournaments are held almost every weekend—call Brandon for battle times at 808/842-7827.

FodorsChoice
★ Kaʻena Point trail is a little longer (at 5 mi round-trip) and hotter than Makapuʻu Point, but it is right next to the beach, and there are spots where you can get in and cool off. Sea-carved cliffs give way to lava-rock beaches and sea arches. Halfway to the point, there is a double blow hole, which is a good indicator of sea conditions. If it is blowing good, stay out of the water. Though the area is hot and dry, there is still much wildlife here, as it is the only nesting ground for many rare sea birds. ■ **TIP→ Keep a lookout for the Laysan albatrosses; these enormous birds have recently returned to the area. Don't be surprised if they come in for a closer look at you, too.** There has been a cave-in of an old lava tube, so be careful when crossing it, but enjoy the view in its enormous mouth. ⊹ *Take Farrington Hwy. to its end at Yokohamas. Hike in on the old 4WD trail.*

When on the North Shore, check out the **Trails at Turtle Bay Resort** (✉ 57-091 Kamehameha Hwy. ☎ 808/293–8811 ⊕ www.turtlebayresort. com) with more than 12 mi of trails and oceanside pathways on this 880-acre resort. You can pick up a trail and ocean guide for a self-guided tour of the 5 mi of coastline and its exotic plants and trees.

Guided Hikes

Hawaiʻi Nature Center. A good choice for families, the center in upper Makīkī Valley conducts a number of programs for both adults and children. There are guided hikes into tropical settings that reveal hidden waterfalls and protected forest reserves. ✉ *2131 Makīkī Heights Dr., Makīkī Heights 96822* ☎ *808/955–0100.*

Oʻahu Nature Tours. Guides explain the native flora and fauna that is your companion on glorious sunrise, hidden waterfall, mountain forest, rain

Continued on page 122

HAWAI'I'S PLANTS 101

Hawai'i is a bounty of rainbow colored flowers and plants. The evening air is scented with their fragrance. Just look at the front yard of almost any home, travel any road, or visit any local park and you'll see a spectacular array of colored blossoms and leaves. What most visitors don't know is that the plants they are seeing are not native to Hawai'i; rather, they were introduced during the last two centuries as ornamental plants, or for timber, shade, or fruit.

Hawai'i boasts every climate on the planet, excluding the two most extreme: arctic tundra and arid desert. The Islands have wine-growing regions, cactus-speckled ranchlands, icy mountaintops, and the rainiest forests on earth.

Plants introduced from around the world thrive here. The lush lowland valleys along the windward coasts are predominantly populated by non-native trees including yellow- and red-fruited **guava**, silvery leafed **kukui**, and orange flowered **tulip trees**.

The colorful **plumeria flower**, very fragrant and commonly used in lei making, and the giant multicolored **hibiscus flower**, are both used by many women as hair adornments, and are two of the most common plants found around homes and hotels. The umbrella-like **monkeypod tree** from Central America provides shade in many of Hawai'i's parks including Kapi'olani Park in Honolulu. Hawai'i's largest tree, found in Lahaina, Maui, is a giant **banyan tree**. It's canopy and massive support roots cover several acres. The native **o'hia tree**, with it's brilliant red brush like flowers, and the **hapu'u**, a giant tree fern, are common in Hawai'i's forests and are also used ornamentally in gardens and around homes.

Bougainvillea

Guava

Monkeypod Tree

Banyan Tree

O'hia Lehua

Tulip Tree

Plumeria

Pandanus

Hibiscus

Anthurium

Kukui Tree

Hapu'u Okina

DID YOU KNOW?

Over 2,200 plant species are found in the Hawaiian Islands, but only about 1,000 are native. Of these, 282 are so rare, they are endangered. Hawai'i's endemic plants evolved from ancestral seeds arriving on the islands over thousands of years as baggage on birds, floating on ocean currents, or drifting on winds from continents thousands of miles away. Once here, these plants evolved in isolation creating many new species known nowhere else in the world.

forest, and volcanic walking tours. ☎ 808/924–2473 ⊕ *www. oahunaturetours.com.*

HORSEBACK RIDING

★ **Happy Trails Hawai'i.** Take a guided horseback ride through the verdant Waimea Valley on the North Shore along trails that offer panoramic views from Ka'ena Point to the famous surfing spots. Rates for a 90-minute trail ride begin at $49. ⊠ *1 mi mauka up Pupakea Rd. on right, Pupakea* ☎ 808/638–7433.

Kualoa Ranch. This ranch across from Kualoa Beach Park on the Windward side leads trail rides in the Ka'a'awa Valley. Rates for a one-hour trail ride begin at $47. Kualoa has other activities such as windsurfing, jet skiing, all-terrain-vehicle trail rides, and children's activities, which may be combined for half- or full-day package rates. ⊠ *49-560 Kamehameha Hwy., Ka'a'awa* ☎ 808/237–8515 ⊕ *www.kualoa.com.*

Turtle Bay Stables. This is the only spot on the Island where you can take the horses on the beach. The stables here are part of the North Shore resort, but can be utilized by nonguests. The sunset ride is a definite must if you are a friend of our four-legged friends. Rates for a 45-minute trail ride begin at $45. ⊠ *4 mi north of Kahuku in the Turtle Bay Resort* ☎ 808/293–8811.

JOGGING

The "Honolulu Walking Map" and "The Fitness Fun Map" are free from the **Hawai'i State Department of Health Community Resources Section** (⌂ 1250 Punchbowl St., Room 217, Honolulu ☎ 808/586–4661). These list more than two-dozen routes and suggested itineraries. If you're looking for jogging companions, show up for the free **Honolulu Marathon Clinic,** which starts at the Kapi'olani Bandstand from March through November, Sunday at 7:30 AM.

In Honolulu, the most popular places to jog are the two parks, **Kapi'olani** and **Ala Moana,** at either end of Waikīkī. In both cases, the loop around the park is just under 2 mi. You can run a 4½-mi ring around **Diamond Head crater,** past scenic views, luxurious homes, and herds of other joggers.

> ## HONOLULU MARATHON
>
> The Honolulu Marathon is a thrilling event to watch as well as to participate in. Join the throngs who cheer at the finish line at Kapi'olani Park as internationally famous and local runners tackle the 26.2-mi challenge. It's held on the second Sunday in December and is sponsored by the **Honolulu Marathon Association** (☎ 808/ 734–7200 ⊕ www. honolulumarathon.org).

Once you leave Honolulu, it gets trickier to find places to jog that are scenic as well as safe. It's best to stick to the well-traveled routes, or ask the experienced folks at the **Running Room** (⊠ 819 Kapahulu Ave., Kapahulu, Honolulu ☎ 808/737–2422) for advice.

TENNIS

O'ahu has 181 public tennis courts that are free and open for play on a first-come, first-served basis; you're limited to 45 minutes of court time if others are waiting to play. A complete listing is free of charge from the **Department of Parks and Recreation** (✉ Tennis Unit, 650 S. King St., Honolulu 96813 ☎ 808/971–7150 ⊕ www.co.honolulu.hi.us).

Kapi'olani Park, on the Diamond Head end of Waikīkī, has two tennis locations. The **Diamond Head Tennis Center** (✉ 3908 Pākī Ave. ☎ 808/971–7150), near Kapi'olani Park, has nine courts open to the public. There are more than a dozen courts for play at **Kapi'olani Tennis Courts** (✉ 2748 Kalākaua Ave. ☎ 808/971–2510). The closest public courts to the 'ewa end of Waikīkī are in **Ala Moana Park** (✉ Ala Moana Blvd. ☎ 808/592–7031).

The **Pacific Beach Hotel** (✉ 2490 Kalākaua Ave., Waikīkī ☎ 808/922–1233) has rooftop tennis courts that are open to nonguests for a fee.

Forty-five minutes from Waikīkī, on O'ahu's 'Ewa Plain, are two championship tennis courts at the **Hawai'i Prince Golf Club** (✉ 91-1200 Ft. Weaver Rd., 'Ewa Beach ☎ 808/944–4567); shuttle service is available from the Hawai'i Prince Hotel Waikīkī for hotel guests.

5

VOLLEYBALL

There are sand volleyball courts in Waikīkī near Fort DeRussy. They are open to the public, so talent levels vary. However, with a winner-plays-on policy, you won't be disappointed with the level as the day progresses. For more advanced play, there is an area at Queen's Beach, but you have to bring your own nets, which leads to a little more court possessiveness. But this is the area where you will find the college kids and pros hitting it while they are in town.

ON THE SIDELINES

Volleyball is an extremely popular spectator sport on the Islands, and no wonder. Both the men's and women's teams of the **University of Hawai'i** have blasted to a number-one ranking in years past. Crowded, noisy, and exciting home games are played from September through December (women's) and from January through April (men's) in the university's 10,000-seat Stan Sheriff Arena. ☎ 808/956–4481 💲 $8.

Shops & Spas

Hot stone massage

WORD OF MOUTH

"We decided to hit the Aloha Swap Meet at Aloha Stadium . . . by the end of the morning, we had so much stuff that I bought a large Hawaiian print suitcase ($28) to carry it all home in!"

—beachgirl86

"Don't get me wrong, I adore Mr. Makai, but there is a certain unrestrained exuberant freedom in shopping alone . . . especially someplace like Chinatown, Honolulu."

—makai1

By Katherine
Nichols

EASTERN AND WESTERN TRADITIONS MEET on O'ahu, where savvy shoppers find luxury goods at high-end malls and scout tiny boutiques and galleries filled with pottery, blown glass, woodwork, and Hawaiian print clothing by local artists. Exploring downtown Honolulu, Kailua on the Windward side, and the North Shore often yields the most original merchandise. Some of these small stores also carry imported clothes and gifts from around the world—a reminder that, on this island half-way between Asia and the United States, shopping is a multicultural experience.

This blend of cultures is pervasive in the wide selection of spas as well. Hawaiian lomi lomi and hot stone massages are as omnipresent as the orchid and plumeria flowers decorating every treatment room. There is a spiritual element to the lomi lomi that calms the soul while muscles release tension. During a hot stone massage, smooth rocks, taken from the earth with permission from Pele, the goddess of volcanoes, are heated and placed at focal points on the body. Others are covered in oil and rubbed over tired limbs, feeling like powerful fingers. For an alternative, refresh skin with mango scrubs so fragrant they seem edible. Savor the unusual sensation of bamboo tapped against the arches of the feet. Indulge in a scalp massage that makes the entire body tingle. Day spas provide additional options to the self-indulgent services offered in almost every major hotel on the island.

SHOPPING IN WAIKĪKĪ

Most hotels and shops are clustered along a relatively short strip in Waikīkī, which can be convenient or overwhelming, depending on one's sensibilities. Clothing, jewelry, and handbags from Europe's top designers sit across the street from the International Marketplace, a conglomeration of booths reminiscent of New York City's Canal Street—with a tropical flair. ■ TIP➜ **It's possible to find interesting items at reasonable prices in Waikīkī, but shoppers have to be willing to search beyond the $4,000 purses and the tacky wooden tikis to find innovation and quality.**

Shopping Centers

DFS Galleria Waikīkī. Hermès, Cartier, and Calvin Klein are among the shops at this enclosed mall, as well as Hawai'i's largest beauty and cosmetic store. An exclusive boutique floor caters to duty-free shoppers only. Amusing and authentic Hawaiian-style shell necklaces, soaps, and printed wraps are rewards for anyone willing to wade through the pervasive tourist schlock along the Waikīkī Walk, an area of fashions, arts and crafts, and gifts. The Kālia Grill and Starbucks offer a respite for weary shoppers. ⊠ *Kalākaua and Royal Hawaiian Aves., Waikīkī* ☎ 808/931–2655.

King Kalākaua Plaza. Banana Republic and Niketown—both two stories high and stocked with the latest fashions—anchor the King Kalākaua Plaza. ⊠ *2080 Kalākaua Ave., Waikīkī* ☎ 808/955–2878.

King's Village. It looks like a Hollywood stage set of monarchy-era Honolulu, complete with a changing-of-the-guard ceremony every evening at 6:15; shops include Hawaiian Island Creations Jewelry, Swim City USA Swimwear, and Island Motor Sports. ✉ *131 Ka'iulani Ave., Waikīkī* ☎ *808/926–7890.*

Royal Hawaiian Shopping Center. Completely renovated in 2006 with a more open and inviting facade, this three-block-long center may still be in flux in 2007. The final tenant mix has more than 100 stores, including Hawaiian Heirloom Jewelry Collection by Philip Rickard, which also has a museum with Victorian pieces. Bike buffs can check out the Harley-Davidson Motor Clothes and Collectibles Boutique, and the Ukulele House may inspire musicians to learn a new instrument. There are restaurants and even a post office. ✉ *2201 Kalākaua Ave., Waikīkī* ☎ *808/922–0588* ⊕ *www.shopwaikiki.com.*

2100 Kalākaua. Tenants of this elegant, town-house-style center include Chanel, Coach, Tiffany & Co., Yves Saint Laurent, Gucci, and Tod's. ✉ *2100 Kalākaua Ave., Waikīkī* ☎ *808/550–4449* ⊕ *www. 2100kalakaua.com.*

Waikīkī Shopping Plaza. This five-floor shopping center is across the street from the Royal Hawaiian Shopping Center. Walden Books, Guess, Clio Blue jewelers, and Tanaka of Tokyo Restaurant are some of its 50 shops and restaurants. ✉ *2270 Kalākaua Ave., Waikīkī* ☎ *808/923–1191.*

Waikīkī Town Center. Free hula shows liven up this open-air complex on Monday, Wednesday, Friday, and Saturday at 7 PM. Shops carry everything from fashions to jewelry. ✉ *2301 Kūhiō Ave., Waikīkī* ☎ *808/ 922–2724.*

Specialty Shops

Books
Bestsellers. This shop in the Hilton's Rainbow Bazaar is a branch of the local independent bookstore chain. They stock novelty Hawai'i memorabilia as well as books on Hawaiian history, local maps and travel guides, and Hawaiian music. ✉ *Hilton Hawaiian Village Beach Resort and Spa, 2005 Kālia Rd. Waikīkī* ☎ *808/953–2378.*

Boutiques
Vera Wang Boutique at Halekūlani. A broad range of luxury goods, from ready-to-wear and accessories to china and crystal, reflects Vera Wang's design and style sensibilities. This lifestyle-themed shop also stocks Wang's new jewelry line, stylish eyewear, fragrances, lingerie, and tableware. ✉ *Halekūlani, 2199 Kālia Rd.* ☎ *808/923–2311* ⊕ *www.halekulani.com.*

Clothing
Cinnamon Girl. Adorable matching mother/daughter dresses in subtle tropical prints, flower-adorned rubber slippers, and fun accessories. Shops also located in Ala Moana Center and Ward Warehouse. ✉ *Sheraton*

Moana Surfrider, 2365 Kalākaua Ave. ☎ *808/922–5536* ⊕ *www. cinnamongirl.com.*

Moonbow Tropics. An elegant selection of silk Tommy Bahama Aloha shirts, as well as tropical styles for women. ⊠ *Sheraton Moana Surfrider 2365 Kalākaua Ave. Waikīkī* ☎ *808/924–1496* ⊕ *www.moonbowtropics.com.*

Newt in the Village. Newt is known for Panama hats and tropical sportswear. ⊠ *Hilton Hawaiian Village Beach Resort and Spa, 2005 Kālia Rd.* ☎ *808/949–4321.*

Reyn's. Reyn's is a good place to buy the aloha print fashions residents wear. This company manufacturers its own label in the islands, has 13 locations statewide, and offers styles for men, women, and children. ⊠ *Sheraton Waikīkī, 2255 Kalākaua Ave., Waikīkī* ☎ *808/923–0331.*

Gifts

Gallery Tokusa. *Netsuke* is a toggle used to fasten small containers to obi belts on a kimono. Gallery Tokusa specializes in intricately carved netsuke, both antique and contemporary, and one-of-a-kind necklaces. ⊠ *Halekūlani, 2199 Kālia Rd., Waikīkī* ☎ *808/923–2311.*

Noeha Gallery. A smaller version of the stores located in Ward Center and Ward Warehouse carries koa bowls and boxes, ceramics, and art glass. ⊠ *Sheraton Moana Surfrider, 2365 Kalākaua Ave.* ☎ *808/923-6644* ⊕ *www.noheagallery.com.*

Norma Kress Gallery. Emerging native Hawaiian and Pacific Island artists show their work at this hotel gallery, highlighted with pottery, sculpture, paintings, drawings, and photography. ⊠ *Hawai'i Prince Hotel, 100 Holomana St., Waikīkī* ☎ *808/952–4761.*

★ **Sand People.** This little shop stocks easy-to-carry gifts, such as fish-shaped Christmas ornaments, Hawaiian-style notepads, charms in the shape of flip-flops (known locally as "slippers"), soaps, and ceramic clocks. Also located in Kailua. ⊠ *Sheraton Moana Surfrider, 2369 Kalākaua, Waikīkī* ☎ *808/924–6773* ⊕ *www.sandpeople.com.*

Jewelry

Bernard Hurtig's. Antique jade and 18-karat gold are the specialties at this fine jeweler. ⊠ *Hilton Hawaiian Village Ali'i Tower, 2005 Kālia Rd., Waikīkī* ☎ *808/947–9399.*

Philip Rickard. The heirloom design collection of this famed jeweler features custom Hawaiian wedding jewelry. ⊠ *Royal Hawaiian Shopping Center, 2201 Kalākaua Ave., Waikīkī* ☎ *808/924–7972.*

Surf Shops & Sporting Goods

Hawaii Five-O. Beach rentals add to a wide array of T-shirts, footwear, bathing suits, and accessories in the store named after the locally-filmed television show that ran from 1968 to 1980. ⊠ *Aston Waikiki Beach Hotel, 2570 Kalākaua Ave.* ☎ *808/923–1243.*

Local Motion. If you plan on surfing or just want to look like a surfer, check out this outfitter's flagship store. They have it all—from surfboards to surf wear. ⊠ *1958 Kalākaua Ave., Waikīkī* ☎ *808/979–7873.*

SHOPPING IN DOWNTOWN HONOLULU & CHINATOWN

Shoppers who know where to look in Honolulu will find everything from designer merchandise to unusual Asian imports.

Three malls in Honolulu provide a combination of the standard department stores and interesting shops showcasing original paintings and woodwork from local artists and craftsmen.

Downtown shopping is an entirely different, constantly changing experience. Focus on the small galleries—which are earning the area a strong reputation for its arts and culture renaissance—and the burgeoning array of hip, home-decor stores tucked between ethnic restaurants. ■ TIP➜ **Don't miss the festive atmosphere on the first Friday of every month, when stores, restaurants, and galleries stay open from 5 PM to 9 PM for the "Downtown Gallery Walk."**

Chinatown offers the typical mix of the tacky and unique, depending on individual taste, but it is an experience not to be missed. The vital, bright colors of fresh fruits and vegetables blend with the distinct scent of recently killed pigs and poultry. Tucked in between are authentic shops with Asian silk clothing at reasonable prices. The bustling, ethnic atmosphere adds to the excitement. Those hungry for a local experience should at least walk through the area, even without plans to purchase questionable herbs from glass jars lining the shelves.

6

TROPICAL FLOWERS & FRUIT

Bring home fresh pineapple, papaya, or coconut to share with friends and family. Orchids also will brighten your home and remind you of your trip to the Islands. By law, all fresh-fruit and plant products must be inspected by the Department of Agriculture before export. Be sure to inquire at the shop about the Department of Agriculture rules so a surprise confiscation doesn't spoil your departure. In most cases, shipping to your home is best.

Kawamoto Nursery. Kawamoto grows all flowers on its three-acre orchid farm near downtown Honolulu. Their specialty is the Cattleylea, a favorite for Mother's day, and they have decades of experience shipping temperamental orchids to the Mainland. ⊠ *2630 Waiomao Rd.* ☎ *808/732–5808* ⊕ *www.kawamotoorchids.com.*

Tropical Fruits Distributors of Hawai'i. Avoid the hassle of airport inspections. This company specializes in packing inspected pineapple and papaya; they will deliver to your hotel and to the airport check-in counter, or ship to the mainland United States and Canada. Think about ordering on the Web, unless you are planning a trip to the North Shore. ⌁ *64-1551 Kamehameha Hwy. 808/847–3234 Ilalo St., Wahiawa* ☎ *800/697–9100* ⊕ *www.dolefruithawaii.com.*

Shopping Centers

Getting to the Ala Moana shopping centers from Waikīkī is quick and inexpensive thanks to **TheBus** and the **Waikīkī Trolley.**

Ala Moana Shopping Center. One of the nation's largest open-air malls is five minutes from Waikīkī by bus. Designer shops in residence include Gucci, Louis Vuitton, Gianni Versace, and Emporio Armani. All of Hawai'i's major department stores are here, including Neiman Marcus, Sears, and Macy's. More than 240 stores and 60 restaurants make up this 50-acre complex. One of the most interesting shops is Shanghai Tang. First opened in Hong Kong, the store imports silks and other fine fabrics, and upholds the tradition of old-style Shanghai tailoring. To get to the mall from Waikīkī, catch TheBus lines 8, 19, or 20; a one-way ride is $2. Or hop aboard the Waikīkī Trolley's pink line, which comes through the area every half-hour. ⊠ *1450 Ala Moana Blvd., Ala Moana* ☎ *808/955–9517 special events and shuttle service.*

Aloha Tower Marketplace. Billing itself as a festival marketplace, Aloha Tower cozies up to Honolulu Harbor. Along with restaurants and entertainment venues, it has 80 shops and kiosks selling mostly visitor-oriented merchandise, from expensive sunglasses to exceptional local artwork to souvenir refrigerator magnets. Don't miss the aloha shirts and fancy hats for dogs at Pet Gear, and the curious mix of furniture, stationery, and clothing in Urban Rejuvenation. To get there from Waikīkī take the E-Transit Bus, which goes along TheBus routes every 15 minutes. ⊠ *1 Aloha Tower Dr., at Piers 8, 9, and 10, Downtown Honolulu* ☎ *808/566–2337* ⊕ *www.alohatower.com.*

Ward Centers. Heading west from Waikīkī toward Downtown Honolulu, you'll run into a section of town with five distinct shopping-complex areas; there are more than 120 specialty shops and 20 restaurants here. The Entertainment Complex features 16 movie theaters. ■ **TIP➔ A "shopping concierge" can assist you in navigating your way through the center, which spans four city blocks.** For distinctive Hawaiian gift stores, visit Nohea Gallery and Native Books/Na Mea Hawaii, carrying quality work from Hawai'i artists, including mu'umu'u, lauhala products, and unparalleled Niihau shell necklaces. Island Soap and Candle Works (808/591–0533) makes all of its candles and soaps on-site with Hawaiian flower scents. Take TheBus routes 19 or 20; fare is $2 one way. Or follow The Waikīkī Trolley yellow line, which comes through the area every 45 minutes. ⊠ *1050–1200 Ala Moana Blvd., Ala Moana.*

Specialty Shops

Books

Bestsellers. Hawai'i's largest independent bookstore has its flagship shop in Downtown Honolulu on Bishop Square. They carry books by both local and national authors. There are also locations of Bestsellers at the Honolulu International Airport and in Waikīkī at the Hilton Hawaiian Village. ⊠ *1001 Bishop St., Downtown Honolulu* ☎ *808/528–2378.*

Borders Books. Borders stocks over 200 books in its Hawaiian section; learn about Hawaiian plants, hula, or surfing. This two-story location has books, music, movies, and a café. ⊠ *Ward Centre, 1200 Ala Moana Blvd.* ☎ *808/591–8995.*

⭐ **Native Books/Na Mea Hawai'i.** In addition to clothing for adults and children and unusual artwork such as Niihau shell necklaces, this boutique's book selection covers Hawaiian history and langauge, and offers children's books set in the Islands. ⊠ *Ward Warehouse, 1050 Ala Moana Blvd.* ☎ *808/596–8885.*

> **KOA KEEPSAKES**
>
> Items handcrafted from native Hawaiian wood make beautiful gifts. Koa and milo have a distinct color and grain. The scarcity of koa forests makes the wood extremely valuable. That's why you'll notice a large price gap between koa wood veneer products and the real thing.

Clothing

⭐ **Anne Namba Designs.** Anne Namba brings the beauty of classic kimonos to contemporary fashions. In addition to women's apparel, she's also designed a men's line and a wedding couture line. ⊠ *324 Kamani St., Downtown Honolulu* ☎ *808/589–1135.*

Hilo Hattie. Busloads of visitors pour in through the front doors of the world's largest manufacturer of Hawaiian and tropical aloha wear. Once shunned by Honolulu residents for its three-shades-too-bright tourist-wear, it has become a favorite source for island gifts, macadamia nut and chocolate packages, and clothing for elegant island functions. Free shuttle service is available from Waikīkī. ⊠ *700 N. Nimitz Hwy., Iwilei* ☎ *808/535–6500.*

Locals Only. This shop carries an exclusive line of rayon aloha shirts in vintage-style patterns by Pineapple Juice and Locals Only sportswear. ⊠ *Ala Moana Shopping Center, Ala Moana* ☎ *808/942–1555.*

Reyn's. Reyn's is a good place to buy the aloha print fashions residents wear. Look for the limited-edition Christmas shirt, a collector's item manufactured each holiday season. Reyn's has 13 locations statewide and offers styles for men, women, and children. ⊠ *Ala Moana Shopping Center, 1450 Ala Moana Blvd., Ala Moana* ☎ *808/949–5929* ⊠ *Kāhala Mall, 4211 Wai'alae Ave., Kāhala* ☎ *808/737–8313.*

⭐ **Shanghai Tang.** First opened in Hong Kong, Shanghai Tang now has its 11th branch at Ala Moana. An emphasis on workmanship and the luxury of fine fabrics upholds the tradition of old-Shanghai tailoring. They do custom work for men, women, and children. ⊠ *Ala Moana Shopping Center, Ala Moana* ☎ *808/942–9800.*

Food

Hilo Hattie (⇨ Clothing, *above*) is another source for packaged food items, including guava jam, macadamia nut cookies and chocolates, coconut-macadamia coffee, pineapples, and anthurium and gift baskets stocked with island specialty snacks.

6

Honolulu Chocolate Company. To really impress those back home, pick up a box of gourmet chocolates here. They dip the flavors of Hawai'i, from Kona coffee to macadamia nuts, in fine chocolate. ✉ *Ward Centre, 1200 Ala Moana Blvd., Ala Moana* ☎ *808/591–2997.*

Longs Drugs. For gift items in bulk, try one of the many outposts of Longs, the perfect place to stock up on chocolate covered macadamia nuts—at reasonable prices—to carry home. ✉ *Ala Moana Shopping Center, 1450 Ala Moana Blvd., 2nd level, Ala Moana* ☎ *808/941–4433* ✉ *Kāhala Mall, 4211 Wai'alae Ave., Kāhala* ☎ *808/732–0784.*

Hawaiian Arts & Crafts

Hawaiian Quilt Collection. Traditional island comforters, wall hangings, pillows, and other Hawaiian-print quilt items are the specialty here. ✉ *Ala Moana Center, 1450 Ala Moana Blvd., Ala Moana* ☎ *808/946–2233.*

> ### GOOD ENOUGH TO EAT
>
> You don't necessarily have to buy a whole pineapple to enjoy Hawai'i's fruit flavors back home. Jams are easy to pack and don't spoil. They come in flavors such as pohā, passion fruit, and guava. Coffee is another option. Kona- and O'ahu-grown Waialua coffee beans have an international following. There are also dried-food products such as saimin, haupia, and teriyaki barbecue sauce. All kinds of cookies are available, as well as exotic teas, drink mixes, and pancake syrups. And don't forget the macadamia nuts, from plain to chocolate-covered and brittled.

Indich Collection. Bring home some aloha you can sink your bare feet into. Designs from this exclusive Hawaiian rug collection depict Hawaiian petroglyphs, banana leafs, and heliconia. ✉ *Gentry Pacific Design Center, 560 N. Nimitz Hwy., Downtown Honolulu* ☎ *808/524–7769.*

Louis Pohl Gallery. Modern works from some of Hawai'i's finest artists. ✉ *1111 Nu'uanu Ave., Downtown Honolulu* ☎ *808/521–1812* ⊕ *www. louispohlgallery.com.*

My Little Secret. The word is out that this is a wonderful selection of Hawaiian arts, crafts, and children's toys. ✉ *Ward Warehouse, 1050 Ala Moana Blvd., Ala Moana* ☎ *808/596–2990.*

Na Hoku. If you look at the wrists of kama'aina women, you are apt to see Hawaiian heirloom bracelets fashioned in either gold or silver in a number of island-inspired designs. Na Hoku sells jewelry in designs, such as these bracelets, that capture the heart of the Hawaiian lifestyle in all its elegant diversity. ✉ *Ala Moana Center, 1450 Ala Moana Blvd., Ala Moana* ☎ *808/946–2100.*

★ **Nohea Gallery.** These shops are really galleries representing over 450 artists who specialize in koa furniture, bowls, and boxes, as well as art glass and ceramics. Original paintings and prints—all with an island theme—add to the selection. They also carry unique hand-made Hawaiian jewelry with ti leaf, maile, and coconut-weave designs. ■ TIP➔ **The koa photo albums in these stores are easy to carry home and make wonderful gifts.** ✉ *Ward Warehouse, 1050 Ala Moana Blvd., Ala Moana* ☎ *808/596–*

0074 ✉ *Ward Center, 1200 Ala Moana Blvd., Ala Moana* ☎ *808/ 591–9001.*

Housewares

INTO. The newest and hippest home decor shop downtown features decorative pillows and Escama handbags and messenger bags. These products are hand-crocheted in Brazil using recycled aluminum tabs. The inventory is always innovative and fresh here. ✉ *40 N. Hotel St., Downtown Honolulu* ☎ *808/536–2211.*

Robyn Buntin Galleries. Chinese nephrite-jade carvings, Japanese lacquer and screens, and Buddhist sculptures are among the international pieces displayed here. ✉ *820 S. Beretania St., Downtown Honolulu* ☎ *808/ 545–5572.*

Leis

⇨ All About Leis, *below.*

Sporting Goods

Boca Hawai'i. This triathlon shop near the Bike Factory offers training gear, racing and mountain bike rentals ($25 per day with a 2-day minimum. $125 per week.), yoga and Spinning classes, and nutritional products. ■ **TIP→ Inquire directly about the latest schedule of fitness and strength sessions at the store, which is owned and operated by top athletes.** ✉ *330 Cooke St., Kaka'ako* ☎ *808/591–9839.*

SHOPPING ELSEWHERE IN HONOLULU

Honolulu offers two distinct types of shopping experiences for visitors: vast malls with the customary department stores, and tiny boutiques with specialty items. Possibilities swarm throughout Honolulu, and a bit of scouting is usually required to get past the items you'll find in your own home town. Industrious bargain hunters can detect the perfect gift in the sale bin of a slightly hidden store at every mall.

Though the areas and shops listed are spread out and often not within walking distance of Waikīkī, access is simple with a rental car and a good map, or industrious use of Honolulu's excellent bus system (www. thebus.org). Since street names are difficult to pronounce and sometimes just as hard to recognize, ask the hotel concierge for landmarks and tips in navigating neighborhoods off the beaten path.

McCully/Mō'ili'ili & the University Area

This neighborhood, while considered separate from the University of Hawai'i's Manoa campus, has a distinct college-town feel. About 3 mi from Waikīkī, the area is extremely tired in some sections and needs updating. However, a look past the exterior reveals a haven for excellent family-owned restaurants, health food stores, and shops that have a loyal following in the residential community.

Continued on page 136

ALL ABOUT LEIS

Leis brighten every occasion in Hawai'i, from birthdays to bar mitzvahs to baptisms. Creative artisans weave nature's bounty—flowers, ferns, vines, and seeds—into gorgeous creations that convey an array of heartfelt messages: "Welcome," "Congratulations," "Good luck," "Farewell," "Thank you," "I love you." When it's difficult to find the right words, a lei expresses exactly the right sentiments.

WHERE TO BUY THE BEST LEIS

The best selections and prices are at the lei shops in Honolulu's Chinatown. Three favorites are: **Cindy's Lei & Flower Shop** (1034 Maunakea St., 808/536-6538); **Lin's Lei Shop** (1017-A Maunakea St., 808/537-4112); and **Lita's Leis** (59 N. Beretania St., 808/521-9065). In Mō'ili'ili, a 10-minute drive from Waikīkī, check out **Flowers by Jr., Lou & T** (2652 S. King St., 808/941-2022); and **Rudy's Flowers** (2357 S. Beretania St., 808/944-8844).

LEI ETIQUETTE

■ To wear a closed lei, drape it over your shoulders, half in front and half in back. Open leis are worn around the neck, with the ends draped over the front in equal lengths.

■ Pīkake, ginger, and other sweet, delicate blossoms are "feminine" leis. Men opt for cigar, crown flower, and carnation, which are sturdier and don't emit as much fragrance.

■ Leis are always presented with a kiss, a custom that supposedly dates back to World War II when a hula dancer fancied an officer at a U.S.O. show. Taking a dare from members of her troupe, she took off her lei, placed it around his neck, and kissed him on the cheek.

■ You shouldn't wear a lei before you give it to someone else. Hawaiians believe the lei absorbs your *mana* (spirit); if you give your lei away, you'll be giving away part of your essence.

ORCHID

Growing wild on every continent except Antarctica, orchids—which range in color from yellow to green to purple—comprise the largest family of plants in the world. There are more than 20,000 species of orchids, but only three are native to Hawai'i—and they are very rare. The pretty lavender vanda you see hanging by the dozens at local lei stands has probably been imported from Thailand.

MAILE

Maile, an endemic twining vine with a heady aroma, is sacred to Laka, goddess of the hula. In ancient times, dancers wore maile and decorated hula altars with it to honor Laka. Today, "open" maile leis usually are given to men. Instead of ribbon, interwoven lengths of maile are used at dedications of new businesses. The maile is untied, never snipped, for doing so would symbolically "cut" the company's success.

'ILIMA

Designated by Hawai'i's Territorial Legislature in 1923 as the official flower of the island of O'ahu, the golden 'ilima is so delicate it lasts for just a day. Five to seven hundred blossoms are needed to make one garland. Queen Emma, wife of King Kamehameha IV, preferred 'ilima over all other leis, which may have led to the incorrect belief that they were reserved only for royalty.

PLUMERIA

This ubiquitous flower is named after Charles Plumier, the noted French botanist who discovered it in Central America in the late 1600s. Plumeria ranks among the most popular leis in Hawai'i because it's fragrant, hardy, plentiful, inexpensive, and requires very little care. Although yellow is the most common color, you'll also find plumeria leis in shades of pink, red, orange, and "rainbow" blends.

PĪKAKE

Favored for its fragile beauty and sweet scent, pīkake was introduced from India. In lieu of pearls, many brides in Hawai'i adorn themselves with long, multiple strands of white pīkake. Princess Kaiulani enjoyed showing guests her beloved pīkake and peacocks at Āinahau, her Waikīkī home. Interestingly, pīkake is the Hawaiian word for both the bird and the blossom.

KUKUI

The kukui (candlenut) is Hawai'i's state tree. Early Hawaiians strung kukui nuts (which are quite oily) together and burned them for light; mixed burned nuts with oil to make an indelible dye; and mashed roasted nuts to consume as a laxative. Kukui nut leis may not have been made until after Western contact, when the Hawaiians saw black beads from Europe and wanted to imitate them.

6

ALL ABOUT LEIS

Hula Supply Center. This family-run business has been around since 1946 and sells everything from hand-crafted Hawaiian implements to lauhala bags, T-shirts, and Hawaiian music. Look for lei that will last a lifetime, made from silk, shell, or nuts. Or splurge for your own hula costume. ✉ *2346 S. King St., Mōʻiliʻili* ☎ *808/941–5379.*

Maui Divers Design Center. For a look into the harvesting and design of coral and black pearl jewelry, visit this shop near the Ala Moana Shopping Center. ✉ *1520 Liona St., Mōʻiliʻili* ☎ *808/946–7979.*

Uyeda Shoe Store. They must be doing something right if they've been in business since 1915. Specializing in sandals and comfort shoes, it's the type of store rarely found in a mall. ✉ *2615 S. King St., Mōʻiliʻili* ☎ *808/941–1331.*

Kapahulu

Kapahulu begins at the Diamond Head end of Waikīkī and continues up to the H-1 freeway. Shops and restaurants are located primarily on Kapahulu Avenue, which like many older neighborhoods, should not be judged at first glance. It is full of variety.

Bailey's Antiques & Aloha Shirts. Vintage aloha shirts are the specialty at this kitschy store. Prices start at $3.99 for the 10,000 shirts in stock, and the tight space and musty smell are part of the thrift-shop atmosphere. ■ TIP➜ Antique hunters can also buy old-fashioned postcards, authentic military clothing, funky hats, and denim jeans from the 1950s. ✉ *517 Kapahulu Ave., Kapahulu* ☎ *808/734–7628.*

Downing Hawaii. Look for old-style Birdwell surf trunks here, along with popular labels such as Quiksilver, which supplement Downing's own line of surf wear. ✉ *3021 Waialae Ave., Kaimuki* ☎ *808/737–9696.*

Surf Shops & Sporting Goods

Go Bananas. Staffers make sure that you rent the appropriate kayak for your abilities, and they also outfit the rental car with soft racks to transport it to the beach. Full-day rates begin at $30 for single kayaks, and $42 for doubles. The store also carries clothing and kayaking accessories. ✉ *799 Kapahulu Ave., Kapahulu* ☎ *808/737–9514.*

Hawaiian Fire. Some of the best-looking firefighters in Honolulu teach surf lessons out of this tiny shop; they transport beginners to the less crowded west side of the island. The store also sells T-shirts and backpacks. ✉ *3318 Campbell Ave., Kapahulu* ☎ *808/737–3473.*

Island Paddler. Fashionable beach footwear, clothing, bathing suits, fun beach bags, and rash guards supplement a huge selection of canoe paddles. ■ TIP➜ Check out the wooden steering paddles: they become works of art when mounted on the wall at home. ✉ *716 Kapahulu Ave., Kapahulu* ☎ *808/737–4854.*

Island Triathlon & Bike. Another source for bikes, sports bathing suits, water bottles, and active clothing. However, they don't rent bicycles. ✉ *569 Kapahulu Ave., Kapahulu* ☎ *808/732–7227.*

Snorkel Bob's. This is a good place to seek advice about the best snorkel conditions, which vary considerably with the season. The company, popular throughout the Islands, sells or rents necessary gear, including fins, snorkels, wetsuits, and beach chairs, and even schedules activities with other suppliers. ✉ *700 Kapahulu Ave., Kapahulu* 🕾 *808/735–7944.*

Kāhala & Hawai'i Kai

★ **Island Treasures.** Local residents come here to shop for gifts that are both unique and within reach of almost every budget, ranging in price from $1 to $5,000. Located next to Zippy's and overlooking the ocean, the store has handbags, toys, jewelry, home accessories, soaps and lotions, and locally-made original artwork. Certainly the most interesting shop in Hawai'i Kai's suburban mall atmosphere, this store is also a good place to purchase CDs of some of the best Hawai'ian music. ✉ *Koko Marina Center, 7192 Kalaniana'ole Hwy., Hawai'i Kai* 🕾 *808/396–8827.*

Kāhala Mall. The upscale residential neighborhood of Kāhala, near the slopes of Diamond Head, is 10 minutes by car from Waikīkī. The only shopping of note in the area is located at the indoor mall, which has 90 stores, including Macy's, Gap, Reyn's Aloha Wear, and Barnes & Noble. Don't miss fashionable boutiques such as **Ohelo Road** (🕾 808/735–5525), where contemporary clothing for all occasions fills the racks. Eight **movie theaters** (🕾 808/733–6233) provide post-shopping entertainment. ✉ *4211 Wai'alae Ave., Kāhala* 🕾 *808/732–7736.*

SHOPPING ON THE WINDWARD SIDE

Shopping on the Windward side is one of O'ahu's best kept secrets. A half-hour by car or about an hour on TheBus, it's definitely a shopping/activity destination. At Windward Mall in Kāne'ohe, stop by the Lomi Shop for authentic Tahitian oils and a 10-minute foot massage in the entrance built to resemble a voyaging canoe. The real treats, however, lie in the small boutiques and galleries in the heart of Kailua—the perfect

---

HAWAIIAN MUSIC

Hawai'i is the only state with its own distinctive music. There's American popular music, but it's not likely you'll see an album called "The Music of Connecticut." Inspired by the landscape and the indigenous Hawaiian culture, it draws inspiration from around the world. Country and western, reggae, and pop influence the sounds. Yet Hawaiian music manages to remain distinctly itself. Tower Records in Kāhala Mall carries most Hawaiian music artists, but small shops and boutiques often have selected the best ones for you, making choices a little easier when you're unsure of what you're buying. Don't miss Israel Kamakawiwo'ole (also known as "Bruddah Iz"), whose "Facing Future" album went platinum long after his 1997 death, Sean Na'auao, Hapa, and slack key guitar compilations for easy listening.

6

place to gather unique gifts. After shopping, enjoy the outdoors in one of the most beautiful beach towns in the world. Kailua is the best place to rent kayaks and paddle out to the Mokulua Islands with a guide, take a windsurfing lesson, or watch the expert kite boarders sailing across the bay. ■ **TIP→ Stop by Kalapawai Market in Lanikai—the only shop in Lanikai, which is right next to Kailua—for sandwiches and cold drinks and souvenirs, and finish the day relaxing on a sparsely populated white sand beach.** The surf here is minimal, making it a perfect picnic spot with the kids, but not the place to learn to ride waves. Save that for Waikīkī.

RAKU POTTERY

Raku is a style of pottery with Japanese origins. It is unique because of the hot and rapid way it's fired, and the resulting crackled look is immediately recognizable even to the untrained eye. Artists create their own glazes to yield distinct blends of colors, and raku glazes in particular are made to withstand intense thermal shock. Because these glazes are liquid glass rather than a coating of color, the hues differ from what's seen on other types of pottery.

The Balcony Gallery. Known almost exclusively to Kailua residents, this small, out-of-the-way gallery features contemporary paintings, photographs, glass, woodwork, ceramics, and jewelry from artists in the Islands. ■ **TIP→ Join them from 2 to 5 PM on the second Sunday of every month for a tour of 15 art venues in the area.** Gallery hours are limited; call before you go. ⊠ *442A Uluniu St., Kailua* ☎ *808/263–4434* ⊘ *Closed Sun.–Mon.*

Bookends. The perfect place to shop for gifts, or just take a break with the family, this bookstore feels more like a small-town library, welcoming browsers to linger for hours. The large children's section is filled with toys and books to read. ⊠ *600 Kailua Rd., Kailua* ☎ *808/261–1996.*

Fodor'sChoice ★ **Global Village.** Tucked into a tiny strip mall near Maui Tacos, this boutique features contemporary apparel for women, Hawai'ian-style children's clothing, and unusual jewelry and gifts from all over the world. Look for Kula Cushions eye pillows (made with lavender grown on Maui), coasters in the shape of flip-flops, a wooden key holder shaped like a surfboard, and placemats made from lauhala and other natural fibers, plus accessories you won't find anywhere else. ⊠ *Kailua Village Shops, 539 Kailua Rd., Kailua* ☎ *808/262–8183* ⊕ *www.globalvillagehawaii.com.*

Fodor'sChoice ★ **Jeff Chang Pottery & Fine Crafts.** With store locations downtown and in Waikīkī, Jeff Chang has become synonymous with excellent craftsmanship and originality in Raku pottery, blown glass, and koa wood. Gift ideas include petroglyph stoneware coasters, photo albums covered in Hawaiian print fabric, blown-glass penholders and business card holders, and Japanese Aeto chimes. The owners choose work from 300 different local and national artists. ⊠ *Kailua Village Shops, 539 Kailua Rd., Kailua* ☎ *808/262–4060.*

Fodor'sChoice ★ **Under a Hula Moon.** Exclusive tabletop items and Pacific home decor, such as shell wreaths, shell night lights, Hawaiian print kitchen towels, and Asian silk clothing, define this eclectic shop. ✉*Kailua Shopping Center, 600 Kailua Rd., Kailua* ☎ *808/261–4252* ⊕ *www.underahulamoon.com.*

Surf Shops & Sporting Goods

Kailua Sailboard and Kayaks Company. Beginners and experts will find everything they need here. Windsurfing lessons start at $69 for a three-hour group lesson, or $35 for a one-hour individual lesson. Transporting gear to the nearby beach is no problem with their help. ✉ *130 Kailua Rd., Kailua* ☎ *808/262–2555.*

Twogood Kayaks Hawai'i. Explore Kailua from the ocean alone or with skilled tour guides who deliver the boats right to the beach (or load them on your car, if you want to go elsewhere on the island), free of charge. Guides are trained in history, geology, and birdlife of the area. Kayak a full day with a guide for $89; this includes lunch, snorkeling gear, and transportation from Waikīkī. The shop is in an open-air market next to O'ahu Dive Center, where scuba divers can rent or buy whatever they need for a successful underwater excursion. ✉ *345 Hahani St., Kailua* ☎ *808/262–5656* ⊕ *www.twogoodkayaks.com.*

SHOPPING ON THE NORTH SHORE

6

A drive to the North Shore takes about one hour from Waikīkī, but allot a full day to explore the beaches and Hale'iwa, a burgeoning attraction that has managed to retain its surf-town charm. The occasional makeshift stand selling delicious fruit or shrimp beside the road adds character to the beach, farm, and artist colony atmosphere. Eclectic shops are the best place to find skin care products made on the North Shore, Hawai'ian music CDs, sea glass and shell mobiles, coffee grown in the Islands, and clothing items unavailable anywhere else. Be sure to chat with the owners in each shop. North Shore residents are an animated, friendly bunch with multiple talents. Stop in for coffee and the shop's owner might reveal a little about his or her passion for creating distinguished pieces of artwork.

★ **Global Creations Interiors.** Look for Hawaiian bath products, pīkake perfume, locally-made jewelry, and a carefully chosen selection of

---

CALABASH

A calabash is a wooden bowl used in ancient Polynesian societies for food and water. Hawaiians elevated it from a utilitarian necessity to a work of art. Carved from one log and hand turned on a lathe in a labor-intensive process, Hawaiian calabash is distinct from other bowls—wider at the sides and narrower at the top. Woods used include koa, kou, mango, milo, kamani, macadamia nut, and pine. The word calabash is derived from the French and Spanish words that mean gourd, or pumpkin—a reference to shape only. Available at Surf Town Coffee Roasters in Hale'iwa, Nohea Gallery at Ward Warehouse, Jeff Chang Pottery and Fine Crafts in Kailua, as well as other galleries.

Hawaiian music CDs. Fun gifts include chip-and-dip plates and spreaders shaped like 'ukuleles. ⊠ 66-079 *Kamehameha Hwy., Hale'iwa* ☎ *808/637–1780* ⊕ *www.globalcreationsinteriors.com.*

★ **The Growing Keiki.** Frequent visitors return to this store year after year. They know they'll find a fresh supply of original, hand-picked, Hawai'ian-style clothing for youngsters. ⊠ 66-051 *Kamehameha Hwy., Hale'iwa* ☎ *808/637–4544* ⊕ *www.thegrowingkeiki.com.*

Matsumoto Shave Ice. Actor Tom Hanks, sumo wrestler Konishiki, and ice skater Kristi Yamaguchi have all stopped in for a cold flavored cone at Mastumoto's. If you're going to the North Shore, it's a must to stop by this legendary shack established in 1951. On average, they produce 1,000 shave ices a day. Mastumoto's also has T-shirts and souvenirs. ⊠ 66-087 *Kamehameha Hwy., Hale'iwa* ☎ *808/637–4827* ⊕ *www. matsumotoshaveice.com.*

North Shore Marketplace. While playing on the North Shore, check out this open-air plaza that includes North Shore Custom and Design Swimwear for mix-and-match bikinis off the rack, as well as Jungle Gems, where they make almost all of the precious and semi-precious gemstone jewelry on the premises. And don't miss the Silver Moon Emporium or Outrigger Trading Company upstairs. ⊠ 66-250 *Kamehameha Hwy., Hale'iwa* ☎ *808/637–7000.*

★ **Outrigger Trading Company.** Though this shop has been in business since 1982, its upstairs location in the North Shore Marketplace often gets bypassed when it shouldn't. Look for Jam's World patchwork tablecloths with an aloha flair, shell boxes, mobiles made of ceramic fish and driftwood, stained-glass ornaments, and beach-glass wind chimes. Other novelties include hula girl and bamboo lamps and silk-screened table runners. ⊠ *North Shore Marketplace, 66-250 Kamehameha Hwy., Hale'iwa.*

Fodor'sChoice
★ **Silver Moon Emporium.** This small boutique carries everything from Brighton accessories and fashionable T-shirts to Betsy Johnson formal wear, and provides attentive yet casual personalized service. Their stock changes frequently, and there's always something wonderful on sale. No matter what your taste, you'll find something for everyday wear or special occasions. ⊠ *North Shore Marketplace, 66-250 Kamehameha Hwy., Hale'iwa* ☎ *808/637–7710.*

★ **Surf Town Coffee Roasters.** Luscious chocolate is made right there in the store, and owners Dave and JulieAnn Hoselton buy coffee beans from Kaua'i, Moloka'i, and the Big Island. Look for their own secret blend called "Dawn Patrol," with a picture of their dog on the package. The Hoseltons are also artists. She creates decorative feather *kahili* (an Hawaiian ceremonial staff), and he makes Hawaiian wooden bowls. Enjoy sipping coffee while shopping for art. ⊠ 66-470 *Kamehameha Hwy., Hale'iwa* ☎ *808/637–3000.*

Surf Shops & Sporting Goods

Surf 'N Sea. A North Shore watersports store with everything under one roof. Purchase rash guards, bathing suits, T-shirts, footwear, hats, and shorts. Rent kayaks, snorkeling or scuba gear, spears for freediving, windsurfing equipment, surfboards, and bodyboards. Experienced surfing instructors will take beginners to the small breaks on the notoriously huge (winter) or flat (summer) North Shore beaches. Warning to fishing enthusiasts: a fishing pole is the one ocean apparatus they don't carry. ✉ *62-595 Kamehameha Hwy.* ☎ *808/637–9887* ⊕ *www. surfnsea.com.*

SHOPPING FOR BARGAINS IN WEST O'AHU

Aloha Stadium Swap Meet. This thrice-weekly outdoor bazaar attracts hundreds of vendors and even more bargain hunters. Every Hawaiian souvenir imaginable can be found here, from coral shell necklaces to bikinis, as well as a variety of ethnic wares, from Chinese brocade dresses to Japanese pottery. There are also ethnic foods, silk flowers, and luggage in aloha floral prints. Shoppers must wade through the typical sprinkling of used and stolen goods to find value. Wear comfortable shoes, use sunscreen, and bring bottled water. The flea market takes place in the Aloha Stadium parking lot Wednesday and weekends from 6 to 3. Admission is 50¢. Several shuttle companies serve Aloha Stadium for the swap meet, including VIP Shuttle (☎ 808/ 839–0911); Rabbi Shuttle (☎ 808/922–4900); Reliable Shuttle (☎ 808/ 924–9292); and Hawaii Supertransit (☎ 808/841–2928). The average cost is $9 per person, round-trip. For a cheaper but slower ride, take TheBus. Check routes at www.thebus.org. ✉ *99-500 Salt Lake Blvd., 'Aiea* ☎ *808/486–6704.*

Waikele Premium Outlets. Anne Klein Factory, Donna Karan Company Store, Kenneth Cole, and Saks Fifth Avenue Outlet anchor this discount destination. You can take a shuttle to the outlets, but the companies do change over frequently. One to try: Moha Shuttle (☎ 808/216–8006); $15 round trip. ✣ *H1 Fwy., 30 min west of Downtown Honolulu* ✉ *Waikele* ☎ *808/676–5656.*

UNDER $20 & PACKABLE

- Hawaiian print dish towels
- Hawaiian music CDs
- Small wooden serving bowls
- Coffee grown in Hawai'i
- Humuhumunukunukuāpua'a fish (Hawai'ian state fish) Christmas ornament at Outrigger Trading Co.
- Soaps, oils, lotions, and candles made in Hawai'i, with scents of pīkake and tuberose
- Eye pillow filled with lavender from Maui

- Island-themed T-shirts
- Kukui nut or shell lei
- Macadamia nuts (chocolate-covered or regular)
- Koa wood pen, bracelet, ring, or bookmark
- Ceramic flip-flop (slipper) magnet
- Dolphin suncatcher
- Hawaiian print cocktail napkins
- Ceramic dishes in the shape of Hawaiian flowers

SPAS

Abhasa Spa. Natural organic skin and body treatments highlight this spa tucked away in the Royal Hawaiian Hotel's coconut grove. Vegetarian-lifestyle spa therapies, color-light therapy, an Ayurveda-influenced Bamboo Facial using Sundari products, and body cocooning are all available. You can choose to have your treatment in any of Abhasa's eight indoor rooms or in one of their three garden cabanas. ⊠ *Royal Hawaiian Hotel, 2259 Kalākaua Ave., Waikīkī* ☎ *808/922–8200* ⊕ *www.abhasa. com* ☞ *$110, 50-min. lomi lomi massage.* ⚴ *Hair salon, indoor hot tub, sauna, showers. Services: massage, body cocoons and scrubs, hydrotherapy, waxing, facials.*

Ampy's European Facials and Body Spa. This 30-year-old spa has kept its prices reasonable over the years thanks to their "no frills" way of doing business. All of Ampy's facials are 75 minutes, and the spa has become famous for custom aromatherapy treatments. Call at least a week in advance because the appointment book fills up quickly here. It's in the Ala Moana Building, adjacent to the Ala Moana Shopping Center. ⊠ *1441 Kapi'olani Blvd., Suite 377, Ala Moana* ☎ *808/946–3838* ☞ *$69, 60-min lomi lomi massage* ⚴ *Sauna. Services: Massage, body treatments, facials, hand and foot care.*

Aveda Salon and Spa. Aveda offers hydrotherm massage, where water-filled cushions cradle your body as a therapist works out your body's kinks. This spa has everything from Vichy showers to hydrotherapy rooms to customized aromatherapy. Ladies, they'll even touch-up your makeup for free before you leave. ⊠ *Ala Moana Shopping Center, 3rd fl., 1450 Ala Moana Blvd., Ala Moana* ☎ *808/947–6141* ⊕ *www.aveda.com* ☞ *$110, 50-min lomi lomi massage* ⚴ *Hair salon, eucalyptus steam room. Services: massage, waxing, facials, body treatments.*

Hawaiian Rainforest Salon and Spa. The most popular treatment at this spa uses pressure and heat from natural Hawaiian lava rocks to massage your pain away. They also have Vichy showers, aromatherapy whirlpool baths, a Korean-style Akasuri body polish, and a wide selection of packages. If you're sleepy from the long flight, try the jet-lag remedy, a 25-minute treatment that includes a neck massage, and scalp rub. ⊠ *Pacific Beach Hotel, 5th fl., 2490 Kalākaua Ave., Waikīkī* ☎ *808/ 441–4890* ⊕ *www.hawaiianrainforest.com* ☞ *$95, 50-min lomi lomi massage* ⚴ *Hair salon, hot tubs, sauna. Services: massage, body wraps, body care, facials, makeup.*

J. W. Marriott 'Ihilani Resort & Spa. Soak in warm seawater among velvety orchid blossoms at this unique Hawaiian hydrotherapy spa. Thalassotherapy treatments combine underwater jet massage with color therapy and essential oils. Specially designed treatment rooms have a hydrotherapy tub, a Vichy-style shower, and a needle shower with 12 heads. The spa's Pua Kai line of natural aromatherapy products includes massage and body oil, bath crystals and body butter, which combine ingredients such as ginger, jasmine, rose petals, and coconut and grape seed oil. ⊠ *J. W. Marriott 'Ihilani Resort & Spa, 92-1001 'Ōlani St.,*

Kapolei ☎ *808/679–0079* ⊕ *www.ihilani.com* ⌖ *$115, 50-min lomi lomi massage* ⚲ *Hair salon, hot tubs (indoor and outdoor), sauna, steam room. Gym with: cardiovascular machines, free weights, weight-training equipment. Services: aromatherapy, body wraps and scrubs, facials, massage, thalassotherapy. Classes and programs: aerobics, body sculpting, dance classes, fitness analysis, guided walks, personal training, Pilates, tai chi, yoga.*

Mandara Spa at the Hilton Hawaiian Village Beach Resort & Spa. From its perch in the Kalia Tower, Mandara Spa, an outpost of the chain that originated in Bali, overlooks the mountains, ocean, and downtown Honolulu. Fresh Hawaiian ingredients and traditional techniques headline an array of treatments. Try an exotic upgrade, such as eye treatments using Asian silk protein and reflexology. The delicately scented, candlelit foyer can fill up quickly with robe-clad conventioneers, so be sure to make a reservation. There are spa suites for couples, a private infinity pool, and a café. ⊠ *Hilton Hawaiian Village Beach Resort and Spa, 2005 Kālia Rd., Waikīkī* ☎ *808/949–4321* ⊕ *www. hiltonhawaiianvillage.com* ⌖ *$115, 50-min lomi lomi massage* ⚲ *Hair salon, hot tubs (indoor and outdoor), sauna, steam room. Gym with: cardiovascular machines, free weights, weight-training equipment. Services: aromatherapy, body wraps and scrubs, facials, massages.*

Nā Hōʻola at the Hyatt Regency Waikīkī Resort & Spa. Nā Hōʻola is the largest spa in Waikīkī, sprawling across the fifth and sixth floors of the Hyatt, with 19 treatment rooms, jet baths, and Vichy showers. Arrive early for your treatment to enjoy the postcard views of Waikīkī Beach. Four packages identified by Hawaiʻi's native healing plants—noni, kukui, awa, and kalo—combine various body, face, and hair treatments and span 2½–4 hours. The Champagne of the Sea body treatment employs self-heating mud wrap to release tension and stress. The small exercise room is for use by hotel guests only. ⊠ *Hyatt Regency Waikīkī Resort and Spa, 2424 Kalākaua Ave., Waikīkī* ☎ *808/921–6097* ⊕ *www. hyattwaikiki.com* ⌖ *$110, for a 50-min lomi lomi massage* ⚲ *Sauna, showers. Gym with: cardiovascular machines. Services: aromatherapy, body scrubs and wraps, facials, hydrotherapy, massage.*

Paul Brown's Spa Olakino at the Waikiki Beach Marriott Resort & Spa. Paul Brown has created a spa facing Waikīkī Beach. Linger with a cup of tea between treatments and gaze through 75-foot-high windows at the activity outside. Lush Hawaiian foliage, sleek Balinese teak furnishings, and a mist of ylang-ylang and nutmeg in the air inspire relaxation. Treatments incorporate Brown's Hapuna line of essential oils, as well as a thermal masking system using volcanic ash. The couples experience lasts four hours and includes massage, massage instruction, and chocolate-covered strawberries at sunset. ⊠ *Waikīkī Beach Marriott Resort & Spa, 2552 Kalākaua Ave., Waikīkī* ☎ *808/922–6611* ⊕ *www.marriottwaikiki.com* ⌖ *$100, 50-min lomi lomi massage* ⚲ *Hair salon, nail care, steam showers. Services: massage, facials, body treatments, waxing.*

Paul Brown Salon and Day Spa. This is one of the few salons where the principal owner still works the floor. Paul Brown's specialized treatments

6

combat everything from cellulite to low energy and dry skin. There's even a facial designed especially for men. ☒ *Ward Centre, 1200 Ala Moana Blvd., Ala Moana* ☎ *808/591–1881* ⊕ *www.paulbrownhawaii.com* ☞ *$65, 50-min lomi lomi massage* ♨ *Hair and nail salon. Services: massage, body scrubs, body wraps, makeup, facials, waxing.*

Serenity Spa Hawai'i. Want to jump start your "just back from Hawai'i" tan without burning to a crisp? Consider the Golden Touch tanning massage, which combines a massage with tan accelerators, sunscreen, and scented oils. Only steps off the beach, this day spa provides aromatherapy treatments, massages, and facials. You can mix and match treatments from the menu to create a specialized package. ☒ *Outrigger Reef on the Beach, 2169 Kālia Rd., Waikīkī* ☎ *808/926–2882* ⊕ *www.serenityspahawaii.com* ☞ *$95, 50-min lomi lomi massage* ♨ *Showers, nail salon, hair station. Services: massage, facials, body treatments, waxing, makeup.*

SpaHalekulani. SpaHalekulani mines the traditions and cultures of the Pacific Islands with massages, body, and facial therapies. Try the Polynesian Nonu, which uses warm stones and healing nonu gel. The invigorating Japanese Ton Ton Amma massage is another popular choice. The exclusive line of bath and body products is scented by maile, lavender orchid, hibiscus, coconut passion, or Manoa mint. ☒ *Halekūlani Hotel 2199 Kālia Rd., Waikīkī* ☎ *808/931–5322* ⊕ *www.halekulani.com* ☞ *$180, 75-min lomi lomi massage* ♨ *Use of facilities is specific to treatment but may include Japanese furo bath, steam shower, or whirlpool tub. Services: hair salon, nail care, massage, facials, body treatments.*

The Spa Luana at Turtle Bay Resort. Luxuriate at the ocean's edge in this serene spa. Don't miss the tropical Pineapple Pedicure ($65), administered outdoors overlooking the North Shore. Tired feet soak in a bamboo bowl filled with coconut milk before the pampering really begins with Hawaiian algae salt, Island bee honey, kukui nut oil, and crushed pineapple. There are private spa suites, an outdoor treatment cabana that overlooks the surf, an outdoor exercise studio, and a lounge area and juice bar. ☒ *Turtle Bay Resort, 57-091 Kamehameha Hwy., North Shore* ☎ *808/447–6868* ⊕ *www.turtlebayresort.com* ☞ *$105, 50-min lomi lomi massage* ♨ *Hair and nail salon, showers, steam room, outdoor whirlpool. Gym with: free weights, cardio and weight-training machines. Services: facials, massages, body treatments, waxing. Classes and programs: hula aerobics, Pilates, yoga.*

Spa Suites at The Kāhala. A footbath begins the pampering process at the elegant yet homey Kahala property favored by celebrities and U.S. Presidents. The new spa suites feature wooden floors, handmade Hawaiian quilts, Kohler infinity-edged whirlpool tubs, private vanity areas, and private gardens in which to relax after treatments with lemongrass-pīkake tea. Custom-designed treatments merge Hawaiian, Asian, and traditional therapies. ☒ *The Kāhala, 5000 Kāhala Ave., Kāhala* ☎ *808/739–8938* ☞ *$165, 75-min lomi lomi massage* ♨ *Hair salon, hot tub, sauna, steam room. Services: facials, massage, body treatments.*

Entertainment & Nightlife

Polynesian Cultural Center Ali'i Lū'au

WORD OF MOUTH

"The Polynesian Cultural Center had the best show, emphasis on *show*, hands down. Paradise Cove Lū'au had the best views; the cove really is pretty and romantic. Germaine's Lū'au had the best atmosphere and wins for me just for that. You are really made to feel a part of the family and not just row 32 seat 6."

–12perfectdays

"Another vote for Zanzabar, if you are looking to go dancing."

–MelissaHI

By Katherine
Young

MANY FIRST-TIME VISITORS ARRIVE in the Islands expecting to see scenic beauty and sandy beaches but not much at night. That might be true on some of the other Islands, but not in Oʻahu. Honolulu sunsets herald the onset of the best nightlife scene in the Islands.

Local artists perform every night of the week along Waikīkī's Kalākaua and Kūhiō avenues and in Downtown Honolulu; the clubs dance to every beat from Top 40 to alternative to '80s.

The arts also thrive alongside the tourist industry. Oʻahu has an established symphony, a thriving opera company, chamber music groups, and community theaters. Major Broadway shows, dance companies, and rock stars also make their way to Honolulu. Check the local newspapers—*MidWeek,* the *Honolulu Advertiser,* the *Honolulu Star-Bulletin,* or the *Honolulu Weekly*—for the latest events.

Whether you make it an early night or stay up to watch that spectacular tropical sunrise, there's lots to do in paradise.

ENTERTAINMENT

Lūʻau

The lūʻau is an experience that everyone, both local and tourist, should have. Today's lūʻau still adhere to traditional foods and entertainment, but there's also a fun, contemporary flair. With most, you can even watch the roasted pig being carried out of its *ʻimu,* a hole in the ground used for cooking meat with heated stones.

Lūʻau cost anywhere from $56 to $195. Most that are held outside of Waikīkī offer shuttle service so you don't have to drive. Reservations are essential.

Note: The Sheraton-Waikīkī Hotel does a Wednesday evening lūʻau in summer only comparable to those at the Sheraton-Waikīkī's sister hotel, the Royal Hawaiian.

Germaine's Lūʻau. Widely regarded as the most folksy and local, this lūʻau is held in Kalaeloa in Leeward Oʻahu. The food is the usual multicourse, all-you-can-eat buffet, but it's very tasty. It's a good lūʻau for first-timers and at a reasonable price. Expect a lively crowd on 35-minute bus ride from Waikīkī. Admission includes buffet, Polynesian show, and shuttle transport from Waikīkī. ☎ 808/949-6626 or 800/367-5655 ⊕ *www.germainesluau.com* ✉ $56 ☉ *Daily at 6. Closed Mon. in winter.*

★ **Paradise Cove Lūʻau.** The scenery is the best here—the sunsets are unbe-

> **SUNSET SPOTS**
>
> Some favor the cool grass and rolling hills of Kakaʻako Park, where you can picnic with a view. Others dine in style and watch nature's beauty from the 32nd floor Hanohano Room in the Sheraton Waikīkī. But a favorite for most is seeing the sun melt into the horizon from a beach blanket, toes curled into the warm sand. Ala Moana Beach Park's Magic Island, while crowded, is a good spot. For a more private view, try Lanikai Beach in Kailua or Sunset Beach on the North Shore.

lievable. Watch Mother Nature's special effects show in Kapolei/Ko Olina Resort in Leeward O'ahu, a good 27 mi from the bustle of Waikīkī. The party-hearty atmosphere is kid-friendly with Hawaiian games, canoe rides in the cove, and lots of pre-dinner activities. The stage show includes a fire-knife dancer, singing emcee, and both traditional and contemporary hula. Basic admission includes buffet, activities and the show, and shuttle transport from Waikīkī. You pay extra for table service and box seating. ☎ *808/842–5911* ⊕ *www.paradisecovehawaii.com* ✉*$65–$110* ⊙ *Daily at 5:30, doors open at 5.*

> ## PŪPŪ
>
> Entertaining Hawaiian style means having a lot of pūpū—the local term for appetizers or hors d'oeuvres. Locals eat these small portions of food mostly as they wind down from their work day, relax, and enjoy a couple of beers. Popular pūpū include sushi, tempura, teriyaki chicken skewers, BBQ meat, and our favorite: poke (pronounced "po-keh"), or raw fish, seasoned with seaweed, shoyu, and other flavorings.

Fodor'sChoice **Polynesian Cultural Center Ali'i Lū'au.** This elaborate lū'au has the sharpest ★ production values but no booze (it's a Mormon-owned facility). It's held amid the seven re-created villages at the Polynesian Cultural Center in the North Shore town of Lā'ie, about an hour's drive from Honolulu. The lū'au includes tours of the park with shows and activities. Package rates vary depending on activities and amenities (personalized tours, reserved seats, buffet vs. dinner service, backstage tour, etc.). Waikīkī transport included. ☎ *808/293–3333 or 800/367–7060* ⊕ *www. polynesia.com* ✉ *$80–$195* ⊙ *Mon.–Sat. center opens at noon; lū'au starts at 5.*

Royal Hawaiian Lū'au. If you don't want to travel too far from the South shore, Waikīkī's only oceanfront lū'au is gracious and relaxed. You won't get to see the 'imu ceremony here because Waikīkī law forbids it. You will, however, get a famous mai tai and a great view of the setting sun, Diamond Head, the Pacific Ocean, and the legendary Pink Palace as a backdrop. Admission includes buffet and music. ☎ *808/931–8383* ⊕ *www.royal-hawaii.com* ✉ *$89* ⊙ *Mon. at 6.*

Cocktail & Dinner Cruises

Dinner cruises depart either from the piers adjacent to the Aloha Tower Marketplace in Downtown Honolulu or from Kewalo Basin, near Ala Moana Beach Park, and head along the coast toward Diamond Head. There's usually dinner, dancing, drinks, and a sensational sunset. ■ **TIP→ Get a good spot on deck early to enjoy the sunset, because everyone tends to pile outside at once.** Except as noted, dinner cruises cost approximately $40–$110, cocktail cruises $25–$40. Most major credit cards are accepted.

Ali'i Kai **Catamaran.** Patterned after an ancient Polynesian vessel, this huge catamaran casts off from Aloha Tower with 1,000 passengers. The deluxe dinner cruise has two bars, a huge dinner, and an authentic Polynesian show with colorful hula music. The food is good, the after-dinner show loud and fun, and everyone dances on the way back to shore. Rates begin

Continued on page 151

MORE THAN A FOLK DANCE

Hula has been called "the heartbeat of the Hawaiian people." Also, "the world's best-known, most misunderstood dance." Both true. Hula isn't just dance. It is storytelling. No words, no hula.

Chanter Edith McKinzie calls it "an extension of a piece of poetry." In its adornments, implements, and customs, hula integrates every important Hawaiian cultural practice: poetry, history, genealogy, craft, plant cultivation, martial arts, religion, protocol. So when 19th century Christian missionaries sought to eradicate a practice they considered depraved, they threatened more than just a folk dance.

With public performance outlawed and private hula practice discouraged, hula went underground for a generation, to rural villages. The fragile verbal link by which culture was transmitted from teacher to student hung by a thread. Even increasing literacy did not help because hula's practitioners were—and, to a degree, still are—a secretive and protected circle.

As if that weren't bad enough, vaudeville, Broadway, and Hollywood got hold of the hula, giving it the glitz treatment in an unbroken line from "Oh, How She Could Wicky Wacky Woo" to "Rock-A-Hula Baby." Hula became shorthand for paradise: fragrant flowers, lazy hours. Ironically, this development assured that hundreds of Hawaiians could make a living performing and teaching hula. Many danced 'auana (modern form) in performance; but taught kahiko (traditional), quietly, at home or in hula schools.

Today, 30 years after the cultural revival known as the Hawaiian Renaissance, language immersion programs have assured a new generation of proficient–and even eloquent–chanters, song-writers, and translators. Visitors can see more, and more authentic, hula than anytime in the last 200 years.

Like the culture of which it is the beating heart, hula has survived.

Lei *po'o*. Head lei. In kahiko, greenery only. In 'auana, flowers.

Face emotes appropriate expression. Dancer should not be a smiling automaton.

Shoulders remain relaxed and still, never hunched, even with arms raised. No bouncing.

Eyes always follow leading hand.

Lei. Hula is rarely performed without a shoulder lei.

Arms and hands remain loose, relaxed, below shoulder level—except as required by interpretive movements.

Traditional hula skirt is loose fabric, smocked and gathered at the waist.

Hip is canted over weight-bearing foot.

Knees are always slightly bent, accentuating hip sway.

In kahiko, feet are flat. In 'auana, may be more arched, but not tiptoes or bouncing.

Kupe'e. Ankle bracelet of flowers, shells, or—traditionally—noise-making dog teeth.

HULA

7

BASIC MOTIONS

Speak or Sing

Moon or Sun

Grass Shack or House

Mountains or Heights

Love or Caress

At backyard parties, hula is performed in bare feet and street clothes, but in performance, adornments play a key role, as do rhythm-keeping implements.

In hula kahiko (traditional style), the usual dress is multiple layers of stiff fabric (often with a pellom lining, which most closely resembles *kapa*, the paper-like bark cloth of the Hawaiians). These wrap tightly around the bosom but flare below the waist to form a skirt. In pre-contact times, dancers wore only kapa skirts. Monarchy-period hula is performed in voluminous Mother Hubbard mu'umu'u or high-necked muslin blouses and gathered skirts. Men wear loincloths or, for monarchy period, white or gingham shirts and black pants—sometimes with red sashes.

In hula 'auana (modern), dress for women can range from grass skirts and strapless tops to contemporary tea-length dresses. Men generally wear aloha shirts, but sometimes grass skirts over pants or even everyday gear. (One group at a recent competition wore wetsuits to do a surfing song!)

SURPRISING HULA FACTS

■ Grass skirts are not traditional; workers from Kiribati (the Gilbert Islands) brought this custom to Hawai'i.

■ In olden-day Hawai'i, *mele* (songs) for hula were composed for every occasion—name songs for babies, dirges for funerals, welcome songs for visitors, celebrations of favorite pursuits.

■ Hula *ma'i* is a traditional hula form in praise of a noble's genitals; the power of the *ali'* (royalty) to procreate gave *mana* (spiritual power) to the entire culture.

■ Hula students in old Hawai'i adhered to high standards: scrupulous cleanliness, no sex, daily cleansing rituals, certain food prohibitions, and no contact with the dead. They were fined if they broke the rules.

WHERE TO WATCH

■ House Without a Key: Live music, graceful solo hula, relaxed seaside stage. Halekūlani, ☎ 808/923-2311.

■ Two worthwhile commercial shows: "Creation-A Polynesian Journey," Sheraton Princess Ka'iulani, ☎ 808/922-5811; Polynesian Cultural Center, ☎ 808/293-3333.

■ Free hula shows: Bishop Museum, ☎ 808/847-3511. Frequent performances and free hula lessons: Royal Hawaiian Shopping Center, ☎ 808/922-0588.

■ Festivals and hō'ike: To find authentic amateur hula, check local media and the gohawaii.com calendar for annual hula school hō'ike (recital/fundraisers) and hula festivals and competitions.

at $66 and include round-trip transportation, the dinner buffet, and one drink. ⊠ *Pier 5, street level, Honolulu* ☎ *808/539–9400 Ext. 5.*

★ **Atlantis Cruises.** The sleekly high-tech *Navatek,* a revolutionary craft designed to sail smoothly in rough waters, powers farther along Waikīkī's coastline than its competitors, sometimes making it past Diamond Head and all the way to Hanauma Bay. Choose from sunset dinner or moonlight cruises aboard the 300-passenger boat where you can feast on beef tenderloin and whole lobster or opt for the downstairs buffet. There's also the option of humpback whale–watch cruises December–mid-April. Tours leave from Pier 6, next to Aloha Tower Marketplace. Rates begin at $75 for the buffet, including one drink; the sit-down dinner, which includes three drinks, starts at $105. ⊠ *Honolulu Harbor* ☎ *808/973–1311* ⊕ *www.atlantisadventures.com.*

Paradise Cruises. Prices vary depending on which deck you choose on the 1,600-passenger, four-deck *Star of Honolulu.* For instance, a seven-course French-style dinner and live jazz on the top deck starts at $165. A steak-and-crab feast on level two starts at $78. This ship also features daily Hawaiiana Lunch cruises that offer lei-making and 'ukulele and hula lessons starting at $45. Evening excursions also take place on the 340-passenger *Starlet I* and 230-passenger *Starlet II,* which offer three-course dinners beginning at $43. Also bring your bathing suits for a morning cruise for $63 complete with ocean fun on a water trampoline and slide, and feast on a BBQ lunch before heading back to shore. ⊠ *1540 S. King St., Honolulu* ☎ *808/983–7827* ⊕ *www.paradisecruises.com.*

Cocktail & Dinner Shows

Cocktail shows run $30 to $43, and the price usually includes one cocktail, tax, and tip. Dinner-show food is usually buffet-style with a definite local accent. Dinner shows are all in the $55 to $99 range. In all cases, reservations are essential. ■ TIP➔ **Artists tend to switch venues, so call in advance to check the evening's lineup.**

Blue Hawai'i: The Show. The King loved the Islands. Jonathan Von Brana sings Elvis Presley tunes that showcase this affection. ⊠ *Waikīkī Beachcomber Hotel, 2300 Kalākaua Ave., Waikīkī* ☎ *808/923–1245* ⊙ *Shows daily at 6:15.*

Creation: A Polynesian Journey. A daring Samoan fire-knife dancer is the highlight of this show that traces Hawai'i's culture and history, from its origins to statehood. ⊠ *'Āinahau Showroom, Sheraton Princess Ka'iulani Hotel, 120 Ka'iulani Ave., Waikīkī* ☎ *808/931–4660* ⊙ *Dinner shows Tues.–Sun. at 6.*

Don Ho. Four decades ago, Don Ho put Waikīkī entertainment on the map, and his song "Tiny Bubbles" became a trademark. His show, a

24-HOUR EATERIES

If it's 3 AM and you're desperate for a snack, avoid the fast-food drive-through and opt to satisfy your munchies the local way. There are several 24-hour eateries on O'ahu that pack in the after-hours crowd: Wailana Coffee House in Waikīkī, Like Like Drive-In by Ala Moana Shopping Center, and Zippy's, of which there are 20 locations open all night. Try Like Like's fried rice and Portuguese sausage or Zippy's saimin, chili frank plate, or an apple napple from the bakery.

Polynesian revue (with a cast of young and attractive Hawaiian performers), has found the perfect home in this intimate club inside the Waikīkī Beachcomber Hotel. ⊠ *Waikīkī Beachcomber Hotel, 2300 Kalākaua Ave., Waikīkī* ☎ *808/923–3981* ⊙ *Shows Sun., Tues., Thurs. at 8, with cocktail and dinner seatings.*

★ **Magic of Polynesia.** Hawai'i's top illusionist, John Hirokawa, displays mystifying sleight of hand in this highly entertaining show, which incorporates contemporary hula and island music into its acts. ⊠ *Waikīkī Beachcomber Hotel, 2300 Kalākaua Ave., Waikīkī* ☎ *808/971–4321* ⊙ *Nightly at 8.*

🖐 **Polynesian Cultural Center.** Easily one of the best on the Islands, this show has soaring moments and an "erupting volcano." The performers are students from Brigham Young University's Hawai'i campus. ⊠ *55-370 Kamehameha Hwy., Lā'ie* ☎ *808/293–3333 or 800/367–7060* ⊕ *www.polynesia.com* ⊙ *Mon.–Sat. 12:30–9:30.*

Society of Seven. This lively, popular septet has great staying power and, after more than 25 years, continues to put on one of the best shows in Waikīkī. They sing, dance, do impersonations, play instruments, and, above all, entertain with their contemporary sound. ⊠ *Outrigger Waikīkī on the Beach, 2335 Kalākaua Ave., Waikīkī* ☎ *808/922–6408* ⊕ *www.outrigger.com* ⊙ *Tues.–Sat. at 8:30.*

Film

Hawai'i International Film Festival. It may not be Cannes, but this festival is unique and exciting. During the weeklong event from the end of November to early December, top films from the United States, Asia, and the Pacific are screened day and night at several theaters on O'ahu to packed crowds. It's a must-see for film adventurers. ☎ *808/528–3456* ⊕ *www.hiff.org.*

Honolulu Academy of Arts. Art, international, classic, and silent films are screened at the 280-seat Doris Duke theater. Though small, the theater is still classy and comfortable. It also has a great sound system. ⊠ *900 S. Beretania St., Downtown Honolulu* ☎ *808/532–8768* ⊕ *www.honoluluacademy.org.*

★ **Sunset on the Beach.** It's like watching a movie at the drive-in, minus the car and the impossible speaker box. Think romantic and cozy; bring a blanket and find a spot on the sand to enjoy live entertainment, food from top local restaurants, and a movie feature on a 40-foot screen. Held twice a month on Waikīkī's Queens Surf Beach across from the Honolulu Zoo, Sunset on the Beach is a favorite event for both locals and tourists. If the weather is blustery, beware of flying sand. ☎ *808/923–1094* ⊕ *www.waikikiimprovement.com.*

Music

Hawai'i Opera Theater. Better known as "HOT," the Hawai'i Opera Theater has been known to turn the opera-challenged into opera lovers. All operas are sung in their original language with projected English translation. Tickets range from $29 to $100. ⊠ *Neil Blaisdell Center Concert Hall, Ward Ave. and King St., Downtown Honolulu* ☎ *808/596–7858* ⊕ *www.hawaiiopera.org.*

Beyond "Tiny Bubbles"

ASK MOST VISITORS about Hawaiian music and they'll likely break into a lighthearted rendition of "Little Grass Shack." When they're finished, lead them directly to a stereo.

First, play them a recording of singer Kekuhi Kanahele, whose compositions combine ancient Hawaiian chants with modern melodies. Then ask them to listen to a CD by guitarist Keola Beamer, who loosens his strings and plays slack-key tunes dating to the 1830s. Amaze them with the 'ukulele stylings of young Jake Shimabukuro. Delight them with a sampling of Sean Na'auao's breezy, often-whimsical local ditties. Treat them to the traditional and contemporary Hawaiian sounds of Keali'i Reichel, a fixture on Billboard Magazine's World Music charts. Enthrall them with the soothing melodies of the Brothers Cazimero, still going strong after more than 30 years in the Hawaiian music industry. Share a recording by falsetto virtuoso Amy Hanaiali'i Gilliom, or play the late Israel Kamakawiwo'ole's version of "What a Wonderful World," which has appeared on scores of feature films and national television series. "Brother Iz," who died in 1997, was a native Hawaiian with a voice so pure, most of his songs were recorded simply with voice and 'ukulele. His last album, *Alone In Iz World*, was released posthumously.

These artists, like many others, are proving just how multifaceted Hawaiian music has become. They're unearthing their island roots in the form of revered songs and chants, and they're reinterpreting them for today's audiences.

Granted, "Little Grass Shack" does have its place in the history books.

After Hawai'i became a U.S. territory in 1900, the world discovered its music thanks to touring ensembles who turned heads with swaying hips, steel guitars, and pseudo-Hawaiian lyrics. Once radio and movies got into the act, dreams of Hawai'i came with a saccharine Hollywood sound track.

But Hawaiian music is far more complex. It harks back to the ancient islanders who beat rough-hewn drums, blew haunting calls on conch shells, and intoned chants for their gods. It recalls the voices of 19th-century Christian missionaries who taught islanders to sing in four-part harmony, a style that's still popular today.

The music takes on international overtones thanks to gifts from foreign immigrants: the 'ukulele from Portuguese laborers, for instance, and the guitar from Mexican traders. And it's enlivened by a million renderings of "Tiny Bubbles," as entertainers such as Don Ho croon Hawaiian-pop hits for Waikīkī tourists.

Island music came full circle in the late 1960s and '70s, when a few dedicated artists began giving voice to a resurgence of interest in Hawaiian culture, history, and traditions.

Today's artistic trailblazers are digging deep to explore their heritage, and their music reflects that thoughtful search. Musicians go one step further by incorporating such time-honored instruments as nose flutes and gourds, helping them keep pace with the past.

Check ads and listings in local papers for information on concerts, which take place in indoor and outdoor theaters, hotel ballrooms, and cozy nightclubs.

7

Honolulu Symphony Orchestra. In recent years, the Honolulu Symphony has worked hard to increase its appeal to all ages. The orchestra performs at the Neil Blaisdell Concert Hall under the direction of the young, dynamic Samuel Wong. The Honolulu Pops series, with performances under the summer stars at the Waikīkī Shell, features top local and national artists under the direction of talented conductor-composer Matt Cattingub. Tickets are $17–$59. ⊠ *Dole Cannery, 650 Iwilei Rd., Suite 202, Iwilei* ☎ *808/792–2000* ⊕ *www.honolulusymphony.com.*

Honolulu Zoo Concerts. For almost two decades, the Honolulu Zoo Society has sponsored Wednesday evening concerts from June to August on the zoo's stage lawn. Listen to local legends play everything from Hawaiian to jazz to Latin music. ■ **TIP➜ At just $1 admission, this is one of the best deals in town.** Take a brisk walk through the zoo exhibits before they close at 5:30 PM or join in the family activities; bring your own picnic for the concert, which starts at 6 PM. It's an alcohol-free event, and there's a food concession for those who come unprepared. ⊠ *151 Kapahulu Ave., Waikīkī* ☎ *808/926–3191* ⊕ *www.honoluluzoo.org* ⊠ *$1* ⊙ *Gates open at 4:30.*

Theater

Hawai'i can be an expensive gig for touring shows and music artists that depend on major theatrical sets. Not many manage to stop here, and those who do sell out fast. O'ahu has developed several excellent local theater companies, which present first-rate entertainment on an amateur and semiprofessional level all year long. Community support for these groups is strong.

Army Community Theatre. This is a favorite for its revivals of musical theater classics presented in an 800-seat house. The casts are talented, and the fare is great for families. ⊠ *Richardson Theater, Fort Shafter, Downtown Honolulu* ☎ *808/438–4480* ⊠ *$14–$20.*

Diamond Head Theater. The repertoire includes a little of everything: musicals, dramas, experimental productions, and classics. This company is in residence five minutes from Waikīkī, right next to Diamond Head. ⊠ *520 Makapu'u Ave., Kapahulu* ☎ *808/733–0274* ⊕ *www. diamondheadtheater.com* ⊠ *$10–$40.*

Hawai'i Theatre Center. Beautifully restored, this Downtown Honolulu theater, built in the 1920s in a neoclassic beaux arts style, hosts a wide variety of performing arts events, including international theatrical productions, international touring acts, festivals, films, and meetings. It's the most beautiful theater in Hawai'i. Historic tours are offered Tuesday at 11 AM for $5. Admission for performances varies. ⊠ *1130 Bethel St., Downtown Honolulu* ☎ *808/528–0506* ⊕ *www.hawaiitheatre.com.*

ᕙ **Honolulu Theater for Youth.** This group stages delightful productions for children around the Islands from September through May. Call for a schedule. ⊠ *2846 Ualena St., Downtown Honolulu* ☎ *808/839–9885* ⊠ *$10.*

Kumu Kahua. This is the only troupe presenting shows and plays written by local playwrights about the Islands. It stages five or six productions a year in a small venue that's perfect for getting up close and personal

Izakaya

JAPANESE PUB-RESTAURANTS, called *izakaya* (ee-ZAH-ka-ya), are sprouting in the Islands like *matsutake* mushrooms in a pine forest. They began as oases for homesick Japanese nationals but were soon discovered by adventurous locals, who appreciated the welcoming atmosphere, sprawling menus, and later dining hours.

Expect to be greeted by a merry, full-staff cry of "Irrashaimase!", offered an *oshibori* (hot towel) and a drink, and handed a menu of dozens of small-plate, made-to-order dishes.

You can find *yakitori* (grilled dishes), tempura (deep-fried dishes), *donburi* (rice bowls), sushi and sashimi, *nabemono* and *shabu-shabu* (hot pots), noodles (both soup and fried), okonomiyaki (chop suey-type omelets), and a bizarre assortment of *yoshoku* dishes (Western foods prepared in Japanese style, such as hamburgers in soy-accented gravy, fried chicken with a mirin glaze, odd gratins, and even pizza).

Full bars are usual; a wide choice of lager-type beers and good-to-great sakes are universal. Many specialize in single-malt scotch, but wine lists are generally short.

Izakaya menus are often confusing, many staff speak marginal English, and outings can get expensive fast (liquor plus small-plate prices equals eyes bigger than stomach). Prices range from $5 for a basket of edamame (steamed soybeans) to $20 or more for wafu (seasoned, grilled steak, sliced for sharing). Start by ordering drinks and *edamame* (salted soybeans) or silky-textured braised *kabocha* pumpkin. This will keep the waiter happy. Then give yourself a quarter of an hour to examine the menu, ogle other people's plates, and seek recommendations. Start with one dish per person and one for the table; you can always call for more.

Imanas Tei. Go early to this cozy, out-of-the-way restaurant for its tasteful, simple decor and equally tasteful and simply perfect sushi, sashimi, *nabe* (hot pots prepared at the table), and grilled dishes; reservations taken from 5 to 7 PM; after that, there's always a line. ⊠ *2626 S. King, Mōʻiliʻili* ☎ *808/941-2626 or 808/934-2727* ⊟ *AE, DC, MC, V* ☞ *$8-$25.*

Izakaya Nonbei. Teruaki Mori designed this pub to put you in mind of a northern inn in winter in his native Japan; dishes not to miss—*karei kara-age* (delicate deep-fried flounder) and *dobinmushi* (mushroom consomme presented in a teapot). ⊠ *3108 Olu St., Kapahulu* ☎ *808/734-5573* ⊟ *AE, D, DC, MC, V* ☞ *$7-$20.*

Tokkuri-Tei. This is a favorite of locals for the playful atmosphere that belies the excellence of the food created by chef Hideaki "Santa" Miyoshi, famous for his quirky menu names (Nick Jagger, Spider Poke); just say "Moriwase, kudasai" ("chef's choice, please"), and he'll order for you. ⊠ *611 Kapahulu Ave., Kapahulu* ☎ *808/739-2800* ⊟ *AE, D, DC, MC, V* ☞ *$13-$25.*

Also worth a visit: **Mr. Oji-san** (⊠ 1018 Kapahulu Ave., Kapahulu ☎ 808/735-4455) for family-style izakaya specialties; and **Kai Okonomi Cuisine** (⊠ 1427 Makaloa, Ala Moana ☎ 808/944-1555) for Osaka-style omlelets.

—Wanda Adams

7

with the cast. ☒ *46 Merchant St., Downtown Honolulu* ☎ *808/536–4441* 📖 *$12–$15.*

NIGHTLIFE

O'ahu is the best of all the islands for nightlife. The locals call it *pau hana* but you might call it "off the clock and ready for a cocktail." The literal translation of the Hawaiian phrase means "done with work." On weeknights, it's likely that you'll find the working crowd still in their casual business attire sipping a few gin and tonics even before the sun goes down. Those who don't have to wake up in the early morning change into a fresh outfit and start the evening closer to 10 PM.

On the weekends, it's typical to have dinner at a restaurant before hitting the clubs around 9:30. Some bar hoppers start as early as 7, but partygoers typically don't patronize more than two establishments a night. That's because getting from one O'ahu nightspot to the next usually requires packing your friends in the car and driving.

You can find a bar in just about any area on O'ahu. Most of the clubs, however, are centralized to Waikīkī, Ala Moana, and Downtown Honolulu. The drinking age is 21 on O'ahu and throughout Hawai'i. Many bars will admit younger people but will not serve them alcohol. By law, all establishments that serve alcoholic beverages must close by 2 AM. The only exceptions are those with a cabaret license, which have a 4 AM curfew. ■ TIP➜ **Most places have a cover charge of $5 to $10, but with some establishments, getting there early means you don't have to pay.**

Bars

Waikīkī

Banyan Veranda. The Banyan Veranda is steeped in history. From this location the radio program *Hawai'i Calls* first broadcast the sounds of Hawaiian music and the rolling surf to a U.S. mainland audience in 1935. Today, a variety of Hawaiian entertainment continues to provide the perfect accompaniment to the sounds of the waves. ☒ *Sheraton Moana Surfrider, 2365 Kalākaua Ave., Waikīkī* ☎ *808/922–3111.*

★ **Cobalt Lounge.** Take the glass elevator up 30 stories to enjoy the sunset. Floor-to-ceiling windows offer breathtaking views of Diamond Head and the Waikīkī shoreline. Leather sofas and cobalt-blue lighting set the "blue" Hawai'i mood. After darkness falls, you can find soft lights, starlight, and dancing in this lounge in the center of the Hanohano Room. ☒ *Sheraton Waikīkī, 2255 Kalākaua Ave., Waikīkī* ☎ *808/922–4422* ⊙ *1st and 3rd Sat. of month.*

★ **Duke's Canoe Club.** Making the most of its oceanfront spot on Waikīkī Beach, Duke's presents "Concerts on the Beach" every Friday, Saturday, and Sunday with contemporary Hawaiian musicians like Henry Kapono. National musicians like Jimmy Buffett have also performed here. At Duke's Barefoot Bar, solo Hawaiian musicians take the stage nightly, and it's not unusual for surfers to leave their boards outside to step in for a casual drink after a long day on the waves. ☒ *Outrigger Waikīkī,*

2335 Kalākaua Ave., Waikīkī ☎ *808/922–2268.*

Formaggio Wine and Cheese Bar. Only people in the know, know where Formaggio is. There's no flashy signage for this establishment on the outskirts of Waikīkī—only the word "Formaggio" painted on the door. This tinted door cloaks a dimly-lighted bar, where young professionals and baby boomers enjoy live jazz nightly. There are more than 40 wines by the glass or taste and a Mediterranean menu with everything from pizzas to paninis. ✉ *Market City Shopping Center, 2919 Kapi'olani Blvd., lower level, Waikīkī* ☎ *808/739–7719* ⊙ *Tues.–Sun.*

★ **Mai Tai Bar at the Royal Hawaiian.** The bartenders sure know how to make one killer mai tai—just one could do the trick. This is, after all, the establishment that came up with the famous drink in the first place. The pink, umbrella-covered tables at the outdoor bar are front-row seating for Waikīkī sunsets and an unobstructed view of Diamond Head. Contemporary Hawaiian music is usually on stage, and the staff is extremely friendly. ✉ *Royal Hawaiian Hotel, 2259 Kalākaua Ave., Waikīkī* ☎ *808/923–7311.*

Fodor's Choice **Moana Terrace.** Three floors up from Waikīkī Beach, this open-air terrace is the home of Aunty Genoa Keawe, the "First Lady of Hawaiian Music." Her falsetto sessions include jams with the finest of Hawai'i's musicians. ✉ *Waikīkī Beach Marriott Resort, 2552 Kalākaua Ave., Waikīkī* ☎ *808/922–6611.*

Moose McGillycuddy's Pub and Cafe. Loud bands play for the beach-and-beer gang in a blue-jeans-and-T-shirt setting. Bikini contests are the thrill on Sunday nights; live bands play late '80s and '90s music the rest of the week. ✉ *310 Lewers St., Waikīkī* ☎ *808/923–0751.*

Shore Bird Oceanside Bar and Grill. This Waikīkī beachfront bar spills right out onto the sand. Local bands play nightly until 1 AM. ✉ *Outrigger Reef on the Beach hotel, 2169 Kālia Rd., Waikīkī* ☎ *808/922–2887.*

Tiki's Grill and Bar. Get in touch with your primal side at this restaurant–bar overlooking Kuhio Beach. Tiki torches, tiki statues, and other South Pacific art set the mood. A twentysomething mix of locals and tourists comes on the weekends to get their fill of kitschy-cool. There's nightly entertainment featuring contemporary Hawaiian musicians. Don't leave without sipping on a "lava flow." It's served in a whole coconut, which is yours to keep at the end of the night. ✉ *Aston Waikīkī Beach Hotel, 2570 Kalākaua Ave., Waikīkī* ☎ *808/923–8454.*

Elsewhere in Honolulu

Anna Bannana's. Generations of Hawai'i college students have spent more than an evening or two at this legendary two-story, smoky dive near the

---

MAI TAIS

The cocktail known around the world as the mai tai recently celebrated its 50th birthday. While the recipe has changed slightly over the years, the original formula, created by bar owner Victor J. "Trader Vic" Bergeron, included two ounces of 17-year-old J. Wray & Nephew rum, over shaved ice, ½ ounce Holland Dekuyper orange curacao, ¼ ounce Trader Vic's rock candy syrup, ½ ounce French Garier orgeat syrup, and the juice of one fresh lime. Done the right way, this tropical drink still lives up to the name "mai tai!" meaning, "out of this world!"

7

University of Hawai'i campus. A living-room atmosphere makes it a comfortable place to hang out. Here, the music is fresh, loud, and sometimes experimental. Live music happens Friday and Saturday, starting at 9 PM. There's also open mike night for amateurs on Monday. ⊠ *2440 S. Beretania St., Mō'ili'ili* ☎ *808/946–5190.*

Chai's Island Bistro. Chai's welcomes some of Hawai'i's top entertainers, such as the Brothers Cazimero (on Wednesday evening), Hapa, and Jake Shimabukuro. Chai's is the perfect place if you're looking to enjoy the signature sounds of Hawai'i while dining on Pacific Rim cuisine. ⊠ *Aloha Tower Marketplace, 1 Aloha Tower Dr., Downtown Honolulu* ☎ *808/585–0011.*

Dave and Buster's. Located in the Ward Centers, this restaurant features a stocked bar and lots of amusements ranging from classic billiards to shuffleboard and the latest in video arcade games. On Wednesday, Friday, and Saturday a DJ spins hip-hop music on the rooftop Sunset Bar starting at 10 PM. ⊠ *Ward Entertainment Complex, 1030 Auahi St., Ala Moana* ☎ *808/589–2215.*

Don Ho's Grill. This popular waterfront restaurant in the Aloha Tower Marketplace houses the Tiny Bubbles Bar, famous for its "suck 'em up" mai tai, a Don Ho classic. The dinner hour features Hawaiian musicians like Jerry Santos and Robert Cazimero. If you're lucky, you might catch a glimpse of the famous Ho, who frequents the restaurant. On the weekend, live bands play reggae music from 10 PM to 2 AM. ⊠ *Aloha Tower Marketplace, 1 Aloha Tower Dr., Downtown Honolulu* ☎ *808/ 528–0807.*

Dragon Room. The best thing about being on vacation is not having to go to work on Monday morning. Sundays at Jackie's Kitchen, the restaurant created by actor Jackie Chan, are a packed house with R&B and neo-soul music from 10:30 PM to 2 AM. Also expect to be amazed by the bar's main attraction: its fantastic flair bartenders who will juggle your drink and then balance it on their forehead. ⊠ *Jackie's Kitchen at Ala Moana Center, 1450 Ala Moana Blvd., Ala Moana* ☎ *808/943–2426.*

Gordon Biersch Brewery Restaurant. This outside bar flanks Honolulu Harbor. Live bands serenade patrons with everything from funk to jazz to rock and roll. Those who feel inspired have been known to strut their stuff in front of the stage, while their friends enjoy a pitcher of the restaurant's own brew from the sidelines. ⊠ *Aloha Tower Marketplace, 1 Aloha Tower Dr., Downtown Honolulu* ☎ *808/599–4877.*

Little Vino. Step inside this small wine bar, and you'd think you have just arrived in Italy. The walls are painted to look like a rustic countryside with beautiful vineyards. Relax on one of the leather couches or at a table and enjoy wines hand-selected by the restaurant's master sommelier and Italian tapas (small plates) if you're hungry. ⊠ *Restaurant Row, 500 Ala Moana Blvd., Kaka'ako* ☎ *808/524–8466* ☉ *Wed. and Thurs. 5:30–9:30 PM, Fri. and Sat. 5:30–10:30 PM.*

Fodor'sChoice
★
Mai Tai Bar at Ala Moana Center. After a long day of shopping, the Mai Tai Bar on the third floor of Ala Moana Center is a perfect spot to relax.

There's live entertainment and two nightly happy hours: one for food items and another strictly for specialty drinks. There's never a cover charge and no dress code, but to avoid waiting in line, get there before 9 PM. ✉ *1450 Ala Moana Blvd., Ala Moana* ☎ *808/947–2900.*

Newjass Quartet at 39 Hotel. In a darkened downtown-loft setting, a collective of young, talented local jazz musicians get down with modern and eclectic set lists. It gets cool from 10 PM to 1:30 AM on Tuesdays. Cover is $3 before 10 PM and $5 afterward. ✉ *39 N. Hotel St., Downtown* ☎ *808/599–2552.*

> ### BLUE HAWAI'I
>
> In 1957 Harry Yee, a bartender at the Hilton Hawaiian Village created the Blue Hawai'i using the Bols company's newest liqueur, Blue Curaçao. It may turn your tongue a tasty shade of blue, but this sweet beverage goes down smoothly. Mix ¾ ounce light rum, ¾ ounce vodka, ½ ounce blue curaçao, 3 ounces pineapple juice, and 1 ounce sweet and sour mix.

Opium Den & Champagne Bar at Indigo's. This bar at the edge of Chinatown resembles a joint right out of a film noir. Jazz plays early in the evening on Tuesday; late-night DJs spin trance, Top 40, funk, disco, and rock on weekends. In addition to champagne, happy hour features sake martinis and complimentary pūpū buffet. ✉ *Indigo Euroasian Cuisine, 1121 Nu'uanu Ave., Downtown Honolulu* ☎ *808/521–2900.*

Pipeline Cafe and Sports Bar. This is two stories of fun with pool, darts, and more. The upstairs sports bar has TVs galore and a skybox view of the dancing below. Music includes both live acts and seasoned DJs. ✉ *805 Pohukaina St., Kaka'ako* ☎ *808/589–1999.*

Spice Lounge. One of the newest night events to hit O'ahu is the Spice Lounge at E&O Trading Company restaurant. The lounge takes on the Far East Asian marketplace feel of the restaurant in a two-phase Friday-night party. In the early evening, a DJ on the outside patio plays '70s and '80s retro music to a crowd of young professionals. After 10 PM, the Spice Lounge takes over the inside restaurant as well, where a DJ spins a mix of R&B and house music. One night a month, the promoter also throws a special themed event, such as the recent Miss Hawaiian Tropic state contest. There are pūpū specials until 11:30 PM, bottle service, and reserved VIP tables. It's a comfortable place to hang. ✉ *E&O Trading Company at Ward Centre, 3rd fl., 1200 Ala Moana Blvd., Kaka'ako* ☎ *808/957–0303.*

Elsewhere in O'ahu
Boardrider's Bar & Grill. Recently renamed Boardriders, this spot tucked away in Kailua Town has long been the venue for local bands to strut their stuff. Renovations have spruced up the space, which now includes pool tables, dart boards, foosball, and eight TVs for sports-viewing with the local and military crowd. Look for live entertainment–reggae to alternative rock to good old-fashioned rock-n-roll–Wednesday through Saturday from 10:30 PM to 1:30 AM. Cover ranges from $3 to $10. ✉ *201-A Hamakua Dr., Kailua* ☎ *808/261–4600.*

Breaker's Restaurant. Just about every surf contest post-party is celebrated at this family-owned establishment, as the owner's son, Benji Weatherly, is a pro surfer himself. Surfing memorabilia, including surfboards hanging from the ceiling, fills the space. The restaurant/bar is open from 11 AM to 9:30 PM with a late-night menu until midnight. But things start to happen around 9 PM on Thursdays for the 18-and-over crowd, who cruise while the DJ spins, and there's live music on Saturdays. The party goes until 2 AM. ✉ *Marketplace Shopping Center, 66-250 Kamehameha Hwy., Hale'iwa* ☎ *808/637–9898.*

The Shack. This sports bar and restaurant is about the only late-night spot you can find in Southeast O'ahu. After a day of snorkeling at Hanauma Bay, stop by to kick back, have a beer, eat a burger, watch some sports, or play a game of pool. It's open until 2 AM nightly. ✉ *Hawai'i Kai Shopping Center, 377 Keahole St., Hawai'i Kai,* ☎ *808/396–1919* ☉ *Nightly until 2 AM.*

Dance Clubs

Waikīkī

Bobby G's. This is a treasure in the middle of the International Marketplace. Bobby G's features nightly entertainment and never has a cover charge. From live reggae music to the mixing of DJ D-Box, get ready for a loud and rowdy time. Doors open at 9 PM. ✉ *International Marketplace Betweeen Kūhiō and Kalākaua Ave., Waikīkī* ☎ *808/926–7066.*

The Cellar Nightclub. The 18-and-over crowd parties underground in this darkened hideaway. Top 40 dance music fills the downstairs space. ✉ *205 Lewers St., Waikīkī* ☎ *808/923–9952* ☉ *Tues.–Sat.*

Esprit Lounge. Soul Cafe plays to a mix of locals and tourists. Spacious and clean, the upscale space overlooks the ocean and has plenty of tables for relaxing. If you feel the need to boogie to the Top 40 music, there's a small dance floor. The exotic fruit martinis are a must-try. ✉ *Sheraton Waikīkī, 2255 Kalākaua Ave., Waikīkī* ☎ *808/922–4422* ☉ *Wed.–Sat.*

Feng Shui Ultralounge. This once-a-week club event is the creation of partymaster Justin Yoshino. After the dinner rush leaves Ciao Mein restaurant, the spacious venue is transformed into the only indoor–outdoor nightlife experience in Honolulu. There are complimentary appetizers and two dance floors featuring everything from deep house to hip-hop. With five bars, it's easy to get a drink; there's also ample space to get away from the booming music and lounge on a pool chair. Dress code—no slippers, shorts, headwear, jerseys, or T-shirts—is strictly enforced. ✉ *Hyatt Regency Waikīkī Resort and Spa, 2424 Kalākaua Ave., Waikīkī* ☎ *808/957–0303* ☉ *Sat. at 9:30 PM.*

Hula's Bar and Lei Stand. Hawai'i's oldest and best-known gay-friendly nightspot offers calming panoramic outdoor views of Diamond Head and the Pacific Ocean by day and a high-energy club scene by night. Check out the soundproof, glassed-in dance floor. ✉ *Waikīkī Grand Hotel, 134 Kapahulu Ave., 2nd fl., Waikīkī* ☎ *808/923–0669.*

Nashville Waikīkī. Country music in the tropics? You bet! Put on your *paniolo* (Hawaiian cowboy) duds and mosey on out to the giant dance floor. There are pool tables, dartboards, line dancing, and free dance lessons (Wednesday at 6:30 PM) to boot. Look for wall-to-wall crowds on the weekend. ⊠ *Ohana Waikīkī West Hotel, 2330 Kūhiō Ave., Waikīkī* ☎ *808/926–7911.*

Scruples Beach Club. After the sun goes down, the beach party moves from the sand to this discotheque right off Waikīkī's strip. Dance to the latest alternative, house, and Top 40 music with a clientele that is as diverse as all Hawai'i. Casual attire is welcome. ⊠ *2310 Kūhiō Ave., at Nahua St., Waikīkī* ☎ *808/923–9530.*

Wave Waikīkī. This venue has stood the test of time, anchoring the Waikīkī entertainment scene for more than two decades. Dance to live rock and roll until 1:30 AM and recorded music after that. It can be a rough scene (the place has seen more than its fair share of drunken fisticuffs), but the bands are tops. Late nights, the music here definitely goes "underground." ⊠ *1877 Kalākaua Ave., Waikīkī* ☎ *808/941–0424.*

Wonder Lounge. The Diamond Head Grill restaurant is also an after-hours nightclub, full of hip, young professionals who enjoy martinis and the chance to do some not-so-serious networking. Look for a younger group on Saturday. Enjoy some fantastic (though pricey) eats until midnight, and keep dancing until 2 AM. ⊠ *2885 Kalākaua Ave., Waikīkī* ☎ *808/ 922–1700* ☉ *Fri. and Sat. at 9 PM.*

Zanzabar. Traverse a winding staircase and make an entrance at Zanzabar where DJs spin top hits, from hip-hop to soul and techno to trance. It's easy to find a drink at this high-energy nightspot with its three bars. Not exactly sure how to get your groove on? Zanzabar offers free Latin dance lessons every Tuesday at 8 PM. Most nights are 21 and over, Sunday, Tuesday, Wednesday, and Thursday allow 18 and over in for $15. ⊠ *Waikīkī Trade Center, 2255 Kūhiō Ave., Waikīkī* ☎ *808/924–3939.*

Elsewhere in Honolulu

Bliss. Several owners of this same location, now known as Bliss, have tried to make the night spot jump over the last few years. These days, Friday nights are the best time to go with no cover charge and reggae and dancehall music from 9 PM to 2 AM for the 18-and-over crowd. ⊠ *327 Keawe St., Kaka'ako* ☎ *808/528–4911.*

Blue Tropix. This nightclub features DJs mixing hip-hop and house for the 18-plus crowd. Upstairs is the Skybox Sports Lounge featuring plenty of pool tables, dart boards, and TVs to watch the big game. The two establishments, though owned by the same person, have separate entrances. ⊠ *1700 Kapi'olani Blvd., Ala Moana* ☎ *808/944–0001.*

Fodor'sChoice **The Ocean Club.** The Ocean Club has withstood the test of time while other ★ local nightclubs have failed. The indoor venue plays mostly Top 40 and hip-hop music. Tuesday is "Ladies' Night" featuring $2 drinks. Thursday is "Paddler's Night" so wear aloha print attire and avoid the cover charge. The last Saturday of every month is the "Piranha Room," where the club is decorated according to various themes, go-go dancers mesmerize, and the place is packed. There is half-price pūpū until 8 PM. All nights are 23 and over except Thursday; dress code—no beach or athletic wear—is strictly enforced. ⊠ *Restaurant Row, 500 Ala Moana Blvd., Kaka'ako* ☎ *808/531–8444* ☷ *Tues., Thurs., Fri. at 4:30 PM, Sat. at 7 PM.*

Rumours. The after-work crowd loves this spot, which has dance videos, disco, and throbbing lights. On Saturday "Little Chill" nights, the club plays oldies from the '70s, '80s, and '90s and serves free pūpū. ⊠ *Ala Moana Hotel, 410 Atkinson St., Ala Moana* ☎ *808/955–4811.*

Venus Nightclub. This high-energy social bar, with leather couches ideal for a night of people-watching, features hip-hop, trance, and reggae with guest DJs five nights a week. Attention, ladies: there's a male dance revue Saturday evenings. ⊠ *1349 Kapi'olani Blvd., Ala Moana* ☎ *808/ 951–8671.*

Where to Eat

Preparing kālua pork

WORD OF MOUTH

"The food was out of this world [at Little Village Noodle House]! My husband and I go to Chinatown in NYC and Philly all the time, and this blew them away . . . It was the best and worth the trip to Chinatown."   –JEC

"Exceptional. We ended up having dinner [at La Mer] twice during our stay. The food, service, staff, etc., were just excellent. The view is probably the best in Honolulu. Very romantic."

–Michael

DINING PLANNER

Take a Tip from Us

With the astronomical cost of living on the Islands, and the fact that many restaurants pool tips, most servers barely get by. The standard for good service is 20%. Cash is kind.

Early to Table

Hawai'i still operates on plantation time, when people were in bed before the average Spaniard had sipped his aperitif. Takeout places still open at dawn and close shortly after mid-day. The most sought-after dinner reservations are between 6 and 6:30, but you can often have your pick of tables at 8. Exceptions: sushi bars and Japanese taverns, a few 24-hour diners, and some younger-spinning restaurants.

Be Warned & Be Mellow

Some of the best food in Hawai'i comes from places that look like they haven't seen a broom or dustcloth since statehood. Cultural differences (language barriers and a general lack of eye contact and engagement) are a fact of life. So are lines out the door and stupid hours at the few Hawaiian food places. Smile, shrug, and no huhu (don't get mad).

Where to Park & What to Bring

In Waikīkī, walk or take a cab; it's cheaper than parking or valet rates. Elsewhere on O'ahu, free, validated, and/or reasonably priced parking is widely available. Exceptions: downtown during the day (hideously expensive–take the trolley or TheBus) and China-town at night (marginally dicey–use valet or park in lighted lots such as Mark's Garage or municipal lots). Leave your smokes at home unless you're eating bar food; smoking is prohibited except in places where liquor revenues exceed food sales. Expect to BYOB to most small, ethnic eateries (except Japanese, which routinely serve beer and sake). Corkage fees are low or non-existent.

What It Costs

Costs are for the average entrée at dinner. As many Island restaurants offer small plates, mix-and-match individual items, and take-out food, the range is considerable, from as little as $1.50 for a dim sum order to $50 for a steak and lobster.

Having Reservations?

If you expect to dine at the holy trinity—Alan Wong's, Chef Mavro, or Roy's—book your table from home, weeks in advance. Also beware brand-new restaurants; they get slammed by migratory hordes for the first few weeks. Otherwise, reserve when you get into town. The practice of charging no-shows has not yet arrived on these shores, but do be considerate if you have to cancel.

WHAT IT COSTS					
	$$$$	**$$$**	**$$**	**$**	**¢**
RESTAURANTS	over $35	$27–$35	$18–$26	$10–$17	under $10
Restaurant prices are for a main course at dinner.					

By Wanda
Adams

O'AHU, WHERE THE MAJORITY of the Islands' 2,000-plus restaurants are located, offers the best of all worlds: it has the foreignness and excitement of Asia and Polynesia, but when the kids need McDonald's, or when you just have to have a Starbucks latte, they're here, too.

Budget for a $$$$ dining experience at the very top of the restaurant food chain, where chefs Alan Wong, Roy Yamaguchi, George Mavrothalassitis, and others you've read about in *Gourmet* put a sophisticated and unforgettable spin on local foods and flavors. Savor seared 'ahi tuna in sea urchin beurre blanc or steak marinated in Korean kim chee sauce.

Spend the rest of your food dollars where budget-conscious locals do: in plate-lunch places and small ethnic eateries, at roadside stands and lunchwagons, or at window-in-the-wall delis. Munch a musubi rice cake, slurp shave ice with red bean paste, order up Filipino pork adobo with two scoops of rice and macaroni salad.

In Waikīkī, where most visitors stay, you can find choices from gracious rooms with a view to surprisingly authentic Japanese noodle shops. But hop in the car, or on the trolley or bus, and travel just a few miles in any direction, and you can save your money and get in touch with the real food of Hawai'i.

Kaimukī's Wai'alae Avenue, for example, offers one of the city's best espresso bars, a hugely popular Chinese bakery, a highly recommended patisserie, an exceptional Italian bistro, a dim sum restaurant, Mexican food (rare here), and a Hawai'i regional cuisine standout, 3660 on the Rise—all in three blocks and 10 minutes from Waikīkī. Chinatown, 10 minutes in the other direction and easily reached by the Waikiki Trolley, is another dining (and shopping) treasure, not only for Chinese but also Vietnamese, Filipino, Malaysian, Indian, and Euroasian food, and even a chic little tea shop.

8

Waikīkī

American–Casual

¢–$ ✕ **Eggs 'n Things.** A favorite of Waikīkī hotel workers for its late hours (11 PM to 2 PM daily), this restaurant on the first floor of an obscure budget hotel has a hearty, country-style menu with a few island touches (tropical pancake syrups, fresh grilled fish) and a permanent line out front. ⊠ *Hawaiian Monarch Hotel, 1911-B Kalākaua Ave., Waikīkī* ☎ *808/949–0820* ▭ *No credit cards* ☉ *No dinner. $7–$14.*

¢–$ ✕ **South Shore Grill.** Just a couple of minutes out of Waikīkī proper on trendy Monsarrat, South Shore Grill is a great place to stoke up before or after sightseeing or beach time. It's inexpensive, and portions are ample. The food, a cut above the usual plate lunch or burgers, includes ciabatta bread sandwiches, entrée salads, and stuffed burritos. ⊠ *3114 Monsarrat Ave., Waikīkī* ☎ *808/734–0229* ▭ *No credit cards. $8–$15.*

¢–$ ✕ **Wailana Coffee House.** Budget-conscious snowbirds, night owls with a yen for karaoke, all-day drinkers of both coffee and the stronger stuff, hearty eaters and lovers of local-style plate lunches contentedly rub shoulders at this venerable diner and cocktail lounge at the edge of Waikīkī.

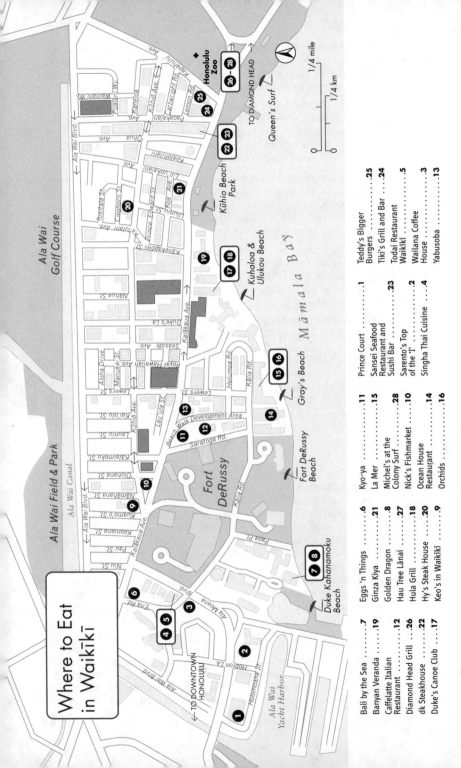

Where to Eat in Waikīkī

Most checks are under $9; $1.95 children's menu. Open 24 hours a day, 7 days a week, 365 days a year. ⊠ *Wailana Condiminium, ground floor, 1860 Ala Moana Blvd. (corner of 'Ena Road and Ala Moana), Waikīkī* ☎ *808/955–1674* ⚄ *Reservations not accepted* ▭ *AE, D, DC, MC, V. $5–$15.*

¢ ✕ **Teddy's Bigger Burgers.** They do but three things at Teddy's—burgers, fries, shakes—but they do them very, very well. The burgers are beefy, the fries crisply perfect, the shakes rich and sweet. The original location in Waikīkī has given birth to two others in Kailua and Hawai'i Kai. ⊠ *134 Kapahulu Ave., Waikīkī* ☎ *808/926–3444* ▭ *No credit cards* ☉ *Open daily. $6–$8.*

Chinese

$$–$$$ ✕ **Golden Dragon.** If you just can't make it to Chinatown, or if you want an English-spoken-here Chinese experience complete with an ocean view and—on some days—charming fortune teller, this lagoon-side hotel restaurant is the place. An expansive menu crosses regional boundaries in both à la carte and multi-course choices. Imperial Peking duck and Imperial beggar's chicken (whole chicken wrapped in lotus leaves and baked in a clay pot) must be ordered 24 hours in advance. ⊠ *Hilton Hawaiian Village, 2005 Kālia Rd., Waikīkī* ☎ *808/946–5336* ⚄ *Reservations essential* ▭ *AE, D, DC, MC, V* ☉ *No lunch.*

Contemporary

$$–$$$$ ✕ **Bali by the Sea.** This many-windowed, multilevel room takes delightful advantage of the restaurant's perch above the beach, facing Diamond Head. Chef Roberto Los Baños creates uncomplicated contemporary cuisine—grilled fish, steaks, and chops accented with East–West fusion flavors. The experienced staff, often called on to serve the VIPs who favor this hotel, extends unruffled and gracious service. ⊠ *Hilton Hawaiian Village, 2005 Kālia Rd., Waikīkī* ☎ *808/941–2254* ⚄ *Reservations essential* ▭ *AE, D, DC, MC, V* ☉ *Closed Sun. No lunch. $25–$43.*

$$–$$$$ ✕ **Banyan Veranda.** Seated on the wide, gracious veranda of Waikīkī's oldest hotel overlooking a courtyard shaded by a tree that's literally a registered historic landmark, you can relive the early days of Hawai'i hotel history. ■ TIP➡ Our favorite meal here is the very pricey but sybaritic Sunday brunch ($42.50), which includes hot and cold buffets, champagne, and strolling musicians. In the evening, there's fine "Pan-Pacific" cuisine, gentle music, and indoor as well as veranda dining. Breakfast is served Monday through Saturday and brunch on Sunday. ⊠ *Sheraton Moana Surfrider, 2365 Kalākaua Ave., Waikīkī* ☎ *808/922–3111* ⚄ *Reservations essential* ▭ *AE, D, DC, MC, V* ☉ *No lunch. $20–$42.*

$$–$$$$ ✕ **Diamond Head Grill.** This beautifully appointed room, with its surprising view across Kapi'olani Park and up the slopes of Diamond Head, has a split personality: quiet dinner house in the early evening, very happening bar in the late evening. New at the helm is award-winning chef Guillaume Burlion; expect contemporary sophistication with a French classic underpinning. ⊠ *2885 Kalākaua Ave., Waikīkī* ☎ *808/922–3734* ⚄ *Reservations essential* ▭ *AE, D, DC, MC, V. $23–$40.*

8

TAKEOUT

FOR LUNCH AT THE BEACH, or a movie night in your hotel room, do as Islanders do: get takeout. (And in the Islands, incidentally, the proper term is always takeout, never take-away or to-go.)

The universality of takeout here stems from traditions imported by plantation workers from Asia. The Chinese had their bakeries, the Japanese, *okazu-ya*, the Asian-style delis. Honolulu is awash in Western-style fast food joints, island-style plate-lunch places, and Asian drive-ins offering Japanese sushi, Korean barbecue, Thai noodles, and Vietnamese spring rolls.

But locals particularly cherish the old-style businesses, now into the third and fourth generation, usually inconveniently located, with no parking and ridiculously quirky hours—and each with a specialty or two that no one else can quite match.

Buy a cheap Stryofoam cooler, pack it with ice to keep the goodies cool, and stop by one of these places. And remember: you'll need cash.

Fukuya Delicatessen. This family operation on the main thoroughfare in charming Mōʻiliʻili, a mile or so out of Waikīkī, offers take-out breakfasts and lunches, Japanese snacks, noodle dishes, even confections. Try *mochi* (sweet rice-flour cakes), *chow fun* (silky noodles flecked with vegetables and barbecue pork), or Asian-style salads. The folks here are particularly patient and helpful to visitors. Open 6 AM–2 PM. ⊠ *2710 S. King, Mōʻiliʻili* ☎ *808/946-2073* ⏲ *Closed Mon. and Tues. No dinner* ▤ *No credit cards* ☞ *$2–$6.*

Kwong On. Minutes from Waikīkī, this Chinese bakery and snack shop is best visited early in the day (open 7 AM to 3 PM Monday through Saturday, but the good stuff is gone by noon). We recommend the curried half-moon pastries, pork hash, and *manapua* (steamed filled buns). ⊠ *3620-A Waiʻalae Ave., Kaimukī* ☎ *808/734-4666* ▤ *No credit cards* ⏲ *Closed Sun. No dinner* ☞ *$1–$6.*

Mitsu-Ken. Trust us. Ignore the downscale neighborhood just north of the city and the unpromising, battered exterior. Just line up and order the garlic chicken (either as a plate lunch, with rice and salad, or chicken only). Crispy, profoundly garlicky, and drizzled with some sweetish glaze that sets the whole thing off, Mitsu-Ken chicken will haunt your dreams. But go early; they open at 4 AM and by 1 PM, they're washing down the sidewalks. It's in Kahili, not far from the Bishop Museum. ⊠ *1223 N. School St., Kapālama* ☎ *808/848-5573* ▤ *No credit cards* ⏲ *Closed Sun. No dinner* ☞ *$1–$5.*

$$–$$$$ ✕ **Prince Court.** Though little heralded, this restaurant overlooking Ala Wai Yacht Harbor is a multifaceted success, offering exceptional high-end lunches and dinners, daily one-price buffets at every meal, and sold-out weekend brunches. The style is contemporary island cuisine (Portobello mushroom and crab hash napoleon, Pacific snapper with wild mushroom ragout) but with many Eastern touches, as this hotel is popular with Japanese nationals. ⊠ *Hawai'i Prince Hotel, 100 Holomoana St., Waikīkī* ☎ *808/944–4494* ⊛ *Reservations essential* ☰ *AE, D, DC, MC, V. $25–$42.*

$$–$$$ ✗ **Ocean House Restaurant.** Guests are greeted on the front porch at this re-creation of a 1900s plantation home. Tables and booths are spaced for views and covered in rich tropical fabrics. The menu puts forth the bounty of the Pacific with such dishes as coconut lobster skewers, seared peppered scallops, and macadamia nut–crusted sea bass. For beef lovers, there's the slow-roasted prime rib. ⊠ *Outrigger Reef on the Beach, 2169 Kālia Rd., Waikīkī* ☎ *808/923–2277* ☰ *AE, D, DC, MC, V* ☾ *No lunch. $19–$28.*

$–$$$ ✗ **Hau Tree Lānai.** The many-branched, vinelike hau tree is ideal for sitting under, and it's said that the one that spreads itself over this beachside courtyard is the very one that shaded Robert Louis Stevenson as he mused and wrote about Hawai'i. In any case, diners are still enjoying the shade, though the view has changed—the gay-friendly beach over the low wall is paved with hunky sunbathers. The food is unremarkable island casual, but we like the place for late afternoon or early-evening drinks, pūpū, and people-watching. ⊠ *New Otani Kaimana Beach Hotel, 2863 Kalākaua Ave., Waikīkī* ☎ *808/921–7066* ⊕ *www.kaimana. com* ⊛ *Reservations essential* ☰ *AE, D, DC, MC, V. $15–$32.*

$–$$ ✗ **Duke's Canoe Club.** Notorious as the spot where Jimmy Buffett did a free, impromptu concert that had people standing six-deep on the beach outside, Duke's is both an open-air bar and a very popular steak-and-seafood grill. It's known for its Big Island pork ribs, huli-huli (rotisserie) chicken, and grilled catch of the day, as well as for a simple and economical Sunday brunch. A drawback is that it's often loud and crowded, and the live contemporary Hawaiian music often stymies conversation. ⊠ *Outrigger Waikīkī on the Beach, 2335 Kalākaua Ave., Waikīkī* ☎ *808/922–2268* ⊛ *Reservations essential* ☰ *AE, DC, MC, V. $12–$25.*

$–$$ ✗ **Tiki's Grill and Bar.** Tiki's, on the second floor of a busy hotel, is the kind of place people come to Waikīkī for: a retro–South Pacific spot designed for fun. It has a back-of-the-bar faux volcano, an open-air lounge with live local-style music, indoor-outdoor dining, and a view of the beach across the street. The menu is—inevitably—contemporary island cuisine (Japanese seven-spice salmon, plate-lunch standards reinterpreted in a sophisticated way), with exceptional desserts and a late-night bar menu. ⊠ *Aston Waikīkī Beach Hotel, 2570 Kalākaua Ave., Waikīkī* ☎ *808/923–8454* ⊛ *Reservations essential* ☰ *AE, D, DC, MC, V. $10–$25.*

¢–$$ ✗ **Hula Grill.** The placid younger sister of boisterous Duke's downstairs, this restaurant and bar resembles a plantation-period summer home: open to the air, outfitted with kitschy decor, stone-flagged floors, warm wood, and floral prints. The food is carefully prepared and familiar—standard breakfast items, steaks and grilled seafood at dinner—but with local and Asian touches that add interest. There's a fabulous Diamond Head view. ⊠ *Outrigger Waikīkī on the Beach, 2335 Kalākaua Ave., Waikīkī* ☎ *808/923–4852* ⊛ *Reservations essential* ☰ *AE, D, DC, MC, V* ☾ *No lunch. $7–$26.*

8

French

★ **$$$$** ✕ **La Mer.** La Mer, like the hotel in which it's housed (Halekūlani, "House Befitting Heaven"), is pretty much heavenly. The softly lighted, low-ceiling room has its windows open to the breeze, the perfectly framed vista of Diamond Head, and the faint sound of music from a courtyard below. The food captures the rich and yet sunny flavors of the south of France in one tiny, exquisite course after another. We recommend the degustation menu; place yourself in the sommelier's hands for wine choices from the hotel's exceptional cellar. ✉ *Halekūlani, 2199 Kālia Rd., Waikīkī* ☎ *808/923–2311* ⚱ *Reservations essential* 🎩 *Jacket required* ▤ *AE, DC, MC, V* ⊘ *No lunch. $38–$48.*

$$$–$$$$ ✕ **Michel's at the Colony Surf.** The wide-open windows are so close to the water that you literally feel the soft mist at high tide. ■ **TIP→ This is arguably the most romantic spot in Waikīkī for a sunset dinner for two.** Venerable Michel's is synonymous with fine dining in the minds of Oahuans who have been coming here for 20 years. The menu is très, très French with both classic choices (escargot, foie gras) and more contemporary dishes (potato-crusted onaga fish). There's dinner nightly, and Sunday brunch. ✉ *Colony Surf, 2895 Kalākaua Ave., Waikīkī* ☎ *808/923– 6552* ⚱ *Reservations essential* ▤ *AE, D, DC, MC, V* ⊘ *No lunch. $28–$40.*

Italian

$$–$$$$ ✕ **Sarento's Top of the 'I'.** Among the best view restaurants in Honolulu, looking toward both the Ko'olau Mountains and the South Shore, 30th-floor Sarento's is an especially favored date-night venue. Regional Italian cuisine is the specialty, and the lobster ravioli and osso buco are local favorites. The wine cellar contains some gems, and there is no more attentive service staff in the city. ✉ *Renaissance 'Ilikai Waikīkī Hotel, 1777 Ala Moana, top fl., Waikīkī* ☎ *808/955–5559* ⚱ *Reservations essential* ▤ *AE, D, DC, MC, V* ⊘ *No lunch. $18–$36.*

$$$ ✕ **Caffelatte Italian Restaurant.** Every dish at this tiny trattoria run by a Milanese family is worth ordering, from the gnocchi in a thick, rich sauce of Gorgonzola to spinach ravioli served with butter and basil. The tiramisu is the best in town, and the sugared orange slices in Russian vodka are a perfect ending to a meal. Each person must order three courses (appetizer, main course, and dessert). There's no parking, so walk here if you can. ■ **TIP→ One drawback: no air-conditioning, so it can be warm and noisy due to open windows.** ✉ *339 Saratoga Rd., 2nd level, Waikīkī* ☎ *808/924–1414* ▤ *AE, DC, MC, V* ⊘ *Closed Tues. $35.*

Japanese

$$–$$$$ ✕ **Kyo-ya.** Tell an Islander that dinner is at Kyo-ya, and you get a long drawn-out "Ooooh," acknowledging both the restaurant's reputation for quality and its top-flight prices. As to authenticity, suffice it to say that you're likely to run into members of the Japanese consular staff. The menu is complete with *teishoku* (combination meals that include salad, soup, sides, and rice), very fresh sushi, noodles, grilled dishes, and hot pots prepared at table. Kyo-ya occupies a striking building with a contemporary teahouse design fronted by an Asian garden. ✉ *2057*

USE YOUR NOODLE

WHEN ISLANDERS ARE HUNGRY, broke, and in need of comfort, they choose noodles.

Three dishes predominate:

Saimin: Saimin is a noodle soup that has roots in similar dishes from China, Japan, and the Philippines, but it is distinctly different from any of its predecessors, being generally sweeter-tasting and heartier. The basic dish is composed of thin wheat noodles in a hot broth (either Japanese dashi, made from bonito flakes, or a pork-based meat broth), garnished with minced green onions and strips of fried egg, slices of bright pink fish cake (surimi), bits of meat (which may be *char siu*–Chinese barbecued pork–ham, luncheon meat, or even the Island favorite, Spam or Portuguese sausage), even pork-stuffed won tons. At its most elaborate, saimin is topped with

hearty "teri-sticks" (grilled chicken or meat skewers). Saimin is on the menu of every fast food shop and family restaurant in the Islands; it's even sold at McDonald's.

Udon and soba: Japanese noodle shops offer hot udon (thick wheat noodles) or cold soba (thin buckwheat strands). These fall on the salty, fishy side of the taste scale and make light, quick, inexpensive meals. Noodle shops are practically the only really cheap option in Waikīkī.

Phô: Phô (pronounced like duh with an "f"), beloved of Vietnamese for any meal of the day, is relatively new to the Islands, but shops specializing in this fragrant beef noodle soup have quickly proliferated. With your steaming noodles, you'll receive herbs and other garnishes to munch alongside or stir into the soup.

8

Kalākaua Ave., Waikīkī ☎ *808/947–3911* ⌕ *Reservations essential* ▤ *AE, D, DC, MC, V* ⊘ *No lunch Sun. $20–$55.*

★ **$–$$$** ✕ **Sansei Seafood Restaurant & Sushi Bar.** D. K. Kodama's "Japanese-based Pacific Rim" cuisine is an experience not to be missed, from early-bird dinners (from 5:30 PM) to late-night appetizers and sushi (until 2 AM Thursday–Saturday, with karaoke). The specialty sushi here—mango-crab roll, foie gras nigiri with eel sauce, and more—leaves California rolls far behind. We fantasize about the signature calamari salad with spicy Korean sauce and crisp-tender calamari. Cleverly named and beautifully prepared dishes come in big and small plates or in a $35 six-course tasting menu. Finish with tempura-fried ice cream or Mama Kodama's brownies. ⊠ *Waikīkī Beach Marriott Resort and Spa, 2552 Kalākaua Ave., Waikīkī* ☎ *808/931–6286* ▤ *AE, D, MC, V. $16–$30.*

Japanese Noodle Shops

¢–$$ ✕ **Yabusoba.** In Japan, noodles are considered an art form, with connoisseurs going to great lengths to find the best soba noodles and the richest broth. In Honolulu, many visiting and resident Japanese nationals consider Yabusoba the place for hand-made buckwheat noodles and well-made tempura. ■ **TIP→ It's also been featured in Japanese magazines** as a great place for celebrity-sighting (you may not recognize Nippon's stars, but watch the folks around you react.). ✉ *255 Beachwalk Ave, Unit No. 2, Waikīkī* ☎ *808/926–5303* ⌙ *Reservations essential* ▭ *No credit cards. $7–$20.*

¢–$ ✕ **Ginza Kiya.** Distinctly unfancy, with linoleum floors and wooden tables, this Tokyo-style spot comes highly recommended for the only thing noodle fanciers care about: authentic, rich broth and fresh *udon* (wheat) and *soba* (buckweat) noodles. Hot noodle soup, cold noodles with dipping sauce, and *donburi* (rice bowls), are offered, plus such specialties as *hiya yakko* (cold tofu topped with ginger and soy sauce) and Western-style green salad on noodles with sesame dressing. Don't worry—there's an English-language menu and a fork will appear on your faux lacquer tray without your even having to ask. Portions are sizable; entrées are served with salad, pickles, and clear soup. The small bar stocks beer, sake, *shochu* (Japanese flavored liquor), and Japanese newspapers. ✉ *Aston Waikiki Circle Hotel, 2464 Kalākaua Ave., Waikīkī* ☎ *808/923–8840* ⌙ *Reservations not accepted* ▭ *No credit cards. $7–$15.*

> ### BEST BREAKFAST
>
> **Big City Diner** (Ala Moana & Kailua). Start the day like a local: rice instead of toast, fish or Portuguese sauce instead of bacon, even noodles.
>
> **Cinnamon's Restaurant** (Kailua). Voted best for breakfast in a local newspaper poll, Cinnamon's does all the breakfast standards.
>
> **Duke's Canoe Club and Hula Grill** (Waikīkī). Duke's has an $11.95 buffet; Hula Grill has a pricier but carefully prepared à la carte breakfast.
>
> **Eggs 'n Things** (Waikīkī). This is a longtime favorite for late hours and country-style food with island touches.

Seafood

$$–$$$$ ✕ **Nick's Fishmarket.** Nick's is like a favorite soap opera—go away for a while, come back and very little has changed. And that's why we like it: the dim lighting, the expansive banquettes, the retro-ish Continental menu, tableside service for Caesar salad or flambéed desserts; it's like a window back to just the good part of the good old days. After the lobster bisque or sautéed abalaone, leave room for signature Vanbana Pie, a decadent combination of bananas, vanilla Swiss-almond ice cream, and hot caramel sauce. ✉ *Waikīkī Gateway Hotel, 2070 Kalākaua Ave., Waikīkī* ☎ *808/955–6333* ⌙ *Reservations essential* ▭ *AE, D, DC, MC, V. $21–$50.*

$$–$$$$ ✕ **Orchids.** Perched along the sea wall at historic Gray's Beach, Orchids is beloved of power breakfasters, ladies who lunch, and family groups celebrating at the elaborate Sunday brunch. La Mer, upstairs, is better known for evening, but we have found dinner at Orchids equally enjoyable. The fold-back walls open to the breezes, the orchids add splashes of color, the seafood is perfectly prepared, and the wine list is intriguing. Plus, it is more casual and a bit less expensive than La Mer. Whatever meal you have here, finish with the hotel's signature coconut layer cake, a longtime favorite of the local-born elite, who consider Halekūlani

Continued on page 177

AUTHENTIC TASTE OF HAWAI'I: LŪ'AU OR LAULAU?

The best place to sample Hawaiian food is at a backyard lū'au. Aunts and uncles are cooking, the pig is from a cousin's farm, and the fish is from a brother's boat.

But even locals have to angle for invitations to those rare occasions. So your choice is most likely between a commercial lū'au and a Hawaiian restaurant.

Most commercial lū'au will offer you little of the authentic diet; they're more about umbrella drinks, laughs, spectacle, and fun. Expect to spend some time—most are far from Waikīkī—and no small amount of cash.

For greater authenticity, folksy experiences, and rock-bottom prices, visit a Hawaiian restaurant (most are in anonymous storefronts in residential neighborhoods). Expect rough edges and some effort negotiating the menu.

In either case, much of what is known today as Hawaiian food would be as foreign to a 16th century Hawaiian as risotto or chow mien. The pre-contact diet was simple and healthy—mainly raw and steamed seafood and vegetables. Early Hawaiians used earth ovens and heated stones to cook seafood, taro, sweet potatoes, and breadfruit and seasoned their food with sea salt and ground kukui nuts. Seaweed, fern shoots, sweet potato vines, coconut, banana, sugarcane, and select greens and roots rounded out the diet.

Successive waves of immigrants added their favorites to the ti leaf-lined table. So it is that foods as disparate as salt salmon and chicken long rice are now Hawaiian—even though there is no salmon in Hawaiian waters and long rice (cellophane noodles) is Chinese.

AT THE LŪʻAU: KĀLUA PORK

The heart of any lūʻau is the *imu*, the earth oven in which a whole pig is roasted. The preparation of an imu is an arduous affair for most families, who tackle it only once a year or so, for a baby's first birthday or at Thanksgiving, when many Islanders prefer to imu their turkeys. Commercial lūʻau operations have it down to a science, however.

THE ART OF THE STONE
The key to a proper imu is the *pohaku*, the stones. Imu cook by means of long, slow, moist heat released by special stones which can withstand a hot fire without exploding. Many Hawaiian families treasure their imu stones, keeping them in a pile in the back yard and passing them on through generations.

PIT COOKING
The imu makers first dig a pit about the size of a refrigerator, then lay down *kiawe* (mesquite) wood and stones, and build a white-hot fire that is allowed to burn itself out. The ashes are raked away, and the hot stones covered with banana and ti leaves. Well-wrapped in ti or banana leaves and a net of chicken wire, the pig is lowered onto the leaf-covered stones. *Laulau* (leaf-wrapped bundles of meats, fish, and taro leaves) may also be placed inside. Leaves—ti, banana, even ginger—cover the pig followed by wet burlap sacks (to create steam). The whole is topped with a canvas tarp and left to steam for the better part of a day.

OPENING THE IMU
This is the moment everyone waits for: The imu is unwrapped like a giant present and the imu keepers gingerly wrestle out the steaming pig. When it's unwrapped, the meat falls moist and smoky-flavored from the bone, looking and tasting just like Southern-style pulled pork, but without the barbecue sauce.

WHICH LŪʻAU?
Germaine's Lūʻau. Widely regarded as most folksy and local.

Paradise Cove. Party-hearty atmosphere, kid-friendly.

Polynesian Cultural Center. The sharpest production values but no booze.

Royal Hawaiian Hotel. Gracious and relaxed, famous mai tais.

AUTHENTIC TASTE OF HAWAI'I: LŪ'AU OR LAULAU?   **8**

MEA 'AI 'ONO.
GOOD THINGS TO EAT.

LAULAU
Steamed meats, fish, and taro leaf in ti-leaf bundles: fork-tender, a medley of flavors; the taro resembles spinach.

LOMI LOMI SALMON
Salt salmon in a piquant salad or relish with onions, tomatoes.

POI (DON'T CALL IT LIBRARY PASTE.)
Islanders are beyond tired of jokes about poi, a paste made of pounded taro root.

Consider: The Hawaiian Adam is descended from *kalo* (taro). Young taro plants are called "keiki"–children. Poi is the first food after mother's milk for many Islanders. 'Ai, the word for food, is synonymous with poi in many contexts.

Not only that. We like it. "There is no meat that doesn't taste good with poi," the old Hawaiians said.

But you have to know how to eat it: with something rich or powerfully flavored. "It is salt that makes the poi go in," is another adage. When you're served poi, try it with a mouthful of smoky kālua pork or salty lomi lomi salmon. Its slightly sour blandness cleanses the palate. And if you don't like it, smile and say something polite. (And slide that bowl over to a local.)

Laulau

Lomi Lomi Salmon

Poi

E HELE MAI 'AI! COME AND EAT!

Hawaiian restaurants tend to be inconveniently located in well-worn storefronts with little or no parking, outfitted with battered tables and clattering Melmac dishes, open odd (and usually limited) hours and days, and often so crowded you have to wait. But they personify aloha, invariably run by local families who welcome tourists who take the trouble to find them.

Many are cash-only operations and combination plates are a standard feature: one or two entrées, a side such as chicken long rice, choice of poi or steamed rice and–if the place is really old-style–a tiny portion of coarse Hawaiian salt and some raw onions for relish.

Most serve some foods that aren't, strictly speaking, Hawaiian, but are beloved of

kama'āina, such as salt meat with watercress (preserved meat in a tasty broth), or *akubone* (skipjack tuna fried in a tangy vinegar sauce).

Our two favorites: **'Ono Hawaiian Foods** and **Helena's Hawaiians Food.**

MENU GUIDE

Much of the Hawaiian language encountered during a stay in the Islands will appear on restaurant menus and lists of lū'au fare. Here's a quick primer.

'ahi: *yellowfin tuna.*

aku: *skipjack, bonito tuna.*

'ama'ama: *mullet; it's hard to get but tasty.*

bento: *a box lunch.*

chicken lū'au: *a stew made from chicken, taro leaves, and coconut milk.*

haupia: *a light, gelatinlike dessert made from coconut.*

imu: *the underground ovens in which pigs are roasted for lū'au.*

kālua: *to bake underground.*

kaukau: *food. The word comes from Chinese but is used in the Islands.*

kimchee: *Korean dish of pickled cabbage made with garlic and hot peppers.*

Kona coffee: *coffee grown in the Kona district of the Big Island.*

laulau: *literally, a bundle. Laulau are morsels of pork, chicken, butterfish, or other ingredients wrapped with young taro shoots in ti leaves for steaming.*

liliko'i: *passion fruit, a tart, seedy yellow fruit that makes delicious desserts and jellies.*

lomi lomi: *to rub or massage; also a massage. Lomi lomi salmon is fish that has been rubbed with onions and herbs, commonly served with minced onions and tomatoes.*

lū'au: *a Hawaiian feast, also the leaf of the taro plant used in preparing such a feast.*

lū'au leaves: *cooked taro tops with a taste similar to spinach.*

mahimahi: *mild-flavored dolphinfish, not the marine mammal.*

mai tai: *potent rum drink with orange and lime juice, from the Tahitian word for "good."*

malassada: *a Portuguese deep-fried doughnut without a hole, dipped in sugar.*

manapua: *dough wrapped around diced pork.*

manō: *shark.*

niu: *coconut.*

'ōkolehao: *a liqueur distilled from the ti root.*

onaga: *pink or red snapper.*

ono: *a long, slender mackerel-like fish; also called wahoo.*

'ono: *delicious; also hungry.*

'opihi: *a tiny shellfish, or mollusk, found on rocks; also called limpets.*

pāpio: *a young ulua or jack fish.*

pohā: *Cape gooseberry. Tasting a bit like honey, the pohā berry is often used in jams and desserts.*

poi: *a paste made from pounded taro root, a staple of the Hawaiian diet.*

poke: *chopped, pickled raw tuna, tossed with herbs and seasonings.*

pūpū: *Hawaiian hors d'oeuvre.*

saimin: *long thin noodles and vegetables in broth, often garnished with small pieces of fish cake, scrambled egg, luncheon meat, and green onion.*

sashimi: *raw fish thinly sliced and usually eaten with soy sauce.*

ti leaves: *a member of the agave family. The fragrant leaves are used to wrap food while cooking and removed before eating.*

uku: *deep-sea snapper.*

ulua: *a member of the jack family that also includes pompano and amberjack. Also called crevalle, jack fish, and jack crevalle.*

something of a private club. ⊠ *Halekūlani, 2199 Kālia Rd., Waikīkī* ☎ *808/923–2311* ⌂ *Reservations essential* ▤ *AE, D, DC, MC, V. $22–$40.*

$–$$$ ✕ **Todai Restaurant Waikīkī.** Bountiful buffets and menus that feature seafood are Islanders' two favorites, so this Japan-based restaurant is a local favorite, despite the difficulties of parking in Waikīkī. It continues to be popular with budget-conscious travelers for the wide range of hot dishes, sushi, and the 160-foot seafood spread, though the emphasis here is more on quantity than quality. Lunch is $14.95 weekdays, $15.95 weekends; dinner is $25.95–$26.95 daily. ⊠ *1910 Ala Moana Blvd., Waikīkī* ☎ *808/947–1000* ⌂ *Reservations essential* ▤ *AE, D, DC, MC, V. $15–$27.*

Steak

$$–$$$$ ✕ **dk Steakhouse.** Around the country, the steak house has returned to prominence as chefs rediscover the art of dry-aging beef and of preparing the perfect Bernaise sauce. D. K. Kodama's chic second-floor restaurant characterizes this trend with such presentations as the sybaritic 22-ounce bone-in rib eye aged 15 days in-house ($32.95) and Oscar of filet mignon with blue crab Bernaise ($29.95). ■ **TIP→ The restaurant shares space, but not a menu, with Kodama's Sansei Seafood Restaurant & Sushi Bar; sit at the bar perched between the two and you can order from either menu.** ⊠ *Waikīkī Beach Marriott Resort and Spa, 2552 Kalākaua Ave., Waikīkī* ☎ *808/931–6280* ▤ *AE, D, MC, V* ☻ *No lunch. $19–$55.*

$$–$$$$ ✕ **Hy's Steak House.** If the Rat Pack reconvened for big steaks and a bigger red, they'd feel right at home at Hy's, which has changed little in the last 30 years. The formula: prime grade beef, old-style service, a men's club atmosphere (but ladies very welcome), and a wine list recognized for excellence by *Wine Spectator.* Specialties include Beef Wellington, Caesar salad, and those tableside flambéed desserts we see so rarely now. ⊠ *Waikīkī Park Heights Hotel, 2440 Kūhiō Ave., Waikīkī* ☎ *808/922–5555* ⌂ *Reservations essential* ▤ *AE, DC, MC, V* ☻ *No lunch. $20–$60.*

Thai

$–$$$ ✕ **Singha Thai Cuisine.** Chai and Joy Chaowasaree's devotion to their native Thailand is evident in the gilt model of the Thai royal palace that graces the entryway of this restaurant just below street level on a busy Waikīkī corner. This is also the only Thai restaurant in the city to showcase Thai dance each evening. We especially like Singha Thai's way with seafood—Siamese Fighting Fish, a whole fish sizzling in garlic-chili oil, or fish in Thai chili ginger and black bean sauce—and the contemporary additions to the menu, such as blackened 'ahi summer rolls. ⊠ *1910 Ala Moana Blvd., Waikīkī* ☎ *808/941–2898* ▤ *AE, D, DC, MC, V* ☻ *No lunch. $13–$35.*

$–$$ ✕ **Keo's in Waikīkī.** Many Islanders—and many Hollywood stars—got their first taste of pad thai noodles, lemongrass, and coconut milk curry at one of Keo Sananikone's restaurants. This one, perched right at the entrance to Waikīkī, characterizes his formula: a bright, clean space awash in flowers with intriguing menu titles and reasonable prices. Evil Jungle Prince, a stir-fry redolent of Thai basil, flecked with chilies and rich

8

with coconut milk, is a classic. Also try the apple bananas in coconut milk. ✉ *2028 Kūhiō Ave., Waikīkī* ☎ *808/951–9355* ☐ *AE, D, DC, MC, V. $10–$18.*

Honolulu: Ala Moana, Downtown & Chinatown

American–Casual

¢–$$ ✕ **Kincaid's Fish, Chop & Chowder House.** Known for Copper River salmon in season, consistently well-made salads and seafood specials, efficient service and appropriate pricing, Kincaid's, a member of the Seattle-based Restaurants Unlimited chain, is business lunch central. But, with its tired, window-fronted room overlooking Kewalo Basin harbor, it's also a relaxing place for a post-shopping drink or intimate dinner. ✉ *Ward Warehouse, 2nd level, 1050 Ala Moana Blvd., Kaka'ako* ☎ *808/591–2005* ☖ *Reservations recommended* ☐ *AE, D, DC, MC, V. $7–$25.*

¢–$$ ✕ **On Jin's Cafe.** To look at this small café, you'd not suspect that restaurateur On Jin Kin had a career as an opera singer and owned a critically acclaimed fine dining restaurant in Honolulu at one time. But her well-traveled background and unerring taste show on the plate in such touches as a perfectly dressed white bean salad with a lunch sandwich, instead of the usual macaroni or greens. Lunch is an order-at-the-counter scramble, but the restaurant becomes a serene sit-down experience at dinner. The East-West menu shows hints of her Korean ethnicity but is unclassifiable as anything other than alluring. ✉ *401 Kamake'e St., Kaka'ko* ☎ *808/589–1666* ☖ *Reservations not accepted* ☐ *AE, D, DC, MC, V. $7–$20.*

¢–$$ ✕ **Ryan's Grill.** An all-purpose food and drink emporium, lively and popular Ryan's offers an exceptionally well-stocked bar with an outdoor deck and sports on TV, plus lunch, dinner, and small plates from late morning (11 ᴀᴍ) to early morning (2 ᴀᴍ). The eclectic menu ranges from an addictive hot artichoke dip with focaccia bread to well-done grilled fresh fish and sophisticated versions of local favorites (Kobe beef hamburger steak), pasta, and salads. ✉ *Ward Center, 1200 Ala Moana Blvd., Kaka'ko* ☎ *808/591-9132* ☖ *Reservations recommended* ☐ *AE, D, DC, MC, V. $6–$21.*

¢–$ ✕ **Contemporary Cafe.** Little known but much appreciated by those who have discovered it, this tasteful lunch spot offers toothsome but light and healthful food of a kind that's woefully rare in Honolulu. The short but well-selected menu runs to housemade soups, crostini of the day, innovative sandwiches garnished with fruit, and a hummus plate with fresh pita. Located in the exclusive Makīkī Heights neighborhood above the city, the restaurant spills out of the ground floor of The Contemporary Museum onto the lawn. ✉ *The Contemporary Museum, 2411 Makīkī Heights Dr., Makīkī* ☎ *808/523–3362* ☖ *Reservations not accepted* ☐ *AE, D, DC, MC, V* ☉ *No dinner. $7–$10.*

¢–$ ✕ **Pavilion Cafe.** The cool courtyards and varied galleries of the Honolulu Academy of Arts are well worth a visit and, afterward, so is Mike Nevin's popular lunch restaurant. The café overflows onto a lanai from which you can ponder Asian statuary and a burbling water feature while you wait for your salade niçoise or signature Piadina Sandwich (fresh-baked flatbread rounds stuffed with arugula, tomatoes, basil, and cheese). Reservations recommended. ⊠ *Honolulu Academy of Arts, 900 S. Beretania St., Downtown* ☎ *808/ 532–8734* ▭ *AE, D, DC, MC, V* ⊘ *No dinner. Closed Sun.–Mon.* *$8–$12.*

★ ¢-$ ✕ **Side Street Inn.** Famous as the place where celebrity chefs gather after hours, local boy Colin Nishida's pub is on an obscure side street near Ala Moana Shopping Center. It is worth searching for, despite annoying smoke and sometimes surly staff, because Nishida makes the best darned pork chops and fried rice in the world. Local-style bar food comes in huge, share-plate portions. ■ TIP→ This is a place to dress any way you like, nosh all night, watch sports on TV, and sing karaoke until they boot you out. Pūpū (in portions so large as to be dinner) is from 4 PM to 12:30 AM daily. Reservations for large parties only. ⊠ *1225 Hopaka St., Ala Moana* ☎ *808/591–0253* ▭ *AE, D, DC, MC, V* ⊘ *No lunch weekends. $8–$15.*

¢ ✕ **Big City Diner.** These unfussy retro diners offer a short course in local-style breakfasts—rice instead of potatoes, fish or Portuguese sausage instead of bacon, steaming bowls of noodles—with generous portions, low prices, and pronounced flavors. Breakfast is served all day. ⊠ *Ward Entertainment Center, 1060 'Auahi St., Ala Moana* ☎ *808/591–8891* ▭ *AE, D, MC, V. $5–$9.*

Barbecue

¢-$$ ✕ **Dixie Grill.** Southern food is hard to come by in Hawai'i, so this eatery and its Pearl City cousin are always crowded with military families and other expats from below the Mason-Dixon line hungry for hush puppies, grits, barbecue (pulled or on the bone, in different styles), and Dixie beer. The odd custom of yelling out the names of certain specials, and clanging a bell to herald their arrival, means the place is loud. ■ TIP→ But it's also family-friendly with a sand box for the kids. ⊠ *404 Ward Ave., Kaka'ako* ☎ *808/596–8359* ▭ *AE, D, DC, MC, V. $5–$21.*

Chinese

¢-$ ✕ **Legend Seafood Restaurant.** Do as the locals do: start your visit to Chinatown with breakfast dim sum at Legend. If you want to be able to hear yourself think, get there before 9 AM, especially on weekends. ■ TIP→ And don't be shy: Use your best cab-hailing technique and sign language to make the cart ladies stop at your table and show you their wares. The pork-filled steamed buns, hearty spare ribs, prawn dumplings, and still-warm custard tarts will fortify you for shopping. ⊠ *Chinese Cultural*

DIM SUM

Dim sum is the original small plates meal, born of roadside tea stands in southern China and served from early morning to mid-afternoon. Dumplings and steamed dishes predominate, with some soup and sweets.

You'll get tea but no menus, and a bill on which your purchases will be marked. As the food carts roll by, be cheerfully forceful: Wave to get the attention of the tea ladies; ask to see what's on the cart and be aware that some things will look odd and taste odder. Popular with all: dumplings, buns, noodles, custard tarts.

8

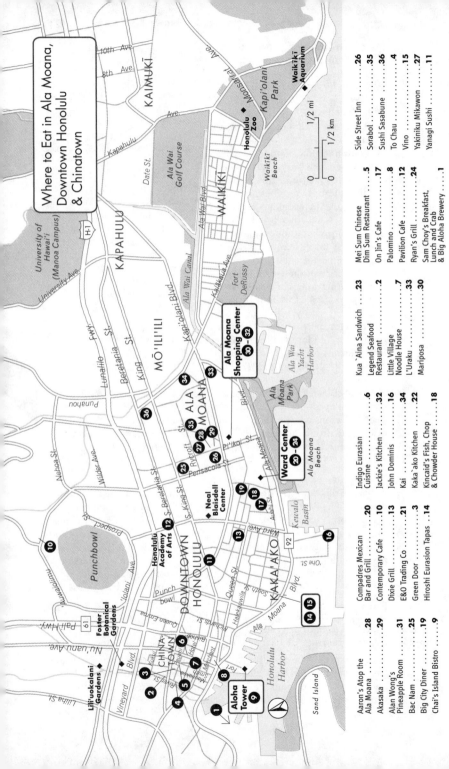

Where to Eat in Ala Moana, Downtown Honolulu & Chinatown

0 ─── 1/2 mi
0 ─── 1/2 km

Plaza, 100 N. Beretania St., Chinatown ☎ *808/532–1868* ☰ *AE, D, DC, MC, V. $5–$15.*

¢–$ ✕ **Little Village Noodle House.** Unassuming and budget-friendly, Little Vil-
Fodor'sChoice lage sets a standard of friendly and attentive service to which every Chi-
★   nese restaurant should aspire. We have roamed the large, pan-China menu and found a new favorite in everything we've tried: shredded beef, spinach with garlic, Shanghai noodles, honey walnut shrimp, orange chicken, dried green beans. Two words: go there. ✉ *1113 Smith St., Chinatown* ☎ *808/545–3008* ☰ *AE, D, MC, V. $7–$15.*

¢–$ ✕ **Mei Sum Chinese Dim Sum Restaurant.** In contrast to the sprawling and noisy halls in which dim sum is generally served, Mei Sum is compact and shiny bright. It's open daily, serving nothing but small plates from 7:45 AM to 8:45 PM. Be ready to guess and point at the color photos of dim sum favorites as not much English is spoken, but the delicate buns and tasty bits are exceptionally well-prepared. ✉ *65 N. Pauahi St., Chinatown* ☎ *808/531–3268* ☰ *No credit cards. $3–$10.*

Contemporary

$$–$$$$ ✕ **The Bistro at Century Center.** You'd think The Bistro had occupied this dim labyrinth of plush spaces for decades, but it opened just a few years ago with the express purpose of bringing back dignified dining: steak Diane and duck à l'orange, tuxedoed waiters, cushy banquettes, a pianist who can perform any request, and bottomless martinis. It was an immediate success and remains so. ✉ *Century Center condominium, 3rd fl., 1750 Kalākaua Ave., Ala Moana* ☎ *808/943–6500* ☰ *AE, D, DC, MC, V. $18–$60.*

$$–$$$$ ✕ **Chai's Island Bistro.** Chai Chaowasaree's stylish, light-bathed and orchid-draped lunch and dinner restaurant expresses the sophisticated side of this Thai-born immigrant. He plays East against West on the plate in signature dishes such as *kataifi* (baked and shredded phyllo), macadamia-crusted prawns, 'ahi *katsu* (tuna steaks dredged crisp Japanese breadcrumbs and quickly deep-fried), crispy duck confetti spring rolls, and seafood risotto. ■ TIP→ **Some of Hawai'i's best-known contemporary Hawaiian musicians play brief dinner shows here Wednesday through Sunday.** ✉ *Aloha Tower Marketplace, 1 Aloha Tower Dr., Downtown Honolulu* ☎ *808/585–0012* ☰ *AE, D, DC, MC, V* ☺ *No lunch Sat.–Mon. $18–$36.*

$–$$$$ ✕ **Alan Wong's Pineapple Room.** This is not your grandmother's department store restaurant. It's über-chef Alan Wong's more casual second spot, where chef de cuisine Neil Nakasone plays intriguing riffs on local food themes. We are frankly addicted to the spicy chili-fried soybeans and the Pineapple Room Baby Back Ribs. Pleasant surroundings and very professional service. Reservations recommended. ✉ *Macy's, Ala Moana Center, 1450 Ala Moana Blvd., Ala Moana* ☎ *808/945–6573* ☰ *AE, D, DC, MC, V. $10–$36.*

$$–$$$ ✕ **Indigo Eurasian Cuisine.** Owner Glenn Chu sets the mood for an evening out on the town: the walls are red brick, the ceilings are high, and from the restaurant's lounge next door comes the sultry sound of late-night jazz. Take a bite of goat cheese won tons with four-fruit sauce followed by rich Mongolian lamb chops. After dinner, duck into the hip Green Room lounge or Opium Den & Champagne Bar for a nightcap.

8

■ TIP→ If you're touring downtown at lunchtime, the Eurasian buffet is an especially good deal at $15.95 per person. ✉ *1121 Nu'uanu Ave., Downtown Honolulu* ☎ *808/521-2900* ▤ *AE, D, DC, MC, V. $19–$30.*

$$–$$$ ✕ **Mariposa.** Yes, the wee little cups of bouillion are there at lunch, and the popovers, but in every other regard, chef Douglas Lum's menu departs from the Nieman Marcus model, incorporating a clear sense of Pacific place. The veranda, open to the breezes and view of Ala Moana Park, twirling ceiling fans, and life-size hula-girl murals say Hawai'i. The popovers come with jam made from native poha berries—a relative of the gooseberry—and local fish are featured nightly in luxuriant specials. ✉ *Nieman Marcus, Ala Moana Center, 1450 Ala Moana, Ala Moana* ☎ *808/951-3420* ⌁ *Reservations essential* ▤ *AE, D, DC, MC, V. $10–$30.*

$–$$$ ✕ **Aaron's Atop the Ala Moana.** Location, location, location, they say, but in this case, it's view, view, view. ■ TIP→ Banquettes and tables around the perimeter of this 36th-floor restaurant offer sparkling night-time vistas of Honolulu and Waikīkī. The contemporary Continental menu is focused on grilled meats and seafood; the wine cellar is deep; and, if you linger, there's dancing. Or go late—the dining room serves until 11:30 on weekends, 2 AM nightly in the bar. ✉ *Ala Moana Hotel, top fl. 410 Atkinson Dr., Ala Moana* ☎ *808/955-4466* ⌁ *Reservations essential* ▤ *AE, D, DC, MC, V* ☉ *No lunch. $14–$28.*

$–$$$ ✕ **L'Uraku.** If you like a little whimsy with your wasabi, then you'll appreciate the decor of this Japanese-European fusion restaurant, which stays sunny with its collection of Kiyoshi hand-painted umbrellas that hang from the ceiling. The Euro-Japanese contemporary food stylings (seared sea scallops with Asian-style beurre blanc) are the perfect complement. Check out L'Uraku's three-course weekender lunch menu. ✉ *1341 Kapi'olani Blvd., Ala Moana* ☎ *808/955-0552* ▤ *AE, D, MC, V. $17–$30.*

¢–$$$ ✕ **Palomino.** A favorite of downtowners for its business lunches and after-work drinks, this art deco Euro-bistro, with handblown glass chandeliers, a grand staircase, and a 50-foot marble-and-mahogany bar, features a menu that fuses Mediterranean cuisines. Entrées include Roma style pizzas, spit-roasted poultry, strombolis, and seafood that includes roasted garlic- or crab-stuffed prawns. The housemade thinbread appetizer with tomato chutney never palls. This is an outlet of the Restaurants Unlimited chain. ✉ *Harbor Court, 66 Queen St., 3rd fl., Downtown Honolulu* ☎ *808/528-2400* ▤ *AE, D, DC, MC, V. $9–$30.*

$–$$ ✕ **La Mariana Restaurant & Sailing Club.** Just past downtown Honolulu, tucked away in the industrial area of Sand Island, is this friendly South Seas–style restaurant. Over the past 50 years, nonagenarian owner Annette Nahinu has bought up kitsch from other restaurants, even importing the piano (and piano player) from the beloved Tahitian Lanai, so it's tikis to the max here. The food–grilled seafood, steaks–is just okay; but go for the sing-along fun and the feeling that Don the Beachcomber might walk in any minute. ✉ *50 Sand Island Rd., Iwilei* ☎ *808/848-2800* ▤ *AE, D, DC, MC, V. $11–$20.*

¢–$$ ✕ **E & O Trading Co.** Named for the colonial-era Eastern & Orient Trading Co., this restaurant's decor recalls a bustling mercantile district in some Asian port. Like a merchant ship, the southeast Asian grill menu hops from Singapore to Korea, Japan to India. The Indonesian corn fritters are a must, as are the Burmese ginger salad and the silky-textured, smoky-flavored marinated Portobello satay. To match the unusual menu, the bar creates some unusual mixtures with infusions and fresh juices. ⊠ *Ward Center, 1200 Ala Moana Blvd., Kaka'ko* ☎ *808/ 591–9555* ☜ *Reservations recommended* ▤ *AE, D, DC, MC, V* ☺ *Lunch and dinner daily. $7–$22.*

¢–$$ ✕ **Hiroshi Eurasion Tapas.** Built around chef Hiroshi Fukui's signature style of "West & Japan" cuisine, this sleek dinner house focuses on small plates to share (enough for two servings each if you're friendly with your dining partner), with an exceptional choice of hard-to-find wines by the glass and in flights. Do not miss Hiroshi's braised veal

> ## MALASSADAS
>
> Donuts without a hole, malassadas are a contribution of the Portuguese, who came to the Islands to work on the plantations. Roughly translated, the name means half-cooked, which refers to the origin of these deep-fried, heavily sugared treats: They are said to have been created as a way to use up scraps of rich, buttery egg dough. A handful of bakeries specialize in malassadas (Leonard's on Kapahulu, Agnes in Kailua, Champion on Beretania); restaurants sometimes serve an upscale version stuffed with fruit puree; they're inevitable at fairs and carnivals. Eat them hot or not at all.

cheeks (he was doing them before everyone else), the locally-raised kampachi fish carpaccio, or the best *misoyaki* (marinated in a rich miso-soy blend, then grilled) butterfish ever. ⊠ *1341 Kapi'olani Blvd., Ala Moana* ☎ *808/955–0552* ▤ *AE, D, MC, V* ☺ *No lunch. $7–$22.*

¢–$ ✕ **Jackie's Kitchen.** The first U.S. outlet of a chain owned by international film star Jackie Chan is a lot like the martial arts movie king's films: surprisingly charming. We didn't expect much but found ourselves enjoying the food, the bartenders flipping bottles about, the silly souvenir glasses, the movies playing on flat screens all over the place. Kids love it, and their parents will find much to enjoy, too. Caution: With all the keepsakes for sale, this could get expensive. ⊠ *Ala Moana Shopping Center, 3rd level, 1450 Ala Moana Blvd., Ala Moana* ☎ *808/943–2426* ☜ *Reservations not accepted* ▤ *AE, D, DC, MC, V. $8–$17.*

★ ¢–$ ✕ **Kaka'ako Kitchen.** Russell Siu was the first of the local-boy fine dining chefs to open a place of the sort he enjoys when he's off-duty, serving high-quality plate lunches (housemade sauce instead of from-a-mix brown gravy, for example). Here you can get your "two scoops of rice" either white or brown and green salad instead of the usual macaroni salad, grilled fresh fish specials, and vegetarian options. Breakfast is especially good with combos like corned beef hash and eggs and exceptional baked goods such as *poi* bread. ⊠ *Ward Center, 1200 Ala Moana Blvd., Kaka'ako* ☎ *808/596–7488* ☜ *Reservations not accepted* ▤ *No credit cards. $7–$15.*

Japanese

$–$$ ✕ **Akasaka.** Step inside this tiny sushi bar tucked behind the Ala Moana Hotel, and you'll swear you're in some out-of-the-way Edo neighborhood in some indeterminate time. Greeted with a cheerful "Iraishaimasu!" (Welcome!), you sink down at a diminutive table or perch at the handful of seats at the sushi bar. It's safe to let the sushi chefs here decide (omakase-style) or you can go for the delicious grilled specialties, such as scallop *battayaki* (grilled in, yes, butter). Award-winning and deservedly so. Reservations accepted for groups only. ⊠ *1646 B Kona St., Ala Moana* ☎ *808/942–4466* ⊟ *AE, D, DC, MC, V* ☉ *No lunch Sun. $9–$25.*

¢–$$ ✕ **Yanagi Sushi.** One of relatively few restaurants to serve the complete menu until 2 AM, Yanagi is a full-service Japanese restaurant offering not only sushi and sashimi around a small bar, but also *taishoku* (combination menus), tempura, stews, and grill-it-yourself shabu shabu. The name refers to the ultra-sharp, sword-like knife used to slice raw fish—and the fish here can be depended on for freshness and variety. Reservations recommended. ⊠ *762 Kapi'olani Blvd., Downtown* ☎ *808/597–1525* ⊟ *AE, D, DC, MC, V. $8–$21.*

¢–$ ✕ **Kai.** This chic little spot opened in 2005 and introduced Honolulu to *okonomiyaki*, the famous savory pancakes that are a specialty of Osaka, with mix-and-match ingredients scrambled together on a griddle then drizzled with various piquant sauces. The combinations may at times strike you as bizarre, but you can always order simpler grilled dishes. Reservations recommended. ⊠ *1427 Makaloa St., Ala Moana* ☎ *808/944–1555* ⊟ *AE, D, DC, MC, V* ☉ *No lunch; closed Mon. $8–$17.*

Korean

$–$$ ✕ **Yakiniku Mikawon.** Korean spoken here—in menu, in cooking style, and in language, but you can make yourself understood with the help of menu translations and pointing. Mikawon is one of few grill-it-yourself restaurants to use real, charcoal-burning grills, considered the sine qua non of this Korean style of cooking which has been adopted by Japan. Their specialty is *wang galbi*–ribs seasoned in the style of Su Won, Korea, a mellower style than the usual soy sauce-soaked kal bi ribs. ⊠ *1726 Kapiolani Blvd., Ala Moana* ☎ *808/947–5454* ⊟ *AE, MC, V. $10–$20.*

¢–$$ ✕ **Sorabol.** The largest Korean restaurant in the city, this 24-hour eatery, with its impossibly tiny parking lot and maze of booths and private rooms, offers a vast menu encompassing the entirety of day-to-day Korean cuisine, plus sushi. English menu translations are cryptic at best. Still, we love it for wee hour "grinds": *bi bim bap* (veggies, meats, and eggs on steamed rice), *kal bi* and *bulgogi* (barbecued meats), and meat or fish *jun* (thin fillets fried in batter). ⊠ *805 Ke'eaumoku St., Ala Moana* ☎ *808/947–3113* ⊟ *AE, DC, MC, V. $6–$20.*

Mexican

¢–$$ ✕ **Compadres Mexican Bar and Grill.** The after-work crowd gathers here for potent margaritas and yummy pūpū. An outdoor terrace is best for cocktails only. Inside, the wooden floors, colorful photographs, and lively paintings create a festive setting. Compadres defines itself as "Western cooking with a Mexican accent": fajitas, baby back ribs, pork *carnitas* (slow-roasted shredded pork), and tortilla-encrusted chicken are specialties. There's a late-night appetizer menu available until midnight. ⊠ *Ward Center, 1200 Ala Moana Blvd., Ala Moana* ☎ *808/591–8307* ⊟ *D, MC, V. $8–$20.*

Seafood

$$–$$$$ ✕ **John Dominis.** Legendary is the word for the Sunday brunch buffet at this long-established restaurant, named for a Hawaiian kingdom chamberlain who became the consort of the last queen, Lili'uokalania. With a network of koi ponds running through the multilevel restaurant, a view of Diamond Head and a favorite surfing area, and over-the-top seafood specials, it's the choice of Oahuans with something to celebrate. An appetizer and small plates menu is available in the bar. ⊠ *580 Nimitz Hwy. Iwilei* ☎ *808/545–7979* ▤ *AE, D, DC, MC, V. $19–$40.*

$$–$$$$ ✕ **Sam Choy's Breakfast, Lunch and Crab & Big Aloha Brewery.** In this casual setting, great for families, diners can down crab and lobster—but since these come from elsewhere, we recommend the catch of the day, the *char siu* (Chinese barbecue), baby back ribs, or Sam's special fried *poke* (flash-fried tuna). This eatery's warehouse size sets the tone for its *bambucha* (huge) portions. ■ **TIP➔ An on-site microbrewery brews five varieties of Big Aloha beer.** Sam Choy's is in Iwilei past Downtown Honolulu on the highway heading to Honolulu International Airport. ⊠ *580 Nimitz Hwy., Iwilei* ☎ *808/545–7979* ▤ *AE, D, DC, MC, V. $19–$40.*

Singaporean/Malaysian

¢–$ ✕ **Green Door.** Closet-sized and fronted by a green door and a row of welcoming Chinese lanterns, this 12-seat café in Chinatown has introduced Honolulu to budget- and tastebud-friendly Malaysian and Singaporean foods, redolent of spices and crunchy with fresh vegetables. ⊠ *1145 Maunakea St., Chinatown* ☎ *808/533–0606* ▤ *No credit cards* ⌆ *Reservations not accepted* ⊙ *Closed Mon. $5–$12.*

Vietnamese

¢ ✕ **To Chau.** If you need proof that To Chau is highly regarded for its authentic *phô* (Vietnamese beef noodle soup), just check the lines that form in front every morning of the week. It's said that the broth is the key, and it won't break the bank for you to find out as the average check is

8

YAKINIKU

A Korean technique with a Japanese name, *yakiniku* is a grill-your-own restaurant concept, and one of the few happy results of the Japanese occupation of Korea. Diners cook their own marinated meats and sliced vegetables on braziers set in the middle of the table.

A yakiniku restaurant may be a chic contemporary pub (Yakiniku Toraji) or a homey family buffet (Camellia Yakiniku). A few, like Yakiniku Mikawon, employ well-vented

charcoal braziers to infuse the ingredients with rich, smoky flavor. Most, however, use gas grills.

Budget yakiniku places charge a flat rate; you serve yourself from a raw buffet. In upscale yakiniku, you order from a menu.

■ **TIP➔ Appoint one griller to prevent mid-table traffic jams. Order or fill your plate in stages to avoid waste and a big bill.**

MUSUBI

Musubi needs translation. Here are cakes of steamed rice like thick decks of cards, topped with something that resembles spoiled luncheon meat, and bound in strip of black like a paper band around a stack of new bills. Swathed in plastic, they sit on the counter of every mom-and-pop store and plate-lunch place in Hawai'i, selling for $1.50, $1.95. And T-shirted surfers with sandy feet, girls in *pareus*, and *tutus* (grandmas) in mu'umu'u are munching these oddities with apparent delight.

"Huh?" says the visitor.

So, a quick dictionary moment: *musubi* (*moo*-sue-bee), a cake of steamed Japanese-style rice topped with some sweet-salty morsel and held together with *nori* (*no*-ree; seaweed). Most common form: Spam musubi, popularized in the early 1980s by vendor Mitsuko Kaneshiro. Kaneshiro turned her

children's favorite snack into a classic—Spam slices simmered in a sugar-soy mixture atop rectangular rice cakes, with nori for crisp contrast. The flavor is surprisingly pleasant and satisfying, like a portable rice bowl.

Musubi has its roots in Japan, where rice cakes are standard festival, funeral, and family fare. But Islanders carried the tradition far afield, topping rice with slices of teriyaki chicken, sandwiching tuna salad between two cakes, dressing the rice in piquant slivers of scarlet pickled plum, toasted sesame, and strips of seaweed.

These ubiquitous tidbits are Hawai'i's go-food, like hot dogs or pretzels on a New York street. Quality varies, but if you visit a craft fair or stumble on a school sale and see homemade musubi—grab one and snack like a local.

less than $10. ⊠ *1007 River St., Chinatown* ☎ *808/533–4549* ▭ *No credit cards. $5–$9.*

Wine Bars

¢–$ ✕ **Vino.** Small plates of Italian-inspired appetizers, a wine list selected by the state's first Master Sommelier, a relaxed atmosphere, and periodic special tastings are the formula for success here. ■ **TIP➔ Vino is well-situated for stopping off between downtown sightseeing and a return to your Waikīkī hotel.** ⊠ *Restaurant Row, 500 Ala Moana Blvd., Downtown* ☎ *808/524–8466* ▭ *AE, D, DC, MC, V* ☾ *Closed Sun.–Tues. $6–$16.*

Honolulu: East & Diamond Head

American–Casual

¢   ✕ **Big City Diner.** These unfussy retro diners offer a short course in local-style breakfasts—rice instead of potatoes, fish or Portuguese sausage instead of bacon, steaming bowls of noodles—with generous portions, low prices, and pronounced flavors. Breakfast is served all day. ⊠ *3569 Wai'alae Ave., Kaimukī* ☎ *808/738–8855* ▭ *AE, D, MC, V. $5–$9.*

¢ ✗ **Cafe Laufer.** Ten minutes from Waikīkī, this is the Island version of a Viennese café. Light meals range from grilled sausage with sauerkraut to soups and salads. Try the classic apple tart, linzer torte, Black Forest cake, or chocolate macadamia-nut pastries. The cafe is open until 10 PM Friday and Saturday for a sweet nightcap. ⊠ *3565 Wai'alae Ave., Kaimukī* ☎ *808/735–7717* ⚠ *Reservations not accepted* ▤ *AE, MC, V. $5–$8.*

Contemporary

$$$–$$$$ ✗ **Alan Wong's.** This worthy restaurant is like that very rare shell you
Fodor'sChoice stumble upon on a perfect day at the beach—well polished and with-
★ out a flaw. We've never had a bad experience here, and we've never heard of anyone else doing so, either. The "Wong Way," as it's not so jokingly called by his staff, includes an ingrained understanding of the aloha spirit, evident in the skilled but unstarched service, and creative and playful interpretations of island cuisine. Try Da Bag (seafood steamed in a Mylar pouch), Chinatown Roast Duck Nachos, and Poki Pines (rice-studded seafood wonton appetizers). With a view of the Ko'olau Mountains, warm tones of koa wood and lauhala grass weaving, you forget you're on the third floor of an office building. Not to be missed. ⊠ *Mc-Cully Court, 1857 S. King St., 3rd fl., Mō'ili'ili* ☎ *808/949–2526* ▤ *AE, MC, V* ⊘ *No lunch. $25–$38.*

$$$–$$$$ ✗ **Chef Mavro.** George Mavrothalassitis, who took two hotel restaurants
Fodor'sChoice to the top of the ranks before founding this James Beard Award-win-
★ ning dinner house, admits he's "crazy." Crazy because of the care he takes to draw out the truest and most concentrated flavors, to track down the freshest fish, to create one-of-a-kind wine pairings that might strike others as mad. But for this passionate Provençal transplant, there's no other way. The menu changes quarterly, every dish (including dessert) matched with a select wine. We recommend the multi-course tasting menus (beginning at $66 for four courses without wine, up to $137 for six courses with wine). Etched-glass windows screen the busy streetcorner scene and all within is mellow and serene with starched white tablecloths, fresh flowers, wood floors, and contemporary island art. ⊠ *1969 S. King St., Mō'ili'ili* ☎ *808/944–4714* ⚠ *Reservations essential* ▤ *AE, DC, MC, V* ⊘ *No lunch. $32–$42.*

★ **$$–$$$$** ✗ **Hoku's at The Kāhala.** Everything about this room speaks of quality and sophistication: the wall of windows with their beach views, the avante-garde cutlery and dinnerware, the solicitous staff and border-busting Pacific Rim cuisine. They do tend to get a bit architectural (lots of edible stacks and towers), but the food invariably tastes every bit as good as it looks. The international breads and the dessert sampler in particular are noteworthy. ⊠ *The Kāhala, 5000 Kāhala Ave., Kāhala* ☎ *808/739–8780* ▤ *AE, D, MC, V* ⊘ *No lunch Sat. $22–$39.*

$–$$$ ✗ **Sam Choy's Diamond Head.** Sam Choy has been called the Paul Prudhomme of Hawai'i and aptly so: Both are big, welcoming men with magic in their hands and a folksy background in small, rural towns. Choy grew up cooking for his parents' lū'au business and now has an empire: restaurants, TV show, cookbooks, commercial products, and his two best chef-friends are Prudhomme and Emeril LaGasse. Here, Choy and staff interpret local favorites in sophisticated ways, and the fresh fish is

8

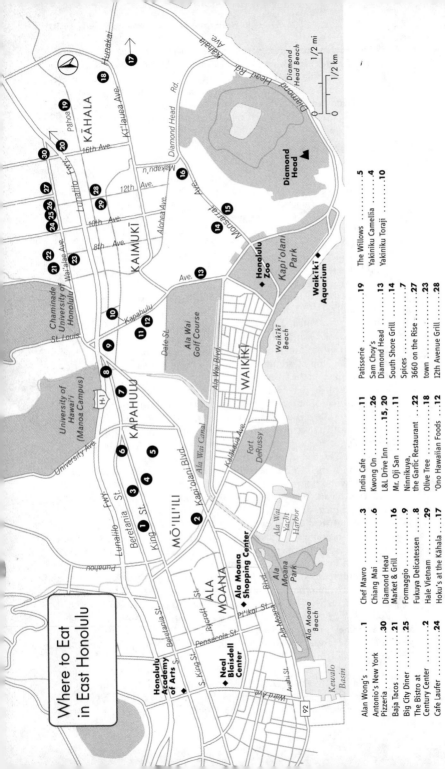

Where to Eat in East Honolulu

the best. The portions, like Sam's smile, are huge. ⊠ *449 Kapahulu Ave.,* *Kapahulu* ☎ *808/732–8645* ▭ *AE, D, DC, MC, V. $15–$35.*

★ **$–$$$** ✕ **3660 on the Rise.** This casually stylish eatery is a 10-minute drive from Waikīkī in the up-and-coming culinary mecca of Kaimukī. Sample Chef Russell Siu's New York Steak Alae'a Alae'a (steak grilled with Hawaiian clay salt), the crab cakes, or the signature 'ahi katsu wrapped in nori and deep-fried with a wasabi-ginger butter sauce. Siu combines a deep understanding of local flavors with a sophisticated palate, making this place especially popular with homegrown gourmands. ■ **TIP→ The dining room can feel a bit snug when it's full (as it usually is); go early or later.** ⊠ *3660 Wai'alae Ave., Kaimukī* ☎ *808/737–1177* ▭ *AE, DC, MC, V. $10–$30.*

¢–$$$ ✕ **12th Avenue Grill.** We love this clean, well-lighted place on a back street where chef Kevin Hanney dishes up diner chic, including macaroni and cheese glazed with house-smoked Parmesan and topped with savory breadcrumbs. The kim chee steak, a sort of teriyaki with kick, is a winner. Go early (5) or late (8:30). Enjoy wonderful, homey desserts. There's a small, reasonably priced wine list. Reservations recommended. ⊠ *1145C 12th Ave., Kaimukī* ☎ *808/732–9469* ⌗ *BYOB* ▭ *MC, V* ☉ *No lunch. Closed Sun. $8–$27.*

¢–$$ ✕ **town.** Tell us how old you are, and we'll tell you whether you're likely to enjoy town (yes, the "t" is lower case). The motto here is "local first, organic whenever possible, with aloha always." Pretty much everyone agrees that chef-owner Ed Kenney's vaguely Mediterranean menu ranges from just fine (pastas and salads) to just fabulous (buttermilk panna cotta). But if you're over 40, you'll probably be put off by the minimalist decor, the shrieking-level acoustics, and the heedlessly careless waitstaff, who have a tendency to get lost. Young people don't seem bothered by either circumstance. The restaurant serves an inexpensive Continental breakfast, as well as lunch and dinner. ⊠ *3435 Wai'alae Ave., Kaimukī* ☎ *808/735–5900* ⌂ *Reservations essential* ⌗ *BYOB* ▭ *MC, V* ☉ *Closed Sun. $4–$20.*

Delicatessens

¢–$ ✕ **Diamond Head Market & Grill.** Kelvin Ro's one-stop spot is a plate-lunch place, a gourmet market, a deli and bakery and espresso bar, too. ■ **TIP→ It's a five-minute hop from Waikīkī hotels.** A take-out window offers grilled sandwiches or plates ranging from teriyaki beef to Portobello mushrooms. The market's deli case is stocked with a range of heat-and-eat entrées from risotto cakes to lamb stew; specials change daily. There are packaged Japanese bento lunchboxes, giant scones, enticing desserts, even a small wine selection. ⊠ *3158 Monsarrat Ave., Diamond Head* ☎ *808/ 732–0077* ⌂ *Reservations not accepted* ▭ *AE, D, MC, V. $5–$15.*

Fast Food

¢–$ ✕ **Antonio's New York Pizzeria.** Thin, crisp, hand-tossed pies sold in 9-inch personal sizes; cannoli shipped over from Little Italy and filled to order; and even—incongruously—Philly cheesesteaks make this an expat's paradise. Stop on the way back to the hotel from snorkeling at Hanauma Bay. ⊠ *4210 Wai'lae Ave., Kāhala* ☎ *808/737–3333* ⌂ *Reservations not accepted* ▭ *No credit cards. $5–$10.*

8

¢–$ ✕ **L&L Drive Inn.** On Monsarrat Avenue in Waikīkī and at more than 60 neighborhood locations throughout the island, the Drive Inn serves up an impressive mix of Asian-American and Hawaiian-style plate lunches. Chicken *katsu* (cutlet), shrimp curry, and seafood mix plates include two scoops of rice-and-macaroni salad. There are also "mini" versions of the large-portion plates that include just one scoop of starch. It's a quick take-out place to pick up lunch before heading to the nearest beach or park. ⊠ *3045 Monsarrat Ave., Diamond Head* ☏ *808/735–1388* ⌲ *Reservations not accepted* ▭ *No credit cards. $5–$10.*

German

¢–$$ ✕ **Patisserie.** By day, this bakery in the Kāhala Mall serves deli food, but five nights a week it turns into a 24-seat restaurant with great German food, a rarity in Hawai'i. The menu is small—only 10 entrées—but any choice is a good one. The Wiener schnitzel is juicy within its crispy crust, and veal ribs are garnished with a sprig of rosemary. Try the potato pancakes, crisp outside and soft inside, joined by a healthy spoonful of applesauce. ⊠ *Kāhala Mall, 4211 Wai'alae Ave., Kāhala* ☏ *808/735–4402* ⌲ *Reservations not accepted* ▭ *MC, V* ☉ *Closed Sun. and Mon.*

Hawaiian

$$–$$$ ✕ **The Willows.** An Island dream, this restaurant is made up of pavilions overlooking a network of ponds (once natural streams flowing from mountain to sea). The Island-style comfort food, served buffet-style, includes the trademark Willows curry along with Hawaiian dishes such as *laulau* (a steamed bundle of ti leaves containing pork, butterfish, and taro tops) and local favorites such as Korean barbecue ribs. In 2005 Chef Jay Matsukawa added a new sit-down restaurant-within-a-restaurant serving rustic French food. ⊠ *901 Hausten St., Mō'ili'ili* ☏ *808/952–9200* ⌲ *Reservations essential* ▭ *AE, D, MC, V. $19–$28.*

¢–$ ✕ **'Ono Hawaiian Foods.** The adventurous in search of a real "local food" experience should head to this no-frills hangout. You know it has to be good if residents are waiting in line to get in. Here you can sample *poi, lomi lomi* salmon (salmon massaged until tender and served with minced onions and tomatoes), laulau, *kālua* pork (roasted in an underground oven), and *haupia* (a light, gelatin-like dessert made from coconut milk). Appropriately enough, the Hawaiian word *'ono* means delicious. ⊠ *726 Kapahulu Ave., Kapahulu* ☏ *808/737–2275* ⌲ *Reservations not accepted* ▭ *No credit cards* ☉ *Closed Sun. $6–$14.*

Indian

¢–$ ✕ **India Cafe.** At this restaurant owned by Indians of Malaysian origin, dosai, griddle breads made of rice and lentil flour, are filled variously with savory and sweet ingredients. Like most such restaurants, this one is very vegetarian-friendly, serving up dahls (lentil stews), curries, and samosas. Reservations recommended. ⊠ *Kilohana Square, 1016 Kapahulu Ave., Kapahulu* ☏ *808/737–4600* ▭ *AE, DC, MC, V* ☉ *No lunch Mon.–Thurs.*

Japanese

$$$$ ✕ **Sushi Sasabune.** You may find this restaurant's approach exasperating and a little condescending. Although it's possible to order from the

menu, you're strongly encouraged to order omakase-style (oh-*mah*-ka-*say*, roughly, "trust me"), letting the chef send out his choices for the night. The waiters keep up a steady mantra: "Please, no shoyu on this one." "One piece, one bite." But then you take the first bite of California baby squid stuffed with Louisiana crab or unctuous *toro* ('ahi belly) smeared with a light soy reduction, washed down with a $20 glass of the smoothest sake you've ever tasted, and any trace of annoyance will vanish. Chef Seiji Kamagawa stands front and center at the counter, his hands—graceful as a conductor's, precise as a surgeon's—

> ## ORDERING SUSHI
>
> In sushi restaurants two terms are helpful:
> *Moriwase* (moe-ree-WA-say) translates to "chef's choice" or "special of the day"–a one-price sushi spread that is supposed to showcase the best fish of the day. *Omakase* (oh-MAH-ka-SAY) is a style of sushi dining in which the sushi chef sends out successive courses of his choosing, at the same time watching to note diner's preferences and eating pace.

forming sushi or slicing sashimi, his eyes sternly examining the room. Caution: the courses come very rapidly; ask to be served every other time. Even bigger caution: the courses, generally two pieces of sushi or 6–8 slices of sashimi, add up fast. It's easy to spend more than $100 in a half hour, not counting drinks. Still, the meal will be as unforgettable as the tab. ✉ *1419 S. King St., Mō'ili'ili* ☎ *808/947–3800* ♨ *Reservations essential* ▤ *AE, D, DC, MC, V* ⊗ *Closed Sun. No lunch Sat. and Mon. $8–$20.*

$–$$$ ✕ **Ninnikuya, the Garlic Restaurant.** Talk about one note: chef-owner Endo Eiyuki picked a powerful one for his charming restaurant in a converted Kaimukī bungalow: garlic. He calls the menu Euro-Asian but the spicing and approach–except for the prevalance of garlic–are distinctly Japanese. Don't miss the Black Angus steak on a sizzling stone. ✉ *3196 Waīalae Ave., Kaimukī* ☎ *808/735–0784* ♨ *Reservations essential* ▤ *AE, D, DC, MC, V* ⊗ *No lunch. Closed Sun. $15–$30.*

¢–$$ ✕ **Yakiniku Toraji.** Trendy Yakiniku Toraji resembles a Japanese country inn and features, in addition to the usual meats and vegetables grilled at the table, *ishikyaki*–meats and vegetables baked on a bed of rice in a stone bowl heated to broiling, forming a delicious crust. ■ **TIP➔ This is a particularly friendly spot, as the menus offer a cartoon to explain yakiniku how-tos.** ✉ *949 Kapahulu Ave., Kapahulu* ☎ *808/732–9996* ♨ *Reservations essential* ▤ *AE, D, MC, V* ⊗ *No lunch. $8–$20.*

Mediterranean

¢–$ ✕ **Olive Tree.** Mediterranean food is scarce in the Islands, so Olive Tree keeps insanely busy; expect a wait for your hummus, fish souvlaki, Greek egg-and-lemon soup, and other specialties at this small spot located behind Kāhala Mall. ✉ *4614 Kīlauea Ave., Kāhala* ☎ *808/737–0303* ♨ *Reservations not accepted* ▤ *No credit cards* ⊗ *No lunch. $8–$15.*

Mexican

¢ ✕ **Baja Tacos.** One of the first California-style taquerias in the Islands, Baja Tacos offers authentic flavors, house-made salsas, Mexican-style small plates, enchiladas, pork carnitas, and adobada (marinated pork) and, of course, tacos—to take out or eat in. Perfect for post-beach. ⊠ *3040 Wai'alae Ave., Kaimukī* ☎ *808/737–5893* ⌨ *Reservations not accepted* 🖃 *No credit cards. $4–$8.*

Southeast Asian

¢–$ ✗ **Bac Nam.** Tam and Kimmy Huynh's menu is much more extensive than most, ranging far beyond the usual *phô* (beef noodle soup) and *bun* (cold noodle dishes). Coconut milk curries, an extraordinary crab noodle soup, and other dishes hail from both from North and South Vietnam. The atmosphere is welcoming and relaxed, and they'll work with you to make choices. Reservations accepted for groups of six or more. ⊠ *1117 S. King St., Downtown* ☎ *808/597–8201* 🖃 *MC, V. $6–$12.*

¢–$ ✗ **Chiang Mai.** Long beloved for its Thai classics, such as spicy curries and stir-fries and sticky rice in woven grass baskets, based on family recipes, Chiang Mai is just a short cab ride from Waikīkī. Some dishes, like the signature Cornish game hen in lemon grass and spices, show how acculturation can create interesting pairings. The space is cozy and decorated with Thai fabrics and artworks. Reservations recommended. ⊠ *2239 S. King St., Mō'ili'ili* ☎ *808/941–1151* 🖃 *AE, D, DC, MC, V* ☾ *No lunch weekends. $7–$15.*

¢–$ ✗ **Hale Vietnam.** One of O'hu's first Vietnamese restaurants, this popular neighborhood spot expresses its friendly character in a name that incorporates the Hawaiian word for house or home, *hale* (hah-lay). They're known for a willingness to help those who don't know much about Vietnamese food, and for their piquant and crunchy green papaya salad. ⊠ *1140 12th Ave., Kaimukī* ☎ *808/735–7581* ⌨ *Reservations not accepted* 🖃 *AE, D, MC, V. $6–$10.*

¢–$ ✗ **Spices.** The creation of a well-traveled trio of friends who enjoy the foods of Southeast Asia, Spices is alluringly decorated in spice-like oranges and reds and offers a menu far from the beaten path, even in a city rich in restaurants of this region. They claim inspiration but not authenticity and use Island ingredients to advantage. Vegetarian-friendly. ⊠ *2671 S. King St., Mō'ili'ili* ☎ *808/949–2679* ⌨ *Reservations essential* 🖃 *MC, V* ☾ *Closed Mon. $8–$12.*

Wine Bars

¢–$ ✗ **Formaggio.** All but invisible on the back side of a strip mall, Formaggio seeks to communicate the feel of a catacomb in Italy, and largely succeeds with dim lighting and soft warm tones. Choose a small sip or an entire bottle from the 40 or so they offer, enjoy the guitar music, then ponder the small-dish menu of pizzas, paninis, and hot and cold specialties such as eggplant Napoleon and melting short ribs in red wine. ⊠ *Market City Shopping Center, rear, lower level, 2919 Kapi'olani Blvd., Kaimukī* ☎ *808/739–7719* ⌨ *Reservations not accepted* 🖃 *AE, MC, V* ☾ *No lunch. Closed Sun. $8–$14.*

Southeast O'ahu: Hawai'i Kai

Austrian

$–$$ ✗ **Chef's Table.** Chef Andreas Knapp creates dishes that are true to his Austrian heritage. Daily specials, including luscious homemade soups,

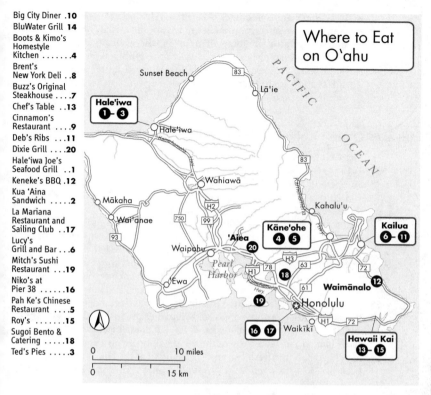

salads, sauerbratens, and schnitzels, combined with an atmosphere that is friendly, fun, and casual, make the Chef's Table a neighborhood favorite. ■ TIP➔ **This tiny eatery is good for a lunch break while touring East O'ahu or as a getaway dinner spot.** A European-style brunch is offered Sunday. ☒ *Hawai'i Kai Towne Center, 333 Keahole St., Hawai'i Kai* ☏ *808/ 394–2433* ▤ *AE, D, DC, MC, V. $12–$22.*

Contemporary

$–$$$ ✗ **BluWater Grill.** Time your drive along Honolulu's South Shore to allow for a stop at this relaxed lunch and dinner restaurant on Kuapa Pond. The savvy chef-manager team left a popular chain restaurant to found this "American eclectic" eatery (wok-seared moi fish, mango and guava ribs, and lots of interesting small dishes $5–$10). They're open until 11 PM Monday through Thursday and on Sunday; until midnight Friday and Saturday. ☒ *Hawai'i Kai Shopping Center, 377 Keahole St., Hawai'i Kai* ☏ *808/395–6224* ▤ *AE, DC, MC, V. $16–$30.*

★ **$–$$$**   ✗ **Roy's.** Roy Yamaguchi's flagship restaurant across the highway from Maunalua Bay attracts food-savvy visitors like the North Shore attracts surfers. But it has a strong following among well-heeled Oahuans from surrounding neighborhoods who consider the place an extension of their homes and Roy's team their personal chefs. For this reason, Roy's is always busy and sometimes overly noisy. It's best to visit later in the evening if you're sensitive to pressure to turn the table. The wide-ranging and ever-interesting "Hawaiian fusion" menu changes daily except for such signature dishes as Szechuan Spiced BBQ Baby Back Ribs, Roy's Original Blackened 'Ahi with Soy Mustard Butter Sauce, and a legendary meat loaf. There's an exceptional wine list. ⊠ *Hawai'i Kai Corporate Plaza, 6600 Kalaniana'ole Hwy., Hawai'i Kai* ☎ *808/396–7697* ⚠ *Reservations essential* ⊟ *AE, D, DC, MC, V. $17–$30.*

Windward O'ahu: Kailua & Kāne'ohe

American–Casual

$–$$$ ✕ **Lucy's Grill and Bar.** This windward eatery offers outdoor seating and an open-air bar that shakes up a mean martini to go with its eclectic and innovative menu. (We prefer the lanai because the indoor seating, though attractive, gets very noisy.) Begin with the deep-fried kālua pig pastry triangles with a mandarin orange-plum dipping sauce. Seafood offerings include grilled mahimahi, and lemongrass-crusted scallops with a yellow Thai curry. For meat lovers, there are baby back ribs in sweet hoisin barbecue sauce. Desserts, such as the coconut-chocolate bar with vanilla gelato, are sinfully rich. There's brunch on Sunday. ⊠ *33 Aulike St., Kailua* ☎ *808/230–8188* ⊟ *MC, V* ☯ *No lunch. $15–$28.*

$–$$ ✕ **Buzz's Original Steakhouse.** Virtually unchanged since it opened in 1967, this cozy maze of rooms opposite Kailua Beach Park is filled with the enticing aroma of grilling steaks. ■ **TIP➔ It doesn't matter if you're a bit sandy (but no bare feet).** Stop at the salad bar, order up a steak, a burger, teri chicken, or the fresh fish special. If you sit at the bar, expect to make friends. ⊠ *413 Kawailoa Rd., Kailua* ☎ *808/261–4661* ⊟ *No credit cards. $13–$23.*

¢–$ ✕ **Brent's New York Deli.** Jewish-style delis are very few in the Islands, and Brent's is a mecca for homesick New Yorkers who need a knish or a reuben. But you don't have to know from blintzes to appreciate Brent Brody's commitment to quality. Breakfasts are particularly scrumptious. Portions are ample and prices right. ⊠ *629-A Kailua Rd., Ste. 108, Kailua* ☎ *808/262–8588* ⚠ *Reservations not accepted* ⊟ *MC, V. $8–$12.*

¢–$ ✕ **Cinnamon's Restaurant.** Known for uncommon variations on common breakfast themes (pancakes, eggs Benedict, French toast, home fries and eggs), this neighborhood favorite is tucked into a hard-to-find Kailua office park; call for directions. Lunch and dinner feature local-style plate lunch and a diner-style menu. ⊠ *315 Uluniu, Kailua* ☎ *808/261–8724* ⊟ *D, DC, MC, V* ☯ *Breakfast and lunch daily; dinner Thurs.-Sat. $3–$10.*

¢ ✕ **Big City Diner.** These unfussy retro diners offer a short course in local-style breakfasts—rice instead of potatoes, fish or Portuguese sausage instead of bacon, steaming bowls of noodles—with generous portions, low prices, and pronounced flavors. Breakfast is served all day. ⊠ *108 Hekuli St., Kailua* ☎ *808/263–8880* ⊟ *AE, D, MC, V. $5–$9.*

¢ ✕ **Boots & Kimo's Homestyle Kitchen.** If you're wondering what aloha spirit is all about, check out this family-owned, local-style restaurant in the industrial backwaters of Kāne'ohe where brothers Ricky and Jesse Ki-

SHAVE ICE

Island-style shave ice (never shaved ice—it's a pidgin thing) is said to have been born when neighborhood kids hung around the ice house, waiting to pounce on the shavings from large blocks of ice, carved with ultra-sharp Japanese planes that created an exceptionally fine-textured granita.

In the 1920s, according to the historian for syrup manufacturer Malolo Beverages Co., Chinese vendors developed sweet fruit concentrates to pour over the ice.

The evolution continued with mom-and-pop shops adding their own touches, such as secreting a nugget of Japanese-style sweet bean paste in the center, or a small scoop of ice cream, adding *li hing* powder (a sweet spice), or deftly pouring multi-toned cones.

There's nothing better on a sticky hot day. Try Waiola on Kapahulu or, in Haleʻiwa, Aoki's or Matsumoto's.

akona treat their guests like family. At breakfast, the signature dish is macadamia nut pancakes; at lunch, pulehu (grilled) ribs. Generous portions at family-friendly prices. ✉ *1321 Heikili St., Ste. 102, Kāneʻohe* ☎ *808/263–7929* ✍ *Reservations not accepted* ▭ *No credit cards. $5–$7.*

Barbecue

¢–$ ✗ **Deb's Ribs.** Though she serves Southern sides from greens to sweet potato pie, it's the ribs that have made Debra Hopkins' small Kailua eatery a draw. Baby back pork ribs are slow, slow cooked, slathered in a slightly spice tomato sauce, then somehow caramelized to finish. We do declare! Stop by after swimming at nearby Kailua Beach Park or on the way back from a North Shore excursion. ✉ *100 Kailua Rd., Kailua, Kailua* ☎ *808/262–3327* ▭ D, DC, MC, V ⊙ *Closed Tues. $3–$10.*

Chinese

$–$$ ✗ **Pah Ke's Chinese Restaurant.** Chinese restaurants tend to be interchangeable but this one—named for the local pidgin term for Chinese—is worth the drive over from Honolulu for its focus on healthier cooking techniques, its seasonal specials such as cold soups and salads made from locally raised produce, and its exceptional East–West desserts. The menu offers all the usual suspects. ■ **TIP➜ Ask host Raymond Siu, a former hotel pastry chef, if he's got anything different and interesting in the kitchen, or call ahead to ask for a special menu.** ✉ *46-018 Kamehameha Hwy., Kāneʻohe* ☎ *808/235–4505* ▭ AE, MC, V. *$13–$23.*

Fast Food

¢ ✗ **Keneke's BBQ.** When you're sightseeing between Hanauma Bay and Makapuʻu, the food pickings are slim. But every day, 365 days a year, there's Keneke's in Waimanālo town. It's the home of plate lunch, shave ice and scriptural graffiti (Keneke—Keith Ward, the burly, weight-lifting, second-generation owner of the place—is born again). The food is

8

SHRIMP SHACKS

NO DRIVE TO THE NORTH SHORE is complete without a shrimp stop. Shrimp stands dot Kamehameha Highway from Kahalu'u to Kahuku. For under $10, you can get a shrimp plate lunch or a snack of chilled shrimp with cocktail sauce, served from a rough hut or converted vehicle (many permanently immobile), with picnic table seating.

The shrimp shack phenomenon began with a lost lease and a determined restaurateur. In 1994, when Giovanni and Connie Aragona couldn't renew the lease on their Hale'iwa deli, they began hawking their best-selling dish—an Italian-style scampi preparation involving lemon, butter, and lots of garlic—from a truck alongside the road. About the same time, aquaculture was gaining a foothold in nearby Kahuku, with farmers raising sweet, white shrimp and huge, orange-whiskered prawns in shallow freshwater ponds. The ready supply and the success of the first shrimp truck led to many imitators.

Though it's changed hands, that first business lives on as Giovanni's Original Shrimp Truck, parked in Kahuku town. Signature dishes include the garlic shrimp and a spicy shrimp sauté, both worth a stop.

But there's plenty of competition—at least seven stands, trucks, or stalls are operating at any given time, with varying menus (and quality).

Don't be fooled that all that shrimp comes fresh from the ponds; much of it is imported. The only way you can be sure you're buying local farm-raised shrimp is if the shrimp is still kicking. Romy's Kahuku Prawns and Shrimp Hut is an arm of one of the longest-running aquaculture farms in the area; they sell live shrimp and prawns along with excellent plate lunches. The pan-fried shrimp and buttery, locally-raised corn from the bright yellow Shrimp Shack, parked at Kaya Store in Punalu'u, is first-rate, too.

diet-busting, piled high, and mostly pretty good, particularly the Asian-style barbecue (including teri chicken or beef and Korean kalbi), Puerto Rican guisantes (pork and peas in tomato gravy), and Filipino adobo (piquant pork stew). If you want a treat, try the shave ice with ice cream. ⊠ *41-855 Kalaniana'ole Hwy., Waimānalo* ☎ *808/259–9800* ▭ *No credit cards. $2–$8.*

The North Shore: Hale'iwa

American/Casual

$–$$ ✕ **Hale'iwa Joe's Seafood Grill.** After the long drive to the North Shore, we like to while away the afternoon on the covered open-air lanai at Hale'iwa Joe's, scoring a couple of cute souvenir glasses, watching the boats and surfers in the harbor, and munching crunchy coconut shrimp, a mahi burger, or whatever's the freshest fish special. It's just past the Anahulu Stream Bridge. A Kāne'ohe location overlooks lush Haiku

Gardens. ⊠ *66-0011 Kamehameha Hwy., Haleʻiwa* ☎ *808/637–8005* ⚶ *Reservations not accepted* ⊟ *AE, DC, MC, V. $13–$20.*

¢ ✕ **Kua ʻAina Sandwich.** A must-stop spot during a drive around the island, this North Shore eatery specializes in large, hand-formed burgers heaped with bacon, cheese, salsa, and pineapple. ■ **TIP→ The crispy shoestring fries alone are worth the trip.** You can also check out Kua ʻAina's south-shore location across from the Ward Centre in Honolulu. ⊠ *66-160 Kamehameha Hwy., Haleʻiwa* ☎ *808/637–6067* ⊠ *1116 Auahi St., Ala Moana* ☎ *808/591–9133* ⚶ *Reservations not accepted* ⊟ *No credit cards. $4–$7.*

¢ ✕ **Ted's Pies.** It's a bakery, yes, famous for its chocolate haupia pie (layered coconut custard and chocolate pudding topped with whipped cream). But it's also favored by surfers and area residents for quick breakfasts, sandwiches, or plate lunches, to go or eaten on a handful of umbrellaed tables outside. ⊠ *59-024 Kamehameha Hwy., Haleʻiwa* ☎ *808/638–8207* ⚶ *Reservations not accepted* ⊟ *DC, MC, V. $4–$7.*

Central & Leeward Oʻahu

American/Casual

¢–$$ ✕ **Dixie Grill.** Casual and family-friendly, this outlet of Dixie Grill is just off the freeway in Pearl City. ■ **TIP→ It's convenient if you're visiting Pearl Harbor or the swap meet.** It brings a taste of the South to the Islands with barbecue, seafood specialties (crab cakes, fried catfish), coleslaw, and hush puppies. ⊠ *99-016 Kamehameha Hwy., ʻAiea* ☎ *808/485–2722* ⚶ *Reservations not accepted* ⊟ *AE, D, DC, MC, V. $5–$21.*

¢ ✕ **Sugoi Bento & Catering.** Sugoi was among the first of a new wave of plate lunch places to take particular care with quality and to recognize that some plate lunch eaters are interested in good health—offering brown rice and green salad instead of the usual white rice and macaroni loaded with mayonnaise. Service is quick and cheerful in this primarily take-out place in a strip mall in industrial Kalihi, north of town. Garlic chicken and mochiko chicken, both adapted from traditional Japanese dishes, are specialties. ⊠ *City Square Shopping Center, 1286 Kalani St., Kalihi* ☎ *808/841–7984* ⚶ *Reservations not accepted* ⊟ *No credit cards* ⊙ *No dinner; closed Sun. $4–$7.*

Seafood

$–$$$$ ✕ **Mitch's Sushi Restaurant.** This microscopic sushi bar (15 seats) is an adjunct of a wholesale seafood market operated by gregarious South African expatriate Douglas Mitchell, who oversees the sushi chefs and keeps customers chatting. The fish, air-freighted from around the world, is ultra-fresh, well-cut, and nicely presented. You can spend as much or as little as you like—$40 for a half-dozen pieces of prime bluefin tuna belly, or just a few dollars for pickled plum sushi. ⊠ *524 Ohohia St., near Honolulu International Airport, Airport area* ☎ *808/837–7774* ⚶ *Reservations essential* ⊟ *MC, V. $4–$40.*

¢ ✕ **Nico's at Pier 38.** Once a chef in one of the city's best-known fine-dining restaurants, Lyon-born Nico Chaiz elected to create a place where he could work the hours he likes and serve people like himself, who love good food at reasonable prices. Where better than a few steps

8

from the city's fish auction? Though its chief clientele is rough-hewn dock workers and fishermen, the café has received universal critical acclaim for its upscale plate lunches of seaweed-crusted tuna steaks, and fish and egg breakfasts. ✉ *1133 N. Nimitz Highway, Pier 38, Downtown* ☎ *808/540–1377* ⌦ *Reservations not accepted* ▭ *AE, D, MC, V. $3–$7.*

Where to Stay

Waikīkī Parc Hotel

WORD OF MOUTH

"Castle Waikīkī Shores: This is the only condo right on the beach in Waikīkī. Very good location."

—dusty56438

"The [J.W. Marriott] 'Ihilani is a beautiful hotel with incredible views, as long as you do not get a high-floor room facing south . . . It is a bit of a hike if you want to spend time in Waikīkī, but we picked this place for that very reason. Nice and quiet, and away from the crowds." —JC

LODGING PLANNER

Hospitality Suites

Many hotels and resorts offer hospitality suites–large lounges with comfortable furnishings, luggage lockers, and shower facilities–for your use before you check in or after you check out. You can set up your laptop or take a quick nap until your hotel room is ready, or you can freshen up there if you choose to spend your last hours on the beach before leaving for the airport. This can save on early check-in and late check-out fees.

Where to Park

Keep in mind that most Waikīkī hotels charge $10 and up per day for parking. Consider renting a car only on the days that you wish to go exploring, or factor the parking costs into your budget.

Under Construction

At this writing, areas of Waikīkī were under much-needed renovation. The Beach Walk development near Fort DeRussy and the revitalization of the Royal Hawaiian Shopping Center and the International Marketplace—both on Kalākaua Avenue in central Waikīkī—are noteworthy. Inquire closely about noise, disruption, and construction when choosing a hotel.

Bargain Hunting

Keep in mind that the prices listed in this guide are the rack rates given by the hotels at this writing. There are always discounts to be had, be it through Internet sites, promotional specials, off-season discounts, combined hotel/car/air packages, special-occasion rates, or by contacting the hotels directly for reservations. Memberships, such as the AARP and AAA, or an affiliation with the military or government, can also earn discounts. It's always smart to ask.

What It Costs

The lodgings we list are the cream of the crop in each price category. Assume that hotels have private bath, phone, and TV and that they do not serve meals unless we state otherwise. We always list facilities but not whether you'll be charged an extra fee to use them, so when pricing accommodations, find out what's included.

Reservations

After your online research but before you book a room, try calling the hotels directly. Sometimes on-property reservationists can hook you up with the best deals, and they usually have the most accurate 411 not only about rooms but also about hotel amenities. If you use a toll-free number, ask for the location of the calling center you've reached. If it's not Oʻahu, double-check information and rates by calling the hotel's local number.

WHAT IT COSTS					
	$$$$	$$$	$$	$	¢
HOTELS	over $340	$261–$340	$181–$260	$100–$180	under $100

Hotel prices are for two people in a standard double room in high season. Condo price categories reflect studio and one-bedroom rates.

By Maggie
Wunsch

THE 2½ MI STRETCH OF SAND KNOWN AS Waikīkī Beach is a 24-hour playground and the heartbeat of Hawai'i's tourist industry. Waikīkī has a lot to offer—namely, the beach, shopping, restaurants, and nightlife, all within walking distance of your hotel.

Business travelers stay on the western edge, near the Hawai'i Convention Center, Ala Moana, and downtown Honolulu. As you head east, Ala Moana Boulevard turns into Kalākaua Avenue, Waikīkī's main drag. This is hotel row (mid-Waikīkī), complete with historic boutique hotels, newer high rises, and megaresorts. Bigger chains like Sheraton, Outrigger, ResortQuest, and Ohana have multiple properties along the strip, so it can get a little confusing. Surrounding the hotels and filling their lower levels is a flurry of shopping centers, restaurants, bars, and clubs. As you get closer to Diamond Head Crater, the strip opens up again, with the Honolulu Zoo and Kapi'olani Park providing green spaces. There's a handful of smaller hotels and condos at this end for those who like their Waikīkī with a "side of quiet."

Waikīkī is still the resort capital of this island and the lodging landscape is constantly changing. As of this writing, by October 2006 the Waikīkī Beach Walk will have opened on 8 acres within the confines of Beach Walk, Lewers and Saratoga streets, and Kālia Road. It comprises a multi-tiered entertainment complex, cultural center, hotels, and vacation ownership properties, all accented by lush tropical landscaping. Also, Ko'Olina Resort and Marina, about 15 minutes from the airport in West O'ahu, looms large on the horizon—this ongoing development already contains the J.W. Marriott 'Ihilani Resort, Marriott Ko Olina Beach Vacation Club, and some outstanding golf courses, but, it is slated, over the coming decade, to see the construction of an extensive planned resort community and marina, an aquarium, dozens of restaurants and shops, more hotels, and extensive vacation-ownership rentals.

Casual Windward and North Shore digs are shorter on amenities but have laid-back charms all their own. O'ahu offers a more limited list of B&Bs than other islands because the state stopped licensing them here in the 1980s; many of those operating here now do so under the radar. If you can't find your match below, contact a reservation service to make reservations at one of O'ahu's reputable B&Bs. The good news is, legislators on O'ahu are taking another look at this industry, and it's possible that B&Bs will flourish here again in the next decade.

For a complete list of every hotel and condominium on the island, write or call the Hawai'i Visitors & Convention Bureau for a free *Accommodation Guide*.

WAIKĪKĪ

Hotels & Resorts

$$$$ ☒ **Halekūlani.** Honeymooners and others seeking seclusion amidst the
FodorśChoice frenetic activity of the Waikīkī scene find it here. Halekūlani exempli-
★ fies the translation of its name—the "house befitting heaven." From the moment you step inside the lobby, the attention to detail and service wraps

you in luxury. It begins with private registration in your guest room and extends to the tiniest of details, such as complimentary tickets to the Honolulu Symphony, Contemporary Art Museum, and Honolulu Academy of Arts. Spacious guest rooms, artfully appointed in marble and wood, have ocean views and extra large lanai. ■ TIP→ If you want to honeymoon in the ultimate style, we recommend the 2,125-square-foot Vera Wang Suite, created by the noted wedding dress designer herself. It's entirely Vera, right down to the signature soft lavender color scheme. Outside, the resort's freshwater pool has an orchid design created from more than 1½ million glass mosaic tiles. Gray's Beach, which fronts the hotel just beyond the pool, is small and has been known to disappear at high tide. ⊠ *2199 Kālia Rd., Waikīkī 96815* ☎ *808/923–2311 or 800/367–2343* 🖷 *808/926–8004* ⊕ *www.halekulani.com* ↝ *412 rooms, 44 suites* △ *3 restaurants, room service, A/C, in-room data ports, Wi-Fi, in-room safes, cable TV, in-room DVD players, pool, health club, hair salon, spa, beach, 3 bars, shops, dry cleaning, Internet room, business services, parking (fee), no-smoking rooms* ▤ *AE, DC, MC, V. $385–$660.*

★ **$$$$** 🏨 **Outrigger Waikīkī on the Beach.** Outrigger's star jewel sits on one of the finest strands of Waikīkī beach, where the hotel plays host to canoe regattas, the World Ocean Games lifeguard competition, and the Honolulu Marathon. The 16-story resort's guest rooms are a tribute to plantation-style living with rich darkwood furnishings, Hawaiian art, and lanai that offer either ocean or Waikīkī skyline views. The popular Duke's Canoe Club has beachfront concerts under the stars. At this writing, the resort's Plantation Spa is slated to open in spring 2006. ⊠ *2335 Kalākaua Ave., Waikīkī 96815* ☎ *808/923–0711 or 800/688–7444* 🖷 *808/921–9798* ⊕ *www.outrigger.com* ↝ *500 rooms, 30 suites* △ *3 restaurants, room service, A/C, in-room broadband, in-room data ports, in-room safes, some kitchenettes, refrigerators, cable TV with movies and video games, pool, gym, hot tub, beach, 6 bars, theater, shops, children's programs (ages 5–13), dry cleaning, laundry facilities, business services, parking (fee), no-smoking rooms* ▤ *AE, D, DC, MC, V. $349–$739.*

$$$$ 🏨 **Royal Hawaiian Hotel.** The high octane mai tais at this resort's outdoor Mai Tai Bar made the drink famous. But the drinks aren't the only thing that's legendary at the Pink Palace of the Pacific, so nicknamed for its cotton-candy color. The Royal was built in 1927 by Matson Navigation Company for its luxury-cruise passengers. A modern tower has since been added, but we're partial to the romance and architectural detailing of the Royal's historic wing with its canopy beds, Queen Anne–style desks, and color motifs that range from soft mauve to soothing sea foam. If you want a lanai for sunset viewing, however, rooms in the oceanfront tower are your best bet. The Royal has bragging rights to a private beach on some of the widest sands in central Waikīkī. ■ TIP→ The Royal's weekly lūʻau–the only oceanfront lūʻau in Waikīkī–is held Monday evenings underneath the stars on the Ocean Lawn. ⊠ *2259 Kalākaua Ave., Waikīkī 96815* ☎ *888/488–3535, 808/923–7311, or 866/500–8313* 🖷 *808/924–7098* ⊕ *www.royal-hawaiian.com* ↝ *472 rooms, 53 suites* △ *2 restaurants, room service, A/C, in-room broadband, Web TV, minibars, cable TV, pool, hair salon, spa, beach, bar, shops, children's pro-*

grams (ages 5–12), Internet, business services, car rental, parking (fee), no-smoking rooms ☰ *AE, DC, MC, V. $395–$680.*

$$$$
Fodor'sChoice
★
🏨 **Waikīkī Beach Marriott Resort.** On the eastern edge of Waikīkī, this flagship Marriott sits across from Kūhiō Beach and close to Kapi'olani Park, the zoo, and the aquarium. Deep Hawaiian woods and bold tropical colors fill the hotel's two towers, which have ample court-yards and public areas open to ocean breezes and sunlight. Rooms in the Kealohilani Tower are some of the largest in Waikīkī, and the Paokalani

> ## LANAI
>
> Islanders love their porches, bal-conies, and verandas–all wrapped up in the single Hawaiian word, "lanai." When booking, ask about the lanai and be sure to specify the view (understanding that top views command top dollars). Also, check that the lanai is not merely a step-out or Juliet balcony, with just enough room to lean against a railing–you want a lanai that is big enough for patio seating.

Tower's Diamond Head–side rooms offer breathtaking views of the crater and Kapi'olani Park. All rooms have private lanai. The outdoor Moana Terrace, three floors up overlooking Waikīkī Beach, presents Hawaiian music in the early evenings. The Friday-evening entertainment lineup on the Pualeilani Terrace includes the Tepatasi luau, complete with fire-knife dancers. ■ **TIP→** **If you want to keep that laid-back vacation spirit to the very end, use Baggage Direct's mobile skycap service in the main lobby.** This TSA certified agency will take your bags and check them through to your final destination right from the hotel. No more schlepping. ⊠ *2552 Kalākaua Ave., Waikīkī 96815* ☎ *808/922–6611 or 800/367–5370* 🖷 *808/921–5222* ⊕ *www.marriottwaikiki.com* 🛏 *1,310 rooms, 13 suites* ⚏ *6 restaurants, room service, A/C, in-room broadband, in-room data ports, Web TV, Wi-Fi, in-room safes, refrigerators, cable TV with movies, 2 pools, gym, spa, 2 bars, business services, parking (fee), no-smoking rooms* ☰ *AE, D, MC, V. $375–$585.*

★ $$$–$$$$
🏨 **Hawai'i Prince Hotel Waikīkī.** This slim high-rise fronts Ala Wai Yacht Harbor at the 'ewa edge of Waikīkī, close to Honolulu's downtown busi-ness districts, the convention center, and Ala Moana's outdoor mall. There's no beach here, but Ala Moana Beach Park is a 10-minute stroll away along the Harbor, and the hotel also offers complimentary shut-tle service around Waikīkī and its surrounding beaches. It's the only re-sort in Waikīkī with a golf course—the 27-hole Arnold Palmer–designed golf course is in 'Ewa Beach, about a 45-minute ride from the hotel. The sleek, modern Prince looks to Asia both in its high-style decor and such pampering touches as the traditional *oshiburi* (chilled hand towel) for re-freshment upon check-in. Floor-to-ceiling windows overlooking the harbor sunsets make up for the lack of lanai. ⊠ *100 Holomoana St., Waikīkī 96815* ☎ *808/956–1111 or 866/774–6236* 🖷 *808/944–4491*

> ## LOOKING FOR BARGAINS
>
> Room prices can vary dramatically within a single property depend-ing on whether or not a room has an ocean view. If you want to save money, ask for mountain or city view.

9

⊕ *www.hawaiiprincehotel.com* ⬂ *521 rooms, 57 suites* ⚴ *3 restaurants, room service, A/C, in-room data ports, in-room safes, minibars, cable TV, 27-hole golf course, pool, gym, hair salon, spa, hot tub, bar, shops, babysitting, business services, parking (fee), no-smoking rooms* ▭ *AE, DC, MC, V. $325–$465.*

$$$–$$$$ ⊡ **Outrigger Reef on the Beach.** Value and a location right on the beach near to Fort DeRussy are the draw here. Beginning in late 2006 or early 2007, this hotel will serve as the beachfront anchor for the new Waikīkī Beach Walk complex. ■ **TIP→ Try to get an ocean view or oceanfront accommodation; the other rooms have less enchanting views of the walls of the Waikīkī Shores condominium next door.** Most rooms have only showers, and all except those in the standard category have lanai. Kids who sign up for the Reef's Island Explorer program get their own backpack and binoculars at check-in. Hawai'i's celebration of culture—Aloha Fridays—finds this hotel brimming with lei makers, entertainers, and artisans. ⊠ *2169 Kālia Rd., Waikīkī 96815* ☎ *808/923–3111 or 800/688–7444* 🖷 *808/ 924–4957* ⊕ *www.outrigger.com* ⬂ *846 rooms, 39 suites* ⚴ *3 restaurants, room service, A/C, in-room data ports, refrigerators, cable TV with movies and video games, pool, gym, beach, 4 bars, nightclub, laundry facilities, children's programs (ages 5–12), business services, parking (fee), no-smoking rooms* ▭ *AE, D, DC, MC, V. $269–$599.*

$$$–$$$$ ⊡ **Sheraton Moana Surfrider.** Outrageous rates of $1.50 per night were the talk of the town when the "First Lady of Waikīkī" opened her doors in 1901. The *Hawai'i Calls* radio program was broadcast from the veranda during the 1940s and '50s. Today the Moana is still a wedding and honeymoon favorite with its sweeping main staircase and period furnishings in its historic main wing, the Moana. You can renew your wedding vows during the Moana's weekly Promise Me Again ceremony held Saturday evenings underneath the stars of the Banyan Courtyard. In the late 1950s, the Diamond Head Tower was built. In the '70s, the Surfrider hotel went up next door— all three merged into one hotel in the 1980s. The newly refurbished Surfrider has oceanfront suites with two separate lanai, one for sunrise and one for sunset viewing. ⊠ *2365 Kalākaua Ave., Waikīkī 96815* ☎ *808/922–3111, 888/488–3535, or 866/500–8313* 🖷 *808/923–0308* ⊕ *www.moana-surfrider.com* ⬂ *793 rooms, 46 suites* ⚴ *2 restaurants, snack bar, room service, A/C, in-room data ports, in-room safes, cable TV, pool, hair salon, beach, 3 bars, shops, children's programs (ages 5–12), dry cleaning, laundry service, parking (fee), no-smoking rooms* ▭ *AE, DC, MC, V. $310–$625.*

> **PRIVATE BEACHES IN HAWAI'I?**
>
> The Royal Hawaiian Hotel and the Sheraton Moana Surfrider are the only hotels in Waikīkī with property lines that extend out into the sand. They have created "private roped off beach areas" that can only be accessed by hotel guests. The areas are adjacent to the hotel properties at the top of the beach.

$$$–$$$$ ⊡ **Sheraton Waikīkī.** Towering over its neighbors on the prow of Waikīkī's famous sands, the Sheraton is center stage on Waikīkī Beach. Designed for the convention crowd, it's big and busy; the ballroom, one of Oʻahu's largest, hosts convention expos, concerts, and boxing matches. A glass-wall elevator, with magnificent views of Waikīkī, ascends 30 stories to the Hano Hano Room's skyline Cobalt lounge and restaurant in the sky. The resort's best beach is on its Diamond Head side, fronting the Royal Hawaiian Hotel. Lanai afford views of the ocean, Waikīkī or mountains. If you don't shy away from crowds, this could be the place. The advantage here is that you have at your vacation fingertips a variety of amenities, venues, and programs, as well as a location smack dab in the middle of Waikīkī. Don't forget, we're talking living large here, so even the walk to your room could hike off a few of those calories consumed in mai tais. ⊠ *2255 Kalākaua Ave., Waikīkī 96815* ☎ *888/488–3535, 808/922–4422, or 866/500–8313* 🖶 *808/923–8785* ⊕ *www.sheratonwaikiki.com* ➳ *1,695 rooms, 128 suites* ♨ *3 restaurants, room service, A/C, in-room broadband, Web TV, refrigerators, cable TV, 2 pools, health club, hair salon, beach, 4 bars, dance club, babysitting, shops, children's programs (ages 5–12), dry cleaning, laundry service, business services, parking (fee), no-smoking rooms* ▭ *AE, DC, MC, V. $300–$620.*

★ **$$–$$$$** ⊞ **Hilton Hawaiian Village Beach Resort and Spa.** Location, location, location. The HHV sprawls over 22 acres on Waikīkī's widest stretch of beach. It has the perfect neighbor in Fort DeRussy, whose green lawns create a buffer zone to the high-rise lineup of central Waikīkī. The Hilton makes the most of its prime real estate—surrounding the five hotel towers with lavish gardens, an aquatic playground of pools, a lagoon, cascading waterfalls, koi ponds, penguins, and pink flamingos. Rainbow Tower, with its landmark 31-story mural, has knockout views of Diamond Head. Rooms in all towers have lanai offering ocean, city, or Waikīkī beach views. More of a city than a village, the HHV has an ABC sundry store, a bookstore, Louis Vuitton, and a post office. Culture comes in the form of an outpost of the Bishop Museum and the contemporary Hawaiian art gracing the public spaces. It even has its own pier, docking point for the Atlantis Submarine. ■ **TIP→ The sheer volume of options, including free stuff (lei-making, poolside hula shows, and fireworks), make the HHV a good choice for families.** This is a megaresort and a convention destination. On the positive side, that means unusual perks, like check-in kiosks (complete with room keys) in the baggage claim area at the airport. On the negative side, it means that there's usually big doings afoot on-site. Be sure to try the family recipe Irish soda bread; it's in the bread baskets at the exclusive Bali by the Sea, but you can also get it at various cafés. ⊠ *2005 Kālia Rd., Waikīkī 96815* ☎ *808/949–4321 or 800/221–2424* 🖶 *808/951–5458* ⊕ *www.hiltonhawaiianvillage.com* ➳ *3,432 rooms, 365 suites, 264 condominiums* ♨ *20 restaurants, room service, A/C, in-room broadband, in-room safes, minibars, cable TV with movies, 5 pools, gym, spa, beach, snorkeling, 5 bars, shops, babysitting, children's programs (ages 5–12), dry cleaning, laundry service, Internet room, business services, car rental, parking (fee), no-smoking rooms* ▭ *AE, D, DC, MC, V. $239–$535.*

$$–$$$$ ⊞ **Hyatt Regency Waikīkī Resort and Spa.** Across the street from the Kūhiō Beach section of Waikīkī, the Hyatt is actually "oceanfront," as there's

9

no resort between it and the Pacific Ocean. A pool deck staircase leads directly to street level, for easy beach access. An open-air atrium with three levels of shopping, a two-story waterfall, and free nightly live entertainment make this one of the liveliest lobbies anywhere. An activity center offers kids' programs, including lei-making lessons, 'ukulele lessons, and field trips to the aquarium and zoo. ⊠ *2424 Kalākaua Ave., Waikīkī 96815* ☎ *808/923–1234 or 800/633–7313* ☒ *808/923–7839* ⊕ *www.hyattwaikiki.com* ⤏ *1,212 rooms, 18 suites* ⟁ *5 restaurants, room service, A/C, in-room data ports, in-room safes, minibars, cable TV with movies, pool, gym, spa, 3 bars, shops, children's programs (ages 5–12), business services, parking (fee), no-smoking rooms* ▭ *AE, D, DC, MC, V. $210–$530.*

$$–$$$$ ⊞ **Renaissance 'Ilikai Waikīkī.** At the 'ewa edge of Waikīkī overlooking the Ala Wai Harbor, this resort has both standard rooms and units with full kitchens, which can save you some bucks if you self-cater occasionally. The atmosphere here is casual thanks to an open-air lobby, cascading waterfalls, and torchlighted walkways perfect for romantic, evening strolls above the Harbor. There are two freshwater pools and a tennis court, but the nearest beach, at Ala Moana Beach Park, is a five-minute walk. Most rooms have lanai. Wanna play tag? Check out the Ultrazone laser adventure facility. ■ **TIP➔ While riding the glass elevator to the top of the "I", note the uppermost penthouse balcony to the west—it's where Jack Lord's character Steve McGarrett turns to face the camera at the beginning of each episode of** *Hawaii 5-0.* ⊠ *1777 Ala Moana Blvd., Waikīkī 96815* ☎ *808/949–3811 or 800/245–4524* ☒ *808/947–4523* ⊕ *www.ilikaihotel. com* ⤏ *728 rooms, 51 suites* ⟁ *3 restaurants, room service, A/C, in-room broadband, some kitchens, refrigerators, cable TV, tennis court, 2 pools, health club, outdoor hot tub, massage, 2 bars, laundry facilities, business services, car rental, parking (fee), no-smoking rooms* ▭ *AE, D, DC, MC, V. $199–$239.*

$$–$$$$ ⊞ **ResortQuest Waikīkī Beach Hotel.** A three-story volcano, backlighted in a faux eruption, crawls up the side of this hotel opposite Kuhio Beach and near Kapi'olani Park. Rooms are hip Hawaiiana, in colors ranging from neon pineapple yellow to hot lava tropical print red. The retro version of '60s island life continues with little touches like hand-painted bamboo curtains on the closets and surfboards used as entry signs. The third-floor pool deck is where all the action takes place. In the early mornings, there's an international food court where guests can choose complimentary breakfast munchies to pack in a takeout cooler bag. In the evenings, the poolside bar breaks out with Hawaiian music that ranges from traditional to Jawaiian (Hawaiian sound with a reggae beat). There's also a Cold Stone Creamery and a Wolfgang Puck's Express, both on the street level. At this writing, new owners are planning additional public-area renovations. ⊠ *2570 Kalākaua Ave., Waikīkī 96815* ☎ *808/922–2511 or 877/997–6667* ☒ *808/923–3656* ⊕ *www.rqwaikikibeachhotel.com* ⤏ *716 rooms, 12 suites* ⟁ *3 restaurants, A/C, in-room safes, refrigerators, cable TV, in-room data ports, pool, shops, laundry facilities, parking (fee), no-smoking rooms* ▭ *AE, D, DC, MC, V. $255–$450.*

Continued on page 210

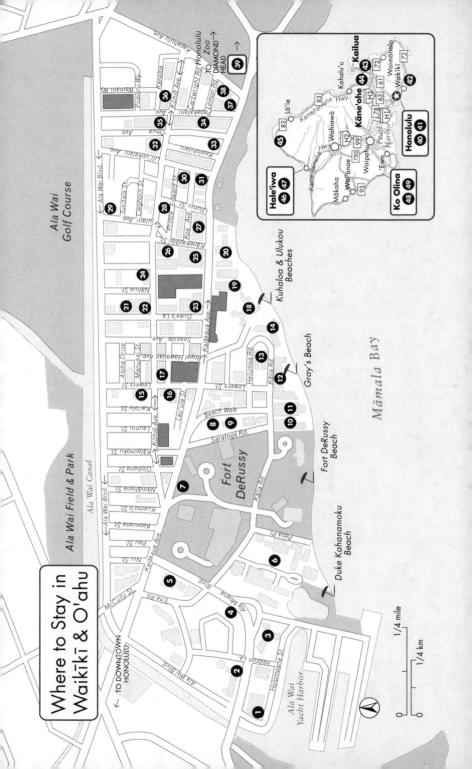

Where to Stay in Waikīkī & Oʻahu

Ala Wai Golf Course

Ala Wai Field & Park

Ala Wai Canal

Fort DeRussy

Māmala Bay

Ala Wai Yacht Harbor

Kuhaloa & Ulukou Beaches

Duke Kahanamoku Beach

Fort DeRussy Beach

Gray's Beach

TO DOWNTOWN HONOLULU

TO Honolulu Zoo / DIAMOND HEAD

1/4 mile

1/4 km

Haleʻiwa

Ko Olina

Honolulu

Kāneʻohe

Kailua

WHERE TO STAY IN WAIKĪKĪ & O'AHU

Hotels & Resorts

★ HOTEL NAME	Worth Noting	Cost $	Pools	Beach	Golf Course	Tennis Courts	Gym	Spa	Children's Programs	Rooms	Restaurants	Other	Location
40 Ala Moana Hotel	Near Ala Moana Shopping	175–570	1				yes			1,217	4		Ala Moana
5 Doubletree Alana Waikīkī	Near Convention Center	140–220	1				yes			313	1		Waikīkī
★ 12 Halekūlani	Great restaurants	385–660	1	yes			yes	yes		456	3	shops	Waikīkī
★ 1 Hawai'i Prince Hotel	Near Ala Moana Shopping	325–465	1		yes		yes	yes	5-12	578	3	shops	Waikīkī
★ 6 Hilton Hawaiian Village	Bishop Museum, fireworks	239–535	5	yes			yes	yes	5-12	4,061	20	shops	Waikīkī
27 Hyatt Regency Waikīkī	Beach across the street	210–530	1				yes	yes	5-12	1,230	5	shops	Waikīkī
49 J.W. Marriott 'Ihilani	Ko'Olina Resort, spa	370–600	2	yes	6		yes	yes	5-12	423	4	shops	West O'ahu
42 The Kāhala	Dolphin Quest	345–735	1	yes			yes	yes		364	5	shops	East Honolulu
2 Marc Hawai'i Polo	Near Ala Moana shopping	99–135	1							106		kitchens	Waikīkī
26 Ohana East	2 blocks to beach	199–209	1				yes			440	3	kitchens	Waikīkī
23 Ohana Waikīkī Beachcomber	1 block to beach, 3 shows	245–295	1						5-12	507	1		Waikīkī
17 Ohana Waikīkī Malia	3 blocks to beach	179–249				1				332	1	kitchens	Waikīkī
24 Ohana Waikīkī West	2 blocks to beach	179–199	1							661	1	kitchens	Waikīkī
11 Outrigger Reef	Good value	269–599	1	yes			yes		5-12	885	3	kitchens	Waikīkī
19 Outrigger Waikīkī	Duke's Canoe Club	349–739	1	yes			yes		5-13	530	3	kitchens	Waikīkī
38 Queen Kapi'olani Hotel	1 block to beach	140–425	1							315	1	kitchens	Waikīkī
32 Radisson Waikīkī Prince K.	2 blocks to beach	199–239	1				yes			620	1		Waikīkī
3 Renaissance 'Ilikai Waikīkī	Short walk to beach	199–239	2			1	yes			779	3	kitchens	Waikīkī
15 ResortQuest Coconut Plaza	3 blocks to beach	105–190	1							80		kitchens	Waikīkī
41 ResortQuest Executive Centre	Near Chinatown, Capitol	200–275	1				yes			116	1	kitchens	Downtown Honolulu
37 ResortQuest Waikīkī Beach	Beach across the street	250–450	1							728	3	shops	Waikīkī
31 ResortQuest Waikīkī Circle	Beach across the street	170–200								104	3		Waikīkī
10 ResortQuest Waikīkī Joy	2 blocks to beach	165–295	1							94	1	kitchens	Waikīkī
30 Royal Grove	Good value	45–75	1							85		no A/C	Waikīkī
18 Royal Hawaiian Hotel	Coconut grove, Mai Tai Bar	395–680	1	yes				yes	5-12	525	2	shops	Waikīkī

	Notes	Price								Rooms			Region
20 Sheraton Moana Surfrider	Landmark historic wing	310–625	1	yes					5–12	839	2	shops	Waikīkī
25 Sheraton Princess Kaiulani	1 block to beach	185–380	1			yes			5–12	1,166	3	shops	Waikīkī
14 Sheraton Waikīkī	30th Floor Cobalt Lounge	300–620	2	yes		yes			5–12	1,823	3	shops	Waikīkī
★ 45 Turtle Bay Resort	Beach cottages, trails	350–780	2	yes	yes	yes	yes		5–12	511	4	shops	North Shore
★ 34 Waikīkī Beach Marriott	Great sushi, spa	375–585	2		10	yes	yes			1,323	6		Waikīkī
★ 13 Waikīkī Parc	1 block to beach	160–333	1			yes				298	2		Waikīkī
29 Waikīkī Sand Villa	3 blocks to beach	109–190	1							212	1	no A/C	Waikīkī

Condos

	Notes	Price								Rooms			Region
8 Aloha Punawai	2 blocks to beach	115–135								19		kitchens	Waikīkī
4 Aqua Palms at Waikīkī	Near Hilton Hawaiian Village	210–275	1			yes				263		kitchens	Waikīkī
9 The Breakers	2 blocks to beach	130	1							64	1	kitchens	Waikīkī
★ 10 Castle Waikīkī Shores	Great value	265–340		yes						168		kitchens	Waikīkī
21 Ilima Hotel	3 blocks to beach	214–249	1			yes				99		kitchens	Waikīkī
★ 7 Outrigger Luana	2 blocks to beach	210–375	1			yes				217		kitchens	Waikīkī
22 Pat Winston's Waikīkī Condos	2 blocks to beach	125–145	1							24		kitchens	Waikīkī
28 ResortQuest Pacific Monarch	3 blocks to beach	170–190	1							152		kitchens	Waikīkī
★ 33 ResortQuest Waikīkī Beach	Beach across the street	505–585	1		1					140		kitchens	Waikīkī
★ 35 ResortQuest Waikīkī Banyan	1 block to beach	200–275	1		1					310		kitchens	Waikīkī
36 ResortQuest Waikīkī Sunset	3 blocks to beach	240–285	1		1					307		kitchens	Waikīkī

B&Bs & Vacation Rentals

	Notes	Price								Rooms			Region
47 Backpackers Vacation Inn	Near Waimea Bay	22–250								25		no A/C	North Shore
39 Diamond Head B&B	Near Diamond Head Crater	130								3		no A/C	Waikīkī
43 Ingrid's	Kailua, Japanese garden	150								2		kitchens	Windward O'ahu
46 Ke Iki Beach Bungalows	Cottages, near Waimea Bay	135–210		yes						11		no A/C	North Shore
48 Marriot Ko Olina Beach	Ko'Olina Resort, spa	319–609	2	yes	6	yes			5–12	200	2	kitchens	Windward O'ahu
44 Schrader's Windward Inn	Near Kāne'ohe Bay	72–144	1	yes						57		no A/C	Windward O'ahu

$$–$$$$ 🏨 **Sheraton Princess Kaiulani.** This hotel sits across the street from its sister property, the Sheraton Moana Surfrider. Kids here can participate in the Keiki Aloha activity program, which is headquartered two blocks down the street at the Sheraton Waikīkī. Rooms are in two towers—some peer over the Moana's low-rise historic wing at the ocean. At night there's poolside hula and live Hawaiian music on the Lava Stage. It's a two-minute stroll to the beach. The hotel's pool is street-side facing Kalākaua Avenue. ✉ *120 Kaiulani Ave., Waikīkī 96815* ☎ *808/922–5811, 888/488–3535, or 866/500–8313* 🖷 *808/931–4577* ⊕ *www.princesskaiulani.com* ⤶ *1,152 rooms, 14 suites* ⚒ *3 restaurants, room service, A/C, in-room data ports, cable TV, pool, gym, bar, children's programs (ages 5–12), business services, no-smoking rooms* ▭ *AE, D, DC, MC, V. $185–$380.*

A SIDE OF CULTURE

Once upon a time you found lei makers and Hollywood-style hula being taught in hotel lobbies. Today, the state is enjoying a renaissance of Hawaiian culture, and you can often connect with programs celebrating this movement for free and without leaving your hotel. Check out hotel music venues featuring some of Hawai'i's most talented musical artists. Watch revered master *kumu* sharing the art of ancient hula. Meet by the ocean for a lesson in the craft of canoe making or join marine reef experts spotting *honu* (Hawaiian sea turtles). Check with your concierge for daily Hawaiiana activities.

$–$$$$ 🏨 **Queen Kapi'olani Hotel.** A half block from the shore on the Diamond Head end of Waikīkī is this older hotel. The Queen "Kap," as she is known by locals, sits right across the street from the zoo, within walking distance of the aquarium, the Waikīkī Concert Shell, Kapio'lani Park, Kapahulu Pier, and Waikīkī Beach. If you're at all a history buff, take a moment to view the historic memorabilia of the Queen and her family—it's displayed throughout the hotel's public areas. Accommodations here are clean and basic and offer a choice among standard rooms, studios with kitchenettes, and one-bedroom suites, all with private lanai and rates that won't break the budget. ✉ *150 Kapahulu Ave., Waikīkī 96815* ☎ *808/ 922–1941 or 800/367–2317* 🖷 *808/924–1982* ⊕ *www.queenkapiolani. com* ⤶ *308 rooms, 7 suites* ⚒ *Restaurant, room service, A/C, in-room safes, kitchenettes, refrigerators, cable TV with video games, pool, bar, laundry facilities, parking (fee)* ▭ *AE, D, DC, MC, V. $140–$425.*

$$–$$$ 🏨 **Ohana Waikīkī Beachcomber Hotel.** This newest addition to the Ohana hotels family is pretty much entertainment central, featuring the legendary Don Ho as well as the popular Blue Hawai'i and Magic of Polynesia revues. Set almost directly across from the Royal Hawaiian Shopping center and adjacent to the International Marketplace, the hotel has a third-floor pool deck that offers the perk of front-row seating for any of Waikīkī's parades or Hoolaulea street party festivals that happen year-round. It's a family-friendly place, with cultural activities that include 'ukulele and hula lessons as well as arts and crafts. Rooms have private lanai and Polynesian motifs. On the hotel's ground level is an entrance to Macy's department store, and across the street is a public accessway that opens up to the beach fronting the Royal Hawaiian hotel. ✉ *2300 Kalākaua Ave., Waikīkī 96815* ☎ *808/922–4646 or 800/462-6262* 🖷 *808/923–4889* 🌐 *www.waikikibeachcomber.com* ✒ *500 rooms, 7 suites* ↺ *Restaurant, snack bar, room service, A/C, minibars, refrigerators, cable TV, in-room data ports, pool, outdoor hot tub, bar, children's programs (ages 5–12), laundry facilities, Internet room, parking (fee), no-smoking rooms* ▭ *AE, DC, MC, V. $245–$295.*

$$–$$$ 🏨 **Ohana Waikīkī Malia.** Close to the 'ewa end of Waikīkī, this older hotel comprises a pair of buildings, one with standard rooms, the other with one-bedroom suites that have kitchenettes. Although almost all rooms and suites here have lanais, the views here are more city and concrete than foliage and ocean. Guests who return here year after year are those who fancy the property's proximity to restaurants and shopping, and its easygoing "come as you are" vibe. During major sporting events on O'ahu, don't be surprised if you share the elevator with a tri-athlete and his bicycle or a marathoner just back from her run. There is a coffee shop on the lobby level, and stops for TheBus and trolley lines are right outside the front door. The hotel's tennis court is on the roof so think carefully before chasing after the longer lobs. ✉ *2211 Kuhio Ave., Waikīkī 96815* ☎ *808/923–7621 or 800/462–6262* 🖷 *808/921–4804* 🌐 *www.ohanahotels.com* ✒ *285 rooms, 47 suites* ↺ *Restaurant, A/C, in-room data ports, in-room safes, some kitchenettes, refrigerators, cable TV with movies and video games, tennis court, laundry facilities, parking (fee), no-smoking rooms* ▭ *AE, D, DC, MC, V. $179–$249.*

$–$$$ 🏨 **ResortQuest Waikīkī Joy.** A trellised open-air lobby of Italian marble and a guava smoothie greet you on arrival at this Lewers Street boutique hideaway. In-room Jacuzzi tubs, slick stereo-entertainment systems, and lighting-sound control bedside panels lend further appeal. One of the hotel's towers contains standard rooms; the other is all suites. Request a room close to the top of the hotel's 11 stories if you want to see the ocean from your lanai. It's about a five-minute stroll to Kalākaua Avenue and through one of the many public accessways to the beach, which can be a bit of a haul if you're carrying beach chairs. Continental breakfast on the lobby veranda is included, and Cappucino's Cafe offers a mix of Asian, American, and Hawaiian treats as well as Internet access. Cappucino's will also cater meals for you and your groupies if you're busy recording your first hit at the hotel's GS Karaoke Studio. ✉ *320 Lewers St., Waikīkī 96815* ☎ *808/923–2300 or 866/774-2924* 🖷 *808/922–8785* 🌐 *www.rqwaikikijoy.com* ✒ *50 rooms, 44 suites* ↺ *Restaurant, A/C, in-room data ports, in-room safes, some kitchenettes, refrigerators, cable TV, pool, sauna, bar, laundry facilities, parking (fee), no smoking rooms* ▭ *AE, D, DC, MC, V. $165–$295.*

★ $–$$$ 🏨 **Waikīkī Parc.** One of the best-kept secrets in Waikīkī is this boutique hotel owned by the same group that manages the Halekūlani across the street. The Waikīkī Parc offers the same attention to detail in service and architectural design as the larger hotel but lacks the beachfront location and higher prices. Guests staying at the Parc have access to most

Lodging Alternatives

APARTMENT & HOUSE RENTAL

If you want a home base that's roomy enough for a family and comes with cooking facilities, consider a furnished rental. These can save you money, especially if you're traveling with a group. Home-exchange directories sometimes list rentals as well as exchanges.

7 International Agents Hideaways International ⊠ 767 Islington St., Portsmouth, NH 03801 ☎ 603/430–4433 or 800/843–4433 📠 603/430–4444 ⊕ www.hideaways.com, annual membership $185. **Vacation Home Rentals Worldwide** ⊠ 235 Kensington Ave., Norwood, NJ 07648 ☎ 201/767–9393 or 800/633–3284 📠 201/767–5510 ⊕ www.vhrww.com.

HOME EXCHANGES

If you would like to exchange your home for someone else's, join a home-exchange organization, which will send you its updated listings of available exchanges for a year and will include your own listing in at least one of them. It's up to you to make specific arrangements.

7 Exchange Clubs HomeLink International ⊠ 2937 NW 9th Terrace, Fort Lauderdale, FL 33311 ☎ 954/566–2687 or 800/638–3841 📠 954/566–2783 ⊕ www.homelink.org; $80 yearly for Web-only membership; $125 with Web access and two directories. **Intervac U.S.** ⊠ 30 Corte San Fernando, Tiburon, CA 94920 ☎ 800/756–4663 📠 415/435–7440 ⊕ www.intervacus.com; $128.88 yearly for a listing, online access, and a catalog; $78.88 without catalog.

HOSTELS

No matter what your age, you can save on lodging costs by staying at hostels. O'ahu hostels cater to a lively international crowd of backpackers, hikers, surfers, and windsurfers; those seeking intimacy or privacy should seek out a B&B.

In some 4,500 locations in more than 70 countries around the world, Hostelling International (HI), the umbrella group for a number of national youth-hostel associations, offers single-sex, dorm-style beds and, at many hostels, rooms for couples and family accommodations. HI has two affiliate members on O'ahu: one near the University of Hawai'i and the other in Waikīkī.

---

of the facilities of the Halekūlani and can sign charges there to their room at the Parc. The pastel guest rooms in this high-rise complex have plantation-style shutters that open out to the lanai. Rooms have sitting areas and flat-screen TVs. The hotel's heated pool and sundeck are eight floors up, affording a bit more privacy and peace for sunbathers. ⊠ 2233 Helumoa Rd., Waikīkī 96815 ☎ 808/921–7272 or 800/422–0450 📠 808/923–1336 ⊕ www.waikikiparc.com 🛏 298 rooms ♨ 2 restaurants, room service, A/C, in-room data ports, in-room safes, cable TV, in-room broadband, pool, gym, business services, parking (fee), no-smoking rooms ⊟ AE, D, DC, MC, V. $160–$333.

$$ ⊞ Ohana East. The flagship property for Ohana Hotels in Waikīkī is next to the Sheraton Princess Kaiulani on the corner of Kaiulani and Kūhiō avenues; it's only two blocks from the beach. It tends to pull in group

Membership in any HI national hostel association, open to travelers of all ages, allows you to stay in HI-affiliated hostels at member rates; one-year membership is about $28 for adults (C$35 for a two-year minimum membership in Canada, £15.95 in the U.K., A$52 in Australia, and NZ$40 in New Zealand); hostels charge about $10–$30 per night. Members have priority if the hostel is full; they're also eligible for discounts around the world, even on rail and bus travel in some countries.

There also are several other hostels in Waikīkī, as well as the Backpackers Vacation Inn and Plantation Village on Oʻahu's North Shore.

🔢 **Organizations Hostelling International—USA** ✉ 8401 Colesville Rd., Suite 600, Silver Spring, MD 20910 ☎ 301/495-1240 🖷 301/495-6697 ⊕ www.hiusa.org. **Hostelling International—Canada** ✉ 205 Catherine St., Suite 500, Ottawa, Ontario K2P 1C3 ☎ 613/237-7884 or 800/663-5777 🖷 613/237-7868 ⊕ www.hihostels.ca. **YHA England and Wales** ✉ Trevelyan House, Dimple Rd., Matlock, Derbyshire DE4 3YH, U.K. ☎ 0870/870-8808, 0870/

770-8868, 01629/592-600 🖷 0870/770-6127 ⊕ www.yha.org.uk. **YHA Australia** ✉ 422 Kent St., Sydney, NSW 2001 ☎ 02/9261-1111 🖷 02/9261-1969 ⊕ www.yha.com.au. **YHA New Zealand** ✉ Level 1, Moorhouse City, 166 Moorhouse Ave., Box 436, Christchurch ☎ 03/379-9970 or 0800/278-299 🖷 03/365-4476 ⊕ www.yha.org.nz.

🔢 **Local Resources Backpackers Vacation Inn and Plantation Village** ✉ 59-788 Kamehameha Hwy. Haleʻiwa 96712 ☎ 808/638-7838 🖷 808/638-7515 ⊕ www.backpackers-hawaii.com. **Pacific Ohana** ✉ 2552 Lemon Rd. Honolulu 96815 ☎ 808/921-8111. **Polynesian Hostel Beach Club** ✉ 2584 Lemon Rd. Honolulu 96815 ☎ 808/922-1340 🖷 808/262-2817 ⊕ www.hawaiihostels.com. **Seaside Hawaiian Hostel** ✉ 419 Seaside Ave. Honolulu 96815 ☎ 808/924-3303 🖷 808/923-2111 ⊕ www.seasidehawaiianhostel.com. **Waikiki Beachside Hostel** ✉ 2556 Lemon Rd. Honolulu 96815 ☎ 866/478-3888 or 808/923-9566 🖷 808/923-7525 ⊕ www.waikikibeachsidehostel.com.

9

travelers. Don't expect any fancy lobbies or outdoor gardens here. Accommodations range from hotel rooms to suites with kitchenettes. Certain rooms on lower floors have no lanai, and some rooms have showers only. Ohana East also offers 14 floors of no-smoking rooms as well as a fitness center and privileges at Outrigger's Serenity Spa in the Outrigger Reef on the Beach. ✉ *150 Kaiulani Ave., Waikīkī 96815* ☎ *808/922-5353 or 800/462-6262* 🖷 *808/926-4334* ⊕ *www.ohanahotels.com* ⤶ *420 rooms, 20 suites* ⚅ *3 restaurants, room service, A/C, in-room broadband, in-room safes, some kitchenettes, refrigerators, cable TV with video games, pool, gym, hair salon, bar, laundry facilities, parking (fee), no-smoking floors* ▭ *AE, D, DC, MC, V. $199–$209.*

$$ 🏨 **Radisson Waikīkī Prince Kūhiō.** You enter the Radisson through a lobby of rich wood detailing, contemporary fabrics, and magnificent tropical floral displays. Two blocks from Kūhiō Beach and across the street from the Marriott Waikīkī, this 37-story high-rise is on the Diamond Head end of Waikīkī. The Lobby Bar mixes up tropical cocktails, an island-style pūpū menu, wireless access, and a wide-screen plasma TV for sports fans and news junkies. If marriage is on your mind, note the wedding gazebo anchoring the hotel gardens. Book on an upper floor if you want to see the ocean from your lanai. ⊠ *2500 Kūhiō Ave., Waikīkī 96815* ☎ *808/922–8811 or 800/333–3333* 🖷 *808/921–5507* ⊕ *www. radisson.com/waikikihi* ↩ *620 rooms* ♨ *Restaurant, room service, A/C, cable TV, in-room broadband, in-room data ports, in-room safes, pool, gym, hot tub, bar, laundry facilities, business services, parking (fee), no-smoking rooms* ▤ *AE, D, DC, MC, V. $199–$239.*

$–$$ 🏨 **Doubletree Alana Waikīkī.** The location (a 10-minute walk from the Hawai'i Convention Center), three phones in each room, and the 24-hour business center meet the requirements of the Doubletree's global business clientele, but the smallness of the property, the staff's attention to detail, the signature Doubletree chocolate chip cookies upon arrival, and the Japanese-style *furo* deep-soaking tubs resonate with vacationers. The mezzanine of this 19-story high-rise has rotating exhibits of local artists' work, and the gym is open round-the-clock. All rooms have lanai, but they overlook the city and busy Ala Moana Boulevard across from Fort DeRussy. To get to the beach, you either cross Fort DeRussy or head through the Hilton Hawaiian Village. ⊠ *1956 Ala Moana Blvd., Waikīkī 96815* ☎ *808/941–7275 or 800/222–8733* 🖷 *808/949–0996* ⊕ *www. alana-doubletree.com* ↩ *268 rooms, 45 suites* ♨ *Restaurant, room service, A/C, in-room data ports, in-room safes, cable TV, pool, gym, bar, business services, car rental, parking (fee), no-smoking rooms* ▤ *AE, D, MC, V. $140–$220.*

$–$$ 🏨 **Ohana Waikīkī West.** Just behind the International Marketplace, this economical hotel offers a third-floor pool and sundeck overlooking all the action of busy Kūhiō Avenue. You can choose a standard room or one with a kitchenette. There are also standard/kitchenette combos consisting of two connecting rooms with either one King and two double beds or four double beds—these sleep a maximum of six. Rooms have showers only. Views from private lanais overlook bustling Kūhiō Avenue or face neighboring high-rises. From the higher-floor rooms, you can catch glimpses of the ocean. The room interiors of soft blues and taro-leaf greens soothe the senses. Favored by group travelers, airline crews, and visiting military, the hotel is just two blocks from the beach and handy for shopping and dining. ⊠ *2330 Kūhiō Ave., Waikīkī 96815* ☎ *808/922–5022 or 800/462–6262* 🖷 *808/924–6414* ⊕ *www. ohanahotels.com* ↩ *645 rooms, 16 suites* ♨ *Restaurant, café, A/C, in-room data ports, in-room safes, some kitchenettes, refrigerators, cable TV with movies and video games, pool, bar, nightclub, laundry facilities, parking (fee), no-smoking rooms* ▤ *AE, D, DC, MC, V* ⦿l *EP. $179–$199.*

$–$$ 🏨 **ResortQuest Coconut Plaza.** Overlooking the Ala Wai Canal, this reasonably priced boutique hotel is more residential than a typical resort, with a cobblestone driveway; a lobby with light rattan, living room–style furnishings; and a wall of French doors that open up to a gazebo garden and a tiny "two-stroke" swimming pool tucked in a backyard. You can choose from hotel rooms or studios with kitchenettes. Accommodations are compact but functional with tile flooring instead of carpets. Views from your lanai include the Canal and its canoers by day and the lights of Honolulu's skyline by night. Complimentary Continental breakfast is served in the lobby overlooking the hotel garden. It's a three-block walk to the beach. ⊠ *450 Lewers St., Waikīkī, 96815* ☎ *808/923–8828 or 866/774–2924* 🖷 *808/923–3473* ⊕ *www.rqcoconutplaza.com* ➷ *80 rooms* ⚓ *A/C, in-room data ports, in-room safes, some kitchenettes, cable TV, pool, laundry facilities, parking (fee), no smoking rooms* ⊟ *AE, D, DC, MC, V. $105–$190.*

$–$$ 🏨 **ResortQuest Waikīkī Circle Hotel.** This unusual 14-story circular hotel is a Waikīkī landmark. A charming interior design scheme brings the Pacific inside, beginning at check-in beneath a seascape mural in the open-air lobby. The elevators are painted a bright sea blue–green, and hallway floors are textured to mimic the sandy beach, complete with appliqued sea shells and sea creatures dotting the circular walkways. Rooms here are small, and every bit of space is utilized. Tiny bathrooms have showers only, but a sandpail and shovel sits on the counter, just begging you to go out and play. And you won't have far to walk—Waikīkī Beach is right down the front stairs and across the street. Honeymooners, snowbirds, and old-timers love this little hotel with a front desk staff that takes the time to get to know you. ⊠ *2464 Kalākaua Ave., Waikīkī 96815* ☎ *808/923–1571 or 866/774–2924* 🖷 *808/926–8024* ⊕ *www. RQwaikikicirclehotel.com* ➷ *104 rooms* ⚓ *Restaurant, in-room data ports, A/C, in-room safes, cable TV, laundry facilities, parking (fee), no-smoking floors* ⊟ *AE, D, DC, MC, V. $170–$200.*

$–$$ 🏨 **Waikīkī Sand Villa.** Families and others looking for an economical rate return to the Waikīkī Sand Villa year after year. It's on the corner of Kaiulani Avenue and Ala Wai Boulevard, a three-block walk to restaurants and the beach. There's a high-rise tower and a three-story walkup building of studio accommodations with kitchenettes. Rooms are small but well-planned. Corner deluxe units with lanai overlook Ala Wai Canal and the golf course. There's a fitness center with 24-hour access. Complimentary Continental breakfast is served poolside beneath shady coconut trees, and the hotel's Sand Bar comes alive at happy hour with a great mix of hotel guests and locals who like to hang out and "talk story." The Sand Bar also has computers and Web cams. ⊠ *2375 Ala Wai Blvd., Waikīkī*

BUDGET-FRIENDLY CHAINS

The following local hotel chains specialize in hotel rooms and condo rentals for value prices. Buildings are older; amenities are limited; and the locations are rarely beachfront. However, you do get a clean place to toss your stuff and lay your head for the night. After all, you didn't come all the way here to stay in your hotel room, now did you?

- **Marc Resorts Hawaii** (☎ 800/ 535–0085 ⊕ www.marcresorts. com).

- **Ohana Hotels** (☎ 800/462– 6262 ⊕ www.ohanahotels. com).

9

96815 ☎ 808/922–4744 or 800/247–1903 🖷 808/923–2541 ⊕ *www. sandvillahotel.com* ✍ *214 rooms* ⚘ *Restaurant, in-room broadband, in-room safes, refrigerators, pool, hot tub, bar, shop, parking (fee), no-smoking rooms; no A/C in some rooms* ☰ *AE, D, DC, MC, V.* $109–$190.

¢–$ 🏨**Marc Hawai'i Polo Inn and Tower.** This small hotel fronts busy Ala Moana Boulevard, one-block from Ala Moana Shopping Center and Ala Moana Beach Park, on the 'ewa end of Waikīkī. Although it doesn't offer much in the way of lobby space, ocean views, or room amenities, it is within walking distance of beach parks, shopping, and restaurants. Here you have the option of standard hotel rooms or studios with kitchenettes. Room interior decor pays tribute to Hawai'i polo enthusiasts, and front desk staff are happy to assist with driving directions to the playing fields at Mokuleia and Waimānalo—pack a picnic if you go. ✉ *1696 Ala Moana Blvd., 96815* ☎ *808/949–0061 or 800/535–0085* 🖷 *808/949–4906* ⊕ *www.marcresorts.com* ✍ *106 rooms* ⚘ *A/C, in-room safes, some kitchenettes, some microwaves, cable TV, pool, shop, laundry facilities, parking (fee), no-smoking rooms* ☰ *AE, DC, MC, V.* $99–$135.

¢ 🏨 **Royal Grove Hotel.** Two generations of the Fong family have put their heart and soul into the operation of this tiny (by Waikīkī standards), six-story hotel. During the hot summer months, seriously consider splurging on the highest-end accommodations, which feature air-conditioning, lanai, and small kitchens. The hotel's pool is its social center in the evenings, where you can usually find at least one or more members of the Fong family strumming a 'ukulele, dancing hula, and singing songs in the old Hawaiian style. On special occasions, the Fongs host a potluck dinner by the pool. Little touches that mean a lot include free use of boogie boards, surfboards, beach mats, and beach towels. The hotel is two blocks from Waikīkī's Kūhiō Beach. On property are a tiny sushi bar, a natural foods deli, and an authentic Korean barbeque plate-lunch place. For extra value, inquire about the Grove's weekly and monthly rates. ✉ *151 Uluniu Ave., Waikīkī 96815* ☎ *808/923–7691* 🖷 *808/922–7508* ⊕ *www.royalgrovehotel.com* ✍ *78 rooms, 7 suites* ⚘ *Kitchenettes, pool; no A/C in some rooms, no parking* ☰ *AE, D, DC, MC, V.* $45–$75.

Condos

★ $$$$ 🏨 **ResortQuest Waikīkī Beach Tower.** Facing Kūhiō Beach, this 40-story resort offers spacious (1,100–1,400 square feet) one- and two-bedroom suites with gourmet kitchens and windows that open to views of Waikīkī and the Pacific Ocean. Amenities include twice-daily maid service, washer-dryers, and spacious private lanai. Valet parking is included. ✉ *2470 Kalākaua Ave., Waikīkī 96815* ☎ *808/926–6400 or 866/774–2924* 🖷 *808/926–7380* ⊕ *www.rqwaikikibeachtower.com* ✍ *140 units* ⚘ *Room service, A/C, in-room data ports, in-room safes, kitchens, cable TV, in-room DVD players, tennis court, pool, outdoor hot tub, sauna, billiards, paddle tennis, laundry facilities, parking, no smoking rooms,* ☰ *AE, D, DC, MC, V. 1-bedroom $540–$585, 2-bedroom $640–$705.*

★ $$–$$$$ 🏨 **Outrigger Luana.** At the entrance to Waikīkī near Fort DeRussy Park, this condo-hotel contains 218 studios and one-bedroom suites. The two-story lobby is appointed in rich, Hawaiian-wood furnishings with island-inspired fabrics, along with a mezzanine lounge. Units are furnished with the same mix of rich woods with etched accents of pineapples and palm trees. At bedside, hula-dancer and beach-boy lamps add another Hawaiian residential touch. The recreational deck features a fitness center, pool, and barbecue area with tables that can be enclosed "cabana-style" for privacy when dining outdoors. One-bedroom suites each have two lanai. ⊠ *2045 Kalākaua Ave., Waikīkī 96815* ☎ *808/955–6000 or 800/688–7444* 🖷 *808/943–8555* ⊕ *www.outrigger.com* ⤴ *217 units* ⏶ *BBQs, A/C, in-room data ports, in-room safes, some kitchens, some kitchenettes, cable TV with movies, pool, gym, laundry facilities, parking (fee), business services* ▭ *AE, D, DC, MC, V. Studios $210–$265, 1-bedroom $325–$375, 2-bedroom $600.*

> ## CONDO COMFORTS
>
> **Foodland** The local chain has 2 locations near Waikīkī: **Market City** (⊠ 2839 Harding Ave., near intersection with Kapahulu Ave. and highway overpass, Kaimukī ☎ 808/734–6303) and **Ala Moana Center** (⊠ 1450 Ala Moana Blvd., ground level, Ala Moana ☎ 808/949–5044).
>
> **Food Pantry** A smaller version of larger Foodland, Food Pantry also has apparel, beach stuff, and tourist-oriented items. ⊠ *2370 Kūhiō Ave., across from Miramar hotel, Waikīkī* ☎ 808/923–9831.
>
> **Blockbuster Video** (⊠ Ala Moana Shopping Center, 451 Piikoi St., Ala Moana ☎ 808/593–2595)
>
> **Pizza Hut** (☎ 808/643–1111 for delivery statewide).

$$$
Fodor'sChoice
★

Castle Waikīkī Shores. Nestled between Fort DeRussy Beach Park and the Outrigger Reef on the Beach, this is the only condo right on Waikīkī Beach. Units include studios and one- and two-bedroom suites, each with private lanai and panoramic views of the Pacific Ocean. The beach directly fronting the building is nothing to write home about, but it's only a few steps to the large expanse of beach at Fort DeRussy. Many of these units have full kitchens, but some only have kitchenettes so be sure you inquire when booking. ⊠ *2161 Kālia Rd., Waikīkī 96815* ☎ *808/952–4500 or 800/367–2353* 🖷 *808/952–4580* ⊕ *www.castleresorts.com* ⤴ *168 units* ⏶ *A/C, in-room data ports, in-room safes, some kitchens, some kitchenettes, cable TV, beach, laundry facilities, parking (fee), no-smoking rooms* ▭ *AE, D, DC, MC, V. 1-bedroom $265–$340, 2-bedroom $425–$595.*

$$–$$$

Aqua Palms at Waikiki. Across from the Hilton Hawaiian Village on Ala Moana Boulevard just as it curves toward Waikīkī's Kalākaua Avenue, the 12-story Aqua Palms completed a $15 million transformation into a "condotel" in 2005 and now offers luxury studio and one-bedroom suite accommodations. The studios include kitchenettes, and the suites feature full kitchens; both have tiled entryways, private lanai, and in-room DVD players. Guests here have signing privileges at restaurants in the Hyatt Regency Waikīkī, located at the Diamond Head end of the strip. ⊠ *1850 Ala Moana Blvd., Waikīkī 96815* ☎ *808/947–7256 or 866/406–2782* 🖷 *808/947–7002* ⊕ *www.aquaresorts.com/palms* ⤴ *263 units* ⏶ *A/C, in-room broadband, in-room safes, some kitchens, some*

9

kitchenettes, cable TV with movies, in-room DVD players, pool, gym, outdoor hot tub, laundry facilities, parking (fee), business services ⊟ *AE, D, DC, MC, V. $210–$275.*

★ **$$–$$$** ▣ **ResortQuest Waikīkī Banyan.** Families looking for condo convenience within walking distance of the beach like this property not only for its one-bedroom suites but also for its recreation deck, which features outdoor grills, a heated swimming pool, two hot tubs, a children's playground, a mini-putting green, and volleyball, basketball, and tennis courts. One-bedroom suites contain island-inspired decor and have complete kitchens and lanai that offer Diamond Head or ocean views. ⊠ *201 Ohua Ave., 96815* ☎ *808/922–0555 or 866/774–2924* ᧒ *808/922–0906* ⊕ *www.rqwaikikibanyan.com* ⇥ *310 units* ⚬ *BBQs, A/C, in-room broadband, in-room data ports, kitchens, cable TV, tennis court, pool, outdoor hot tub, sauna, basketball, volleyball, shop, playground, parking (fee), laundry facilities, no-smoking rooms* ⊟ *AE, D, DC, MC, V. 1-bedroom $200–$275.*

$$–$$$ ▣ **ResortQuest Waikīkī Sunset.** This 38-story high-rise condominium resort is near Diamond Head, one block from Waikīkī Beach and on The-Bus line. Without leaving the property, you can swim, take a sauna break, throw some steaks on the outdoor grill, have access to a computer in the hospitality lounge, and end your day with night play on the condo's volleyball, basketball, and tennis courts. One- and two-bedroom suites are light, bright, and airy with tropical furnishings, complete kitchens, daily maid service, private lanai, and terrific views through floor-to-ceiling windows. There are coin-op washers/dryers on each guest floor for added convenience. ⊠ *229 Paoakalani Ave., Waikīkī 96815* ☎ *808/922–0511 or 866/774–2924* ᧒ *808/922–8580* ⊕ *www.rqwaikikisunset.com* ⇥ *307 units* ⚬ *BBQs, A/C, in-room data ports, kitchens, cable TV, tennis court, pool, sauna, shop, laundry facilities, no-smoking rooms* ⊟*AE, D, DC, MC, V. 1-bedroom $240–$285, 2-bedroom $440–$680.*

$$ ▣ **Ilima Hotel.** Tucked away on a residential side street near Waikīkī's Ala Wai Canal, this locally owned 17-story condominium-style hotel is a gem. The glass-wall lobby with koa-wood furnishings, original Hawaiian artwork, and friendly staff creates a Hawaiian home-away-from-home. One of the selling points of this place is the decent rate for its spacious studios with kitchenettes, as well as its one- and two-bedroom suites with full kitchens, Jacuzzi baths, cable TV with free HBO and Disney channels, multiple phones, and spacious lanai. It's a two-block walk to Waikīkī Beach. The parking is free but limited. When the spots are full, you park on the street. ⊠ *445 Nohonani St., Waikīkī 96815* ☎ *808/923–1877 or 800/801–9366* ᧒ *808/924–2617* ⊕ *www.ilima.com* ⇥ *99 units* ⚬ *A/C, in-room data ports, in-room safes, kitchens, cable TV, some in-room broadband, pool, gym, sauna, laundry facilities, parking, no-smoking rooms* ⊟ *AE, DC, MC, V. 1-bedroom $214–$249, 2-bedrooms $302–$325.*

$–$$ ▣ **ResortQuest Pacific Monarch.** One block from Waikīkī Beach on the 'ewa end of Waikīkī, this 34-story high-rise condominium resort features a rooftop deck with a freshwater pool, hot tub, and sauna and affords a panoramic view spanning the length of Waikīkī. Studio and one-bedroom suites are available, plus some larger units with full

Condo + Hotel = "Condotel"

Hawai'i's newest alternative in vacation lodging is a hybrid of condominium vacation rental and hotel services and amenities. The condo concept is not a new one in the Islands, but the time of just picking up your keys from a nameless agent or from underneath the welcome mat has passed.

Today many people invest in hotel condominium units as vacation homes. Unlike many single-family condos, these units can be rented out easily and require less maintenance, since the units are managed by hotel companies.

Condotels give both owners and renters the spaciousness, convenience, and privacy of a vacation home along with the amenities of full-service hotel resorts. Just consider the possibilities: amenities can include pre-arrival grocery-delivery service, daily maid service, a newspaper at your doorstep each morning, Wi-Fi, DVD entertainment systems, plasma TVs, and in-room massage and spa treatments. Concierges can assist with restaurant reservations, sightseeing tours, and car rentals.

No longer is it just you, your condo, and a swimming pool. At many of these properties, you have access to golf courses, tennis courts, horse stables, hot tubs, spas, and fitness centers. Forget mere barbecue pits— you may have access to private cabanas, where you can dine with a view. You can do your laundry on property, or even in some condos outfitted with washers and dryers, or

send it out. There's typically 24-hour front desk and business services, if you just can't keep the office at bay.

Consider what your needs are in terms of location, size of unit, bedding, family desires, amenities, architectural style, and character. Is a view hugely important? Do you want a lanai that offers sunbathing privacy or patio furniture for outdoor dining? Do you need peace and quiet or do you prefer a high-energy, kid-friendly compound? Is it important to have the ocean outside your door or the city? Know what you want before you book. It isn't as easy to change a condo unit as it is a hotel room.

Since condotels contain units with individual owners and are rented out through management companies, inquire when booking about furniture and decor standards. Are units individually furnished? Are furnishings maintained and upgraded by the condotel management? If you have 21st-century tastes, you might not feel comfortable in a unit last gussied-up in the late '70s. Also inquire as to bedding configurations. Will you be sleeping in regular beds or in bedding created from a pullout sofa? If your unit has a kitchen or kitchenette, consider which appliances and equipment you need. Some kitchens come furnished with as little as a tiny microwave and mini-refrigerator, but fancy full-service ones might contain convection ovens, wine coolers, dishwashers, and wet bars.

Many of Waikīkī's older hotels are enjoying resurgences as they've been transformed into hotel condominiums.

9

kitchens. All accommodations have lanai. There's a hospitality lounge with showers available to early arrivals and late departures. The only drawback here is that the rooftop pool deck is accessible only via a single flight of stairs after you exit the elevator on the top floor; however, the view is worth the climb. ⊠ *2427 Kūhiō Ave., Waikīkī 96815* ☎ *808/ 923–9805 or 866/774–2924* 🖷 *808/924–3220* ⊕ *www.rqpacificmonarch. com* 🛏 *152 units* ☉ *A/C, some kitchens, some kitchenettes, cable TV, pool, outdoor hot tub, sauna, laundry facilities, parking (fee), no smoking rooms* ▭ *AE, D, DC, MC, V. $170–$265.*

$ 🖼 **Aloha Punawai.** Punawai provides all the basics for those on a budget. This family-operated apartment hotel is across busy Saratoga Road from Fort DeRussy Beach. Each unit comes with a full kitchen and a lanai. Studios have bathrooms with showers only. One-bedroom units have either two twins or a king-size bed, while one-bedroom deluxe units have one queen, one twin and a sofa bed. Furnishings are simple, and decor is spartan. You can opt for telephone service or forgo the distraction. ⊠ *305 Saratoga Rd., Waikīkī 96815* ☎ *808/923–5211 or 866/713– 9694* 🖷 *808/923–5211* ⊕ *www.alternative-hawaii.com/alohapunawai* 🛏 *19 units* ☉ *A/C, kitchens, cable TV, laundry facilities; no phones in some rooms* ▭ *AE, DC, MC, V. 1-bedroom $115–$135.*

$ 🖼 **The Breakers.** For a taste of Hawai'i in the '60s, right after Statehood, go retro at this low-rise hotel a mere half-block from Waikīkī Beach. The Breakers' six two-story buildings surround its pool and overlook gardens filled with tropical flowers. Guest rooms have Japanese-style *shoji* doors that open to the lanai, kitchenettes, and bathrooms with showers only. Units 130, 132, and 134 have views of the Urasenke Teahouse. This tiny haven is in the shadow of the on-going construction, expected to last through 2006, of the Waikīkī Beach Walk, and all the sounds that go with it. Once Beach Walk is finished, however, The Breakers will enjoy enviable proximity to this new entertainment and retail complex. The resort is very popular thanks to its reasonable prices and great location. Parking is limited, but it's free. ⊠ *250 Beach Walk, Waikīkī 96815* ☎ *808/ 923–3181 or 800/426–0494* 🖷 *808/923–7174* ⊕ *www.breakers-hawaii. com* 🛏 *64 units* ☉ *Restaurant, A/C, kitchenettes, pool, bar, parking* ▭ *AE, DC, MC, V. 1-bedroom $130, 2-bedroom $145.*

$ 🖼 **Pat Winston's Waikīkī Condos.** This five-story condominium complex is just off Kūhiō Avenue near the International Marketplace and two blocks from Waikīkī Beach. All units have full kitchens, ceiling fans, sofa beds, and lanai. Interior designs vary, with units to accommodate families, honeymooners, business travelers, and nostalgia buffs (check out the Blue Hawaii, *Hawaii 5-0,* or Asian-inspired Mount Fuji theme suites). Owner Pat Winston provides everything from exercise equipment to rice cookers to tips on the best places to dine on the island. There's no maid service, but basic cleaning supplies are provided. Parking (fee) is available at the condo next door on Ala Wai Boulevard. ⊠ *417 Nohonani St., Waikīkī 96815* ☎ *808/922–3894 or 800/545–1948* 🖷 *808/924–3332* ⊕ *www. winstonswaikikicondos.com* 🛏 *24 units* ☉ *A/C, in-room data ports, fans, kitchens, pool, exercise equipment, laundry facilities, parking (fee).* ▭ *AE, DC, MC, V. 1-bedroom $125–$145, 2-bedroom $145–$165.*

B&Bs & Vacation Rentals

$ ⚏ **Diamond Head Bed and Breakfast.** Many a traveler and resident would love to own a home like this art-filled B&B at the base of Waikīkī's famous Diamond Head crater, one of the city's most exclusive neighborhoods. Each of the three guest rooms feature koa-wood furnishings and private bath, and they open to a lanai and a big backyard filled with the sounds of birds and rustling trees. For a bit more privacy, book the ground-floor suite, which offers a separate living room and a bedroom with a queen bed. If you want to experience a bit of Hawaiian history, request the room that includes the extra-large hand-carved koa bed that once belonged to a Hawaiian princess. The closest beach is the intimate Sans Souci near the Natatorium; it's hard to imagine that busy Waikīkī is a short stroll from the house. Reservations should be made three to four months in advance. ⊠ *3240 Noela Dr., Waikīkī 96815* ① *Reservations: Hawai'i's Best Bed and Breakfasts, Box 485, Laupahoehoe, 96767* ☎ *808/962–0100, 800/262–9912 reservations* 🖷 *808/962–6360* ⊕ *www.bestbnb.com* ⤢ *2 rooms, 1 suite* ⚭ *No A/C, no room phones, no smoking* ⊟ *No credit cards.* $130, 2-night minimum.

> ### CHOOSING A VACATION RENTAL
>
> **Hawai'i's Best Bed and Breakfasts** (☎ 808/962–0100 or 800/262–9912 ⊕ www.bestbnb.com) inspects and selects the top B&B's island-wide for its booking service; they also have vacation rentals and condos on all of the other major islands.
>
> **Pat's Kailua Beach Properties** (☎ 808/261–1653 or 808/262–4128 🖷 808/261–0893 ⊕ www.patskailua.com) books beachfront accommodations in the windward community of Kailua.
>
> **Team Real Estate** (☎ 808/637–3507 or 800/982–8602 🖷 808/637–8881 ⊕ www.teamrealestate.com) manages cottages, oceanfront homes, and condos on the North Shore.

HONOLULU BEYOND WAIKĪKĪ

$$$$ ⚏ **The Kāhala.** Hidden away in the wealthy residential neighborhood of Kāhala (on the other side of Diamond Head from Waikīkī), this elegant oceanfront hotel has played host to both presidents and princesses as one of Hawai'i's very first luxury resorts. The Kāhala is flanked by the exclusive Waialae Golf Links and the Pacific Ocean—surrounding it in a natural tranquillity. Pathways meander out along a walkway with benches tucked into oceanfront nooks for lazy viewing. The reef not far from shore makes the waters here calm enough for young swimmers to try their water wings. You can also sign up for dolphin interactions in the 26,000-square-foot-lagoon. Rooms combine touches of Asia and old Hawai'i, with mahogany furniture, teak parquet floors, hand-loomed area rugs, local art, and grass-cloth wall coverings. Culinary buffs should inquire if the Kahala Culinary Academy is in session. Here you can learn everything from cooking basics to party planning in classes taught by master chefs. If you plan to visit the second week of January and love golf, ask for a view of the course so you can have a bird's eye view of the PGA Sony Open from

9

your lanai. ✉ *5000 Kāhala Ave., Kāhala 96816* ☎ *808/739–8888 or 800/367–25285* 🖨 *808/739–8000* ⊕ *www.mandarinoriental.com/ kahala* ⇨ *331 rooms, 33 suites* ♿ *5 restaurants, room service, A/C, in-room broadband, in-room data ports, in-room safes, minibars, cable TV with movies, pool, gym, hair salon, spa, beach, bike rentals, 2 bars, shops, babysitting, children's program (ages 5–12) business services, parking (fee), no-smoking rooms* ▭ *AE, D, DC, MC, V. $345–$735.*

$–$$$$ 🏨 **Ala Moana Hotel.** Shoppers might wear out their Manolos here; the hotel is connected to O'ahu's biggest mall, the Ala Moana Shopping Center, by a pedestrian ramp, and it's a four-block stroll away from the Victoria Ward Centers. Business travelers are walking one block in the opposite direction to the Hawai'i Convention Center. Swimmers, surfers, and beachgoers make the two-minute walk to Ala Moana Beach Park across the street. Studio accommodations have cherrywood furnishings, kitchenettes, flat-screen wall-mounted TVs, and lanai with glass railings and outdoor seating. One- and two-bedroom suites are also available. Most units in this 36-story high-rise have a view of Ala Moana Beach, the ocean, or the mountains. ✉ *410 Atkinson Dr., Ala Moana 96814* ☎ *808/955–4811 or 888/367–4811* 🖨 *808/944–6839* ⊕ *www.alamoanahotel.com* ⇨ *1,150 studios, 67 suites* ♿ *4 restaurants, A/C, room service, in-room safes, minibars, cable TV, pool, gym, bar, 2 bars, dance club, nightclub, parking (fee), no-smoking rooms* ▭ *AE, DC, MC, V. $175–$570.*

$$–$$$ 🏨 **ResortQuest at the Executive Centre Hotel.** Downtown Honolulu's only hotel is an 89-unit, all-suite high-rise in the center of the business district, within walking distance of the historic Capitol District, Honolulu's Chinatown, and a 10-minute drive from Honolulu International Airport. Embarking on an inter-island cruise? This hotel is three blocks from Aloha Tower Marketplace and the cruise ship terminal at Pier 10. Accommodations occupying the top 10 floors of a 40-story glass tower afford magnificent views of downtown Honolulu and Honolulu Harbor. Many hotels offer their guests free Continental breakfast each morning, but here it's served in the top-floor Executive Club with views so mesmerizing, you might linger over your morning coffee past sunset. Each spacious suite has a separate living area, three phones, deep whirlpool tubs, and kitchenette stocked with cold beverages. Some units have washer-dryers. The major disadvantage is that, after work hours, there are few nearby dining options, so if you like to dine out, you might want to consider renting a car. ✉ *1088 Bishop St., Downtown Honolulu 96813* ☎ *808/539–3000 or 866/774–2924* 🖨 *808/523–1088*

KID STUFF

Children's curiosity never takes a vacation, so while in Hawai'i let 'em have at it with such activities as dolphin encounters, "sea-faris," horseback riding, lei making, and cultural activities created with young tastes in mind. Most major hotel chains on O'ahu have children's activity centers and sessions that range from a few hours to a full day—they're typically geared toward kids ages 5-12.]. W. Marriott 'Ihilani Resort has a teen program that focuses on fitness and fun, and teens 16 and older can enroll in The Kāhala Culinary Academy.

⊕ *www.rqexecutivecentre.com* ⇗ *116 suites* ⚉ *Restaurant, A/C, in-room safes, kitchenettes, cable TV, in-room broadband, in-room data ports, pool, gym, laundry facilities, business services, parking (fee), no-smoking rooms* ▤ *AE, DC, MC, V. $200–$275.*

WINDWARD O'AHU

$ 🏨 **Ingrid's.** This B&B in the windward bedroom community of Kailua features a one-bedroom upstairs studio with decor that mimics those found in traditional Japanese inns, with *shoji* screen doors and black-tile counters. Ingrid is one of the island's most popular hosts, and she has created a little Zen of tranquillity in this unit that also features a kitchenette, deep soaking tub, and has its own private entrance. Guests have access to the pool, and Kailua Beach is less than 1 mi away. Three- to four-month advance reservations are advised. ⊠ *Pauku St., Kailua 96734* ☎ *Reservations: Hawai'i's Best Bed and Breakfasts, Box 485, Laupahoehoe, 96767* ☎ *808/962–0100, 800/262–9912 reservations* 🖷 *808/962–6360* ⊕ *www.bestbnb.com* ⇗ *2 rooms* ⚉ *A/C, TV, kitchenettes; no room phones* ▤ *No credit cards. $150, 4-night minimum.*

¢–$ 🏨 **Schrader's Windward Country Inn.** If you're looking for an alternative to staying in Waikīkī and you aren't fussy about amenities, consider Schrader's, which is in Kāne'ohe, 30 minutes from both Waikīkī and the North Shore. Though billed as "cottages by the sea," the setting is actually more roadside motel than resort. However, Schrader's provides a moderately priced lodging option with amenities you won't find in Waikīkī, including complimentary biweekly ocean-reef tours that include snorkeling and kayaking the scenic windward coastline. One- to four-bedroom accommodations are available. Units feature microwaves and refrigerators, and some have full kitchens. Complimentary breakfast on the main building's veranda is included. Ask for the units that open onto Kāne'ohe Bay if you relish the possibility of fishing right off your lanai. ⊠ *47-039 Lihikai Dr., Kāne'ohe 96744* ☎ *808/239–5711 or 800/735–5711* 🖷 *808/239–6658* ⊕ *www.hawaiiscene.com/schrader* ⇗ *57 units* ⚉ *BBQs, kitchenettes, pool, outdoor hot tub; no a/c in some rooms* ▤ *AE, D, DC, MC, V. 1-bedroom $72–$144, 2-bedroom $127–$215.*

NORTH SHORE

$$$$ 🏨 **Turtle Bay Resort.** Some 880 acres of raw natural Hawai'i landscape is
Fodor'sChoice your playground at this resort on O'ahu's North Shore. Set out on the
★ edge of Kuilima Point, Turtle Bay has spacious guest rooms averaging nearly 500 square feet, with lanai that showcase stunning peninsula views. In winter, when the big waves roll ashore, you get a front-row seat for watching the powerful surf. The sumptuous oceanfront beach cottages come complete with Brazilian walnut floors and teak rockers on the lanai. If you prefer a vacation home, Turtle Bay's gated community, the Ocean Villas, offers three- and four-bedroom units with plenty of cushy accoutrements and a host of amenities, from private butlers to chefs to in-home spa treatments. Turtle Bay has a Hans Heidemann Surf School, horse stables, a spa, and the only 36-hole golf facility on O'ahu to keep you busy.

9

There are two swimming pools, one with an 80-foot water slide. While out exploring Turtle Bay's 12 mi of nature trails, don't be surprised if you suddenly find yourself "Lost." The hit television series has been known to frequent the resort's beaches, coves, and natural forests for location filming. ✉ *57-091 Kamehameha Hwy., Box 187, Kahuku 96731* ☎ *808/293-8811 or 800/203-3650* 🖷 *808/293-9147* ⊕ *www.turtlebayresort.com* ☞ *373 rooms, 40 suites, 42 beach cottages, 56 ocean villas* ♨ *4 restaurants, room service, A/C, refrigerators, cable TV, 2 18-hole golf courses, 10 tennis courts, 2 pools, gym, spa, beach, horseback riding, 2 bars, shops, children's programs (ages 5–12), no-smoking rooms* ☰ *AE, D, DC, MC, V. $350–$780.*

HOPELESSLY ROMANTIC

It might seem odd that the eight islands that comprise some of the world's most famous honeymooning turf have a native language lacking a word that means "romance." Could it be that Hawaiians don't need one? Everywhere you turn, the essence of the word brushes your shoulder like a caressing tradewind. Whether you are celebrating a honeymoon or a lifetime of romance, Hawaiian hospitality welcomes with a loving embrace. When booking, inquire about honeymoon and romance room packages. Many include extras ranging from champagne upon arrival to spa treatments and vow renewal ceremonies.

$–$$ ▦ **Ke Iki Beach Bungalows.** Ke Iki Road runs parallel to Kamehameha Highway and is the site of this 1½-acre sloped beachfront lot with six duplex beach bungalows operated by Greg Gerstenberger and his wife Annie. You can choose from studios to one- or two-bedroom units outfitted with breezy beach-house furnishings, individual grills and picnic tables, and access to a 200-foot strand of creamy white-sand beach running between the North Shore's famous Waimea Bay and Banzai Pipeline. Swimming is best here in summer as the rest of the year the North Shore is slammed with monster waves best tackled by only professional surfers. There are outdoor showers, an outdoor meditation area, and beachfront seating for nightly stargazing. Ke Iki is popular with families for reunions and weddings. There's a bikepath fronting the property that meanders along the ocean into Hale'iwa Town. If you want more surf than street sounds, reserve one of the beachside bungalows. ✉ *59-579 Ke Iki Rd., Hale'iwa 96712* ☎ *808/638-8829* 🖷 *808/637-6100* ⊕ *www.keikibeach.com* ☞ *11 units* ♨ *BBQs, Kitchens, cable TV, beach, laundry facilities, parking; no a/c* ☰ *AE, MC, V. Studio $135, 1-bedroom $150–$210, 2-bedroom $170–$230.*

¢–$$ ▦ **Backpackers Vacation Inn and Plantation Village.** Here's laid-back Hale'iwa surfer chic at its best. Spartan in furnishings, rustic in amenities, and definitely very casual in spirit, Backpackers is at Pūpūkea Beach Marine Sanctuary, otherwise known as Three Tables Beach. It's a short stroll to Waimea Bay. Accommodations include hostel-type dorm rooms, double rooms (some with a double bed, others with two single beds), studios, and cabins. Some have kitchenettes; it's a three-minute walk to the supermarket. ✉ *59-788 Kamehameha Hwy., Hale'iwa 96712* ☎ *808/638-7838* ⊕ *www.backpackers-hawaii.com* 🖷 *808/638-7515* ☞ *25 rooms* ♨ *BBQs, some kitchenettes, laundry facilities;*

no A/C, no phones in some rooms, no TV in some rooms ⊟ *MC, V.*
$22–$250.

WEST O'AHU

$$$$ ▦ **J. W. Marriott 'Ihilani Resort & Spa.** Forty-five minutes and a world
away from the bustle of Waikīkī, this sleek, 17-story resort anchors the
still-developing Ko'Olina Resort and Marina on O'ahu's leeward coastline. Honeymooners, NFL Pro Bowlers, and even local residents looking for a "neighbor island" experience without the hassle of catching a
flight come to 'Ihilani for first-class R&R. The resort sits on one of Ko
Olina's seven lagoons and features a lū'au cove, tennis garden, wedding
chapel, yacht marina, and a Ted Robinson–designed 18-hole championship golf facility. Rooms here are spacious with 650 square feet; marble bathrooms with deep soaking tubs; spacious private lanai with teak
furnishings, in-room CD players; and high-tech control systems (lights,
temperature controls). Most have ocean views. A rental car is pretty much
a necessity here. ⊠ *92-1001 'Ōlani St., Kapolei 96707* ☎ *808/679–0079*
or 800/626–4446 ⊟ *808/679–0080* ⊕ *www.ihilani.com* ⤴ *387 rooms,*
36 suites ♨ *4 restaurants, room service, A/C, minibars, cable TV, 18-*
hole golf course, 6 tennis courts, 2 pools, health club, spa, beach, shops,
babysitting, children's programs (ages 5–12), business services, no-
smoking rooms ⊟ *AE, DC, MC, V.*

$$$–$$$$ ▦ **Marriott Ko Olina Beach Vacation Club.** If you have your heart set on
getting away to O'ahu's western shores, check out the Marriott, which
is primarily a vacation-ownership property. This property does offer
nightly rental rates for its rooms, which range from hotel-style standard
guest rooms to expansive and elegantly appointed one- or two-bedroom
guest villa apartments. The larger villas (1,240 square feet) have three
TVs, full kitchens, and separate living and dining areas. Situated on 30
acres of Ko Olina, fronting a lagoon, this resort has two pools (one with
sandy-beach bottom), a fitness center, four outdoor hot tubs (including
one overlooking the ocean that's ideal for sunset soaks). Breakfast is of-
fered at Kolohe's poolside bar and grill where, after sundown, there's
live music nightly under the stars. Tuesday evenings, check out the
oceanfront Fia Fia–An Evening in Samoa Lū'au, whose featured performer
is one of the island's champion fire-knife dancers. ⊠ *92-161 Waipahe*
Pl., Kapolei 96707 ☎ *808/679–4900 or 877/229–4484* ⊟ *808/679–4910*
⊕ *www.marriottvacationclub.com* ⤴ *200 units* ♨ *2 restaurants, A/C,*
Wi-Fi, in-room safes, kitchens, cable TV, in room DVD players, 18-hole
golf course, 6 tennis courts, 2 pools, outdoor hot tubs, gym, beach, ma-
rina, bar, shops, children's programs (ages 5–12), parking (fee) ⊟ *AE,*
DC, MC, V. $319–$609.

9

UNDERSTANDING O'AHU

HAWAI'I AT A GLANCE

**HAWAIIAN
VOCABULARY**

HAWAI'I AT A GLANCE

Fast Facts

Nickname: Aloha State
Capital: Honolulu
State song: "Hawai'i Pono'i"
State bird: The nēnē, an endangered land bird and variety of goose
State flower: Yellow Hibiscus Brackenridgii
State tree: Kukui (or candlenut), a Polynesian-introduced tree
Administrative divisions: There are four counties with mayors and councils: City and County of Honolulu (island of O'ahu), Hawai'i County (Hawai'i Island), Maui County (islands of Maui, Moloka'i, Lāna'i, and Kahoolawe), and Kaua'i County (islands of Kaua'i and Ni'ihau)
Entered the Union: August 21, 1959, as the 50th state
Population: 1,334,023
Life expectancy: Female 82, male 76
Literacy: 81%

Ethnic groups: Hawaiian/part Hawaiian 22.1%; Caucasian 20.5%; Japanese 18.3%; Filipino 12.3%; Chinese 4.1%
Religion: Roman Catholic 22%; Buddhist, Shinto, and other East Asian religions 15%; Mormon 10%; Church of Christ 8%; Assembly of God and Baptist 6% each; Episcopal, Jehovah's Witness, and Methodist 5% each
Language: English is the first language of the majority of residents; Hawaiian is the native language of the indigenous Hawaiian people and an official language of the state; other languages spoken include Samoan, Chinese, Japanese, Korean, Spanish, Portuguese, Filipino, and Vietnamese

The loveliest fleet of islands that lies anchored in any ocean.

Mark Twain

Geography & Environment

Land area: An archipelago of 137 islands encompassing a land area of 6,422.6 square mi in the north-central Pacific Ocean (about 2,400 mi from the west coast of the continental U.S.)
Coastline: 750 mi
Terrain: Volcanic mountains, tropical rain forests, verdant valleys, sea cliffs, canyons, deserts, coral reefs, sand dunes, sandy beaches
Natural resources: Dimension limestone, crushed stone, sand and gravel, gemstones
Natural hazards: Hurricanes, earthquakes, tsunamis
Flora: More than 2,500 species of native and introduced plants throughout the islands
Fauna: Native mammals include the hoary bat, Hawaiian monk seal, and Polynesian rat. The humpback whale migrates to Hawaiian waters every winter to mate and calve. More than 650 fish and 40 different species of shark live in Hawaiian waters. Freshwater streams are home to hundreds of native and alien species. The humuhumunukunukuāpua'a (Hawaiian triggerfish) is the unofficial state fish.
Environmental issues: Plant and animal species threatened and endangered due to hunting, overfishing, overgrazing by wild and introduced animals, and invasive alien plants

Hawai'i is not a state of mind, but a state of grace.

Paul Theroux

Economy

Tourism and federal defense spending continue to drive the state's economy. Efforts to diversify in the areas of science and technology, film and television production, sports, ocean research and development, health and education, tourism, agriculture, and floral and specialty food products are ongoing.

GSP: $40.1 billion
Per capita income: $30,000
Inflation: 1%
Unemployment: 4.3%
Work force: 595,450
Debt: $7.3 billion
Major industries: Tourism, Federal government (defense and other agencies)
Agricultural products: Sugar, pineapple, papayas, guavas, flower and nursery products, asparagus, alfalfa hay, macadamia nuts, coffee, milk, cattle, eggs, shellfish, algae
Exports: $616 million
Major export products: Aircraft and parts, naphthas, medical equipment and supplies, fruit, steel scrap, electronic components, unleaded gasoline, artwork, cocoa, coffee, flowers, macadamia nuts
Imports: $2.6 billion
Major import products: Crude oil, electronic and digital equipment, coal, passenger motor vehicles

In what other land save this one is the commonest form of greeting not "Good day," or How d'ye do," but "Love?" That greeting is "Aloha"–love, I love, my love to you . . .It is a positive affirmation of the warmth of one's own heart, giving.

Jack London

Debate has waxed and waned for more than a century over how and when to return to native Hawaiians more than 1 million acres of land and other assets seized when American business interests overthrew the island monarchy in 1893. Certain native factions still advocate a return to independent nationhood. Sovereignty gained new momentum in the 1990s with the passage of a federal law formally apologizing for the overthrow and urging reconciliation. Momentum has since fizzled. Hawai'i's current governor has renewed efforts to have Congress recognize Hawaiians as an indigenous people, much like Native Americans and Alaskans. The governor also has pledged to support continued funding of health care, language, and other cultural programs, and to achieve state and federal obligations to distribute homestead lands to qualified Hawaiians.

Did You Know?

- Hawai'i is home to the world's most active volcano: Kīlauea, on the Big Island.

- 'Iolani Palace had electricity and telephones installed several years before the White House, and is the only palace on U.S. soil.

- Hawai'i has about 12% of all endangered plants and animals in the U.S.;

75% of the country's extinct plants and birds were Hawaiian.

- The Royal Hawaiian Band is the only intact organization from the time of Hawaiian monarchy that is fully functional and still preserves Hawai'i's musical history.

HAWAIIAN VOCABULARY

Although an understanding of Hawaiian is by no means required on a trip to the Aloha State, a *malihini*, or newcomer, will find plenty of opportunities to pick up a few of the local words and phrases. Traditional names and expressions are widely used in the Islands, thanks in part to legislation enacted in the early '90s to encourage the use of the Hawaiian language. You're likely to read or hear at least a few words each day of your stay.

With a basic understanding and some uninhibited practice, anyone can have enough command of the local tongue to ask for directions and to order from a restaurant menu. One visitor announced she would not leave until she could pronounce the name of the state fish, the *humuhumunukunukuāpua'a*. Luckily, she had scheduled a nine-day stay.

Simplifying the learning process is the fact that the Hawaiian language contains only eight consonants—H, K, L, M, N, P, W, and the silent *'okina*, or glottal stop, written '—plus one or more of the five vowels. All syllables, and therefore all words, end in a vowel. Each vowel, with the exception of a few diphthongized double vowels such as *au* (pronounced "ow") or *ai* (pronounced "eye"), is pronounced separately. Thus *'Iolani* is four syllables (ee-oh-la-nee), not three (yo-la-nee). Although some Hawaiian words have only vowels, most also contain some consonants, but consonants are never doubled.

Pronunciation is simple. Pronounce *A* "ah" as father; *E* "ay" as in weigh; *I* "ee" as in marine; *O* "oh" as in no; *U* "oo" as in true.

Consonants mirror their English equivalents, with the exception of W. When the letter begins any syllable other than the first one in a word, it is usually pronounced as a V. *'Awa*, the Polynesian drink, is pronounced "ava," *'ewa* is pronounced "eva."

Nearly all long Hawaiian words are combinations of shorter words; they are not difficult to pronounce if you segment them into shorter words. *Kalaniana'ole*, the highway running east from Honolulu, is easily understood as *Kalani ana 'ole*. Apply the standard pronunciation rules—the stress falls on the next-to-last syllable of most two- or three-syllable Hawaiian words—and Kalaniana'ole Highway is as easy to say as Main Street.

Now about that fish. Try *humu-humu nuku-nuku āpu a'a*.

The other unusual element in Hawaiian language is the *kahakō*, or macron, written as a short line (ˉ) placed over a vowel. Like the accent (´) in Spanish, the kahakō puts emphasis on a syllable that would normally not be stressed. The most familiar example is probably *Waikīkī*. With no macrons, the stress would fall on the middle syllable; with only one macron, on the last syllable, the stress would fall on the first and last syllables. Some words become plural with the addition of a macron, often on a syllable that would have been stressed anyway. No Hawaiian word becomes plural with the addition of an S, since that letter does not exist in the *'ōlelo Hawai'i* (which is Hawaiian for "Hawaiian language").

What follows is a glossary of some of the most commonly used Hawaiian words.

'a'ā: rough, crumbling lava, contrasting with *pāhoehoe*, which is smooth.
'ae: yes.
aikane: friend.
āina: land.
akamai: smart, clever, possessing savoir faire.
akua: god.
ala: a road, path, or trail.
ali'i: a Hawaiian chief, a member of the chiefly class.
aloha: love, affection, kindness; also a salutation meaning both greetings and farewell.
'ānuenue: rainbow.

ʻaʻole: no.

ʻapōpō: tomorrow.

ʻauwai: a ditch.

auwē: alas, woe is me!

ʻehu: a red-haired Hawaiian.

ʻewa: in the direction of ʻEwa plantation, west of Honolulu.

hala: the pandanus tree, whose leaves (*lau hala*) are used to make baskets and plaited mats.

hālau: school.

hale: a house.

hale pule: church, house of worship.

ha mea iki or ha mea ʻole: you're welcome.

hana: to work.

haole: ghost. Since the first foreigners were Caucasian, *haole* now means a Caucasian person.

hapa: a part, sometimes a half; often used as a short form of *hapa haole,* to mean a person who is part-Caucasian; thus, the name of a popular local band, whose members represent a variety of ethnicities.

hauʻoli: to rejoice. *Hauʻoli Makahiki Hou* means Happy New Year. *Hauʻoli lā hānau* means Happy Birthday.

heiau: an outdoor stone platform; an ancient Hawaiian place of worship.

holo: to run.

holoholo: to go for a walk, ride, or sail.

holokū: a long Hawaiian dress, somewhat fitted, with a yoke and a train. Influenced by European fashion, it was worn at court, and at least one local translates the word as "expensive muʻumuʻu."

holomū: a post–World War II cross between a *holokū* and a muʻumuʻu, less fitted than the former but less voluminous than the latter, and having no train.

honi: to kiss; a kiss. A phrase that some tourists may find useful, quoted from a popular hula, is *Honi Kaʻua Wikiwiki:* Kiss me quick!

honu: turtle.

hoʻomalimali: flattery, a deceptive "line," bunk, baloney, hooey.

huhū: angry.

hui: a group, club, or assembly. A church may refer to its congregation as a *hui* and a social club may be called a *hui.*

hukilau: a seine; a communal fishing party in which everyone helps to drive the fish into a huge net, pull it in, and divide the catch.

hula: the dance of Hawaiʻi.

iki: little.

ipo: sweetheart.

ka: the. This is the definite article for most singular words; for plural nouns, the definite article is usually *nā.* Since there is no *S* in Hawaiian, the article may be your only clue that a noun is plural.

kahuna: a priest, doctor, or other trained person of old Hawaiʻi, endowed with special professional skills that often included the gift of prophecy or other supernatural powers; the plural form is kāhuna.

kai: the sea, saltwater.

kalo: the taro plant from whose root poi is made.

kamaʻāina: literally, a child of the soil; it refers to people who were born in the Islands or have lived there for a long time.

kanaka: originally a man or humanity in general, it is now used to denote a male Hawaiian or part-Hawaiian, but is occasionally taken as a slur when used by non-Hawaiians. *Kanaka maoli,* originally a full-blooded Hawaiian person, is used by some native Hawaiian rights activists to embrace part-Hawaiians as well.

kāne: a man, a husband. If you see this word on a door, it's the men's room. If you see *kane* on a door, it's probably a misspelling; that is the Hawaiian name for the skin fungus tinea.

kapa: also called by its Tahitian name, *tapa,* a cloth made of beaten bark and usually dyed and stamped with a repeat design.

kapakahi: crooked, cockeyed, uneven. You've got your hat on *kapakahi.*

kapu: keep out, prohibited. This is the Hawaiian version of the more widely known Tongan word *tabu* (taboo).

kapuna: grandparent; elder.

kēia lā: today.

keiki: a child; *keikikāne* is a boy, *keikiwahine* a girl.

kona: the leeward side of the Islands, the direction (south) from which the *kona* wind and *kona* rain come.

kula: upland.

kuleana: a homestead or small plot of ground on which a family has been installed for some generations without necessarily owning it. By extension, *kuleana* is used to denote any area or department in which one has a special interest or prerogative. You'll hear it used this way: If you want to hire a surfboard, see Moki; that's his *kuleana*. And conversely: I can't help you with that; that's not my *kuleana*.

lā: sun.

lamalama: to fish with a torch.

lānai: a porch, a balcony, an outdoor living room. Almost every house in Hawai'i has one. Don't confuse this two-syllable word with the three-syllable name of the island, Lāna'i.

lani: heaven, the sky.

lau hala: the leaf of the *hala*, or pandanus tree, widely used in Hawaiian handicrafts.

lei: a garland of flowers.

limu: sun.

lolo: stupid.

luna: a plantation overseer or foreman.

mahalo: thank you.

makai: toward the ocean.

malihini: a newcomer to the Islands.

mana: the spiritual power that the Hawaiian believed inhabited all things and creatures.

manō: shark.

manuwahi: free, gratis.

mauka: toward the mountains.

mauna: mountain.

mele: a Hawaiian song or chant, often of epic proportions.

Mele Kalikimaka: Merry Christmas (a transliteration from the English phrase).

Menehune: a Hawaiian pixie. The *Menehune* were a legendary race of little people who accomplished prodigious work, such as building fishponds and temples in the course of a single night.

moana: the ocean.

mu'umu'u: the voluminous dress in which the missionaries enveloped Hawaiian women. Now made in bright printed cottons and silks, it is an indispensable garment in a Hawaiian woman's wardrobe.

Culturally sensitive locals have embraced the Hawaiian spelling but often shorten the spoken word to "mu'u." Most English dictionaries include the spelling "muumuu," and that version is a part of many apparel companies' names.

nani: beautiful.

nui: big.

ohana: family.

'ono: delicious.

pāhoehoe: smooth, unbroken, satiny lava.

Pākē: Chinese. This *Pākē* carver makes beautiful things.

palapala: document, printed matter.

pali: a cliff, precipice.

pānini: prickly pear cactus.

paniolo: a Hawaiian cowboy, a rough transliteration of *español,* the language of the Islands' earliest cowboys.

pau: finished, done.

pilikia: trouble. The Hawaiian word is much more widely used here than its English equivalent.

puka: a hole.

pupule: crazy, like the celebrated Princess Pupule. This word has replaced its English equivalent in local usage.

pu'u: volcanic cinder cone.

waha: mouth.

wahine: a female, a woman, a wife, and a sign on the ladies' room door; the plural form is *wāhine.*

wai: freshwater, as opposed to saltwater, which is *kai.*

wailele: waterfall.

wikiwiki: to hurry, hurry up (since this is a reduplication of *wiki,* quick, neither *W* is pronounced as a *V*).

Note: Pidgin is the unofficial language of Hawai'i. It is a Creole language, with its own grammar, evolved from the mixture of English, Hawaiian, Japanese, Portuguese, and other languages spoken in 19th-century Hawai'i, and it is heard everywhere: on ranches, in warehouses, on beaches, and in the hallowed halls (and occasionally in the classrooms) of the University of Hawai'i.

SMART TRAVEL TIPS

Finding out about your destination before you leave home means you won't spend time organizing everyday minutiae once you've arrived. You'll be more streetwise when you hit the ground as well, better prepared to explore the aspects of Oʻahu that drew you here in the first place. The organizations in this section can provide information to supplement this guide; contact them for up-to-the-minute details. Happy landings!

AIR TRAVEL

Hawaiʻi is a major destination link for flights traveling to and from the U.S. mainland, Asia, Australia, New Zealand, and the South Pacific. All of the major airline carriers fly directly into Honolulu. For international travelers, Oʻahu is a gateway to the United States.

BOOKING

When you book, look for nonstop flights and remember that "direct" flights stop at least once. Try to avoid connecting flights, which require a change of plane. Two airlines may operate a connecting flight jointly, so ask whether your airline operates every segment of the trip; you may find that the carrier you prefer flies you only part of the way. To find more booking tips and to check prices and make online flight reservations, log on to www.fodors.com.

CARRIERS

From the U.S. mainland, ATA, America West, American, Continental, Delta, Northwest, and United serve Honolulu.

Aloha Airlines flies from California (Oakland, Orange County, Sacramento, and San Diego) and Nevada (Las Vegas and Reno). Hawaiian Airlines serves Honolulu from California (Los Angeles, Sacramento, San Diego, San Francisco, and San Jose), Las Vegas, Phoenix, Portland, and Seattle.

🔢 **Major Airlines Aloha Airlines** ☎ 800/367–5250 ⊕ www.alohaairlines.com. **American** ☎ 800/433–7300 ⊕ www.aa.com. **America West** ☎ 800/327–7810 ⊕ www.americawest.com. **ATA** ☎ 800/435–9282 ⊕ www.ata.com. **Continental** ☎ 800/523–3273 ⊕ www.continental.com. **Delta** ☎ 800/221–1212 ⊕ www.delta.com. **Hawaiian Airlines** ☎ 800/

367–5320 ⊕ www.hawaiianair.com. **Northwest**
☎ 800/225–2525 ⊕ www.nwa.com. **United**
☎ 800/241–6522 ⊕ www.united.com.
🔗 **Direct Flights from the U.K. to Honolulu American** ☎ 0208/572–5555 ⊕ www.aa.com. **Continental** ☎ 0800/776–464 ⊕ www.continental.com.
Delta ☎ 0800/414–767 ⊕ www.delta.com. **United**
☎ 0845/844–4777 ⊕ www.united.com.

CHECK-IN & BOARDING

Like most city airports, Honolulu International can be quite busy during peak times.
Allot extra travel time to all airports during morning and afternoon rush-hour traffic periods.

Always **find out your carrier's check-in
policy.** Plan to arrive at the airport about
two hours before your scheduled departure time for domestic flights and 2½ to 3
hours before international flights. You
may need to arrive earlier if you're flying
from one of the busier airports or during
peak air-traffic times.

To avoid delays at airport-security check-
points, try not to wear any metal. Jewelry,
belt and other buckles, steel-toe shoes,
barrettes, and underwire bras are among
the items that can set off detectors.

Assuming that not everyone with a ticket
will show up, airlines routinely overbook
planes. When everyone does, airlines ask
for volunteers to give up their seats. In return, these volunteers usually get a several-
hundred-dollar flight voucher, which can
be used toward the purchase of another
ticket, and are rebooked on the next available flight out. If there are not enough volunteers, the airline must choose who will
be denied boarding. The first to get
bumped are passengers who checked in
late and those flying on discounted tickets,
so get to the gate and check in as early as
possible, especially during peak periods.

Always **bring a government-issued photo
I.D.** to the airport; even when it's not required, a passport is best.

AGRICULTURAL INSPECTION

Plants and plant products are subject to
regulation by the Department of Agriculture, both on entering and leaving O'ahu.
Upon leaving, you'll have to have your

bags X-rayed and tagged at the airport's
agricultural inspection station before you
proceed to check-in. Pineapples and coconuts with the packer's agricultural inspection stamp pass freely; papayas must
be treated, inspected, and stamped. All
other fruits are banned for export to the
U.S. mainland. Flowers pass except for
gardenia, rose leaves, jade vine, and
mauna loa. Also banned are insects,
snails, soil, cotton, cacti, sugarcane, and
all berry plants.

You'll have to **leave dogs and other pets
at home.** A 120-day quarantine is imposed
to keep out rabies, which is nonexistent in
Hawai'i. If specific pre- and post-arrival
requirements are met, animals may qualify
for a 30-day or 5-day-or-less quarantine.
🔗 **U.S. Customs and Border Protection** ✉ for inquiries and equipment registration, 1300 Pennsylvania Ave. NW, Washington, DC 20229 ⊕ www.cbp.
gov ☎ 877/287–8667, 202/354–1000 ✉ for complaints, Customer Satisfaction Unit, 1300 Pennsylvania Ave. NW, Room 5.2C, Washington, DC 20229.

CUTTING COSTS

The least expensive airfares to Honolulu
are often priced for round-trip travel and
must usually be purchased in advance.
Airlines generally allow you to change
your return date for a fee; most low-fare
tickets, however, are nonrefundable. It's
smart to call a number of airlines and
check the Internet; when you are quoted a
good price, book it on the spot—the same
fare may not be available the next day, or
even the next hour. Always check different
routings and look into using alternate airports. Also, price off-peak flights and red-
eye, which may be significantly less
expensive than others. Travel agents, especially low-fare specialists (⇨ Discounts &
Deals), are helpful. Trailfinders can arrange bargain flights from the U.K.

Consolidators are another good source.
They buy tickets for scheduled flights at reduced rates from the airlines, then sell
them at prices that beat the best fare available directly from the airlines. (Many also
offer reduced car-rental and hotel rates.)
Sometimes you can even get your money
back if you need to return the ticket. Care-

fully read the fine print detailing penalties for changes and cancellations, purchase the ticket with a credit card, and confirm your consolidator reservation with the airline.

When you fly as a courier, you trade your checked-luggage space for a ticket deeply subsidized by a courier service. There are restrictions on when you can book and how long you can stay. Some courier companies list with membership organizations, such as the Air Courier Association and the International Association of Air Travel Couriers; these require you to become a member before you can book a flight.

◪ **Consolidators** AirlineConsolidator.com ⊕ www.airlineconsolidator.com, for international tickets. **Best Fares** ⊕ www.bestfares.com; $59.90 annual membership. **Cheap Tickets** ⊕ www. cheaptickets.com. **Expedia** ⊕ www.expedia.com. **Hotwire** ⊕ www.hotwire.com. **LuxuryLink** ⊕ www. luxurylink.com. has auctions (surprisingly good deals) as well as offers for high-end travel. **Onetravel.com** ⊕ www.onetravel.com. **Orbitz** ⊕ www.orbitz.com. **Priceline.com** ⊕ www. priceline.com. **Travelocity** ⊕ www.travelocity.com.

◪ **Courier Resources** Air Courier Association/ **Cheaptrips.com** ☎ 800/461-8856 ⊕ www. aircourier.org or www.cheaptrips.com; $39 annual membership. **Courier Travel** ☎ 303/570-7586 ⊕ www.couriertravel.org; $40 one-time membership fee. **International Association of Air Travel Couriers** ☎ 308/632-3273 ⊕ www.courier.org; $45 annual membership.

◪ **Direct Flights from the U.K.** Trailfinders ✉ 194 Kensington High St., London W8 7RG ☎ 0845/058-5858 ⊕ www.trailfinders.com.

ENJOYING THE FLIGHT

State your seat preference when purchasing your ticket, and then repeat it when you confirm and when you check in. For more legroom, you can request one of the few emergency-aisle seats at check-in, if you're capable of moving obstacles comparable in weight to an airplane exit door (usually between 35 pounds and 60 pounds)—a Federal Aviation Administration requirement of passengers in these seats. Seats behind a bulkhead also offer more legroom, but they don't have underseat storage. Don't sit in the row in front of the emergency aisle or in front of a

bulkhead, where seats may not recline. SeatGuru.com has more information about specific seat configurations, which vary by aircraft.

Ask the airline whether a snack or meal is served on the flight. If you have dietary concerns, request special meals when booking. These can be vegetarian, low-cholesterol, or kosher, for example. It's a good idea to pack some healthful snacks and a small (plastic) bottle of water in your carry-on bag. On long flights, try to maintain a normal routine, to help fight jet lag. At night, get some sleep. By day, eat light meals, drink water (not alcohol), and **move around the cabin** to stretch your legs. For additional jet-lag tips consult *Fodor's FYI: Travel Fit & Healthy* (available at bookstores everywhere).

Smoking policies vary from carrier to carrier. Most airlines prohibit smoking on all of their flights; others allow smoking only on certain routes or certain departures. Ask your carrier about its policy.

FLYING TIMES

Flying time is about 10 hours from New York, 8 hours from Chicago, 5 hours from Los Angeles, and 15 hours from London, not including layovers.

HOW TO COMPLAIN

If your baggage goes astray or your flight goes awry, complain right away. Most carriers require that you **file a claim immediately.** The Aviation Consumer Protection Division of the Department of Transportation publishes *Fly-Rights*, which discusses airlines and consumer issues and is available online. You can also find articles and information on mytravelrights.com, the Web site of the nonprofit Consumer Travel Rights Center.

◪ **Airline Complaints** Aviation Consumer Protection Division ✉ U.S. Department of Transportation, Office of Aviation Enforcement and Proceedings, C-75, Room 4107, 400 7th St. SW, Washington, DC 20590 ☎ 202/366-2220 ⊕ airconsumer.ost.dot.gov. **Federal Aviation Administration Consumer Hotline** ✉ for inquiries: FAA, 800 Independence Ave. SW, Washington, DC 20591 ☎ 800/835-5322 ⊕ www.faa.gov.

RECONFIRMING

Check the status of your flight before you leave for the airport. You can do this on your carrier's Web site, by linking to a flight-status checker (many Web booking services offer these), or by calling your carrier or travel agent.

FLYING TO THE NEIGHBOR ISLANDS

If you've allotted more than a week for your vacation, you may want to consider visiting a neighbor island. From Honolulu, there are departing flights to the Neighbor Islands leaving almost every half-hour from early morning until evening. Since each flight is only 30–60 minutes in length, you can watch the sunrise on Oʻahu and look for the green flash at sunset while on either the Big Island, Kauaʻi, Lānaʻi, Maui, or Molokaʻi. To simplify your vacation, schedule your return flight to Oʻahu so that it coincides with your flight home.

Check local and community newspapers when you're on Oʻahu for package deals and coupons on interisland flights. Both Hawaiian Airlines and Aloha Airlines have stopped offering the once-popular multi-island air passes, but there are other ways to save money on interisland fares. Sign up for either airlines' free frequent-flyer programs, and you'll be eligible for excellent online specials that aren't available by phone or elsewhere. There also are a number of wholesalers that offer neighbor island packages including air, hotel, rental car, and even visitor attractions.

🛪 **Interisland Flights Aloha Airlines** ☎ 800/367-5250 ⊕ www.alohaairlines.com. **Hawaiian Airlines** ☎ 800/367-5320 ⊕ www.hawaiianair.com. **Island Air** ☎ 800/323-3345 ⊕ www.islandair.com. **Pacific Wings** ☎ 888/575-4546 ⊕ www.pacificislandtravel.com. **Paragon Airlines** ☎ 808/244-3356 ⊕ www.paragon-air.com.

🛪 **Wholesalers Pleasant Holidays** ☎ 800/742-9244 ⊕ www.pleasantholidays.com. **Roberts Overnighters** ☎ 800/899-9323 ⊕ www.robertsovernighters.com.

AIRPORTS

Honolulu International Airport (HNL) is 20 minutes (9 mi) west of Waikīkī, and is served by most of the major domestic and international carriers. It is "open-air," meaning you can enjoy those tradewind breezes up until the moment you step on the plane.

If you have time after you've checked in for your flight home, visit the Pacific Aerospace Museum, open daily, in the main terminal. It includes a 1,700-square-foot, three-dimensional, multimedia theater presenting the history of flight in Hawaiʻi, and a full-scale space-shuttle flight deck. Hands-on exhibits include a mission-control computer program tracing flights in the Pacific.

🛪 **Honolulu International Airport (HNL)** ☎ 808/836-6413.

TO & FROM THE AIRPORT

Some hotels have their own pickup service. Check when you book.

A cumbersome and inefficient airport taxi system requires you to line up to a taxi wrangler, who radios for cars. At $2.50 start-up plus $2.30 for each mile, the fare to Waikīkī will run approximately $25–$35, plus tip. If your baggage is oversized, there is an additional charge of $3.50.

Roberts Hawaiʻi runs a 24-hour airport shuttle from the airport to most of the major hotels in Waikīkī. The fare is $8 one-way, $14 round-trip. Look for a representative at the baggage claim. Call for return reservations only. TheBus, the municipal bus, will take you into Waikīkī for only $2, but you are allowed only one bag, which must fit on your lap.

🛪 **Roberts Hawaiʻi** ☎ 808/539-9400. **TheBus** ☎ 808/848-5555 ⊕ www.thebus.org.

BIKE TRAVEL

Oʻahu's natural beauty, breathtaking coastal routes, and year-round fair weather make it attractive to explore by bike. However, on many roads, bicycle lanes are limited or nonexistent, and cyclists must contend with heavy traffic. You can rent bikes for some solo cruising, join local cycling clubs for their weekly rides, or hit the road with outfitters for tours that go beyond the well-traveled paths.

🛪 **Bike Maps Honolulu City and County Bike Coordinator** ☎ 808/527-5044.

◪ Tours & Rentals Banfield's Raging Isle Surf & Cycle ☎ 808/637-7707 on the North Shore. **Bike Hawai'i** ☎ 877/682-7433 ⊕ www.bikehawaii.com. **The Bike Shop** ☎ 808/596-0588 in Honolulu ⊕ www.bikeshophawaii.com. **Blue Sky Rentals** ☎ 808/947-0101 in Waikīkī.

BIKES IN FLIGHT

Most airlines accommodate bikes as luggage, provided they are dismantled and boxed; check with individual airlines about packing requirements. Some airlines sell bike boxes, which are often free at bike shops, for about $20 (bike bags can be considerably more expensive). International travelers often can substitute a bike for a piece of checked luggage at no charge; otherwise, the cost is about $100. Most U.S. and Canadian airlines charge $40–$80 each way.

BUSINESS HOURS

Even people in paradise have to work. Generally local business hours are weekdays 8–5. Banks are usually open Monday–Thursday 8:30–3 and until 6 on Friday. Some banks have Saturday-morning hours.

Many self-serve gas stations stay open around-the-clock, with full-service stations usually open from around 7 AM until 8 PM. U.S. post offices are open weekdays 8:30 AM–4:30 PM and Saturday 8:30–noon. On O'ahu, the Ala Moana post office branch is the only branch, other than the main Honolulu International Airport facility, that stays open until 4 PM on Saturday.

MUSEUMS & SIGHTS

Most museums generally open their doors between 9 AM and 10 AM and stay open until 5 PM Tuesday–Saturday. Many museums operate with afternoon hours only on Sunday and close on Monday. Visitor-attraction hours vary, but most sights are open daily with the exception of major holidays such as Christmas. **Check local newspapers upon arrival for attraction hours and schedules if visiting over holiday periods.** The local dailies carry a listing of "What's Open/What's Not" for those time periods.

SHOPS

Stores in resort areas sometimes open as early as 8, with shopping-center opening hours varying from 9:30 to 10 on weekdays and Saturday, a bit later on Sunday. Bigger malls stay open until 9 weekdays and Saturday and close at 5 on Sunday. Boutiques in resort areas may stay open as late as 11.

BUS TRAVEL

Getting around by bus is a wonderfully affordable option on O'ahu. In Waikīkī, in addition to TheBus and the Waikīkī Trolley, there are a number of brightly painted private buses, many free, that will take you to such commercial attractions as dinner cruises, garment factories, and the like.

THEBUS

You can go all around the island or just down Kalākaua Avenue for $2 on Honolulu's municipal transportation system, affectionately known as TheBus. It's one of the island's best bargains. Taking TheBus in the Waikīkī and downtown Honolulu areas is especially convenient, with buses making stops in Waikīkī every 15 minutes to take passengers to nearby shopping areas, such as Ala Moana Center.

You're entitled to one free transfer per fare if you ask for it when boarding. Exact change is required, and dollar bills are accepted. A four-consecutive-day pass for visitors costs $20 and is available at ABC convenience stores in Waikīkī and in the Ala Moana Shopping Center. Monthly passes cost $40.

There are no official bus-route maps, but you can find privately published booklets at most drugstores and other convenience outlets. The important route numbers for Waikīkī are 2, 4, 8, 19, 20, 58 and City Express Route B. If you venture afield, you can always get back on one of these.

◪ TheBus ☎ 808/848-5555 ⊕ www.thebus.org.

WAIKĪKĪ TROLLEY

The Waikīkī Trolley has three lines and dozens of stops that allow you to design your own itinerary while riding on brass-trimmed, open-air trolleys. The Honolulu City Line (Red Line) travels between

Waikīkī and the Bishop Museum and includes stops at Aloha Tower, Ala Moana,
and downtown Honolulu, among others.
The Ocean Coast Line (Blue Line) provides a tour of O'ahu's southeastern coastline, including Diamond Head Crater,
Hanauma Bay, and Sea Life Park. The Ala
Moana Shuttle Line (Pink Line) stops at
Ward Center and Ala Moana Shopping
Center. The trolleys depart from the DFS
Galleria Waikīkī. A one-day, three-line
ticket costs $25. Four-day tickets, also
good for any of the three lines, are $45.

🚋 **Waikīkī Trolley** ☎ 808/591-2561 or 800/824-
8804 ⊕ www.waikikitrolley.com.

CAMERAS & PHOTOGRAPHY

Today's underwater "disposable" cameras
can provide terrific photos for those once-
in-a-lifetime underwater experiences.
Many hotel–resort sundries stores offer
film developing, and larger department
stores, such as Long's Drugs, have one-
hour service for regular film developing
and overnight service for panoramic film.
The *Kodak Guide to Shooting Great
Travel Pictures* (available at bookstores
everywhere) is loaded with tips.

🚋 **Photo Help Kodak Information Center** ☎ 800/
242-2424 ⊕ www.kodak.com.

EQUIPMENT PRECAUTIONS

**Don't pack film or equipment in checked
luggage,** where it is much more susceptible to damage. X-ray machines used to
view checked luggage are extremely powerful and therefore are likely to ruin your
film. Try to ask for hand inspection of
film, which becomes clouded after re-
peated exposure to airport X-ray machines, and keep videotapes and computer
disks away from metal detectors. Always
keep film, tape, and computer disks out of
the sun. Carry an extra supply of batteries,
and be prepared to turn on your camera,
camcorder, or laptop to prove to airport
security personnel that the device is real.

CAR RENTAL

You can rent anything from an econobox
to a Ferrari. It's wise to make reservations
in advance, especially if visiting during
peak seasons or for major conventions or
sporting events.

Rates in Honolulu begin at about $25 a
day for an economy car with air-conditioning, automatic transmission, and unlimited mileage. This does not include
vehicle registration fee and weight tax, insurance, sales tax, and a $3-per-day
Hawai'i state surcharge.

🚋 **Major Agencies Alamo** ☎ 800/327-9633
⊕ www.alamo.com. **Avis** ☎ 800/331-1212, 800/
879-2847 or 800/272-5871 in Canada, 0870/606-
0100 in the U.K., 02/9353-9000 in Australia, 09/526-
2847 in New Zealand ⊕ www.avis.com. **Budget**
☎ 800/527-0700 ⊕ www.budget.com. **Hertz**
☎ 800/654-3131, 800/263-0600 in Canada, 0870/
844-8844 in the U.K., 02/9669-2444 in Australia,
09/256-8690 in New Zealand ⊕ www.hertz.com.
National Car Rental ☎ 800/227-7368 ⊕ www.
nationalcar.com.

CUTTING COSTS

If you are staying in Waikīkī, you may
want to rent a car only on the days you
plan to sightsee around the island. Since
you don't really need a car in the Waikīkī
resort area and hotel parking garage
charges can add up, this is one way to
keep your ground transportation costs affordable.

Many rental companies offer coupons for
discounts at various attractions that could
save you money later on in your trip.

For a good deal, book through a travel
agent who will shop around. Also, price
local car-rental companies—whose prices
may be lower still, although their service
and maintenance may not be as good as
those of major rental agencies—and research rates on the Internet. Consolidators
that specialize in air travel can offer good
rates on cars as well (⇨ Air Travel). Remember to ask about required deposits,
cancellation penalties, and drop-off
charges if you're planning to pick up the
car in one city and leave it in another. If
you're traveling during a holiday period,
also make sure that a confirmed reservation guarantees you a car.

🚋 **Local Agencies AA Aloha Cars-R-Us** ☎ 800/
655-7989 ⊕ www.hawaiicarrental.com. **JN Car and
Truck Rentals** ☎ 800/475-7522, 808/831-2724 on
O'ahu ⊕ www.jnautomotive.com. **VIP Car Rentals**
☎ 808/922-4605 in Waikīkī.

INSURANCE

When driving a rented car you are generally responsible for any damage to or loss of the vehicle. You also may be liable for any property damage or personal injury that you may cause while driving. Before you rent, see what coverage you already have under the terms of your personal auto-insurance policy and credit cards.

For about $9 to $25 a day, rental companies sell protection, known as a collision- or loss-damage waiver (CDW or LDW), that eliminates your liability for damage to the car; it's always optional and should never be automatically added to your bill. In most states you don't need a CDW if you have personal auto insurance or other liability insurance. However, **make sure you have enough coverage to pay for the car.** If you do not have auto insurance or an umbrella policy that covers damage to third parties, purchasing liability insurance and a CDW or LDW is highly recommended.

REQUIREMENTS & RESTRICTIONS

In Hawai'i you must be 21 years of age to rent a car and you must have a valid driver's license and a major credit card. Those under 25 will pay a daily surcharge of $15–$25.

In Hawai'i your unexpired mainland driver's license is valid for rental for up to 90 days.

SURCHARGES

Before you pick up a car in one city and leave it in another, ask about drop-off charges or one-way service fees, which can be substantial. Also inquire about early-return policies; some rental agencies charge extra if you return the car before the time specified in your contract while others give you a refund for the days not used. Most agencies note the tank's fuel level on your contract; to avoid a hefty refueling fee, return the car with the same tank level. If the tank was full, refill it just before you turn in the car, but be aware that gas stations near the rental outlet may overcharge. It's almost never a deal to buy a tank of gas with the car when you rent it; the understanding is that you'll return it empty, but some fuel usually remains.

Surcharges may apply if you're under 25 or if you take the car outside the area approved by the rental agency. You'll pay extra for child seats (about $8 a day), which are compulsory for children under five, and usually for additional drivers (up to $25 a day, depending on location).

CAR TRAVEL

O'ahu can be circled except for the roadless west-shore area around Ka'ena Point. Elsewhere, major highways follow the shoreline and traverse the island at two points. Rush-hour traffic (6:30 to 8:30 AM and 3:30 to 6 PM) can be frustrating around Honolulu and the outlying areas, as many thoroughfares allow no left turns due to contra-flow lanes. Parking along many streets is curtailed during these times, and towing is strictly practiced. Read curbside parking signs before leaving your vehicle, even at a meter.

Asking for directions will almost always produce a helpful explanation from the locals, but you should be prepared for an island term or two. Instead of using compass directions, remember that Hawai'i residents refer to places as being either *mauka* (toward the mountains) or *makai* (toward the ocean) from one another. Other directions depend on your location: in Honolulu, for example, people say to "go diamondhead," which means toward that famous landmark, or to "go 'ewa," meaning in the opposite direction. A shop on the mauka–Diamond Head corner of a street is on the mountain side of the street on the corner closest to Diamond Head. It all makes perfect sense once you get the lay of the land.

GASOLINE

You can pretty much count on having to pay more at the pump for gasoline on O'ahu than on the U.S. mainland.

ROAD CONDITIONS

O'ahu is a relatively easy island to navigate. Roads and streets, although they may challenge the visitor's tongue, are well marked; just watch out for the many one-way streets in Waikīkī. Keep an eye open for the Hawai'i Visitors and Convention Bureau's red-caped King Kamehameha signs, which mark major attractions and scenic spots. Ask for a map at the car-rental counter. Free publications containing good-quality road maps can be found at most hotels and resorts and throughout Waikīkī.

RULES OF THE ROAD

Be sure to **buckle up.** Hawai'i has a strictly enforced seat-belt law for front-seat passengers. Children under five must be in a car seat (available from car-rental agencies). Children 18 and under, riding in the backseat, are also required by state law to use seat belts. The highway speed limit is usually 55 mph. In-town traffic moves from 25 to 40 mph. Jaywalking is very common, so be particularly watchful for pedestrians, especially in congested areas such as Waikīkī. Unauthorized use of a parking space reserved for persons with disabilities can net you a $150 fine.

O'ahu's drivers are generally courteous, and you rarely hear a horn. People will slow down and let you into traffic with a wave of the hand. A friendly wave back is customary. If a driver sticks a hand out the window in a fist with the thumb and pinky sticking straight out, this is a good thing: it's the *shaka*, the Hawaiian symbol for "hang loose," and is often used to say "thanks," as well.

CHILDREN IN O'AHU

Sunny beaches and many family-oriented cultural sites, activities, and attractions make O'ahu a very *keiki-* (child-) friendly place. Here kids can swim with a dolphin, soar in a glider, surf with a boogie board, hike to the top of Diamond Head, or walk the decks of the "Mighty Mo" battleship. Parents should **use caution on beaches and during water sports.** Even waters that appear calm can harbor powerful rip currents. Be sure to **read any beach-warning guides your hotel may provide. Ask around for kid-friendly beaches** that might have shallow tide pools or are protected by reefs. And remember that the sun's rays are in operation full-force year-round here. Sunblock for children is essential.

Most major resort chains on O'ahu offer activity programs for children ages 5 to 12. These kid clubs provide opportunities

to learn about local culture, make friends with children from around the world, and experience age-appropriate activities while giving moms and dads a "time-out." Upon arrival, check out the daily local newspapers for children's events. The *Honolulu Advertiser's* "TGIF" section each Friday includes a section on keiki activities with a local flavor.

If you are renting a car, don't forget to arrange for a car seat when you reserve. For general advice about traveling with children, consult *Fodor's FYI: Travel with Your Baby* (available in bookstores everywhere).

FLYING

If your children are two or older, ask about children's airfares. As a general rule, infants under two not occupying a seat fly at greatly reduced fares or even for free. But if you want to guarantee a seat for an infant, you have to pay full fare. Consider flying during off-peak days and times; most airlines will grant an infant a seat without a ticket if there are available seats. Experts agree that it's a good idea to use safety seats aloft for children weighing less than 40 pounds. Airlines set their own policies: if you use a safety seat, U.S. carriers usually require that the child be ticketed, even if he or she is young enough to ride free, because the seats must be strapped into regular seats. And even if you pay the full adult fare for the seat, it may be worth it, especially on longer trips. Do **check your airline's policy about using safety seats during takeoff and landing.** Safety seats are not allowed everywhere in the plane, so get your seat assignments as early as possible.

When reserving, request children's meals or a freestanding bassinet (not available at all airlines) if you need them. But note that bulkhead seats, where you must sit to use the bassinet, may lack an overhead bin or storage space on the floor.

LODGING

Families can't go wrong choosing resort locations that are part of larger hotel chains such as Hilton, Hyatt, Outrigger, and Sheraton. Many of these resorts are centrally located on beautiful beaches and have activities created for children. Outrigger's "Ohana" brand hotels are off the beachfront but provide great value at good prices. Many condominium resorts now also offer children's activities and amenities during holiday periods.

Most hotels allow children under a certain age to stay in their parents' room at no extra charge, but others charge for them as extra adults; be sure to find out the cutoff age for children's discounts. Also **check for special seasonal programs,** such as "kids eat free" promotions.

Hilton ☎ 800/445-8667 ⊕ www.hilton.com. **Hyatt Hotels & Resorts** ☎ 888/591-1234 ⊕ www. hyatt.com. **Marriott** ☎ 888/236-2427 ⊕ www. marriott.com. **Outrigger Hotels & Resorts** ☎ 800/ 688-7444 ⊕ www.outrigger.com. **ResortQuest Hawaii** ☎ 877/997-6667 ⊕ www. resortquesthawaii.com. **Starwood Hotels and Resorts** ☎ 888/625-5144 for Sheraton, 800/325-3589 for Luxury Collection ⊕ www.starwood.com. **Turtle Bay Resort** ☎ 800/203-3650 ⊕ www. turtlebayresort.com.

SIGHTS & ATTRACTIONS

Places that are especially appealing to children are indicated by a rubber-duckie icon (☺) in the margin. Top picks for children run the gamut from natural attractions kids can enjoy for free to some fairly expensive amusements. On O'ahu, favorites include surfing lessons at Waikīkī Beach, hiking Diamond Head, snorkeling Hanauma Bay, learning about marine life at Sea Life Park, splashing about the 29-acre Hawaiian Waters Adventure Park, and touring through South Pacific cultures at the Polynesian Cultural Center.

CONCIERGES

Concierges, found in many hotels, can help you with theater tickets and dinner reservations: a good one with connections may be able to get you seats for a hot show or prime-time dinner reservations at the restaurant of the moment. You can also turn to your hotel's concierge for help with travel arrangements, sightseeing plans, services ranging from aromatherapy to zipper repair, and emergencies. **Always**

tip a concierge who has been of assistance (⇨ Tipping).

CONSUMER PROTECTION

Whether you're shopping for gifts or purchasing travel services, **pay with a major credit card** whenever possible, so you can cancel payment or get reimbursed if there's a problem (and you can provide documentation). If you're doing business with a particular company for the first time, contact your local Better Business Bureau and the attorney general's offices in your state and (for U.S. businesses) the company's home state as well. Have any complaints been filed? Finally, if you're buying a package or tour, always consider travel insurance that includes default coverage (⇨ Insurance).

BBBs Council of Better Business Bureaus ✉ 4200 Wilson Blvd., Suite 800, Arlington, VA 22203 ☎ 703/276-0100 🖷 703/525-8277 ⊕ www. bbb.org.

CRUISE TRAVEL

When Pan Am's amphibious *Hawai'i Clipper* touched down on Pearl Harbor's waters in 1936, it marked the beginning of the end of regular passenger-ship travel to the Islands. From that point on, the predominant means of transporting visitors would be by air, not by sea. Today, however, cruising to Hawai'i is making a comeback.

Norwegian Cruise Lines offers four "freestyle" cruises (no set meal times, less formal clothing, more nightlife choices) with seven-day Hawai'i itineraries on three U.S.-flagged ships, *Pride of Aloha, Pride of America,* and the newest, *Pride of Hawaii.*

Carnival, Celebrity, Holland America, Princess, and Royal Caribbean cruise lines circle Hawai'i in a number of itineraries that typically begin and end on the U.S. west coast. Most of these itineraries include a port of call in Honolulu.

Even if you choose, as most travelers do, to travel by air to the Islands, you can get the flavor of what the luxury-cruise era in Hawai'i was like by checking out Aloha Tower Marketplace's Boat Day Celebrations in Honolulu. Vessels stopping here are met upon arrival by hula dancers and the kind of entertainment and floral festivities that once greeted travelers almost a century ago. Contact Aloha Tower Marketplace for a boat-day schedule upon arrival.

To get the best deal on a cruise, **consult a cruise-only travel agency.** To learn how to plan, choose, and book a cruise-ship voyage, consult *Fodor's FYI: Plan & Enjoy Your Cruise* (available in bookstores everywhere).

⌗ Aloha Tower Marketplace ⌧ 1 Aloha Tower Dr., at Piers 8, 9, and 10, Honolulu ☏ 808/528-5700 ⊕ www.alohatower.com.

⌗ Cruise Lines Carnival ☏ 888/227-6482 ⊕ www.carnival.com. **Celebrity** ☏ 800/647-2251 ⊕ www.celebritycruises.com. **Holland America** ☏ 877/724-5425 ⊕ www.hollandamerica.com. **Princess** ☏ 800/774-6237 ⊕ www.princess.com. **Royal Caribbean Cruise Line** ☏ 866/562-7625 ⊕ www.royalcaribbean.com.

CUSTOMS & DUTIES

IN AUSTRALIA

Australian residents who are 18 or older may bring home A$900 worth of souvenirs and gifts (including jewelry), 250 cigarettes or 250 grams of cigars or other tobacco products, and 2.25 liters of alcohol (including wine, beer, and spirits). Residents under 18 may bring back A$450 worth of goods. If any of these individual allowances are exceeded, you must pay duty for the entire amount (of the group of products in which the allowance was exceeded). Members of the same family traveling together may pool their allowances. Prohibited items include meat products. Seeds, plants, and fruits need to be declared upon arrival.

⌗ Australian Customs Service ⌗ Customs House, 10 Cooks River Dr., Sydney International Airport, Sydney, NSW 2020 ☏ 02/6275-6666 or 1300/363263, 02/8334-7444 or 1800/020-504 quarantine-inquiry line ☐ 02/8339-6714 ⊕ www.customs.gov.au.

IN CANADA

Canadian residents who have been out of Canada for at least seven days may bring in C$750 worth of goods duty-free. If you've been away fewer than seven days

but more than 48 hours, the duty-free allowance drops to C$200. If your trip lasts 24 to 48 hours, the allowance is C$50; if the goods are worth more than C$50, you must pay full duty on all of the goods. You may not pool allowances with family members. Goods claimed under the C$750 exemption may follow you by mail; those claimed under the lesser exemptions must accompany you. Alcohol and tobacco products may be included in the seven-day and 48-hour exemptions but not in the 24-hour exemption. If you meet the age requirements of the province or territory through which you reenter Canada, you may bring in, duty-free, 1.5 liters of wine *or* 1.14 liters (40 imperial ounces) of liquor *or* 24 12-ounce cans or bottles of beer or ale. Also, if you meet the local age requirement for tobacco products, you may bring in, duty-free, 200 cigarettes, 50 cigars or cigarillos, and 200 grams of tobacco. You may have to pay a minimum duty on tobacco products, regardless of whether or not you exceed your personal exemption. Check ahead of time with the Canada Border Services Agency or the Department of Agriculture for policies regarding meat products, seeds, plants, and fruits.

You may send an unlimited number of gifts (only one gift per recipient, however) worth up to C$60 each duty-free to Canada. Label the package UNSOLICITED GIFT—VALUE UNDER $60. Alcohol and tobacco are excluded.

⌗ Canada Border Services Agency ⌧ Customs Information Services, 191 Laurier Ave. W, 15th fl., Ottawa, Ontario K1A 0L5 ☏ 800/461-9999 in Canada, 204/983-3500, 506/636-5064 ⊕ www.cbsa.gc.ca.

IN NEW ZEALAND

All homeward-bound residents may bring back NZ$700 worth of souvenirs and gifts; passengers may not pool their allowances, and children can claim only the concession on goods intended for their own use. For those 17 or older, the duty-free allowance also includes 4.5 liters of wine or beer; one 1,125-ml bottle of spirits; and either 200 cigarettes, 250 grams of tobacco, 50 cigars, *or* a combination of the three up to 250 grams. Meat products, seeds, plants, and fruits must be declared upon arrival to the Agricultural Services Department.

New Zealand Customs ✉ Head office: The Customhouse, 17–21 Whitmore St., Box 2218, Wellington ☎ 04/473-6099 or 0800/428-786 ⊕ www.customs. govt.nz.

IN THE U.K.

From countries outside the European Union, including the United States, you may bring home, duty-free, 200 cigarettes, 50 cigars, 100 cigarillos, or 250 grams of tobacco; 1 liter of spirits or 2 liters of fortified or sparkling wine or liqueurs; 2 liters of still table wine; 60 ml of perfume; 250 ml of toilet water; plus £145 worth of other goods, including gifts and souvenirs. Prohibited items include meat and dairy products, seeds, plants, and fruits.

HM Customs and Excise ✉ Portcullis House, 21 Cowbridge Rd. E, Cardiff CF11 9SS ☎ 0845/010-9000 or 0208/929-0152 advice service, 0208/929-6731 or 0208/910-3602 complaints ⊕ www.hmce. gov.uk.

DISABILITIES & ACCESSIBILITY

The Society for the Advancement of Travel for the Handicapped has named Hawai'i the most accessible vacation spot for people with disabilities. Ramped visitor areas and specially equipped lodgings are relatively common. Travelers with vision impairments who use a guide dog don't have to worry about quarantine restrictions. All you need to do is present documentation that the animal is a trained guide dog and has a current inoculation record for rabies. Access Aloha Travel is the state's only travel planner specializing in the needs of Hawai'i-bound travelers with disabilities. The company can arrange accessible accommodations, sightseeing, dining, activities, personal care attendants, and rentals of medical equipment, wheelchairs, and scooter vans.

Local Resources Access Aloha Travel ✉ 414 Kuwili St., Suite 101, Honolulu 96817 ☎ 800/480-1143 or 808/545-1143 🖷 808/545-7657 ⊕ www. accessalohatravel.com. **Disability and Communication Access Board** ✉ 919 Ala Moana Blvd., Room 101, Honolulu 96814 ☎ 808/586-8121 🖷 808/586-8129 ⊕ www.hawaii.gov/health/dcab.

LODGING

Despite the Americans with Disabilities Act, the definition of accessibility seems to differ from hotel to hotel. Some properties may be accessible by ADA standards for people with mobility problems but not for people with hearing or vision impairments, for example.

If you have mobility problems, ask for the lowest floor on which accessible services are offered. If you have a hearing impairment, check whether the hotel has devices to alert you visually to the ring of the telephone, a knock at the door, and a fire/emergency alarm. Some hotels provide these devices without charge. Discuss your needs with hotel personnel if this equipment isn't available, so that a staff member can personally alert you in the event of an emergency.

If you're bringing a guide dog, get authorization ahead of time and write down the name of the person with whom you spoke.

RESERVATIONS

When discussing accessibility with an operator or reservations agent, ask hard questions. Are there any stairs, inside *or* out? Are there grab bars next to the toilet *and* in the shower/tub? How wide is the doorway to the room? To the bathroom? For the most extensive facilities meeting the latest legal specifications, opt for newer accommodations. If you reserve through a toll-free number, consider also calling the hotel's local number to confirm the information from the central reservations office. Get confirmation in writing when you can.

SIGHTS & ATTRACTIONS

Many of O'ahu's sights and attractions are accessible to travelers with disabilities. The Honolulu Department of Parks and Recreation provides "all-terrain" wheelchairs and beach mats at several beach parks on O'ahu.

Therapeutic Recreation Unit of the Honolulu Department of Parks and Recreation ☎ 808/692-5461 Therapeutic Recreation Unit ⊕ www.co. honolulu.hi.us/parks/programs/beach.

TRANSPORTATION

Paratransit Services (TheHandi-Van) will take you to a specific destination on

O'ahu–not on sightseeing outings—in shared-ride vans with lifts and lock-downs. With TheHandi-Van Pass, one-way trips cost $2. Passes are free and can be obtained from the Honolulu Department of Transportation Services, which is open weekdays 7:45–4:30; you'll need a doctor's written confirmation of your disability or a Paratransit ID card. Application forms also can be obtained in advance of your visit by calling the Department of Transportation Services or going online. Handi-Cabs of the Pacific is a private company that provides a wheelchair accessible taxi and tour service. Fares are $9 plus $2 per mile for curbside service and $19 plus $2 per mile for door-to-door service. Reservations at least 24 hours in advance are required by both companies, so plan ahead.

Those who prefer to do their own driving may rent hand-controlled cars from Alamo, Avis, Budget, Hertz, and National. You can use the windshield card from your own state to park in spaces reserved for people with disabilities. All require at least 48 hours notice.

The U.S. Department of Transportation Aviation Consumer Protection Division's online publication *New Horizons: Information for the Air Traveler with a Disability* offers advice for travelers with a disability, and outlines basic rights. Visit DisabilityInfo.gov for general information.

🚹 Buses & Vans Department of Transportation Services ✉ 711 Kapiolani Blvd., Suite 250, Honolulu 96813 ☎ 808/523-4083 ⊕ www.co.honolulu.hi.us/dts/. Handi-Cabs of the Pacific ☎ 808/524-3866. Paratransit Services (TheHandi-Van) ☎ 808/456-5555.

🚹 Cars Alamo ☎ 800/651-1223 ⊕ www.alamo.com. Avis ☎ 800/321-3712 ⊕ www.avis.com. Budget ☎ 800/526-6408 ⊕ www.budget.com. Hertz ☎ 800/654-3011 ⊕ www.hertz.com. National ☎ 800/227-7368 ⊕ www.nationalcar.com.

🚹 Information & Complaints Aviation Consumer Protection Division (⇨ Air Travel) for airline-related problems; ⊕ airconsumer.ost.dot.gov/publications/horizons.htm for airline travel advice and rights. Departmental Office of Civil Rights ✉ for general inquiries, U.S. Department of Transportation, S-30, 400 7th St. SW, Room 10215, Wash-ington, DC 20590 ☎ 202/366-4648, 202/366-8538 TTY 🖶 202/366-9371 ⊕ www.dotcr.ost.dot.gov. Disability Rights Section ✉ NYAV, U.S. Department of Justice, Civil Rights Division, 950 Pennsylvania Ave. NW, Washington, DC 20530 ☎ ADA information line 202/514-0301, 800/514-0301, 202/514-0383 TTY, 800/514-0383 TTY ⊕ www.ada.gov. U.S. Department of Transportation Hotline ☎ for disability-related air-travel problems, 800/778-4838 or 800/455-9880 TTY.

TRAVEL AGENCIES

In the United States, the Americans with Disabilities Act requires that travel firms serve the needs of all travelers. Some agencies specialize in working with people with disabilities.

🚹 Travelers with Mobility Problems Access Adventures/B. Roberts Travel ✉ 1876 East Ave., Rochester, NY 14610 ☎ 800/444-6540 ⊕ www.brobertstravel.com, run by a former physical-rehabilitation counselor. Access Aloha Travel ✉ 414 Kuwili St., Suite 101, Honolulu, HI 96817 ☎ 800/480-1143 🖶 808/545-7657 ⊕ www.accessalohatravel.com. Accessible Vans of Hawaii ✉ 355 Hukilike St., Suite 121A, Kahului, HI 96732 ☎ 808/871-7785 or 800/303-3750 🖶 808/871-7536 ⊕ www.accessiblevanshawaii.com. CareVacations ✉ No. 5, 5110–50 Ave., Leduc, Alberta, Canada, T9E 6V4 ☎ 780/986-6404 or 877/478-7827 🖶 780/986-8332 ⊕ www.carevacations.com, for group tours and cruise vacations. Flying Wheels Travel ✉ 143 W. Bridge St., Box 382, Owatonna, MN 55060 ☎ 507/451-5005 🖶 507/451-1685 ⊕ www.flyingwheelstravel.com.

🚹 Travelers with Developmental Disabilities New Directions ✉ 5276 Hollister Ave., Suite 207, Santa Barbara, CA 93111 ☎ 805/967-2841 or 888/967-2841 🖶 805/964-7344 ⊕ www.newdirectionstravel.com. Sprout ✉ 893 Amsterdam Ave., New York, NY 10025 ☎ 212/222-9575 or 888/222-9575 🖶 212/222-9768 ⊕ www.gosprout.org.

DISCOUNTS & DEALS

Be a smart shopper and compare all your options before making decisions. A plane ticket bought with a promotional coupon from travel clubs, coupon books, and direct-mail offers or purchased on the Internet may not be cheaper than the least expensive fare from a discount ticket agency. And always keep in mind that what you get is just as important as what you save.

DISCOUNT RESERVATIONS

To save money, look into discount reservations services with Web sites and toll-free numbers, which use their buying power to get a better price on hotels, airline tickets (⇨ Air Travel), even car rentals. When booking a room, always **call the hotel's local toll-free number** (if one is available) rather than the central reservations number—you'll often get a better price. Always ask about special packages or corporate rates.

Hotel Rooms Accommodations Express ☎ 800/444-7666 or 800/277-1064. **Hotels.com** ☎ 800/219-4606 or 800/364-0291 ⊕ www.hotels.com. **Quikbook** ☎ 800/789-9887 ⊕ www.quikbook.com. **Steigenberger Reservation Service** ☎ 800/223-5652 ⊕ www.srs-worldhotels.com. **Turbotrip.com** ☎ 800/473-7829 ⊕ w3.turbotrip.com.

PACKAGE DEALS

Don't confuse packages and guided tours. When you buy a package, you travel on your own, just as though you had planned the trip yourself. Fly/drive packages, which combine airfare and car rental, are often a good deal. In cities, ask the local visitor's bureau about hotel and local transportation packages that include tickets to major museum exhibits or other special events.

ECOTOURISM

Hawai'i's connection to its environment is spiritual, cultural, and essential to its survival. You'll find a rainbow of natural attractions to explore on O'ahu, from the ribbons of beaches to lush mountain valleys. Ecotouring on O'ahu gives you the opportunity to learn from local guides who are familiar with the *aina* (land) and Hawai'i's unique cultural heritage. Many of these tours take clients to locations less traveled, so it helps to be in good physical shape. The views at the ends of these roads are an exceedingly rich reward.

Nature and all its ornaments are sacred to Hawaiians, so before taking pieces of lava rock home for souvenirs, listen to what residents (and some vacationers) will tell you: don't touch! Hapless travelers who take "souvenir" rocks speak of "bad-luck" consequences in the form of stalled cars, travel delays, and bouts of illness. Visitor bureau staff spin tales about rocks mailed from around the world with attached tales of woe and pleas for the rocks to be put back. If nothing else, with millions of visitors a year, there aren't enough cool rocks to go around.

During the winter months, be sure to watch the beachfronts for endangered sea turtles, or recently laid nests. If you spot one, notify local authorities—they'll be thankful for your help in tracking these elusive creatures.

There are dozens of organizations that offer programs to explore the island's breathtaking environment, as well as volunteer opportunities to help preserve the fragile ecosystem.

Alternative-Hawai'i ☎ 808/695-5113 ⊕ www. alternative-hawaii.com. **Hawai'i Department of Land and Natural Resources, Division of State Parks** ☎ 808/587-0400 ⊕ www.hawaii.gov/dlnr/dsp/index.html. **Hawai'i Ecotourism Association** ☎ 877/300-7058 ⊕ www.hawaiiecotourism.org. **Hawai'i Forest & Trail** ☎ 800/464-1993 ⊕ www.hawaii-forest.com. **Hawai'i Nature Center** ☎ 888/955-0104 ⊕ www.hawaiinaturecenter.org. **Nā Ala Hele Trail & Access Program** ☎ 808/973-9782 ⊕ www.hawaiitrails.org. **The Nature Conservancy** ☎ 808/537-4508 ⊕ www.nature.org/hawaii. **Sierra Club** ☎ 808/538-6616 ⊕ www.hawaii.sierraclub.org.

EMERGENCIES

To reach the police, fire department, or an ambulance in an emergency, dial **911**.

A doctor, laboratory-radiology technician, and nurses are always on duty at Doctors on Call. Appointments are recommended but not necessary. Dozens of medical insurances are accepted, including Medicare, Medicaid, and most kinds of travel insurance.

Kūhiō Pharmacy is Waikīkī's only pharmacy and handles prescription requests only until 4:30 PM. Longs Drugs is open evenings at its Ala Moana location and 24 hours at its South King Street location (15 minutes from Waikīkī by car). Pillbox Pharmacy, located in Kaimukī, will deliver prescription medications for a small fee.

Doctors & Dentists Doctors on Call ✉ Sheraton Princess Kaiulani Hotel, 120 Kaiulani Ave., Waikīkī ☎ 808/971-6000.

🚹 **Emergency Services Coast Guard Rescue Center** ☎ 808/541-2450.

🚹 **Hospitals Castle Medical Center** ✉ 640 Ulukahiki, Kailua ☎ 808/263-5500. **Kapiolani Medical Center for Women and Children** ✉ 1319 Punahou St., Makiki Heights, Honolulu ☎ 808/983-6000. **Queen's Medical Center** ✉ 1301 Punchbowl St., Downtown Honolulu, Honolulu ☎ 808/538-9011. **Saint Francis Medical Center-West** ✉ 91-2141 Ft. Weaver Rd., 'Ewa Beach ☎ 808/678-7000. **Straub Clinic** ✉ 888 S. King St., Downtown Honolulu, Honolulu ☎ 808/522-4000.

🚹 **Pharmacies Kūhiō Pharmacy** ✉ Outrigger West Hotel, 2330 Kūhiō Ave., Waikīkī ☎ 808/923-4466. **Longs Drugs** ✉ Ala Moana Shopping Center, 1450 Ala Moana Blvd., 2nd level, near Sears Ala Moana ☎ 808/949-4010 ✉ 2220 S. King St., Mō'ili'ili ☎ 808/947-2651. **Pillbox Pharmacy** ✉ 1133 11th Ave., Kaimukī ☎ 808/737-1777.

ETIQUETTE & BEHAVIOR

Hawai'i was admitted to the Union in 1959, so residents can be pretty sensitive when visitors refer to their own hometowns as "back in the States." Remember, when in Hawai'i, refer to the contiguous 48 states as "the mainland" and not as the United States. When you do, you won't appear to be such a *malahini* (newcomer).

GAY & LESBIAN TRAVEL

A few small hotels and some bed-and-breakfasts on O'ahu are favored by gay and lesbian visitors; Purple Roofs is a listing agent for gay-friendly accommodations. Pacific Ocean Holidays specializes in prearranging package tours for independent gay travelers. The organization also offers an online directory of gay-owned and gay-friendly businesses and community resources.

For details about the gay and lesbian scene, consult *Fodor's Gay Guide to the USA* (available in bookstores everywhere).

🚹 **Local Resources Pacific Ocean Holidays** ☞ Box 88245, Honolulu 96830 ☎ 808/923-2400 or 800/735-6600 ⊕ www.gayHawaiivacations.com and www.gayHawaii.com. **Purple Roofs** ⊕ www.purpleroofs.com.

🚹 **Gay- & Lesbian-Friendly Travel Agencies Different Roads Travel** ✉ 155 Palm Colony, Palm Springs, CA 92264 ☎ 310/289-6000 or 800/429-8747 🖷 310/855-0323 ✉ lgernert@tzell.com.

Skylink Travel and Tour/Flying Dutchmen Travel ✉ 1455 N. Dutton Ave., Suite A, Santa Rosa, CA 95401 ☎ 707/546-9888 or 800/225-5759 🖷 707/636-0951; serving lesbian travelers.

HEALTH

Hawai'i is known as the Health State. The life expectancy here is 79 years, the longest in the nation. Balmy weather makes it easy to remain active year-round, and the low-stress aloha attitude certainly contributes to general well-being. When visiting the Islands, however, there are a few health issues to keep in mind.

The Hawai'i State Department of Health recommends that you drink 16 ounces of water per hour to avoid dehydration when hiking or spending time in the sun. **Use sunblock, wear UV-reflective sunglasses, and protect your head with a visor or hat for shade.** If you're not acclimated to warm, humid weather you should allow plenty of time for rest stops and refreshments. When visiting freshwater streams, be aware of the tropical disease leptospirosis, which is spread by animal urine and carried into streams and mud. Symptoms include fever, headache, nausea, and red eyes. If left untreated it can cause liver and kidney damage, respiratory failure, internal bleeding, and even death. To avoid this, don't swim or wade in freshwater streams or ponds if you have open sores and **don't drink from any freshwater streams or ponds.**

On the Islands, fog is a rare occurrence, but there can often be "vog," an airborne haze of gases released from volcanic vents on the Big Island. During certain weather conditions such as "Kona Winds," the vog can settle over the Islands and wreak havoc with respiratory and other health conditions, especially asthma or emphysema. If susceptible, stay indoors and get emergency assistance if needed.

PESTS & OTHER HAZARDS

The Islands have their share of bugs and insects that enjoy the tropical climate as much as visitors do. Most are harmless but annoying. When planning to spend time outdoors in hiking areas, **wear long-**

sleeved clothing and pants and use mosquito repellent containing deet. In very damp places you may encounter the dreaded local centipede. On the Islands they usually come in two colors, brown and blue, and they range from the size of a worm to an 8-inch cigar. Their sting is very painful, and the reaction is similar to bee- and wasp-sting reactions. When camping, shake out your sleeping bag before climbing in, and check your shoes in the morning, as the centipedes like cozy places. If planning on hiking or traveling in remote areas, always carry a first-aid kit and appropriate medications for sting reactions.

HOLIDAYS

Major national holidays are New Year's Day (Jan. 1); Martin Luther King Day (3rd Mon. in Jan.); Presidents' Day (3rd Mon. in Feb.); Memorial Day (last Mon. in May); Independence Day (July 4); Labor Day (1st Mon. in Sept.); Columbus Day (2nd Mon. in Oct.); Thanksgiving Day (4th Thurs. in Nov.); Christmas Eve and Christmas Day (Dec. 24 and 25); and New Year's Eve (Dec. 31).

INSURANCE

The most useful travel-insurance plan is a comprehensive policy that includes coverage for trip cancellation and interruption, default, trip delay, and medical expenses (with a waiver for preexisting conditions).

Without insurance you'll lose all or most of your money if you cancel your trip, regardless of the reason. Default insurance covers you if your tour operator, airline, or cruise line goes out of business—the chances of which have been increasing. Trip-delay covers expenses that arise because of bad weather or mechanical delays. Study the fine print when comparing policies.

U.K. residents can buy a travel-insurance policy valid for most vacations taken during the year in which it's purchased (but check preexisting-condition coverage).

Always **buy travel policies directly from the insurance company**; if you buy them from a cruise line, airline, or tour operator that goes out of business you probably won't be covered for the agency or operator's default, a major risk. Before making any purchase, review your existing health and home-owner's policies to find what they cover away from home.

🗂 Travel Insurers In the U.S.: **Access America** ✉ 2805 N. Parham Rd., Richmond, VA 23294 ☎ 800/729-6021 🖷 804/673-1469 or 800/346-9265 ⊕ www.accessamerica.com. **Travel Guard International** ✉ 1145 Clark St., Stevens Point, WI 54481 ☎ 800/826-4919 or 715/345-1041 🖷 800/955-8785 or 715/345-1990 ⊕ www.travelguard.com.

FOR INTERNATIONAL TRAVELERS

For information on customs restrictions, *see* Customs & Duties.

CAR RENTAL

When picking up a rental car, non-U.S. residents need a reservation voucher for any prepaid reservations that were made in the traveler's home country, a passport, a driver's license, and a travel policy that covers each driver.

Your driver's license may not be recognized outside your home country. International driving permits (IDPs) are available from the American and Canadian automobile associations and, in the United Kingdom, from the Automobile Association and Royal Automobile Club. These international permits, valid only in conjunction with your regular driver's license, are universally recognized; having one may save you a problem with local authorities.

CAR TRAVEL

Stations are plentiful. Most stay open late (24 hours along large highways and in big cities), except in rural areas, where Sunday hours are limited and where you may drive long stretches without a refueling opportunity. Highways are well paved. State police and tow trucks patrol major highways and lend assistance.

Driving in the United States is on the right. Do obey speed limits posted along roads and highways. Watch for lower limits in small towns and on back roads. On weekdays between 6 and 10 AM and again between 4 and 7 PM expect heavy traffic. To encourage carpooling, some freeways have special lanes for so-called high-occupancy vehicles (HOV)—cars carrying more than one passenger.

Bookstores, gas stations, convenience stores, and rest stops sell maps (about $3) and multiregion road atlases (about $10).

CONSULATES & EMBASSIES

🚩 **Australia** Australian Consulate ✉ 1000 Bishop St., Honolulu 96813 ☎ 808/524–5050.

🚩 **Canada** Canadian Consulate ✉ 1000 Bishop St., Honolulu 96813 ☎ 808/524–5050.

🚩 **New Zealand** New Zealand Consulate ✉ 900 Richards St., Room 414, Honolulu 96813 ☎ 808/543–7900.

🚩 **United Kingdom** British Consulate ✉ 1000 Bishop St., Honolulu 96813 ☎ 808/524–5050.

CURRENCY

The dollar is the basic unit of U.S. currency. It has 100 cents. Coins are the copper penny (1¢); the silvery nickel (5¢), dime (10¢), quarter (25¢), and half-dollar (50¢); and the golden $1 coin, replacing a now-rare silver dollar. Bills are denominated $1, $5, $10, $20, $50, and $100, all mostly green and identical in size; designs and background tints vary. In addition, you may come across a $2 bill, but the chances are slim. The exchange rate at this writing is US$1.73 per British pound, .85¢ per Canadian dollar, .74¢ per Australian dollar, and .70¢ per New Zealand dollar.

ELECTRICITY

The U.S. standard is AC, 110 volts/60 cycles. Plugs have two flat pins set parallel to each other.

EMERGENCIES

For police, fire, or ambulance, **dial 911** (0 in rural areas).

INSURANCE

Britons and Australians need extra medical coverage when traveling overseas.

🚩 **Insurance Information** In the U.K.: **Association of British Insurers** ✉ 51 Gresham St., London EC2V 7HQ ☎ 020/7600–3333 🖷 020/7696–8999 ⊕ www.abi.org.uk. In Australia: **Insurance Council of Australia** ✉ Level 3, 56 Pitt St., Sydney, NSW 2000 ☎ 02/9253–5100 🖷 02/9253–5111 ⊕ www.ica.com.au. In Canada: **RBC Insurance** ✉ 6880 Financial Dr., Mississauga, Ontario L5N 7Y5 ☎ 800/387–4357 or 905/816–2559 🖷 888/298–6458 ⊕ www.rbcinsurance.com. In New Zealand: **Insurance**

Council of New Zealand ✉ Level 7, 111–115 Customhouse Quay, Box 474, Wellington ☎ 04/472–5230 🖷 04/473–3011 ⊕ www.icnz.org.nz.

MAIL & SHIPPING

You can buy stamps and aerograms and send letters and parcels in post offices. Stamp-dispensing machines can occasionally be found in airports, bus and train stations, office buildings, drugstores, and the like. You can also deposit mail in the stout, dark blue, steel bins at strategic locations everywhere and in the mail chutes of large buildings; pickup schedules are posted. You can deposit packages at public collection boxes as long as the parcels are affixed with proper postage and weigh less than one pound. Packages weighing one or more pounds must be taken to a post office or handed to a postal carrier.

For mail sent within the United States, you need a 39¢ stamp for first-class letters weighing up to 1 ounce (24¢ for each additional ounce) and 24¢ for postcards. You pay 84¢ for 1-ounce airmail letters and 75¢ for airmail postcards to most other countries except Canada and Mexico. For mail to Canada and Mexico, you need a 63¢ stamp for a 1-ounce letter and 55¢ for a postcard. An aerogram—a single sheet of lightweight blue paper that folds into its own envelope, stamped for overseas airmail—costs 75¢.

To receive mail on the road, have it sent c/o General Delivery at your destination's main post office (use the correct five-digit ZIP code). You must pick up mail in person within 30 days and show a driver's license or passport.

PASSPORTS & VISAS

When traveling internationally, carry your passport even if you don't need one (it's always the best form of I.D.) and **make two photocopies of the data page** (one for someone at home and another for you, carried separately from your passport). If you lose your passport, promptly call the nearest embassy or consulate and the local police.

Visitor visas aren't necessary for Canadian or European Union citizens, or for citizens of Australia who are staying fewer than 90 days.

⚡ Australian Citizens Passports Australia ☎ 131-232 ⊕ www.passports.gov.au. **United States Consulate General** ✉ MLC Centre, Level 59, 19-29 Martin Pl., Sydney, NSW 2000 ☎ 02/9373-9200, 1902/941-641 fee-based visa-inquiry line ⊕ usembassy-australia.state.gov/sydney.

⚡ Canadian Citizens Passport Office ✉ to mail in applications: Foreign Affairs Canada, Gatineau, Québec K1A 0G3 ☎ 800/567-6868 ⊕ www.ppt.gc.ca.

⚡ New Zealand Citizens New Zealand Passports Office ✉ For applications and information, Level 3, Boulcott House, 47 Boulcott St., Wellington ☎ 0800/22-5050 or 04/474-8100 ⊕ www. passports.govt.nz. **Embassy of the United States** ✉ 29 Fitzherbert Terr., Thorndon, Wellington ☎ 04/462-6000 ⊕ usembassy.org.nz. **U.S. Consulate General** ✉ Citibank Bldg., 3rd fl., 23 Customs St. E, Auckland ☎ 09/303-2724 ⊕ usembassy. org.nz.

⚡ U.K. Citizens U.K. Passport Service ☎ 0870/521-0410 ⊕ www.passport.gov.uk. **American Consulate General** ✉ Danesfort House, 223 Stranmillis Rd., Belfast, Northern Ireland BT9 5GR ☎ 028/9038-6100 🖷 028/9068-1301 ⊕ www.usembassy. org.uk. **American Embassy** ✉ for visa and immigration information or to submit a visa application via mail (enclose an SASE), Consular Information Unit, 24 Grosvenor Sq., London W1A 2LQ ☎ 090/5544-4546 or 090/6820-0290 for visa information (per-minute charges), 0207/499-9000 main switchboard ⊕ www.usembassy.org.uk.

TELEPHONES

All U.S. telephone numbers consist of a three-digit area code and a seven-digit local number. Within many local calling areas, you dial only the seven-digit number. Within some area codes, you must dial "1" first for calls outside the local area. To call between area-code regions, dial "1" then all 10 digits; the same goes for calls to numbers prefixed by "800," "888," "866," and "877"—all toll free. For calls to numbers preceded by "900" you must pay—usually dearly.

For international calls, dial "011" followed by the country code and the local number. For help, dial "0" and ask for an overseas operator. The country code is 61 for Australia, 64 for New Zealand, 44 for the United Kingdom. Calling Canada is

the same as calling within the United States, although you might not be able to get through on some toll free numbers. Most local phone books list country codes and U.S. area codes. The country code for the United States is 1.

For operator assistance, dial "0." To obtain someone's phone number, call directory assistance at 555–1212 or occasionally 411 (free at many public phones). To have the person you're calling foot the bill, phone collect; dial "0" instead of "1" before the 10-digit number.

At pay phones, instructions often are posted. Usually you insert coins in a slot (usually 25¢–50¢ for local calls) and wait for a steady tone before dialing. When you call long-distance, the operator tells you how much to insert; prepaid phone cards, widely available in various denominations, are easier. Call the number on the back, punch in the card's personal identification number when prompted, then dial your number.

If you're taking your cell phone on vacation with you, make sure roaming is included, otherwise, your minutes and bill will quickly add up. Prepaid phone cards are convenient and cost-effective.

LANGUAGE

English is the primary language on the Islands. Making the effort to learn some Hawaiian words can be rewarding, however. Despite the length of many Hawaiian words, the Hawaiian alphabet is actually one of the world's shortest, with only 12 letters: the five vowels, *a, e, i, o, u,* and seven consonants, *h, k, l, m, n, p, w.* Hawaiian words you are most likely to encounter during your visit to the Islands are *aloha, mahalo* (thank you), *keiki* (child), *haole* (Caucasian or foreigner), *mauka* (toward the mountains), *makai* (toward the ocean), and *pau* (finished, all done). Hawaiian history includes waves of immigrants, each bringing their own language. To communicate with each other, they developed a sort of slang known as "pidgin." If you listen closely, you will know what is being said by the inflections and by the extensive use of body language. For example, when you know what you want to say but don't know how to say it, just say "you know, da kine." (⇨ *See* Hawaiian Vocabulary *in* Understanding O'ahu)

For an informative and somewhat-hilarious view of things Hawaiian, check out Jerry Hopkins's series of books titled *Pidgin to the Max* and *Fax to the Max,* available at most local bookstores in the Hawaiiana sections.

LEI GREETINGS

When you walk off a long flight, perhaps a bit groggy and stiff, nothing quite compares with a Hawaiian lei greeting. The casual ceremony ranks as one of the fastest ways to make the transition from the worries of home to the joys of your vacation. Though the tradition has created an expectation that everyone receives this floral garland when they step off the plane, the state of Hawai'i cannot greet each of its nearly 7 million annual visitors.

Still, it's easy to **arrange for a lei ceremony for yourself or your companions before you arrive.** Contact Kama'āina Leis, Flowers & Greeters if you have not signed up with a tour company that provides it. If you really want to be wowed by the experience, request a lei of plumeria, some of the most divine-smelling blossoms on the planet. Kama'āina requires two days' notice and charges $13.30 for a standard lei greeting at the gate upon arrival into Honolulu.

🎋 **Kama'āina Leis, Flowers & Greeters** ☎ 808/836-3246 or 800/367-5183 🖷 808/836-1814.

MEDIA

NEWSPAPERS & MAGAZINES

O'ahu's daily newspapers are available through most hotel bell desks; in sundry stores, restaurants, and cafés; and at newsstands. Many hotels will deliver one to your room upon request. The *Honolulu Advertiser* is O'ahu's morning and Sunday paper; the *Honolulu Star-Bulletin* is O'ahu's evening paper and also prints on Sundays. *Honolulu Weekly* is a great guide for arts and alternative events, and *Pacific Business News* provides the latest in business news. The monthly *Honolulu*

Magazine focuses on O'ahu issues and happenings.

RADIO & TELEVISION

For Hawaiian music on the island, tune your FM radio dial to 98.5 KDNN, 100.3 KCCN, 99.5 KHUI, or 105.1 KINE. News junkies can get their fill of news and talk by tuning to 830 KHVH, 870 KHNR, 990 KHBZ, 1080 KWAI, or 1500 KUMU on the AM radio dial. National Public Radio enthusiasts can tune to the FM dial for NPR programming on 88.1 KHPR and 89.3 KIPO.

Many residents wake up with Perry & Price on KSSK AM 59 or FM 92.3. The lively duo provides news, traffic updates, and weather reports between "easy-listening" music and phone calls from listeners from 5 to 10 AM.

On O'ahu, you can find the following network programming with its channel and local affiliate call sign: FOX (2) KHON, ABC (4) KITV, UPN/WB (5) KHVE, CBS (9) KGMB, PBS (10) KHET, and NBC (13) KHNL. You can also find your favorite cable channel programs, as well.

MONEY MATTERS

Prices throughout this guide are given for adults. Substantially reduced fees are almost always available for children, students, and senior citizens. For information on taxes, *see* Taxes.

ATMS

Automatic teller machines, for easy access to cash, can be found at many locations throughout O'ahu including shopping centers, small convenience and grocery stores, inside hotels and resorts, as well as outside most bank branches. For a directory of locations, call 800/424-7787 for the Master-Card/Cirrus/Maestro network or 800/843-7587 for the Visa/Plus network.

CREDIT CARDS

Throughout this guide, the following abbreviations are used: **AE,** American Express; **D,** Discover; **DC,** Diners Club; **MC,** MasterCard; and **V,** Visa.

🎋 **Reporting Lost Cards American Express** ☎ 800/992-3404. **Diners Club** ☎ 800/234-6377. **Discover** ☎ 800/347-2683. **MasterCard** ☎ 800/622-7747. **Visa** ☎ 800/847-2911.

NATIONAL PARKS & STATE PARKS

On the island of O'ahu, the USS *Arizona* Memorial at Pearl Harbor is overseen by the National Park Service.

The State Parks Division of the Hawai'i State Department of Land and Natural Resources oversees 23 state parks and historic areas on O'ahu including Diamond Head State Monument, Hanauma Bay State Underwater Park, Kahana Valley State Park, Makapu'u Point, and Pu'u o Mahuka Heiau State Monument. Many of these parks and monuments offer excellent opportunities for shore fishing, swimming, picnicking, camping, and hiking; to say nothing of the spectacular views.

Look into discount passes to save money on park entrance fees. For $50, the National Parks Pass admits you (and any passengers in your private vehicle) to all national parks, monuments, and recreation areas, as well as other sites run by the National Park Service, for a year. (In parks that charge per person, the pass admits you, your spouse and children, and your parents, when you arrive together.) Camping and parking are extra. The $15 Golden Eagle Pass, a hologram you affix to your National Parks Pass, functions as an upgrade, granting entry to all sites run by the NPS, the U.S. Fish and Wildlife Service, the U.S. Forest Service, and the Bureau of Land Management. The upgrade, which expires with the parks pass, is sold by most national-park, Fish-and-Wildlife, and BLM fee stations. A major percentage of the proceeds from pass sales funds National Parks projects.

Both the Golden Age Passport ($10), for U.S. citizens or permanent residents who are 62 and older, and the Golden Access Passport (free), for persons with disabilities, entitle holders (and any passengers in their private vehicles) to lifetime free entry to all national parks, plus 50% off fees for the use of many park facilities and services. (The discount doesn't always apply to companions.) To obtain them, you must show proof of age and of U.S. citizenship or permanent residency—such as a U.S. passport, driver's license, or birth certificate—and, if requesting Golden Access, proof of disability. The Golden Age and Golden Access passes are available only at NPS-run sites that charge an entrance fee. The National Parks Pass is also available by mail and phone and via the Internet.

National Park Foundation ⊠ 11 Dupont Circle NW, Suite 600, Washington, DC 20036 ☎ 202/238-4200 ⊕ www.nationalparks.org. **National Park Service** ⊠ National Park Service/Department of Interior, 1849 C St. NW, Washington, DC 20240 ☎ 202/208-6843 ⊕ www.nps.gov. **National Parks Conservation Association** ⊠ 1300 19th St. NW, Suite 300, Washington, DC 20036 ☎ 202/223-6722 or 800/628-7275 ⊕ www.npca.org.

Passes by Mail & Online National Park Foundation ⊕ www.nationalparks.org. **National Parks Pass** National Park Foundation ✉ Box 34108, Washington, DC 20043 ☎ 888/467-2757 ⊕ www.nationalparks.org; include a check or money order payable to the National Park Service, plus $3.95 for shipping and handling (allow 8 to 13 business days from date of receipt for pass delivery), or call for passes.

State Parks State Parks Division, Hawai'i State Department of Land and Natural Resources ⊠ 1151 Punchbowl St., Room 310, Honolulu 96813 ☎ 808/587-0400 ⊕ www.hawaii.gov.

PACKING

O'ahu is casual: sandals, bathing suits, and comfortable, informal clothing are the norm. In summer synthetic slacks and shirts, although easy to care for, can be uncomfortably warm.

Probably the most important thing to tuck into your suitcase is sunscreen. This is the tropics, and the ultraviolet rays are powerful, even on overcast days. Doctors advise putting on sunscreen when you get up in the morning, whether it's cloudy or sunny. Don't forget to **reapply sunscreen periodically during the day,** since perspiration can wash it away. Consider using sunscreens with a sun protection factor (SPF) of 15 or higher. There are many tanning oils on the market in Hawai'i, including coconut and *kukui* (the nut from a local tree) oils, but they can cause severe burns. Too many Hawaiian vacations have been spoiled by sunburn and even sun poisoning. Hats and sunglasses offer important sun protection, too. Both are easy to find in island shops, but if you already have a favorite packable hat or sun visor, bring it with you, and don't forget to wear it. All major hotels on Oʻahu provide beach towels.

As for clothing, there's a saying that when a man wears a suit during the day, he's either going for a loan or he's a lawyer trying a case. Only a few upscale restaurants require a jacket for dinner. The aloha shirt is accepted dress on Oʻahu for business and most social occasions. Shorts are acceptable daytime attire, along with a T-shirt or polo shirt. There's no need to buy expensive sandals on the mainland—here you can get flip-flops for a couple of dollars and off-brand sandals for $20. Golfers should remember that many courses have dress codes requiring a collared shirt; call courses you're interested in for details. If you're not prepared, you can pick up appropriate clothing at resort pro shops. If you're visiting in winter or planning to visit a high-altitude area, **bring a sweater or light- to medium-weight jacket.** A polar fleece pullover is ideal, and makes a great impromptu pillow.

In your carry-on luggage, pack an extra pair of eyeglasses or contact lenses and enough of any medication you take to last a few days longer than the entire trip. You may also ask your doctor to write a spare prescription using the drug's generic name, as brand names may vary from country to country. In luggage to be checked, **never pack prescription drugs, valuables, or undeveloped film.** And don't forget to carry with you the addresses of offices that handle refunds of lost traveler's checks. Check *Fodor's How to Pack* (available at online retailers and bookstores everywhere) for more tips.

To avoid customs and security delays, carry medications in their original packaging. Don't pack any sharp objects in your carry-on luggage, including knives of any size or material, scissors, nail clippers, and corkscrews, or anything else that might arouse suspicion.

To avoid having your checked luggage chosen for hand inspection, don't cram bags full. The U.S. Transportation Security Administration suggests packing shoes on top and placing personal items you don't want touched in clear plastic bags.

CHECKING LUGGAGE

You're allowed to carry aboard one bag and one personal article, such as a purse or a laptop computer. Make sure what you carry on fits under your seat or in the overhead bin. Get to the gate early, so you can board as soon as possible, before the overhead bins fill up.

Baggage allowances vary by carrier, destination, and ticket class. On international flights, you're usually allowed to check two bags weighing up to 50 pounds (23 kilograms) each, although a few airlines allow checked bags of up to 88 pounds (40 kilograms) in first class. Some international carriers don't allow more than 66 pounds (30 kilograms) per bag in business class and 44 pounds (20 kilograms) in economy. If you're flying to or through the United Kingdom, your luggage cannot exceed 70 pounds (32 kilograms) per bag. On domestic flights, the limit is usually 50 to 70 pounds (23 to 32 kilograms) per bag. In general, carry-on bags shouldn't exceed 40 pounds (18 kilograms). Most airlines won't accept bags that weigh more than 100 pounds (45 kilograms) on domestic or international flights. Expect to pay a fee for baggage that exceeds weight limits. Check baggage restrictions with your carrier before you pack.

Airline liability for baggage is limited to $2,500 per person on flights within the United States. On international flights it amounts to $9.07 per pound or $20 per kilogram for checked baggage (roughly $540 per 50-pound bag), with a maximum of $634.90 per piece, and $400 per passenger for unchecked baggage. You can buy additional coverage at check-in for about $10 per $1,000 of coverage, but it often excludes a rather extensive list of items, shown on your airline ticket.

Before departure, itemize your bags' contents and their worth, and label the bags with your name, address, and phone number. (If you use your home address, cover it so potential thieves can't see it readily.) Include a label inside each bag and **pack a**

copy of your itinerary. At check-in, make sure each bag is correctly tagged with the destination airport's three-letter code. Because some checked bags will be opened for hand inspection, the U.S. Transportation Security Administration recommends that you leave luggage unlocked or use the plastic locks offered at check-in. TSA screeners place an inspection notice inside searched bags, which are re-sealed with a special lock.

If your bag has been searched and contents are missing or damaged, file a claim with the TSA Consumer Response Center as soon as possible. If your bags arrive damaged or fail to arrive at all, file a written report with the airline before leaving the airport.

🔢 Complaints **U.S. Transportation Security Administration Contact Center** ☎ 866/289-9673 🌐 www.tsa.gov.

SAFETY

O'ahu is generally a safe tourist destination, but it's still wise to follow the same common sense safety precautions you would normally follow in your own hometown. Hotel and visitor-center staff can provide information should you decide to head out on your own to more remote areas. **Rental cars are magnets for break-ins, so don't leave any valuables in the car, not even in a locked trunk.** Avoid poorly lighted areas, beach parks, and isolated areas after dark as a precaution. When hiking, **stay on marked trails,** no matter how alluring the temptation might be to stray. Weather conditions can cause landscapes to become muddy, slippery, and tenuous, so staying on marked trails will lessen the possibility of a fall or getting lost. Ocean safety is of the utmost importance when visiting an island destination. **Don't swim alone, and follow the international signage posted at beaches** that alerts swimmers to strong currents, man-of-war jellyfish, sharp coral, high surf, sharks, and dangerous shore breaks. At coastal lookouts along cliff tops, heed the signs indicating that waves can climb over the ledges. Check with lifeguards at each beach for current conditions, and **if the red flags are up, indicating swimming and surfing are not allowed, don't go in.** Waters that look calm on the surface can harbor strong currents and undertows, and not a few people who were just wading have been dragged out to sea.

LOCAL SCAMS

Be wary of those hawking "too good to be true" prices on everything from car rentals to attractions. Many of these offers are just a lure to get you in the door for timeshare presentations. When handed a flyer, read the fine print before you make your decision to participate.

WOMEN IN HAWAI'I

Women traveling alone are generally safe on the Islands, but always follow the safety precautions you would use in any major destination. When booking hotels, **request rooms closest to the elevator,** and always keep your hotel-room door and balcony doors locked. Stay away from isolated areas after dark; camping and hiking solo are not advised. If you stay out late visiting nightclubs and bars, **use caution when exiting night spots** and returning to your lodging.

SENIOR-CITIZEN TRAVEL

Hawai'i is steeped in a tradition that gives great respect to elders, or *kupuna,* and considers them "keepers of the wisdom." Visitors may not be so esteemed, but senior citizens traveling in Hawai'i will find discounts, special senior citizen–oriented activities, and buildings with easy access. Many lodging facilities have discounts for members of the American Association of Retired Persons (AARP).

To qualify for age-related discounts, mention your senior-citizen status up front when booking hotel reservations (not when checking out) and before you're seated in restaurants (not when paying the bill). Be sure to have identification on hand. When renting a car, ask about promotional car-rental discounts, which can be cheaper than senior-citizen rates.

🔢 Educational Programs **Elderhostel** ✉ 11 Ave. de Lafayette, Boston, MA 02111 ☎ 877/426-8056, 978/323-4141 international callers, 877/426-2167 TTY 📠 877/426-2166 🌐 www.elderhostel.org.

SHOPPING

SMART SOUVENIRS

Aloha shirts and resort wear, Hawaiian-music recordings, shell leis, coral jewelry, traditional quilts, island foods, Kona coffee, and koa-wood products are just a few of the gifts that visitors to Hawai'i treasure. For the more elegant gift items, check out the Hawaiian boutiques in shopping centers, as well as those tucked away in smaller shopping areas in residential districts. Island crafts fairs and swap meets offer a bargain bazaar of standard items such as T-shirts and tiki statues as well as the original works of local artisans.

WATCH OUT

Souvenirs made from coral or tortoise shell may not have been harvested legally, so in the interest of preserving Hawai'i's environment, it's best to avoid these.

SPORTS & OUTDOORS

If you like to swim, hike, fish, bike, scuba dive, windsurf, or play golf, O'ahu is your kind of place. The O'ahu Visitors Bureau's Web site provides detailed information on land, sky, and water adventure outfitters on the island. The environment is particularly fragile here, so whatever you do outdoors, don't forget to tread lightly.

🔲 **O'ahu Visitors Bureau** ☎ 877/525-6248 ⊕ www.visit-oahu.com.

BEACHES

Hawai'i's beaches are the stuff of legend, with white sand wedged between palm trees and turquoise water, or even colorful black-and-green stretches of sand. All beaches are free and open to the public unless otherwise noted—even the most luxurious hotels have to share their beachfronts. Note that riptides and strong undertows can challenge even the strongest swimmers, so if you see a beach where no one is swimming, ask a local about its safety before diving in. **Use care when diving into lagoons** as well, as they often are not as deep as they appear. Alcohol is not permitted on most beaches.

GOLF

There are more golf courses on O'ahu than on any other Hawaiian island. O'ahu hosts one of Hawai'i's premier golf events, the Sony Open, at the prestigious Waialae Country Club. To experience great golf with spectacular scenery as your backdrop, check with your hotel concierge or golf shop to arrange tee times, or call the courses directly.

HIKING & CAMPING

Hiking is a wonderful way to explore O'ahu, but **don't stray off trails,** and be sure to **wear sturdy hiking shoes.** It's also prudent to bring along a cellular phone, and it's especially helpful if it has GPS tracking. When camping, **be prepared for radical weather shifts,** especially at high altitudes. Fog, wind, and rain can and do blow in with little or no warning. Ask local outdoor shops which areas are best for you based on your fitness level and camping experience. Note that O'ahu doesn't have drive-to camping sites; most locations require a hike in or a night on the beach.

KAYAKING

Kayaking is an excellent low-impact way to enjoy the scenery. Kayak rentals are available for solo trips, or you can arrange guided trips. **Remain close to shore** if you don't want to be whooshed out to sea. Check with the kayak rental shop for weather advisories.

SCUBA DIVING & SNORKELING

Underwater O'ahu is breathtaking, but diving tends to be pricey. You can arrange trips with countless outfitters, or rent equipment on your own. Whether snorkeling or diving, remember **never to go alone,** and be sure to **ask at the dive shop about rip currents and places to avoid.** Undersea life is extremely fragile, so **don't touch (or take) the coral,** and **watch that your fins don't hit the reefs** behind you.

STUDENTS IN HAWAI'I

Hawai'i is a popular destination for exchange students from around the world, who mainly attend the University of Hawai'i in Honolulu. Contact your hometown university about study and internship possibilities. To check out the student scene on the Island, stop by any of the University of Hawai'i campuses or community college campuses, and read the *Honolulu Weekly* upon arrival for club and event information. Be sure to ask about discounts for students at all museums and major attractions and be prepared to show ID to qualify.

🔢 **IDs & Services STA Travel** ✉ 10 Downing St., New York, NY 10014 ☎ 212/627-3111, 800/781-4040 24-hr service center in the U.S. ⊕ www.sta.com. **Travel Cuts** ✉ 187 College St., Toronto, Ontario M5T 1P7, Canada ☎ 800/592-2887 in the U.S., 416/979-2406 or 888/359-2887 in Canada ⊕ www. travelcuts.com.

TAXES
SALES TAX
There's a 4.16% state sales tax on all purchases, including food. A hotel room tax of 7.25%, combined with the sales tax of 4%, equals an 11.41% rate added onto your hotel bill. A $3-per-day road tax is also assessed on each rental vehicle.

TAXIS
Taxis can be found at the airport, through your hotel doorman, in the more popular resort areas, or by contacting local taxi companies by telephone. Rates are $2.50 at the drop of the flag and each additional mile is $2.30. Drivers are generally courteous and the cars are in good condition, many of them air-conditioned. Most companies will also provide a car and driver for half-day or daylong island tours if you absolutely don't want to rent a car, and a number of companies also offer personal guides. Remember, however, that rates are quite steep for these services, ranging from $100 to $200 or more per day.

TIME
Hawai'i is on Hawaiian Standard Time, 5 hours behind New York, 2 hours behind Los Angeles, and 10 hours behind London.

When the U.S. mainland is on daylight saving time, Hawai'i is not, so add an extra hour of time difference between the Islands and U.S. mainland destinations. You may also find that things generally move more slowly here. That has nothing to do with your watch—it's just the laid-back way called Hawaiian time.

TIPPING
Tip cab drivers 15% of the fare. Standard tips for restaurants and bar tabs run from 15% to 20% of the bill, depending on the standard of service. Bellhops at hotels usually receive $1 per bag, more if you have bulky items such as bicycles and surfboards. Tip the hotel room maid $1 per night, paid daily. Tip doormen $1 for assistance with taxis; tips for concierge vary depending on the service. For example, tip more for "hard-to-get" event tickets or dining reservations.

TOURS & PACKAGES
Because everything is prearranged on a prepackaged tour or independent vacation, you spend less time planning—and often get it all at a good price.

BOOKING WITH AN AGENT
Travel agents are excellent resources. But it's a good idea to collect brochures from several agencies, as some agents' suggestions may be influenced by relationships with tour and package firms that reward them for volume sales. If you have a special interest, find an agent with expertise in that area. The American Society of Travel Agents (ASTA) has a database of specialists worldwide; you can log on to the group's Web site to find one near you.

Make sure your travel agent knows the accommodations and other services of the place being recommended. Ask about the hotel's location, room size, beds, and whether it has a pool, room service, or programs for children, if you care about these. Has your agent been there in person or sent others whom you can contact?

Do some homework on your own, too: local tourism boards can provide information about lesser-known and small-niche operators, some of which may sell only direct.

BUYER BEWARE
Each year consumers are stranded or lose their money when tour operators—even large ones with excellent reputations—go out of business. So check out the operator. Ask several travel agents about its reputation, and try to **book with a company that**

has a consumer-protection program.
(Look for information in the company's
brochure.) In the United States, members
of the United States Tour Operators Association are required to set aside funds (up
to $1 million) to help eligible customers
cover payments and travel arrangements in
the event that the company defaults. It's
also a good idea to choose a company that
participates in the American Society of
Travel Agents' Tour Operator Program;
ASTA will act as mediator in any disputes
between you and your tour operator.

Remember that the more your package or
tour includes, the better you can predict
the ultimate cost of your vacation. Make
sure you know exactly what is covered,
and beware of hidden costs. Are taxes,
tips, and transfers included? Entertainment
and excursions? These can add up.

🖪 **Tour-Operator Recommendations American
Society of Travel Agents** (⇨ Travel Agencies).
**CrossSphere–The Global Association for Pack-
aged Travel** ⊠ 546 E. Main St., Lexington, KY
40508 ☎ 859/226-4444 or 800/682-8886 🖷 859/
226-4414 ⊕ www.CrossSphere.com. **United States
Tour Operators Association** (USTOA) ⊠ 275 Madi-
son Ave., Suite 2014, New York, NY 10016 ☎ 212/
599-6599 🖷 212/599-6744 ⊕ www.ustoa.com.

TRANSPORTATION AROUND O'AHU

Waikīkī and downtown Honolulu can realistically be done without a car. Waikīkī
itself is walkable, and public shuttles and
buses connect it with the downtown area
and the most important sites (Pearl Harbor, Polynesian Cultural Center, etc.).

If you plan to further your explorations on
O'ahu, rent a car. **Reserve your vehicle in
advance,** particularly during peak travel
times and during major special events.
Most large rental car companies have airport counters and complimentary transportation for pickup/drop-off back at the
airport upon departure.

If you are staying in Waikīkī, consider
renting a car only on the days you plan to
use it. You don't need a car in Waikīkī itself, and hotel parking garages charge
everyone (even hotel guests) close to $20 a
day, plus tips. Parking is another reason to
consider taking TheBus or a shuttle to
downtown Honolulu.

TRAVEL AGENCIES

A good travel agent puts your needs first.
Look for an agency that has been in business at least five years, emphasizes customer service, and has someone on staff
who specializes in your destination. In addition, **make sure the agency belongs to a
professional trade organization.** The
American Society of Travel Agents (ASTA)
has more than 10,000 members in some
140 countries, enforces a strict code of
ethics, and will step in to mediate agent-
client disputes involving ASTA members.
ASTA also maintains a directory of agents
on its Web site; ASTA's TravelSense.org, a
trip planning and travel advice site, can
also help to locate a travel agent who
caters to your needs. (If a travel agency is
also acting as your tour operator, *see*
Buyer Beware *in* Tours & Packages.)

🖪 **Local Agent Referrals American Society of
Travel Agents** (ASTA) ⊠ 1101 King St., Suite 200,
Alexandria, VA 22314 ☎ 703/739-2782 or 800/965-
2782 24-hr hotline 🖷 703/684-8319 ⊕ www.
astanet.com and www.travelsense.org. **Association
of British Travel Agents** ⊠ 68-71 Newman St.,
London W1T 3AH ☎ 0901/201-5050 ⊕ www.abta.
com. **Association of Canadian Travel Agencies**
⊠ 350 Sparks St., Suite 510, Ottawa, Ontario K1R
7S8 ☎ 613/237-3657 🖷 613/237-7052 ⊕ www.acta.
ca. **Australian Federation of Travel Agents** ⊠ Level
3, 309 Pitt St., Sydney, NSW 2000 ☎ 02/9264-3299
or 1300/363-416 🖷 02/9264-1085 ⊕ www.afta.com.
au. **Travel Agents' Association of New Zealand**
⊠ Level 5, Tourism and Travel House, 79 Boulcott
St., Box 1888, Wellington 6001 ☎ 04/499-0104
🖷 04/499-0786 ⊕ www.taanz.org.nz.

VISITOR INFORMATION

Before you go, contact the O'ahu Visitors
Bureau (OVB) for a free vacation planner
and map. You can also request brochures
on the island's romance, golf, and family
activities. The Web site provides detailed
information on the island, including an
online yellow page listing of accommodations, activities and sports, attractions,
dining venues, services, transportation,
travel professionals, and wedding information. The Hawai'i Visitors Bureau Web site
has a calendar section that allows you to

see what local events will be taking place during your stay.

7 **Tourist Information** Hawai'i Visitors & Convention Bureau ✉ 2270 Kalakaua Ave., Suite 801, Honolulu 96815 ☎ 808/923-1811, 800/464-2924 for brochures ⊕ www.gohawaii.com. In the U.K. contact the **Hawai'i Visitors & Convention Bureau** ✆ 36 Southwark Bridge Rd., London, SE1 9EU ☎ 020/7202-6384 🖷 020/7928-0722. **O'ahu Visitors Bureau** ☎ 877/525-6248 ⊕ www.visit-oahu.com.

7 **Government Advisories** Consular Affairs Bureau of Canada ☎ 800/267-6788 or 613/944-6788 ⊕ www.voyage.gc.ca. **U.K. Foreign and Commonwealth Office** ✉ Travel Advice Unit, Consular Directorate, Old Admiralty Building, London SW1A 2PA ☎ 0845/850-2829 or 020/7008-1500 ⊕ www.fco.gov.uk/travel. **Australian Department of Foreign Affairs and Trade** ☎ 300/139-281 travel advisories, 02/6261-3305 Consular Travel Advice ⊕ www.smartraveller.gov.au. **New Zealand Ministry of Foreign Affairs and Trade** ☎ 04/439-8000 ⊕ www.mft.govt.nz.

WEB SITES

Do check out the World Wide Web when planning your trip. You'll find everything from weather forecasts to virtual tours of famous cities. Be sure to visit Fodors.com (⊕ www.fodors.com), a complete travel-planning site. You can research prices and book plane tickets, hotel rooms, rental cars, vacation packages, and more. In addition, you can post your pressing questions in the Travel Talk section. Other planning tools include a currency converter and weather reports, and there are loads of links to travel resources.

The Web site ⊕ www.search-hawaii.com has an engine that can search all linked Hawaiian Web pages by topic or word.

Visit ⊕ www.co.honolulu.hi.us/menu/, the official Web site of the City and County of Honolulu; ⊕ www.hshawaii.com for the Hawai'i State vacation planner; ⊕ www.honoluluweekly.com for a weekly guide to the arts, entertainment, and dining in Honolulu; and ⊕ www.hawaii.gov, the state's official Web site, for all information on the destination, including camping.

INDEX

DINING INDEX

LODGING INDEX

PHOTO CREDITS

Cover Photo (North Shore): *Ken Ross/viestiphoto.com.* F4, *Tor Johnson/Photo Resource Hawaii/Alamy.*
Chapter 1: Experience Oahu: 1, *Stuart Pearce/World Pictures/Alamy.* 2 (top), *Ken Ross/viestiphoto.com.*
2 (bottom left), *Michael S. Nolan/age fotostock.* 2 (bottom right), *Superstock/age fotostock.* 3 (top), *Oahu Visitors Bureau.* 3 (bottom left), *Corbis.* 3 (bottom right), *Oahu Visitors Bureau.* 4, *Superstock/age fotostock.* 5, *Oahu Visitors Bureau.* 6 (left), *Douglas Peebles Photography/Alamy.* 6 (top right), *David Franzen/ Doris Duke Foundation for Islamic Art.* 6 (bottom left), *Tor Johnson/Photo Resource Hawaii/Alamy.* 6 (bottom right), *Deborah Davis/Alamy.* 7 (top left), *Oahu Visitors Bureau.* 7 (bottom left), *David L. Moore/ Alamy.* 7 (right), *Ann Cecil/Photo Resource Hawaii/Alamy.* 8 (left), *Ed Watamura.* 7 (top right), *Bill Gleasner/viestiphoto.com.* 7 (bottom right), *David Schrichte/Photo Resource Hawaii/Alamy.* 9 (left), *Tor Johnson/Photo Resource Hawaii/Alamy.* 9 (top right), *Tomas del Amo/Alamy.* 9 (bottom right), *Joe Viesti/viestiphoto.com.* 11, *Surfpix/Alamy.* 12, *Oahu Visitors Bureau.* 13, *Starwood Hotels and Resorts.* 14, *Corbis.* 15 (left), *Hideo Kurihara/Alamy.* 15 (right), *Tor Johnson/Photo Resource Hawaii/Alamy.* 16, *Andre Seale/Alamy.* 17 (left), *Oahu Visitors Bureau.* 17 (right), *Douglas Peebles/age fotostock.* **Chapter 2: Exploring Oahu:** 19, *David Schrichte/Alamy.* 27, *J.D. Heaton/Picture Finders/age fotostock.* 28, *Oahu Visitors Bureau.* 29 (left and center), *Walter Bibikow/viestiphoto.com.* 29 (right), *Douglas Peebles/age fotostock.* 30, *Stuart Westmorland/age fotostock.* 31 (left), *The Royal Hawaiian.* 31 (center), *Atlantide S.N.C./age fotostock.* 31 (right), *Liane Cary/age fotostock.* 47, *Library of Congress Prints and Photographs Division.* 49 (top), *Corbis.* 49 (bottom), *USS Arizona Memorial Photo Collection/NPS.* 50 (top), *USS Missouri Memorial Association.* 50 (bottom), *Army Signal Corps Collection/National Archives.* 51, *USS Bowfin Submarine Museum and Park.* 61–63, *Pierre Tostee/ASP Tostee.* 64, *Carol Cunningham/ cunninghamphotos.com.* **Chapter 3: Beaches:** 71, *J.D. Heaton/Picture Finders/age fotostock.* **Chapter 4: Water Activities & Tours:** 85, *Dave Bjorn/Photo Resource Hawaii/Alamy.* 96, *Ron Dahlquist/HVCB.* **Chapter 5: Golf, Hiking & Outdoor Activities:** 105, *David Schrichte/Photo Resource Hawaii/Alamy.* 120, *Luca Tettoni.* 121, *Jack Jeffrey.* **Chapter 6: Shops & Spas:** 125, *Beauty Photo Studio/age fotostock.* 134 (top), *Linda Ching/HVCB.* 134 (bottom), *Sri Maiava Rusden/HVCB.* 135 (top), *leisofhawaii.com.* 135 (second from top), *kellyalexanderphotography.com.* 135 (third, fourth, and fifth from top), *leisofhawaii.com.* 135 (bottom), *kellyalexanderphotography.com.* **Chapter 7: Entertainment & Nightlife:** 145, *Polynesian Cultural Center.* 148, *HVCB.* 149, *Thinkstock LLC.* **Chapter 8: Where to Eat:** 163, *Dana Edmunds/Polynesian Cultural Center.* 173, *Polynesian Cultural Center.* 174 (top), *Douglas Peebles Photography.* 174 (top center), *Douglas Peebles Photography/Alamy.* 174 (center), *Dana Edmunds/ Polynesian Cultural Center.* 174 (bottom center), *Douglas Peebles Photography/Alamy.* 174 (bottom), *Purcell Team/Alamy.* 175 (top, top center, and bottom center), *HTJ/HVCB.* 175 (bottom), *Oahu Visitors Bureau.* **Chapter 9: Where to Stay:** 199, *Waikiki Parc Hotel.* **Color Section:** View of Windward Oahu from the Nuuanu Pali Lookout: *David Schrichte/Photo Resource Hawaii/Alamy.* Kayaking in Kaneohe Bay: *Douglas Peebles Photography/Alamy.* Sunrise over Manana Island (Rabbit Island) off Makapuu Point: *Kenny Williams/Alamy.* Surf lesson on Waikiki Beach: *David Schrichte/Photo Resource Hawaii/Alamy.* Iolani Palace in downtown Honolulu: *Ken Ross/viestiphoto.com.* Aerial view of Honolulu and Waikiki, looking east to Diamond Head: *Corbis.* Aerial view of the Koolau Range in Windward Oahu: *Joe Viesti/viestiphoto.com.* Lanikai Beach in Windward Oahu: *Peebles/Mauritius/age fotostock.* Leis: *Michael Soo/Alamy.* Surfing the Banzai Pipeline: *Karen Wilson.* Chinese New Year celebrations in downtown Honolulu: *David L. Moore/Alamy.* Keiki hula dancers from Halau Hula O Hokulani in Kapiolani Park: *Ann Cecil/Photo Resource Hawaii/Alamy.* Relaxing with a view of Waikiki and Diamond Head: *Tor Johnson/Photo Resource Hawaii/Alamy.* USS *Arizona* Memorial in Pearl Harbor: *Studiolab/allphoto/age fotostock.* Waikiki Beach: *Alan Seiden/Oahu Visitors Bureau.*

ABOUT OUR WRITERS

Wanda A. Adams was born and raised on Maui and now makes her home on O'ahu. She has been a newspaper reporter for more than 25 years, specializing in food, dining, and travel.

Don Chapman is the editor of the award-winning *MidWeek*, Hawai'i's largest-circulated newspaper. The golf writer for this guide, Don has played 88 golf courses in Hawai'i and writes about golf for a variety of national publications. He is also the author of four books.

Katherine Nichols is a writer in the Features department of the *Honolulu Star-Bulletin*. She has won four awards from the Society of Professional Journalists and has written for numerous publications, including *Town & Country*, *Runner's World*, *Shape*, and the Associated Press.

Chad Pata has been covering the beaches and sports of Hawai'i for *MidWeek* and *The Honolulu Advertiser* for six years. Originally from Atlanta, Georgia, he moved to O'ahu in 1993, married a local girl, and now lives for his two kids, Honu and Calogero.

Cathy Sharpe was born and reared on O'ahu. For 13 years, she worked at a Honolulu public relations agency representing major travel industry clients. Now living in Maryland, she is a marketing consultant. Cathy returns home once a year to visit family and friends, relax at her favorite beaches, and enjoy island cuisine.

After 20 years as a Hawai'i hotel executive, **Maggie Wunsch** now covers Hawai'i for a variety of radio, print, and broadcast media. She is an unabashed fan of room service, sandy beaches, and the delicious scents of her state—from pikake jasmine to teriyaki barbeque.

Hawai'i resident **Katie Young** has spent five years as a writer, columnist, and editor for *MidWeek*, covering everything from entertainment to island living. Her work has also appeared in *Makai* magazine and the *Honolulu Star-Bulletin*. She enjoys dancing hula and watching the sunset with her dog, Pono.